The
COMPLETE
BOOK OF
French
Cooking

French edition
Editorial director: Ronite Tubiana
Editor: Clélia Ozier-Lafontaine
Layout adaptation: Alice Leroy

English edition
Editorial director: Kate Mascaro
Editor: Helen Adedotun
Cover design: Audrey Sednaoui
Translation from the French: Carmella Abramowitz-Moreau
Additional translation: Ansley Evans
Typesetting: Gravemaker+Scott
Copyediting and proofreading: Penelope Isaac
Indexing: JMS/Chris Bell

Production: Julie Hautecourt, Marylou Deserson,
Louisa Hanifi
Color Separation: IGS-CP, L'Isle d'Espagnac
Printed in China by Toppan Leefung

Simultaneously published in French as
Le Grand livre de la gastronomie française
© Éditions Flammarion, Paris, 2023

English-language edition
© Éditions Flammarion, Paris, 2023
First edition published in 2010

editions.flammarion.com
@flammarioninternational

24 25 26   4 3 2

ISBN: 978-2-08-042193-7

Legal Deposit: 06/2023

HUBERT DELORME AND VINCENT BOUÉ ～ PHOTOGRAPHY BY CLAY McLACHLAN
FOREWORD BY PAUL BOCUSE

The COMPLETE BOOK OF French Cooking

Flammarion

Contents

Foreword

By Paul Bocuse

This book is an invaluable companion in the kitchen. Whether we are professionals or home chefs, we need to check proportions or a particular technique, or we wish to prepare a forgotten classic or reinvent a dish, we all have to return to our books at some point to consult the culinary advice of experts. Yet books alone are not enough, and therein lies the complexity of our profession, which is both manual and scientific. Books certainly perpetuate recipes, but without the requisite skills, there can be no fine cuisine. Just knowing that an onion must be finely chopped or that sweetbreads must be prepared before cooking is no guarantee of successful results. A great deal of training is required, as well as regular practice, to transform the theory in books into expertise. In times past, mothers transmitted precious culinary knowledge to their daughters. The youth of today have to seek out other mentors. Fortunately, opportunities abound, and what better starting point than this volume—an indispensable reference for everyone, from aspiring cooks intent on learning the basics to those honing their skills to master the fundamentals of French cuisine.

There is no doubt that this exceptional work is a continuation of the tradition of reference books that will contribute to the prestige of French cuisine worldwide. Many of these already occupy a prominent place in the kitchens of self-respecting chefs. Notable examples are *L'Art de la cuisine française au XIXᵉ siècle* (The Art of French Cooking in the Nineteenth Century) by Antonin Carême, as well as the 1903 work *Guide culinaire d'Auguste Escoffier* (published in English as *The Complete Guide to the Art of Modern Cookery*), the 1907 *La Gastronomie pratique* (The Encyclopedia of Practical Gastronomy) by Ali-Bab, and *L'Art culinaire français par nos grands maîtres de la cuisine* (The Art of French Cooking). It is no coincidence that Flammarion published the original French edition of the latter three works. Today, once again, Flammarion is taking a bold step by bringing together the two dimensions of cuisine in this book: knowledge and savoir faire. The volume is divided into two distinct parts and, with its numerous photos, takes you step by step through the techniques, before presenting one hundred and sixty-five recipes that make up the very foundation of French cooking.

This book is distinctive in another way, too. It called on teachers at a professional school for the hospitality industry to explain the techniques, to enable you to successfully prepare the thousands of recipes from the French terroirs. Contributions from nine renowned chefs open each recipe chapter: Anne-Sophie Pic for appetizers, Alain Passard for vegetables, Gérald Passédat for fish, Jean-François Piège for poultry, Régis Marcon for meat, Xavier Thuret for cheese, Yves Thuriès and Didier Stéphan for desserts, and Stéphane Augé for frozen desserts. Their contributions may be interpreted as a homage to the men and women who are at the forefront of today's cuisine. This volume is, in essence, the transmission of the numerous techniques and recipes that have built up the framework of French cuisine since the nineteenth century.

The publication of a book of this scope gives me more than one reason for profound satisfaction: it pays tribute to our ability to transmit our unique savoir faire. For me, the passing on of knowledge is one of the fundamental values of the cooking profession. In my restaurant, I have a constant intake of apprentices and cooks from all over the world. They come for hands-on learning experience: how to truss a chicken, prepare a fillet, put together elaborate desserts, and make a perfect soufflé. They observe my chefs, who are officially acknowledged to be some of the finest artisans in France, and repeat their every action. At the Institut Paul Bocuse, founded thirty years ago in Écully, cooking instructors teach all of these techniques to young students, who also learn management and hospitality skills.

Who could have imagined, when Jack Lang, minister of culture at the time, and I launched the project, that gastronomy would inspire such passion in the twenty-first century? Even the most optimistic were convinced that technology would reduce cuisine to little more than mechanized "ready meals," dealing a fatal blow to flavorsome food. Technology has certainly made its presence felt, but in no way like the imaginary food synthesizers of *Star Trek*. On the contrary, it has widened our creativity and extended our range of possibilities. The food processors, siphons, slow-cooking ovens, sous vide machines, and *planchas* (electric griddles) that come to us from the food industry have not only facilitated the work of cooks, they have also raised the profession—which was so disparaged after World War II—to new heights.

This book forms part of a movement that is fighting for authentic taste. Significant changes in outlook mean that people from all walks of life are now happy to spend hours busying themselves in the kitchen with the sole aim of delighting a table of guests. Television programs, cooking lessons given in an ever-increasing number of cooking schools, practical and teaching books, lectures, debates, and gastronomical encounters all inevitably lead back to the home kitchen. We are all seeking to take control of what is on our plates, selecting the healthiest and tastiest ingredients. Never before have cooks and those who consume their food had such a close relationship.

With this new culinary bible, French cuisine will no longer hold any secrets for you. At last, all of the intricacies of preparing great French classics are explained from A to Z. So, peel, chop, slice, grill, braise, prepare stocks and sabayon, cook sea bass in a salt crust, tuck goat cheese into pastry parcels, and put together unforgettable vol-au-vents. As long as you wield your kitchen utensils, cooking will live on. And as long as there is cooking, there is hope!

TECHNIQUES

Basic Doughs and Batters

Firm doughs

Shortcrust pastry (*pâte brisée*) ✳

Shortcrust pastry is very often baked simultaneously with the filling, and is used both for savory and sweet dishes. This shortcrust pastry is used mainly to hold a relatively liquid filling, so is used for dishes such as quiches, flans, pies, or fruit tarts such as apple and pear. For sweet tarts, add 3 ½ tablespoons (40 g) sugar.

INGREDIENTS

2 ¾ cups (250 g) cake flour
1 generous teaspoon (5 g) salt
3 ½ tablespoons (40 g) sugar (for sweet tarts)
1 stick (125 g) unsalted butter, room temperature
1 egg yolk
4 ½ tablespoons (50 ml) water

Sift the flour and add the salt and sugar if using. Blend the butter and the flour together with your fingertips until the mixture forms coarse crumbs.

Incorporate the egg yolk and water, working lightly with your hands (1). Do not overwork the dough as it will become too elastic. Form the dough into a ball and chill, covered in plastic wrap, for about 30 minutes.

Cut in half and roll each half into a ball. Lightly sprinkle your working surface with flour and roll the dough into a disk shape with a thickness of about ⅛ inch (3 mm).

Roll the dough over your pastry roller to transfer it from the working surface to line your circle or tart dish (2). Decorate the edges.

CHEF'S NOTES

– Alternatively, the egg yolk and water may be mixed with the sifted flour, salt, and sugar (if using) first, followed by the butter.
– Make sure you leave time to chill the dough to reduce elasticity; it will be far easier to roll out.
– Leftover pieces of dough may be used for other purposes.

RECIPE IDEAS

Quiche Lorraine **280**
Apple upside-down cake (tarte Tatin) **478**
Apricot tartlets **455**

1

2

Crumbled sweet short pastry (*pâte sablée*) ✳

Because the butter and flour are worked together, this is a crumbly pastry. It is often blind-baked before being filled or topped. It is used for sweet pastry making only. You may also use it on its own, in individual portions, to make shortbread cookies. Many regions and towns in France, such as Brittany, Normandy, and Nantes, have their own specialty shortbread cookies.

INGREDIENTS

2 ¾ cups (250 g) cake flour
1 generous teaspoon (5 g) salt
1 stick (125 g) unsalted butter, softened
⅔ cup (125 g) sugar
1 egg

Sift the flour with the salt. Dice the butter and blend it in with your fingers until it forms coarse crumbs **(1, 2)**. Incorporate the sugar, make a well, and then work in the egg **(3, 4)**.

Chill for around 30 minutes. Roll out the dough to form a disk about ⅛ inch (3 mm) thick.

Place it in a tart dish **(5)** and blind-bake at 350°F (180°C) for about 20 minutes (if making a tart for 8 servings).

CHEF'S NOTES

– For an optimal crumbly texture, do not work the butter in for too long.
– Add variety to your recipes by adding spices such as cinnamon or allspice, or candied ginger, dry ingredients such as shredded coconut, citrus zest, or cocoa powder, or liquid ingredients such as orange-blossom water, honey, or other flavor essences.

RECIPE IDEA

Lemon meringue tartlets **460**

Creamed sweet short pastry (*pâte sucrée*) ✳

This dough is used as a sweet tart base. Blind-bake it or fill it with almond cream, custard filling, or other sweet cream filling for baking.

INGREDIENTS

1 stick (125 g) unsalted butter, softened
½ cup (100 g) granulated sugar
1 egg
2 ¾ cups (250 g) cake flour
1 teaspoon (5 ml) salt

Place the butter, sugar, and egg in the bowl of a food processor (**1**) and cream together until smooth. Sift the flour and add it with the salt (**2**) to process for 1–2 minutes further, until smooth.

Press down the dough with the palm of your hand, pushing it away from you, until the ingredients are thoroughly blended. Chill, covered, for about 30 minutes.

Roll out the dough very thinly (to about ⅛ inch or 3 mm) to form a disk. Use your rolling pin to transfer it from the working surface to the baking pan or circle: drape it round the pin and then unroll it over the tart mold (**3**).

Make decorative patterns around the edge (**4**).

CHEF'S NOTES

– This method uses creaming to combine the butter with the egg and sugar, which means it has a softer texture than the crumbly pastry dough in the previous method. If you make it ahead of time, keep it covered in plastic wrap so that it does not absorb any tastes or odors.
– If you use just the egg yolk you may need to add a little water (about 3 ½ tablespoons [50 ml]).

RECIPE IDEAS

Alsatian mirabelle plum
  tart **504**
Mixed berry tart **472**
Raspberry ganache tart **487**

Pasta and noodle dough ✳

Pasta has played an important role in the history of food for humankind. China is the country with the highest consumption of noodles in the world. In Europe, Italy is the leading consumer and producer, exporting a wide variety of pasta types. Several regions in France—Alsace, Savoy, Dauphiné—have traditional dishes that use pasta, like *spätzles* (small dumplings), *crozets* (small squares of dough made with wheat or buckwheat), and the *ravioles* of Royans (small stuffed cases of dough). This smooth, dry dough should be rolled out very thinly for its various uses.

INGREDIENTS

2 eggs
1 ¼ tablespoons (20 ml) oil
1 teaspoon (5 g) salt
2 ½ cups (220 g) cake flour

Beat the eggs and combine with the oil and salt. Sift the flour, then make a well in the center and pour in the liquid ingredients.

Rapidly knead the ingredients so that they form a ball. Do not overwork or else the dough will become too elastic **(2, 3)**.

Chill, covered, for 30 to 45 minutes.

Roughly spread the dough out using a pastry roller, then process it through a pasta maker **(4)**.

Use a cutter or laminator to cut the desired shapes **(5, 6)**. Allow the pasta to dry for several hours before using it.

CHEF'S NOTE

– To make ravioli, pass the dough through a pasta maker until it is very thin. This will prevent it from having a floury taste when eaten. The dough can be prepared ahead of time, but it will lose its elasticity. If you wish to prepare it ahead, cover it in plastic wrap to protect it from other tastes and odors.

DID YOU KNOW?

Using a flavored oil in the dough gives it an original touch.
Pasta dough may also be colored:
· black: cuttlefish ink
· red: tomato paste
· yellow: turmeric
· orange: ground saffron
· green: parsley chlorophyll

RECIPE IDEA

Snail ravioli and garlic cream **277**

Puff pastry ✳ ✳ ✳

Puff pastry is made by creating successive layers of fat (here, butter) and dough, each one as thin and even as possible. This is done by making a series of folds. The pastry puffs up because of the steam caught in the leaves of dough mixture that have been softened by the addition of fat or butter.

INGREDIENTS

2 ¾ cups (250 g) cake flour
1 teaspoon (5 g) salt
½ cup (125 ml) water
10 ½ tablespoons (185 g)
  unsalted butter

Sift the flour and add the salt. Make a well in the center and pour the water into the flour. Blend the ingredients together rapidly until thoroughly mixed. You should have a smooth paste, known as the *détrempe*. Form it into a ball and chill, covered, for about 20 minutes.

Check that the butter has the identical consistency of the dough mixture. Flatten it, if necessary, between 2 sheets of parchment paper, using your rolling pin. This enables it to be incorporated more easily into the dough, and gives it a longer rectangular shape.

Now roll out the dough mixture to form a cross shape, leaving the center—where you will place the butter—thicker (about ⅓ inch or 8 mm) than the four other parts. The butter should fit over this part of the dough.

Place the butter in the center of the dough **(1)** and fold over each of the four parts of the cross (similarly to the back of an envelope).

Lightly dust your cool working counter with flour (use as little as possible each time, so that the pastry does not become too hard). Roll out the dough (called a *paton*) to form a rectangle whose length is three times greater than its width **(2)**.

Fold this into three, starting at each end (three layers) **(3)**. Rotate the folded dough a quarter-turn and roll out again to form the same shape as previously, a rectangle three times its width. Repeat the folding operation. Cover with plastic wrap and chill again for about 20 minutes.

Repeat this procedure— rolling out and folding—five more times (a total of six times), chilling for 20 minutes between each stage.

CHEF'S NOTES

The quantity of fat to incorporate into this pastry is equal to half the weight of your dough mixture (water and flour).
– Not all puff pastries are made with six turns. The fewer turns you make, the more it will puff up. However, the end result after baking will be less regular.
There are three other types of puff pastry:
– inverted puff pastry (*feuilletage inverse*), where the dough is incorporated into a mixture of fat and flour
– quick puff pastry, where the fat is cubed and incorporated into the dough mixture and four turns are made;
– Viennese puff pastry, using a slightly sweet dough to which milk is added.

DID YOU KNOW?

A simple form of puff pastry has been in existence for a long time. The Arabs and Greeks prepared it using oil. The French artist known as Claude Lorrain is said to have invented it in the seventeenth century when he was working as a pastry maker's apprentice. In the eighteenth century, Feuillet, a cook working for the princely Condé family, used and improved the recipe, as did Antonin Carême, recognized as the founder of French haute cuisine, some decades later.

Does a mille-feuille have one thousand leaves?

Mille-feuilles means, literally, one thousand leaves, and basing our calculations on a six-turn puff pastry, it is possible to calculate the number of leaves created by layering dough and fat.
After the first folding into three, there are three layers of butter and six layers of dough. However, two layers of dough are in direct contact and so form only one layer. Here's the calculation:
1st turn: $3 \times 3 = 9 - 2 = 7$
2nd: $7 \times 3 = 21 - 2 = 19$
3rd: $19 \times 3 = 57 - 2 = 55$
4th: $55 \times 3 = 165 - 2 = 163$
5th: $163 \times 3 = 489 - 2 = 487$
6th: $487 \times 3 = 1,461 - 2 = 1,459$
Three layers of pastry are normally used to make a mille-feuille, so altogether there will be $1,459 \times 3 = 4,377$ leaves.

RECIPE IDEAS

Batters and dough pastes

Crêpe batter ✳

In France, crêpes are a special treat for the Candlemas festival in February, and may be enjoyed plain, sweet, or savory. Use them, too, as a base for other recipes. The batter is smooth, liquid, and a yellow color.

INGREDIENTS

2 ¾ cups (250 g) cake flour
1 teaspoon (5 g) salt
3 eggs
2 cups (500 ml) low-fat (semi-skimmed) milk, room temperature
Your own choice of flavoring, such as vanilla, orange-blossom water, or a hint of rum
3 tablespoons (40 g) unsalted butter, melted until brown
Oil for the skillet

Sift the flour and salt into a mixing bowl **(1)**. Crack the eggs into the mixture one by one. Incorporate the melted butter into the milk without heating. Whisk the mixture briskly while pouring on a little of the milk and melted butter **(2)**.

Incorporate the remaining milk, beating energetically until the batter is smooth and fluid.

Add the flavor of your choice and strain through a fine-mesh sieve **(3)**.

Chill for about 30 minutes.

Heat a skillet or crêpe pan over high heat. Drizzle a little oil in and cook the crêpes one by one, turning them over when they go golden-brown at the edges **(4)**.

CHEF'S NOTES

– To avoid lumps forming, use a whisk as you gradually pour the milk into the mixture of flour, eggs, and salt. If lumps form nevertheless, strain the batter through a fine-mesh sieve.
– You may replace some or all of the milk with beer or hard cider: you may also substitute wheat flour with other types of flour such as buckwheat or spelt.
– For savory crêpes, think of adding finely chopped herbs, spices, or even finely shredded vegetables to the batter.
– You can also add the melted brown butter at the end of the preparation, after straining.

DID YOU KNOW?

Plain, simple galettes date back to approximately 7,000 BCE. Crêpes as we know them were first made considerably later, in the thirteenth century. Blinis come to us from Russia. They are thick, leavened crêpes made with wheat and buckwheat.

In France, savory crêpes are known as galettes. They are of Celtic origin, and in Brittany are made using buckwheat flour, water, and salt.

HOW TO USE THEM:

Aumonière (almoner's purse): sweet or savory filling in a crêpe that is tied up to form a pouch or parcel.

Crêpe Suzette: a crêpe flavored with curaçao and caramelized with sugar cubes rubbed on the skin of unsprayed tangerines.

Crêpe soufflée: a crêpe filled with a soufflé batter and then baked.

Gâteau de crêpes (crêpe cake): a pile of crêpes interspersed with a garnish, such as preserves, pastry cream, almond cream, ganache, and so on, to form a cake shape.

Pannequet: a crêpe holding a sweet or savory filling and folded into four, forming a small cushion shape.

RECIPE IDEA

Rolled Picardy crêpes **428**

21

Choux pastry ✳✳

Choux pastry may be used for sweet or savory recipes, on its own or with a purée, béchamel sauce, pastry cream, and so on. It is cooked by frying, poaching, or baking. This pastry is firm and sticky but smooth, and swells when cooked or baked.

INGREDIENTS

1 ¼ cups (125 g) all-purpose flour
1 cup (250 ml) water
1 teaspoon (5 g) salt
1 scant tablespoon (15 g) sugar (optional)
7 tablespoons (100 g) unsalted butter, diced
4 eggs, and an additional egg for basting

Sift the flour. In a saucepan, bring the water, salt, sugar (if using), and diced butter to a boil.

Pour all the sifted flour in **(1)** and beat energetically with a rubber spatula until the moisture has evaporated.

Transfer the mixture to a mixing bowl. Spread it out with the spatula so that it adheres (it will not stick, however) to the sides of the bowl.

Add the four eggs, one by one, using the spatula to mix **(2)**. Stir in thoroughly each time.

Spoon the batter into a piping bag and pipe out the shapes you will need (puffs, éclairs, or profiteroles) **(3)**.

Beat the remaining egg with a small pinch of salt and baste the shapes with a pastry brush.

Dip the tines of a fork into water and lightly press them in, in a cross pattern, to smooth out the surface of the choux pastry so that it bakes evenly **(4)**.

Choux pastry bakes in two stages, first at 350°F (180°C) for 15 minutes (until the pastry is nicely swelled and is uniformly golden), and then at 325°F (160°C), for 10 minutes (the all-important drying-out stage). The exact time will of course depend on the size of the pastries you are baking. During the second stage, leave the oven door slightly ajar (use the handle of a wooden spoon) to facilitate the evaporation of the moisture in the pastries.

CHEF'S NOTES

– For best results, have your butter at room temperature so that it melts as the same time as the water starts boiling. If too much evaporation occurs at this stage, the pastry will be too hard.
– If your batter is not sufficiently dried out, only use three eggs so that you will be able to pipe it out with a pastry bag.

USE FOR:

Cream puffs, éclairs, *chouquettes* (small, sugar-coated puffs), *religieuses*, *glands* (small acorn-shaped pastries), soufflé doughnuts, and cakes such as the croquembouches, Paris-Brest, and Saint-Honoré.

RECIPE IDEAS

Florentine-style gnocchi **412**
Mushroom *gougères* **289**

4

Waffle batter ✳

Waffles are light, airy, honeycomb-shaped delicacies with a rectangular form. Enjoy them on their own or with fruit preserves, Chantilly cream, or chocolate sauce.

INGREDIENTS

3 ¾ cups (340 g) cake flour
Scant ½ cup (80 g) sugar
Scant ½ teaspoon (2 g) salt
2 slightly heaped teaspoons
  (10 g) baking powder
2 eggs
1 cup (¼ liter) milk
7 tablespoons (100 g) butter,
  melted and cooled
A few drops of vanilla extract

Combine the flour, sugar, salt, and baking powder in a mixing bowl. Make a well in the center.

Break the eggs into the well and whisk them into the dry ingredients with a little milk.

Gradually add the rest of the milk, whisking so that there are no lumps.

Stir in the melted butter and vanilla extract.

Chill the batter for about 30 minutes. Cook your waffles in a waffle maker according to instructions.

CHEF'S NOTES

– If you wish, you may substitute beer or hard cider for some or all of the milk.
– You can also use beaten egg whites to make waffles, or even baking powder or yeast. Follow the instructions according to the weight of your ingredients.
– Try out different flavors, such as orange-blossom water, rum, and so on.

DID YOU KNOW?

The ancestor of the waffle was the *oublie*, a small, flat wafer. Like waffles, they were cooked between two hot iron plates by *oubloyeurs* or *oublieux*, members of the guild who sold *oublies*. When irons were made with a honeycomb indentation, the resulting offerings became known as *gaufres* after the word for honeycomb; the Old French version of this word, *wafla*, is the origin of the name by which we know them today.

RECIPE IDEA

Tutti-frutti waffles **490**

Frying batter ✳

Batter for frying is light and airy. It is used to coat food before it is dipped in oil.

INGREDIENTS

2 cups (200 g) all-purpose flour
1 teaspoon (5 g) salt
2 eggs
4 teaspoons (20 ml) sunflower seed oil
¾ cup (200 ml) milk or beer
3 egg whites

Sift the flour into a mixing bowl and add the salt (1). Break the whole eggs one by one, and whisk them in to the dry ingredients. Incorporate the oil.

Pour in the liquid (milk or beer) and whisk until the mixture is smooth. Stiffly beat the egg whites.

Gently fold in the beaten egg whites using a flexible rubber spatula (2).

CHEF'S NOTES

– Fold in the egg whites just before you coat the food you will be frying so that it does not deflate.
– The pan or pot must be perfectly clean. If you have prepared fish or fruit in it beforehand, make sure there are no traces left as the taste could permeate what you are frying.

DID YOU KNOW?

Fritters appeared in France as early as the thirteenth century. Each region had its own specialty with a specific shape, batter, and filling. Some examples are the *bugne* of Lyon, the *bottereau* of the Charentes regions, the *roussette* of Strasbourg, the *merveilles* of Gascony, the *tourtisseau* of Anjou, the *bignes* of the Auvergne region, and the *oreillette* of Montpellier.

RECIPE IDEA

Apple fritters with apricot coulis **474**

Yeast doughs

Brioche dough ✳✳

This is a yeast dough that gets its lovely yellow color from the eggs and fat included. The proportion of each determines just how delicate the brioche is.

INGREDIENTS

⅙ oz. (5 g) fresh (compressed) yeast
2 teaspoons milk or water
2 ½ cups (250 g) all-purpose flour
1 teaspoon (5 g) salt
2 tablespoons (25 g) granulated sugar
3 eggs
1 stick (125 g) unsalted butter, softened

Dilute the yeast in 2 teaspoons (10 ml) milk or water at room temperature. Sift the flour onto a flat surface and make a well in the center. Sprinkle the salt and sugar outside the well so that they do not come into direct contact with the yeast (1). Beat the eggs and incorporate them into the mixture using a rubber scraper (2).

Knead the dough energetically to give it elasticity. You may use a stand mixer with the dough hook to do this, in which case use medium speed for about 10 minutes. Then knead in the butter at room temperature until it is completely incorporated and the dough is smooth (3), and place the dough in a mixing bowl.

Cover with plastic wrap or a slightly damp tea towel and leave to rise for 30 to 40 minutes at a temperature of 77°F–82°F (25°C–28°C) with a bowl of water. (If left uncovered the dough will form a crust.) When the dough has doubled in volume, remove from the bowl and turn out onto a lightly floured surface. Flatten it and fold into three. This is known as deflating (or knocking back in the UK). Form a ball and then make the desired shapes. Leave to rise again (covered with a damp tea towel or plastic wrap) until it reaches the top of the mold (4), which should take 30 to 40 minutes.

Preheat the oven to 375°F (190°C), or slightly hotter, if you know your oven well, as high heat gives the impetus for the best result. Bake the brioche. Allow about 40 minutes for a single brioche using this recipe, less for smaller ones. It should be well risen and the crust will have a nice golden color. Test for doneness: the tip of a knife should come out dry.

CHEF'S NOTES

– The dough will also rise at a lower temperature than that stated in the recipe but will take more time.
– For a faster rising, all the ingredients should be at room temperature.
– Never allow the salt to come into direct contact with the yeast as this will kill it.

DID YOU KNOW?

The brioche has a long history. There are numerous regional specialties in France, and it is one of the Viennoiserie pastries that has the most variations. Kugelhopf dough is closely related to brioche dough.

Brioches differ in both shape and filling. Some examples are:
• the Nanterre brioche, made of two parallel lines of balls in a rectangular baking pan;
• the braided brioche, made with two, three, or four strands;
• the Swiss brioche, rolled with raisins, a type of raisin loaf made with brioche dough and pastry cream;
• the Parisian brioche, which has a little "head," and is probably the best-known type, popular for breakfast;
• the Bordelaise brioche, a crown shape with candied fruit and incisions on the top.

RECIPE IDEA

French brioche toast and vanilla stewed rhubarb **485**

Savarin or baba dough ✳✳

This leavened dough is distinct from brioche dough: it does not use the same quantities of egg and fat, and it is shaped differently. For the babas, you will need to soak the raisins in the rum one day before baking.

INGREDIENTS

³/₅ oz. (17 g) fresh (compressed) yeast
Scant ½ cup (100 ml) water
2 ¾ cups (250 g) cake flour
1 teaspoon (5 g) salt
2 ½ teaspoons (10 g) sugar
2 eggs, room temperature, beaten
7 tablespoons (100 g) unsalted butter, plus a little extra to grease the pan

For rum babas, add
Generous ¾ cup (125 g) currants or raisins
3 tablespoons (50 ml) amber rum

Syrup
2 cups (500 ml) water
1 ¼ cup (250 g) granulated sugar
¾ cup (200 ml) amber rum

A day ahead: If you are making babas, plump up the raisins by soaking them in the rum.

Dilute the yeast in a scant ½ cup (100 ml) water at room temperature. Sift the flour and make a well in the center. Sprinkle the salt outside the well so that it does not come into direct contact with the yeast. Add the sugar, combine the ingredients using a scraper, and gradually pour in the beaten eggs.

Knead the dough energetically to give it elasticity. You may use a stand mixer with the dough hook to do this. Stop when the dough detaches from your fingertips or from the sides of the bowl.

Melt the butter (ensure it is warm, not hot) and mix it into the dough. Cover with plastic wrap and set aside to rise for 30–40 minutes at a temperature of 77°F–82°F (25°C–28°C).

When the dough has doubled in volume, remove it from the bowl and turn out onto a lightly floured surface. Flatten it and fold into three, punching it to remove the air. This is known as deflating. If you are making rum babas, stir in the rum-soaked raisins.

Butter the baking pans **(1)**. Spoon the dough into a pastry bag, or use a scraper to fill the buttered pans halfway **(2)**. Leave to rise, covered with a cloth or plastic wrap, until the dough reaches the top of the pan.

Preheat the oven to 375°F (190°C). When the dough has doubled in volume, place the pan or pans in the oven. Bake for about 40 minutes; check for doneness with the tip of a knife, which should come out dry. Keep a close eye on your cakes as they bake: the crust must be a nice golden color.

Prepare a syrup (see p. 172). For best absorption of the syrup, prepare it while the cake cools, and pour it over while still warm. You may place your baba or savarin in a special grid, known as a *candissoire*, to glaze it.

CHEF'S NOTES

– The dough will also rise at a lower temperature than 77°F–82°F (25°C–28°C) but will take more time. For a faster rising, all the ingredients should be at room temperature.
– Never allow the salt to come into direct contact with the yeast, as this will kill it.
– The raisins can be soaked in cool liquid a day ahead, or in tepid liquid for 2 hours.

DID YOU KNOW?

Savarins are completely open in the center, forming a crown shape (4), whereas baba molds are not, and are indented (3). Stanislaw Leszczynski (1677–1766), King of Poland and father-in-law of Louis XV, found the kugelhopf too dry, so thought it would be a good idea to soak it with rum. He is said to have given it the name of "baba" in honor of Ali Baba, the hero of *One Thousand and One Nights*, a favorite book of his.
Auguste Jullien created the savarin in 1845 in homage to Brillat-Savarin, the renowned author of a work on gastronomy, *La Physiologie du goût* (*The Physiology of Taste*), published twenty years earlier.

Bread dough ✳✳

This is a dough that rises twice. It comes out of the oven with a lovely crust and a soft crumb.

INGREDIENTS

⁴/₅ oz. (25.5 g) fresh (compressed) yeast
2 cups plus 1 scant ½ cup (600 ml) water
2 ¼ lb. (1 kg) all-purpose flour
4 teaspoons (20 g) salt
5 teaspoons (20 g) sugar (optional)

For best results, prepare this recipe using a stand mixer with the dough hook.

Dilute the yeast in tepid water, or slightly warm water, i.e., around 85°F (30°C).

Sift the flour onto a flat surface and make a well. Pour the yeast into the center. Add the sugar, if using. Knead the dough on low speed for 3 minutes until it is smooth and slightly elastic.

Continue kneading the dough at medium speed for about 10 minutes, adding the salt 5 minutes before the end.

Form the dough into a ball and cover the bowl with plastic wrap or a clean, slightly damp tea towel.

Heat the oven to a temperature of 77°F–82°F (25°C–28°C) and place a bowl of water at the bottom. Place the dough in the oven to rise until it doubles in volume (1, 2).

Split the dough into pieces and shape it to make individual rolls, loaves, or baguettes (3).

Cover the shaped dough and return to the oven until it again doubles in volume.

Make regular, shallow incisions, ¹/₁₀–¹/₅ inch (0.3–0.5 cm) deep at the top using the blade of a cutter or scissors. This will allow the bread to expand without cracking.

Preheat the oven to 450°F (230°C). When you are ready to place the bread in the oven, spray the bottom of the oven with water and immediately put the loaves in to bake. When baked, the crust will be golden brown and crisp.

Test for doneness by rapping on the bottom of the bread: this should make a hollow sound.

Remove the bread from the baking tray immediately so that it does not reabsorb any moisture.

CHEF'S NOTES

– The dough will rise also at a lower temperature than 77°F–82°F (25°C–28°C) but will take more time. For a faster rising, all the ingredients should be at room temperature.
– Never allow the salt to come into direct contact with the yeast, as this will kill it.
– Experiment with different types of flour, wholewheat or other, whatever you enjoy best. Should you want to add ingredients such as nuts, chopped onions, bacon bits, and so on, incorporate them when you split up the dough after the first rising.

DID YOU KNOW?

There are three main techniques in bread-making:

• the use of leaven or sourdough culture as a starter. This involves natural fermentation of flour and water at room temperature. It is a slow technique.

• the use of a *poolish*, or wet starter. This involves two stages: a dry flour-and-water paste (*la détrempe*) is added to a liquid paste that is fermented with yeast.

• the direct technique: the flour, water, and yeast are fermented together. This is the easiest and fastest of the methods.
Yeast is a live organism and its Latin name is *Saccharomyces cerevisiae*.

Sandwich loaf ✳ ✳ ✳

A yeast dough whose white crumb has fine, closely knit holes.

INGREDIENTS
(for one 15-inch [38-cm] loaf)

¼ cup (25 g) powdered milk
1 ¼ cups (300 ml) water, room temperature
¾ oz. (22 g) fresh (compressed) yeast
5 ½ cups (500 g) cake flour
5 teaspoons (20 g) sugar
5 ¼ tablespoons (75 g) unsalted butter, softened, plus a little extra to grease the pan
2 ½ teaspoons (12 g) salt

Special equipment: a covered loaf pan (a Pullman pan), or aluminum foil, a baking sheet, and a weight to cover the loaf pan

Combine the milk powder with the water at room temperature and dilute the yeast in the liquid. Sift the flour, make a well in the center and pour in the liquid. Add the sugar.

Knead the dough at low to medium speed until the mixture is smooth and slightly elastic (1). Knead for about 5 minutes. Add the softened butter and the salt and knead for a further 5 minutes.

Shape the dough into a ball and cover it with a clean, damp cloth or plastic wrap.

Heat the oven to 77°F–82°F (25°C–28°C) and place a bowl of water at the bottom. Place the dough in the oven to rise until it doubles in volume.

Butter a baking pan. Now break the dough and punch it down to evacuate any air. Shape it to fit into the loaf pan.

Return it to the oven, cover with a damp cloth or plastic wrap, and leave it to double in volume with the cover slightly open (2). When it has reached this volume, preheat the oven to 425°F (220°C).

If you wish, you may make regular, shallow incisions, ¹/₁₀–¹/₅ inch (0.3–0.5 cm) deep at the top using the blade of a cutter or scissors. This will allow the bread to expand without cracking.

When you are ready to bake the bread, spray the bottom of the oven with water and immediately put the loaf in with the lid closed or the top of the pan covered to prevent the bread from rising. Bake for about 30–40 minutes.

Test for doneness by rapping on the bottom of the bread. It should make a hollow sound. Turn it out of the pan so that it does not reabsorb any moisture (3).

CHEF'S NOTES

– For best results, make this recipe using a stand mixer with the dough hook.
– The dough will also rise at a lower temperature than 77°F–82°F (25°C–28°C) but will take more time. For a faster rising, all the ingredients should be at room temperature.
– Never allow the salt to come into direct contact with the yeast, as this will kill it.

DID YOU KNOW?

A French sandwich loaf and brioched bread differ in that the brioched bread has more fat. In France, sandwich loaves are used as a base for canapés, for toasts, and to make croutons. They are also used for croque monsieur, a popular toasted ham and cheese sandwich snack served in cafés.

Croissant dough ✳ ✳ ✳

This quintessentially French breakfast treat is a yeast-based puff pastry, cut out into triangles and rolled from the base to the top, then shaped into a crescent. The same dough is used for many of the other pastries collectively known as *viennoiseries*, such as *pains au chocolat* (chocolate croissants) and *pains au raisins* (raisin rolls, usually made with pastry cream).

INGREDIENTS
(for about 25 croissants)

5 cups (500 g) all-purpose flour
2 teaspoons (10 g) salt
¼ cup (50 g) granulated sugar
1 ¼ cups (300 ml) milk, at room
 temperature
³/₅ oz. (17 g) fresh (compressed)
 yeast
2 ²/₃ sticks (300 g) unsalted
 butter

Sift the flour and salt together and combine with the sugar. Dissolve the yeast in the milk. Make a well in the center of the flour. Rapidly work the liquid into the dry ingredients until the mixture is smooth. (If you are using a stand mixer with the dough hook, this will take 4–5 minutes at medium speed.)

Chill for about 20 minutes.

Then allow the dough to rise for 40 minutes in a warm, draft-free place at 77°F–86°F (25°–30°C). It should double in volume.

Fold the dough over itself and rap to evacuate any air. Cover in plastic wrap and chill again for 30 minutes.

The butter should be at the same temperature as the dough.

Roll the dough out into a cross shape, leaving the center thicker than the four sides, about ¹/₅ inch (5 mm).

Place the slab of butter between two sheets of parchment paper and flatten it with a rolling pin until it takes on a square shape. Place the butter in the center of the cross and wrap the four sides of the dough around it.

Roll out the dough until it forms a rectangle. The length should be three times the width.

Fold it into three, rotate the folded dough a quarter-turn and roll out again to form the same shape as previously. Repeat the folding and rotating operation three times, chilling between each stage. The dough will be folded a total of six times, just as for the basic puff pastry recipe.

Roll the dough out to a thickness of ¹/₅ inch (0.5 cm). Cut out triangles measuring about 4 inches at the base with sides about 6 inches long (10 cm base/15 cm sides). Roll up the croissants (**1, 2, 3**) starting from the base.

Leave to rise again for at least 40 minutes and bake for about 20 minutes at 350°F (180°C).

DID YOU KNOW?

Croissants were created in Austria, and introduced in France when Marie-Antoinette arrived, around 1770. With the Universal Exhibition of 1889, their popularity really took off.

1

2

3

Batters with chemical raising agents

French fruit cake ✳

Basic Doughs and Batters

In French, this loaf cake is simply known as "*un cake*." It has less fruit than the traditional holiday or dark fruit cake baked in the English-speaking world, and a light batter.

INGREDIENTS

1 ½ sticks (6 oz. or 175 g) unsalted butter, softened, and a little extra for the pan
⅔ cup (125 g) granulated sugar
½ teaspoon (3 g) fine sea salt
3 eggs
A few drops of fruit brandy or other strong alcohol
2 ½ cups (250 g) all-purpose flour
1 slightly heaped teaspoon (5 g) baking powder
7 oz. (200 g) candied fruit
3 ½ oz. (100 g) sultanas or raisins
A little flour or confectioners' sugar for coating the fruit

Place a baking tray in the center of the oven and preheat it to 400°F (200°C). Butter a loaf pan and/or line it with parchment paper.

Cream the butter, sugar, and salt together very thoroughly. Add the eggs, one by one, and combine. Flavor with fruit brandy. Sift the flour and salt together into the batter and combine (**1**) until just mixed.

Coat the fruit lightly in flour or confectioners' sugar so that the pieces don't fall to the bottom of the pan during baking. Add the candied fruit and sultanas or raisins (**2**). Pour the batter into the loaf pan and place it on the baking tray.

Bake for 5 minutes, then reduce the temperature to 300°F (150°C). Bake for a further 40–50 minutes,

depending on the size and shape of the cake pan, or until the tip of a knife comes out clean.

Turn out onto a rack to cool.

CHEF'S NOTES

– In general, allow 4 slightly heaped teaspoons (20g) of baking powder for 4 ¼ cups (1 kg) of flour.
– Place the loaf pan on a well-heated baking pan in the oven, not on a rack.
– You can also make savory versions of this recipe. Loaves with olives, diced ham, onions, cheese, and bacon bits are popular in France at buffets, for picnics, or with drinks.

RECIPE IDEA

French fruit loaf **459**

Marble cake ✳✳

Each portion of the batter is colored and flavored differently, then piped alternately into the loaf tin to create an attractive "marbled" effect.

INGREDIENTS

1 stick (125 g) unsalted butter, softened, plus extra for the mold
1 scant cup (125 g) confectioners' sugar
3 eggs
1 ¾ cups (160 g) cake flour
1 teaspoon (4 g) baking powder
A few drops of vanilla essence
Grated zest of 1 unsprayed or organic lemon
3 tablespoons (20 g) cocoa powder, unsweetened

Preheat the oven to 400°F (200°C). Place a baking tray on the middle rack on which to set the loaf pan for baking.

Butter a loaf pan and/or line it with parchment paper.

Cream the softened butter with the sugar in a mixing bowl. Add the eggs, one by one, and mix thoroughly.

Sift the flour and baking powder together into the mixture and blend.

Divide the batter into two parts. Flavor one half with the vanilla essence and lemon zest (the color should remain light). Incorporate the cocoa powder into the other half.

Spoon the mixtures into two pastry bags. Pipe the two mixtures into the loaf pan alternately **(1)** and smooth the top with the back of a spoon **(2)**.

Bake immediately for 5 minutes at 400°F (200°C), then lower the temperature to 300°F (150°C). Continue baking for 40–50 minutes depending on the size of the pan. Test for doneness: the tip of a knife should come out clean.

When done, turn out and cool on a rack **(3)**.

CHEF'S NOTES

– For optimal flavor contrast and so that the batter does not become too liquid, use dry flavoring ingredients such as cocoa powder, and/or very concentrated essence.
– Cakes that use chemical leavening agents should be baked as soon as the batter is in the loaf pan.

Madeleines ✳

A raised dough that is baked to form small cakes in a special mold. The grooved base of each mold resembles a scallop shell. Nothing is added to the basic madeleine batter—madeleines are not filled, just flavored.

INGREDIENTS
(for about 30 standard-sized madeleines)

4 eggs
1 scant cup (175 g) granulated sugar
2 scant cups (175 g) cake flour
1 stick (125 g) unsalted butter, softened, plus extra for molds
2 slightly heaped teaspoons (10 g) baking powder
A few drops of vanilla essence
Zest of ½ unsprayed or organic lemon or orange (optional)

Special equipment: a madeleine baking pan

Preheat the oven to 375°F (190°C). Place a baking tray large enough to hold your madeleine pan on the middle rack while the oven heats up. (If possible, use two trays, one on top of the other, to increase the amount of heat the madeleines come into contact with.)

Whisk the eggs and sugar together until the mixture becomes pale and thick.

Sift in the flour and combine. Then add the butter, followed by the baking powder, the vanilla essence, and the citrus zest if using. The consistency should be thick. Place the batter in the refrigerator.

Grease the molds and fill them to two-thirds with a pastry bag or a spoon (1).

Place the baking pan on the hot tray to ensure that the characteristic mound on top of the cakes forms. To ensure that the madeleines do not dry out, lower the oven temperature to 350°F (170°C) as soon as you place them in the oven, or spray a little water on the oven wall.

Baking time will depend on the size of your madeleines. For the standard size, allow about 10 minutes. They are done when the top is a nice golden-brown color.

Remove from the oven, test for doneness, and turn out from the pan immediately. Leave to cool on a rack.

CHEF'S NOTES

– It is best to place the filled madeleine baking pan on a tray that is already hot in the oven.
– Turn them out of their molds as soon as you remove them from the oven so that no condensation forms between the cakes and the mold.

DID YOU KNOW?

The first madeleines are commonly believed to have been baked by Madeleine Paumier at the Château of Commercy in the Lorraine region around 1730. She made them for Stanislaw Leszczynski, King of Poland and father-in-law of Louis XV, who later made them famous.

The tops of the cakes are shaped like a scallop shell, a symbol of the pilgrims' route on Saint James's Way, El Camino de Santiago.

1

Basic Doughs and Batters

Eggs

How to choose eggs

The color of the eggshell— white or brown—depends on the breed of the hen, and is not a result of the hen's feed.

An egg is composed of:
· the white (1 oz. or 28 g on average): 87% water, 11% albumen;

· the yolk (0.98 oz. or 20 g on average): 50% water, 31% lipids, and 16% protein.

Eggs are not only a good, reasonably priced source of nutrition, delicious served on their own as in the recipes set out here, they are also a multipurpose foodstuff with a wide range of uses. Well beaten, they help cakes and soufflés rise; whisked into sauces, they prevent them from separating; they also play a key role in pastry making.

Eggs must always be stored in the refrigerator once they are bought, preferably in their cartons and with their larger end facing upward. For optimal quality, both in terms of taste and culinary use, use them within a week of their laying date, but if their shells are in perfect condition you may store them for up to one month.

Hard-boiled eggs ✳

INGREDIENTS

2 fresh eggs per person
A few drops of vinegar

Bring water to boil in a saucepan or pot. Add a few drops of vinegar just as you immerse the eggs (1). Allow them to cook for 11 to 12 minutes from the moment the water starts to boil again.

Remove them from the water and cool immediately under cold running water.

Remove the shells, taking care to remove the thin membrane covering the egg along with the shells (2, 3, 4).

Rinse the eggs to remove any remaining pieces of shell.

If storing them, leave them still slightly damp, on a tray or plate, covered with plastic wrap, in the refrigerator.

CHEF'S NOTE

– Keep an eye on cooking times for eggs; an overcooked egg will have a greenish streak around the yolk.

RECIPE IDEA

Salade Niçoise **420**

Soft-boiled eggs (*oeufs mollets*) ✳

See hard-boiled eggs (p. 41).

Use the same method but shorten the cooking time so that the yolk does not cook and remains runny.

COOKING TIME

5 to 6 minutes from the time the water starts to boil again. Shell the eggs before serving.

RECIPE IDEA

Soft-boiled eggs on a bed of artichokes with eggplant caviar **424**

Lightly boiled eggs in their shells (*oeufs à la coque*) ✳

See soft-boiled eggs (left).

Lightly boiled eggs are served in their shells to crack open at the table, hence their French name (coque means "shell").

COOKING TIME

3 minutes from the time the water starts to boil again.

CHEF'S NOTE

– Do not bring the water to a fast boil as this causes the eggs to move around too much. If they come into contact with one another, or with the sides of the pot, they may crack, causing the white to escape during the cooking process.

Shirred eggs ✳

INGREDIENTS

2 fresh eggs per person
A little butter
Fine sea salt, white pepper

If you are using the traditional oven method, preheat the oven to just below 195°F (90°C).

Butter two egg dishes (they should have small handles) using a pastry brush. Use one dish per person (1). Otherwise, melt the butter in a frying pan.

Season the cooking dishes (2).

Break the eggs carefully, one by one, into the dish or frying pan, ensuring that you do not break the yolks. If using dishes, place two eggs in each.

Cook gently without coloring the white. It should coagulate, and the yolk should remain runny (3).

CHEF'S NOTES

– The low temperature (below 195°F [90°C]) of the oven ensures that the eggs will not dry out or form unsightly bubbles.
– Brush your eggs with butter just before serving to give them an attractive sheen.
– Season the dish or pan rather than the top of the eggs so that there are no white or black spots.

43

Scrambled eggs ✳

INGREDIENTS

2 fresh eggs per person
2 teaspoons (10 g) butter, cubed,
    and/or cream, plus a little
    butter for the pan
To garnish: chopped fresh herbs,
    mushrooms, chopped
    tomatoes.
Salt, pepper

Break the eggs into a mixing bowl. Season and beat them with a fork or a whisk.

Melt some butter in the pan over low heat. Pour the eggs into the hot pan. Stir constantly with a spatula or wooden spoon. The last moments of cooking are crucial. The eggs should not be completely cooked, so remove the skillet from the heat and add the butter cubes and/or a drizzle of cream to stop the cooking. The final texture should be creamy.

Add your garnish and serve immediately.

CHEF'S NOTE

– You can also add the garnish (herbs, chopped tomatoes, or mushrooms) before you cook the eggs if you prefer.

RECIPE IDEA

Scrambled eggs with a mini-ratatouille **293**

Eggs en cocotte ✳

INGREDIENTS

A little butter, melted
Fresh eggs
To garnish: port sauce, sautéed
  mushrooms, tomato sauce, etc.
Salt, pepper

Special equipment: ramekins, a
  large flameproof dish or pan

Grease the ramekins with the
butter using a pastry brush **(1)**.
Season the bottom of the
ramekins with salt and
pepper.

Break the eggs carefully, one
into each ramekin, making
sure you do not break the
yolks **(2)**.

Line a shallow flameproof
baking dish with parchment
paper and place the ramekins
in this.

Half fill the dish with water.

Begin cooking the eggs on low
heat, until the water simmers.

Remove from the heat when
the white is coagulated, but
the yolk still creamy **(3)**.
Pour your sauce over the eggs,
or add the garnish, and serve
immediately.

CHEF'S NOTES

– The egg white should not be
colored at all, and the yolk
should not be covered by a dry
film. It must be shiny, and this is
why the result is called *miroir*—
mirror—in French.
– Eggs en cocotte may be
accompanied by many sauces
and side dishes. They are a real
treat for breakfast.
– Quail eggs are also excellent
when cooked using this method.

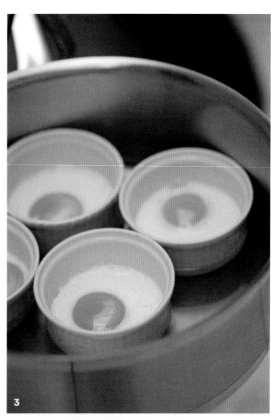

Deep-fried eggs ✳ ✳

INGREDIENTS

Oil for frying
Very fresh eggs

Special equipment: oil
thermometer

Accompany with: bacon,
eggplant caviar, fried
mushroom, etc.

Heat the oil in a deep pan to a
temperature of 350°F (180°C).
Check the temperature with a
thermometer.

Break the eggs, one by one,
into separate ramekins or
small cups. Be careful not to
break the yolks **(1)**.

Use two spatulas, one in each
hand, to gently immerse each
egg into the hot oil. Roll them
gently so that they maintain
an oval shape in the pan **(2)**.

When the egg turns a nice
light yellow color, remove it
from the pan with a slotted
spoon **(3)**. Repeat the
procedure with the remaining
eggs. Drain on kitchen paper.
Place on the plate with the
accompaniment of your
choice and serve immediately.

CHEF'S NOTES

– These eggs should be cooked
only at the last minute, just
before serving.
– Be careful of the hot oil, which
may splatter during cooking.
– Only cook one egg at a time.

Eggs in aspic ✳✳

INGREDIENTS
(serves 4)

Aspic powder for 1 scant cup
  (200 ml) aspic
4 fresh eggs
To garnish: a slice of ham, leek
  greens, tomato skin, black
  olives, carrot, long turnip, etc.

Prepare the aspic according to the package instructions.

Bring salted water to a boil and poach the eggs for about 3 minutes (see p. 49).

Drain them and allow them to cool. Trim the eggs so that the edges are regular.

Prepare the differently colored elements you will be using for decoration, either raw or cooked (1).

Pour a thin layer of aspic into the bottom of the ramekins and put them in the refrigerator to set. Make sure the dishes are placed perfectly horizontally.

To decorate, place the various elements on the set aspic, bearing in mind that this will be uppermost when the dish is unmolded.

Pour in another thin layer of aspic and chill to set.

Place the egg at the center of the ramekin and pour in the remaining aspic.

Return to the refrigerator to set.

Dip the ramekins briefly in boiling water to unmold them.

Arrange attractively on a plate (2).

Omelet ✳

INGREDIENTS

2–3 fresh eggs per person
A little butter or oil for the pan
A little clarified butter to brush
  the omelet
To garnish: chopped fresh herbs,
  cheese, sautéed mushrooms,
  slow-cooked bell peppers with
  tomatoes, etc.
Salt, pepper

If you are making a flat omelet, add the garnish at this stage. Melt a little butter or pour the oil into a hot pan and pour the mixture in. Keeping the heat high, cook the omelet, drawing the cooked edges towards the center so the still-liquid part can cook. The texture should be creamy.

Place a plate over the pan and turn it over with a rapid movement. Slip the other side of the omelet into the pan to finish cooking.

Brush with clarified butter for a nice shine and serve on a plate.

If you are making a rolled omelet, heat the pan with butter or oil and pour the beaten eggs in. Cook over high heat, drawing the cooked edges towards the center so that the still-liquid eggs can cook. The texture should be creamy.

Add the garnish (2), tilt the pan downward (handle upward) and, using a fork, roll the omelet downward over itself. Brush with clarified butter for a nice shine and serve on a plate.

CHEF'S NOTE

– The best omelet is a pale color. When omelets are overdone, they become dry and rubbery. Take 2–3 eggs per person (1) and break into a mixing bowl. Season with salt and pepper and whisk with a fork.

DID YOU KNOW?

Omelets and hard-boiled eggs are probably the oldest dishes made only with eggs. Mention is made of them in a book written in 1398, *Le Mesnagier de Paris* (*The Good Wife's Guide*, translated by Gina L. Greco and Christine M. Rose, Ithaca: Cornell University Press, 2009), a medieval treatise for women.

RECIPE IDEA

Rolled mushroom omelet **269**

Poached eggs ✳✳

INGREDIENTS

1 fresh egg per person
A few drops of vinegar

Bring the water to a boil (1).

Break the eggs, one by one, into individual ramekins. Take care not to break the yolks (2).

Add the vinegar to the water and gently slip the eggs in. Use a skimmer to shape the white as evenly as possible.

Cook for about 3 minutes.

Remove with a skimmer, refresh very briefly under cold water, drain (3), and trim so that the edges are nice and neat.

DID YOU KNOW?

Eggs may be poached in red wine (the dish is called *oeufs meurette* or *oeufs à la bordelaise*) as well as in milk.

Poached eggs go well with very different accompaniments, from mushrooms, bacon bits, and croûtons to shellfish and salad.

French meringue ✳

This is also known as simple meringue. It is prepared cold, that is to say without cooking the sugar, and then usually baked. French meringue is used to make plain or flavored meringues, and for the shells that hold ice cream in the frozen dessert called vacherin. The French meringue technique is also used to make mousses: the eggs are whisked stiffly and sugar is added to make them very firm and shiny.

INGREDIENTS

4 egg whites
Scant ½ cup (80 g) sugar
1 pinch salt

First, liquefy the egg whites by beating them in a semi-spherical bowl with a pinch of salt.

Whisk them energetically, making sure to lift the beaters or whisk high to incorporate as much air as possible.

Briskly whisk the sugar in with a circular movement so that the mixture takes on a firm texture.

The meringue must be compact and smooth, and peaks must form when you lift it up with the whisk.

RECIPE IDEAS

Floating islands with spun caramel **488**
Frozen blackberry vacherin **528**

Italian meringue ✳✳

This hot preparation, made with cooked sugar, is widely used for decoration because of its firm texture. It is also used for making ice cream, and is an essential component of almond macarons.

INGREDIENTS

2 tablespoons (30 ml) water
⅔ cup (120 g) granulated sugar
4 egg whites
1 pinch of salt

Special equipment: sugar thermometer

To prepare the syrup, heat the water and sugar in a saucepan.

Meanwhile, put the egg whites in the bowl of a stand mixer, ensuring it is perfectly clean and dry first.

When the temperature of the syrup reaches 230°F (110°C), begin beating the egg whites with a pinch of salt. When the temperature of the syrup reaches 243°F–250°F (117°C–120°C), take the pan off the heat and start pouring it in a slow, steady stream into the egg whites. Continue beating until the meringue has cooled down completely. It will be dense and shiny, and will form many small peaks.

RECIPE IDEAS

Lemon meringue tartlets **460**
Baked Alaska **532**
Frozen banana soufflé **531**

Swiss meringue ✳

This is a hot preparation made over a bain-marie. It is firm meringue used for the small pastries known as *rochers* (rocks) and for decoration. The origins of this dish are disputed, but one version claims that it was invented in 1720 in the town of Meiringen, Switzerland, giving meringues their name.

INGREDIENTS

4 egg whites
1 pinch of salt
½ cup (100 g) granulated sugar

Special equipment: sugar thermometer

Prepare a pot half filled with hot water to make a bain-marie. The water should be between 122°F and 131°F (50°C–55°C) when you are ready to use it.

Liquefy the whites by beating them with a pinch of salt in a semi-spherical bowl. Pour the sugar in and whisk energetically, making sure you lift the whites high into the air. When the mixture begins to foam, place the bowl over the hot water.

Whisk continuously until the mixture thickens, increases to three times its volume, and becomes shiny. At this point, the meringue should be at a maximum temperature of 113°F (45°C). When it reaches this temperature, remove it from the heat and continue to whisk until it cools down completely to room temperature.

Sabayon (zabaglione) ✳✳

INGREDIENTS

6 egg yolks
Generous ½ cup (150 ml) liquid,
  for example water, liqueur, or wine
⅔ cup (125 g) sugar (optional)

Place the egg yolks in a saucepan. Add the liquid and sugar (1), if using, and whisk energetically.

Place the saucepan over a low heat (low flame or hot water bath). Whisk the mixture continuously until it is creamy (2).

DID YOU KNOW?

Sweet sabayon is excellent with strawberries or as a base for a fruit gratin. Savory sabayon pairs well with asparagus and fish.

RECIPE IDEAS

Strawberry gratin with sabayon **503**
Hot oyster gratin **266**

1

2

Preparing Garnishes, Fish, and Meat

Garnishes

Canelling ✳

This technique can be used for decorative elements and aromatic ingredients (for example, in a court bouillon).

Use this technique for carrots, zucchini, citrus fruits, and so on.

Wash, dry, and trim the ends of the fruit or vegetable. Using a canelle knife, make regular incisions lengthwise along the fruit or vegetable (**1, 2, 3**).

Dicing ✳✳

It is important to dice regularly to obtain pieces that are uniformly sized. This ensures even cooking.
If, however, you do find you have some large pieces, do not chop them any further as they will lose their juice and flavor.

Use this technique for shallots, large onions, and so on.

Cut the product in half through its thickest part, i.e. vertically, from top to bottom, to the root (**1**).

Taking each half separately, slice regularly lengthwise, but stop before you reach the base. (**2**).

Make two or three horizontal incisions, depending on the thickness of the product, without going as far as the root (**3**).

Hold the vegetable firmly and slice finely from top to root through the other cuts to create dice (**4**).

Chopping tomatoes ✳✳

This technique entails roughly chopping tomatoes.

Remove the tomato skin using the boiling water technique (see p. 63), not forgetting to make a cross incision at the base. Cut in half from the stem to the cross you have made. Remove the seeds by gently squeezing each half in the palm of your hand.

Cut and cube the tomato halves into the size that suits your recipe.

RECIPE IDEA

Provençal-style sardine *tartes fines* **290**

Simple slicing (*émincer à la paysanne*) ✳

This cutting technique is used for several aromatic bases. Depending on the vegetable, you can make shapes such as squares and triangles.

Use this technique for leeks, carrots, turnips, and so on.

Cut the vegetable into chunks, depending on its length **(1)**.

Slice it lengthwise in two, or four if it is thick.

Hold the vegetable firmly and cut finely at right angles to the slices **(2)**.

Slicing into rings (*émincer en bracelets*) ✳

Rings are fine cuts, used as garnish and as an aromatic base. It is important to keep to the cooking time specified in the recipe so that they maintain their shape.

Use this technique for large onions, shallots, and so on.

Choose a vegetable with a nice round shape.

Hold it firmly and cut regular fine slices. **(1)**

Detach the rings **(2, 3)**.

CHEF'S NOTE

– You can also use a Japanese mandoline to prepare rings.

1

2

1

2

3

Shredding (chiffonade) ✳

Use for leafy vegetables such as lettuce, spinach, and cabbage.

Remove the central part (rib or stalk) **(1)** and place several leaves on top of one another **(2)**.

Fold them over themselves. Shred them as finely as you need for your recipe **(3)**.

CHEF'S NOTE

– Use the shredded vegetables as soon as you have cut them, whether raw or cooked, because they will wilt rapidly.

RECIPE IDEAS

Creamed lettuce soup (*velouté Choisy*) **299**
Sweetbread vol-au-vents with cider and
 apples **283**

Cutting round slices ✳

Use this technique for vegetables such as carrots, zucchini, and long turnips.

Slice rounds to the thickness required for your recipe using either a Japanese mandoline **(1)** or a vegetable slicing knife **(2)**.

CHEF'S NOTE

– The thickness of the slices depends on whether you are using the vegetable as an aromatic base or for garnish. If using several vegetables, it's best to cook them separately and combine them when you serve them, as each one has a specific cooking time and a particular taste that should be preserved.

RECIPE IDEA

Provençal shoulder of lamb and vegetable *tian* **379**

Cutting on the oblique ✳

This technique is widely used for garnishes of mixed vegetables.

Use for vegetables such as carrots, zucchini, and long turnips.

Cut or slice the vegetables at a slight angle. Make regular slices of a thickness suitable for the recipe you will be preparing. Use either a Japanese mandoline **(1)** or a vegetable slicing knife **(2)**. For an added attractive touch, canelle the product beforehand.

Peeling ✳

Use this technique for fruit and vegetables such as carrots, large onions, asparagus, apples, and pears.

Remove the skin from a raw fruit or vegetable using a paring knife, a double-bladed vegetable peeler, or a peeler with a single blade.

Special care should be paid when preparing asparagus, black salsify (black oyster plant), and white salsify (white oyster plant).

Hold the vegetable firmly at its base.

Asparagus should be peeled from the tip towards the base, which should then be broken off. Asparagus is a fragile vegetable, so tie a bunch together and trim them before cooking so that they are all the same height.

CHEF'S NOTE

Lemon juice should be squeezed over certain fruit, such as apples and pears, as soon as they are peeled so that they do not go brown. Potatoes should simply be left in water to await cooking.

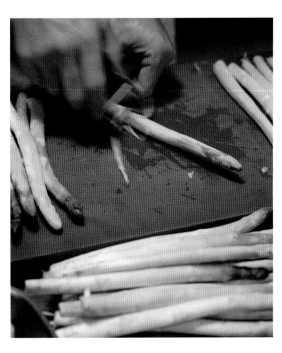

Quartering button mushrooms ✳

Use this technique for button mushrooms.

Separate the stalk from the cap by cutting just below the cap **(1)**.

Cut the cap in half, holding the blade of the knife at an angle. This will ensure that you have an esthetically pleasing cut, not one that is too straight or severe.

Rotate the cap a quarter turn and cut at an angle as before **(2)**.

CHEF'S NOTE

– Squeeze a little lemon juice over the cut mushrooms so that they do not darken. Even with the lemon juice, it is important to use them rapidly.

RECIPE IDEA

Rolled mushroom omelet **269**

Rubbing with kosher salt ✳

Use this technique for Chinese artichokes.

Top and tail the Chinese artichokes. Place them on a tea cloth with a handful of kosher salt. Wrap them up in the cloth and rub them briskly.

Kosher salt eliminates the thin skin and any remaining earth between the folds.

Rinse well under running water.

CHEF'S NOTE

– You may also leave the Chinese artichokes to soak overnight, brush them, and then top and tail them.

Zigzag cut (Vandyke technique) ✳

This technique is mainly used for citrus fruits, but is very similar to fruit and vegetable sculpture.

Wash and dry the citrus fruit and slice off the two ends **(1)**.

Insert the blade of the knife at the widest point of the fruit, and make your way around the circumference by creating zigzag incisions. The size of the angle will depend on the number of zigzags you wish to make **(2)**.

Continue round the fruit, cutting right into the center so the halves will come apart easily. Separate the two halves carefully and remove the pips **(3)**.

Cutting into julienne strips ✳✳

Julienne strips must be very finely sliced. Julienned citrus zests may be up to 1 ½ in. (4 cm) in length, but they should always be very fine.

Use this technique for vegetables such as carrots, turnips, the whites of leeks, and pickled cucumbers.

Thinly slice the vegetable using a Japanese mandoline. You may use a slicing knife instead.

Place the slices one on top of another. Then cut very fine strips with a slicing knife.

For leeks:

First, cut chunks about 4 in. (10 cm) long. Cut them in half lengthwise.

Flatten the halves well so that you can place them on top of one another. Slice fine strips lengthwise with the same slicing knife.

CHEF'S NOTE

– To prepare citrus zests, remove the skin with a double-bladed vegetable peeler (see p. 62 for the technique of cutting citrus segments) and then slice it very finely.

RECIPE IDEA

Mixed garden vegetables **416**

Scooping ✳

Use this technique for fruits and vegetables such as potatoes, apples, melon, turnips, carrots, zucchini, and so on.

Place the melon baller on the surface of the fruit or vegetable and press it right in, pivoting it as you do so. This will form a ball that you can then scoop out.

CHEF'S NOTE

– Apple balls make a nice change from apple slices on a tart, and may also be used to garnish a poultry dish.

RECIPE IDEA

Fish papillotes with vegetable scoops **311**

Cutting citrus segments ✳

A fan of citrus segments and other cut fruits makes a spectacular platter, or you can use citrus segments as decoration on a dish.

Wash and dry your fruit. Cut off the top and bottom of the fruit, and stand it firmly on one of the cut ends.

Use a knife with a flexible edge. Hold it at an angle so that it follows the curve of the fruit. Make sure that all the pith is removed from the outside of the fruit (it tastes bitter and looks unattractive).

Using the same knife, remove the segments of flesh between the white membranes.

Arrange the segments and drizzle with the juice that has come out from the fruit.

CHEF'S NOTE

– The segments of citrus fruit are very fragile once they are cut, and do not hold together when cooked.

RECIPE IDEA

Duckling à l'orange with sautéed potatoes and artichokes **353**

Peeling using hot water ✳

Use this technique for fruits such as plums, tomatoes, almonds, and peaches.

Remove the stalk of the fruit **(1)** and make a cross-shaped incision at the other end with a kitchen knife.

Prepare a saucepan of boiling water and drop the fruit in for about ten seconds, or until the skin begins to peel off at the cross incision **(2)**.

Remove from the water using a slotted spoon **(3)** and place immediately in a bowl of ice water. The difference in temperature will prevent the fruit from cooking further.

Peel with a paring knife **(4)** and place on paper towel to drain any excess water.

CHEF'S NOTE

– The skin may be kept to use for decoration (fried), and the seeds can be added to a stock.

RECIPE IDEA

Provençal-style sardine *tartes fines* **290**

Peeling using oil ✳

Use this technique for bell peppers.

Preheat the oven to 480°F–520°F (250°C–270°C), or to the maximum temperature your oven will reach.

Place the bell peppers on a baking tray and drizzle with oil **(1)**. Cook until the skin begins to separate from the flesh and form bubbles.

Remove from the oven; allow to cool sufficiently that you are able to handle them, and remove the skin using a paring knife **(2)**. Don't wait until they are completely cool as the skin will be hard to remove.

Cutting into batons (*jardinière*) ✳✳

Use this technique for vegetables such as carrots and turnips.

Cut chunks about 4 in. (10 cm) long (**1**). Place the chunks lengthwise against the mandoline to make slices $^1/_6$–$^1/_5$ in. (4 mm–5 mm) thick (**2**).

Place the slices one above another and cut sticks about $^1/_6$–$^1/_5$ in. (4–5 mm) wide (**3**).

CHEF'S NOTE

– Use good-sized vegetables to facilitate cutting.

RECIPE IDEA

Roasted rack of lamb with garden vegetables **389**

Cutting into fine dice (*brunoise*) ✳

Use this technique for all fruits and vegetables with firm flesh.

Cut chunks about 4 in. (10 cm) long (**1**).

Place the chunks lengthwise against the mandoline to make slices that are about $^1/_8$ in. (2–3 mm) thick (**2**).

Place the slices above one another and cut sticks about $^1/_8$ in. (2–3 mm) wide.

Cut them into regularly shaped $^1/_8$-in. (2–3-mm) cubes.

DID YOU KNOW?

To make a *macédoine* (mixed diced vegetables or fruit), use the method above for *brunoise* but make slightly larger cubes, with cuts about $^1/_5$ in. (4–5 mm).

A *mirepoix* is a mixture of vegetables such as carrots, onions, and celery, in larger cubes measuring about $^1/_2$ in.–$^1/_3$ in. (1.5 cm) and often used as an aromatic base.

RECIPE IDEA

Rabbit and pistachio terrine with exotic fruit chutney **270**

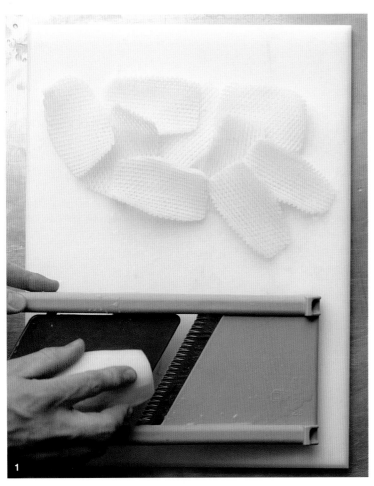

Cutting wafers ✳

Use this technique for vegetables such as potatoes, turnips, zucchini (courgettes), and celery root (celeriac).

Place a medium-sized vegetable on a mandoline with a wavy blade (1).

Each time you scrape the vegetable against the blade, rotate it a quarter-turn to obtain the fine open-work result (2).

CHEF'S NOTE

– Rinse the wafers well, then dab them to dry thoroughly so that they don't stick together when fried.

RECIPE IDEA

Grilled cockerel and *diable* sauce **369**

Turning vegetables ✳✳

Use this technique for vegetables such as potatoes, turnips, zucchini (courgettes), and carrot.

Cut chunks and then cut them lengthwise into two or four pieces, depending on the size (1, 2).

Hold the vegetable piece firmly between the thumb and index of one hand and, with the other, use a paring knife or a special shaping knife to shape curved sides, like the oval shape of a rugby or American football ball (3, 4).

CHEF'S NOTES

– For zucchini (courgettes), keep one side flat.
– When using turning vegetables as a garnish, allow seven to nine pieces per person.
– Generally, the trimmings are puréed to be used for another dish, so that there's no wastage.

1

2

3

4

For artichokes:

Break off the stems of the artichokes. Remove the outside leaves using a knife with a short, rigid blade (1, 2).

Trim the base neatly to remove any traces of green—these parts are very bitter (3).

Trim the head an inch or so (a few centimeters) from the bottom, where the feathery "choke" is.

Remove the choke using a spoon or scoop if need be (4). You can also remove it after cooking.

Sprinkle the entire artichoke bottom with lemon juice so it does not oxidize. You may also tie a slice of lemon to the base for cooking (5).

Reserve the bottoms in water with lemon juice until you need them. Cook them in a *blanc* (salted water with lemon juice and flour, see p. 108) or braise them (see p. 98).

RECIPE IDEA

Soft-boiled eggs on a bed of artichokes with eggplant caviar **424**

Fish, shellfish, and crustaceans

What to keep in mind when selecting seafood

A checklist for fresh, whole fish:

· the eyes must be shiny, bulging, and transparent; the gills should be damp and bright pink or red.
· the scales must be shiny and adhere to the flesh. They should be covered with a transparent, film of mucus.
· the smell should be fresh and inoffensive— not "fishy."

A whole fish often yields little flesh.

For fish such as John Dory, sea bream, and flat varieties, there may be as much as two-thirds wastage. The same is true of shellfish.

Type	Variety	Characteristics	Substitutes	Recipes
Cod family	Cod	Dense white flesh, mild flavor	Halibut, pollock, hake, haddock	Salt cod purée (brandade) and mashed potatoes (p. 312)
	Pollock/black cod	Firm white flesh	Cod, haddock, halibut, hake	Pollack fillets bonne femme (p. 319)
	Whiting	Delicate sweet flavor	Cod, pollock, any white fish	Fish papillotes with vegetable scoops (p. 311)
Bony	Gurnard	Firm white dense flesh	Cod	Bouillabaisse (p. 322)
	Salmonette/dogfish/rock salmon/huss	Well flavored firmish pink flesh	Any firm white fish	Dogfish stew in red wine with Brussels sprouts (p. 305)
Freshwater	Trout	Pink tender flesh, mild nutty flavor	Salmon	Trout with almonds (p. 306)
	Salmon	Pink oily flesh, distinctive flavor	Trout	Grilled salmon steaks with braised fennel (p. 325)
	Pike and pickerel	Sweet and fine-textured flesh	Any firm white fish	Pike quenelles and crayfish sauce (p. 272)
Small	Sea bass	White flesh with a medium sweet flavor and medium texture	Sea bream, snapper	Sea bass in a salt crust (p. 317)
	Sole	Mild, buttery sweet flavor	Halibut, lemon sole, flounder, plaice	Sole meunière and potatoes cocotte (p. 336)
	Plaice	Mild sweet flavor and soft texture	Dab, flounder, sole	Plaice *goujonnettes* with tartare sauce (p. 330)
Large	Turbot	Bright white firm flesh, delicate flavor	Halibut, Dover sole	Turbot poached in cardamom-infused milk, with hollandaise sauce (p. 335)
	John Dory/St. Pierre	Nutty, sweet flavor with flaky meat	Sole, turbot, halibut	Sautéed John Dory fillets with seaweed (p. 329)
Meaty	Monkfish	Firm, meaty texture	Lobster	Braised bacon-wrapped monkfish (p. 328) Monkfish medallions *à l'américaine* and rice pilaf (p. 338)
	Tuna	Oily, rich dark pink flesh, meat-like texture	Swordfish, marlin, or other firm-fleshed fish	Tuna rillettes with horseradish p. 261)
Thin-bodied	Sea bream	Medium sweet flavor, texture similar to bass	Sea bass, snapper	Aniseed-flambéed sea bream (p. 308)
	Mackerel	Pale and firm oily flesh	Herring, sardines	Mackerel in *escabèche* (p. 332)
Long-bodied	Eel	Firm flesh, distinctive flavor	Alaskan or Canadian black cod	Rockfish soup (p. 278)
Other	Anchovy	Very strong salty flavor (preserved)	Sardines (if using fresh)	Salade Niçoise (p. 420)

Shelling crustaceans ✴✴

The procedure is far easier when the crustacean is still alive.

Use this technique for shellfish such as langoustine and crayfish.

Hold the crustacean in the palm of your hand with the abdomen facing upward. Remove the central intestinal vein by pulling on the central part of the tail (1).

Use a pair of pointed scissors to make an incision all along the membrane of the abdomen.

Pull the abdominal shell away from the flesh and remove it (2). Rinse, drain, and chill.

CHEF'S NOTE

– You may remove the gut or intestinal vein after you shell the crustacean: make a small incision on the back to expose it.

RECIPE IDEA

Langoustine and pineapple skewers **314**

Preparing monkfish ✴✴

In French, the whole fish is known as *baudroie* and the edible part *lotte*. The whole fish is generally not sold at the fish counter, but the cheeks, which are considered a delicacy, are sometimes available.

Firmly grasp the black skin and use a knife to remove it, starting from the tail and moving toward the top of the bone (1, 2).

Cut the fillets away from the spine, and remove the thin membranes and violet-colored parts of the tails (these are very elastic) using a sole filleting knife (3).

Trim the rest of the tail so that it is as white as possible.

RECIPE IDEA

Monkfish medallions *à l'américaine* and rice pilaf **338**

Cutting fish steaks ✳

Use this technique for large fish such as salmon, conger or sea eel, and hake.

Take a prepared fish (scaled, gutted, fins removed, and washed) with the skin still on. Start at the head and work toward the tail, cutting perpendicularly to make thick slices weighing about 7 oz. (200 g).

Reserve the tail for other uses, such as escalopes, rillettes or terrines, cubes, or small morsels.

Tie the steaks with twine so that they hold together when cooked.

Remove the skin when they are ready to eat.

CHEF'S NOTE

– If possible, do not rinse the steaks, particularly if they are to be grilled.

DID YOU KNOW?

In French, these steaks are called *darnes*, from the Breton word for "piece."

RECIPE IDEA

Grilled salmon steaks with braised fennel **325**

Cutting medallions ✳

A medallion should, as its name indicates, be round. Use this technique for most firm varieties of fish.

Using a fish steak:

Take a fish steak, cut it in two, and remove the central bone.
Fold the abdominal section over the fleshy section. Tie them together with twine so that you have a nice, round piece.

Using a fillet:

Remove the bones from the fillet. If you wish, you may remove the skin.

Use a round pastry cutter to cut out pieces. An average piece should weigh about 3 oz. (80 g). Allow two medallions per person for a main dish.

RECIPE IDEA

Monkfish medallions *à l'américaine* and rice pilaf **338**

Cutting fish and shellfish into chunks ✳✳

For thick flat fish such as turbot, brill, and halibut:

Take a flat fish that is already prepared (scaled, gutted, fins removed, and washed) and remove its head, working carefully so that you remove the least possible amount of flesh.

Using a large knife with a rigid blade, slice the fish in two along the fine mark that indicates the central bone (a lateral line) (**1**).

Begin cutting from the tail.

Cut chunks weighing about 10 to 12 oz. (300 to 350 g) taking into account the variable thicknesses of the two quarters (back and belly) (**2**).

For elongated fish such as eel, lamprey, and dogfish:

Remove the head and skin of the fish.

Cut thick slices, 3–4 ½ in. (8–12 cm) long, depending on the diameter of the fish.

The average weight of a chunk should be between 7–9 oz. (200–250 g) for a main dish.

For crustaceans such as lobster, crayfish, royal langoustine, large prawns, and so on:

Split the head (cephalothorax) in two.

Separate it from the abdomen and remove the pouch on one side of the head. Set aside the greenish matter (known as the tomalley) for another use—a sauce, for example.

Remove the legs and claws.

Slice the abdomen along the segments using a knife with a rigid blade (**3**).

RECIPE IDEAS

Turbot poached in cardamom-infused milk, with hollandaise sauce **335**
Langoustines with tarragon **327**

Cutting strips (*goujonnettes*) ✳

Use this technique for average-sized flat fish, such as sole, plaice, and lemon sole.

Take a flat fish that is already prepared (scaled, gutted, fins removed, and washed) and skinned.

Fillet it as explained below. Hold your knife to cut thin, angled slices in the fillets.

DID YOU KNOW?

The French word for these strips, *goujonnettes*, is derived from their resemblance to the goujon, a small, spindle-shaped freshwater fish.

RECIPE IDEA

Plaice *goujonnettes* with tartare sauce **330**

Filleting a fish (two round, flat fillets) ✳✳

Use this technique for fish such as salmon, cod, trout, sea bass, sea bream, and pollack.

Take a fish that is already prepared (gutted, trimmed, and washed). Descale it with a knife (**1**) and make an incision along the back through to the central bone. Cut around the head, then cut through the side facing upward along the central bone, pressing on it as you work toward the tail (**2**).

Turn the fish around and repeat the procedure on the other side to make the other fillet.

Trim the fillets so that they are neat and clean. If necessary, remove the skin: place the fillet skin side downward and, starting from the tail, slip the blade of a flexible knife between the skin and the flesh. Make back- and forward

movements with the knife as you work toward the head (**3**).

Use tweezers to remove the bones from the fillets.

Rinse, drain, and chill until needed.

CHEF'S NOTES

– If there is any flesh remaining along the central bone, scrape it off with a teaspoon and use it for stuffing, rillettes, and so on.
– Use fillets to make escalopes, medallions, strips, and thick slices.
– John Dory is the only fish in this category to yield two flat fillets.

RECIPE IDEA

Pollack fillets bonne femme **319**

Filleting a fish (four flat fillets) ✳

Use this technique for fish such as sole, lemon sole, plaice, and turbot.

Dress the fish **(1)** and, if preparing sole, remove the skin at this stage. Starting at the tail, slip the blade of a flexible knife between the skin and the flesh and then pull away the skin **(2)**.

Using a knife with a flexible blade, make an incision along the sides, from the head to the tail. Take special care when rounding the head, so that there is minimum wastage.

Starting from the central bone, cut away the fillets **(3)**.

Turn the fish over and repeat the procedure.

Trim the fillets neatly: remove the barbell, an elongated, hair-like projection, usually around the mouth, chin, or nose, as well as any part that has bloody stains, and any fatty flesh.

If working with lemon sole, plaice, and turbot, remove the skin now. If there are any sinews left, make incisions with your knife. This will prevent the fish from retracting or twisting during cooking. If you need to flatten them, particularly if you are going to roll the fillets, use the smooth side of a tenderizer.

CHEF'S NOTES

– The four fillets will not be identically sized.
– Choose good-sized fish to make fillets using this technique.
– These fillets have no bones and so children will like them!

DID YOU KNOW?

Flat fish like sole, lemon sole, turbot, and plaice only spend the first four weeks after hatching in a vertical position. After this, they adopt their distinctive horizontal position.

RECIPE IDEA

Plaice *goujonnettes* with tartare sauce **330**

1

2

3

Opening oysters and other shellfish ✳✳

Opening at the side (use this technique for hollow oysters and mussels):

Don a protective glove or use a folded tea towel to cover your hand and place the oyster in your palm with the hinge toward you.

Using a rigid oyster knife, insert the tip on the right-hand side, two-thirds of the way along, between the two shells.

Use a horizontal, small in-and-out movement with the knife to cut through the connecting muscle.

Lift the upper shell and separate the two shells at the hinge.

Check that no flesh is left on the upper shell. Check the oyster for freshness, and ensure that there are no shards of shell remaining.

For the finest taste, we recommend that you discard the brine in the shell and leave the oyster for 3 to 5 minutes while it secretes more liquid.

Opening from the hinge (flat oysters, mollusks, and varieties of clams):

Don a protective glove or use a folded tea towel to cover your hand and place the oyster in your palm with the hinge facing away you.

Place the center of the blade of the rigid shucking knife at the hinge and press hard, bending your fingers to lever the knife. You must also cut the connecting muscle joining the oyster to the shell, which is to the right of its center.

Ensure that no flesh is left on the upper shell. Check the oyster for freshness, and ensure that there are no shards of shell remaining.

For the finest taste, we recommend that you discard the brine in the shell and leave the oyster for 3 to 5 minutes while it secretes more liquid.

CHEF'S NOTE

– If you are going to replace the mollusks in their shells to cook them, clean them first and boil them for 2 minutes to eliminate any debris.

DID YOU KNOW?

To check that oyster are fresh, the first rule is to buy them live. Their shells must be closed, or else they must close as soon as they are tapped. Discard any that don't meet this criterion. Today, oysters are almost always eaten live, but they may be baked or poached, and served hot or cold.

RECIPE IDEA

Hot oyster gratin **266**

Opening scallops ✳✳

Don a protective glove or use thick fabric to protect your hand. Place the scallop shell in the cup of your hand with the hinge facing away from you and the flat side facing up.

Insert the tip of a rigid knife into one of the two openings on either side of the hinge.

Cut the connecting muscle (the scallop), keeping the knife as close as possible to the flat part of the upper shell to avoid wasting flesh. Lift off the upper shell and discard it (1).

Scoop out the scallop, the corral, the beards, and black innards with a spoon (2).

Take the beards and rinse them several times. They can be used later to make a sauce.

Discard the black innards (3).

Separate the scallop from the coral (4). You may want to use the coral for another recipe.

Remove the white muscle at the end of the scallop.

Rinse, drain, and chill the coral and the scallop.

DID YOU KNOW?

You can cook the coral in exactly the same way as the scallop itself, or incorporate it in the sauce.

RECIPE IDEA

Luted scallops on a bed
of vegetables **284**

Meat and offal

Barding a fillet ✳

Barding meat prevents it from drying out when it is cooked, and enriches it with fat. Another, less frequently used method involves larding it—threading small strips of fat through the lean flesh of meat using a larding needle. Bard is made from fatback, a thick piece of fat that covers the back of a pig.

Prepare the meat to be barded and remove any nerves and sinews.

Cut the bard into strips. If you're cooking individual pieces of meat, such as tournedos or medallions, wrap the meat completely (**1**), or if you're using large pieces such as the tenderloin (filet) or a sizeable roast, envelop it only partially with bard, and tie it with individual pieces of kitchen twine (**2**).

CHEF'S NOTES

– You can decorate the bard by making cut-out patterns before you drape it round your meat.
– Do not keep bard in the freezer for more than three months: it goes rancid, oxidizes, and absorbs smells.

RECIPE IDEA

Beef tournedos with foie gras **404**

Encrusting poultry ✳

This involves slipping flavorsome ingredients such as truffle slices or bay leaves between the skin and the flesh of poultry.

RECIPE IDEA

Bay leaf-infused young guinea hen with canapés **350**

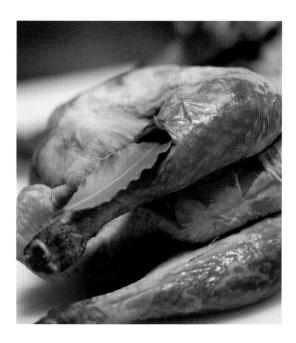

Cutting up raw, dressed poultry ✷✷✷

This technique involves separating the wings and thighs from the carcass before cooking.

Hold the bird firmly and make an incision in the skin between the thigh and the abdomen. Then disjoint the thigh at the articulation **(1, 2)**.

Cut along the backbone to separate the thigh from it. Make sure you include the choice morsel known as the oyster, which is found in the cavity just in front of the thigh.

Repeat the procedure for the other thigh. Turn the bird over.

Cut along both sides of the wishbone to separate the fillets and the wings **(3, 4)**. Trim off the tips of the wings and thighs.

RECIPE IDEA

Stuffed chicken legs with
  chestnuts **365**

Jointing rabbit ✳✳

Rabbit meat is low in fat and is used much like most poultry and small game. Hare is cooked in the same way as rabbit, but it is best in dishes with a red wine sauce. These are known as *civets*, game stews. An average rabbit weighs between 3 lb. 5 oz. and 4 lb. 6 oz. (1.5–2 kg).

Remove the head and take out the giblets (heart, liver, and lungs).

Cleave the hind legs at the hip. Separate the two hind legs by removing the tip of the backbone (the coccyx). If the hind legs are a good size, you may want to cut each of them into two.

Make a cut at the base of the rib cage, then cleave the backbone in half to separate the two forelegs. Cut the saddle into two or three pieces, depending on its size.

CHEF'S NOTES

– Ensure that you make clean, sharp cuts so that there are no bone splinters in the flesh.
– The saddle can be boned and stuffed like a saddle of lamb.

RECIPE IDEA

Rabbit stew with puréed Golden Hubbard squash **361**

Boning a shoulder of lamb ✳✳

When preparing a shoulder of lamb, bear in mind that 3 ½ lb.–4 ½ lb. (1.6–2 kg) will serve five to six people.

Place the shoulder of lamb on a chopping board (1). Remove the thin membrane on the outside of the shoulder.

Turn the shoulder over. Take a boning knife and make an incision in the flat part of the shoulder blade to free the meat below (2).

Cut round the shoulder bone (it has a triangular shape) and remove it by sectioning the nerve at the articulation.

Scrape the two remaining bones so that there is a minimum amount of meat left on them, and remove them (3).

The shoulder can be used whole, rolled and tied (either roasted or pan-cooked) or cut into 2-oz. (50-g) pieces to make a stew.

RECIPE IDEA

Provençal shoulder of lamb and vegetable *tian* **379**

Boning a saddle of lamb ✳ ✳

Choose a saddle (loin) weighing 3 lb.–3 ½ lb. (1.2–1.6 kg) to serve four. In the USA, the term "saddle" may mean the whole loin, the hip, and the leg. Here, you will need the top of the hind leg.

Release the tenderloin (filet mignon) from the backbone, leaving it attached to the skin. Cut carefully around each vertebra. Be careful not to pierce the meat or make open holes in it.

Trim the flanks so that they are all the same length.

The saddle of lamb may be used plain, trussed and roasted. You may also stuff it (see recipes for duxelles, mousseline, and so on).

COOKING TIMES FOR A BONED SADDLE OF LAMB

– Pink: 20–25 minutes at 350°F–370°F (180°C–190°C).
– Well done: approximately 40 minutes at 350°F–370°F (180°C–190°C).

In order for the meat not to shrink during cooking, remove the sciatic nerve on the backbone.

DID YOU KNOW?

In France, the finest lamb is salt marsh lamb. They graze on the grasses and plants on the coast of the Atlantic and the Channel. The plants, sprayed by the sea, are rich in iodine and impart a particular, much appreciated flavor to the meat.

Preparing foie gras ✳ ✳

Mistakenly termed "removing the nerves" of the foie gras, this technique involves removing the blood vessels, not the nerves.

If you are preparing a hot recipe (such as a sautéed slice), it is not necessary to remove the veins.

Allow 2 ½–2 ¾ oz. (70–80 g) per person for a cold terrine served as a starter, and 3 ½–4 ¼ oz. (100–120 g) for sautéed escalopes served as a hot starter.

Remove the foie gras from the refrigerator about 1 hour before you begin preparing it (1).

Separate the two lobes and remove any traces of green matter, the bile.

Make an incision along the length of the long vein so that you can remove it. Use your thumb or a round-tipped knife to adjust the movement of the knife, keeping it as precise as possible (2).

To make a terrine, marinate the deveined foie gras in milk in the refrigerator for 12 hours to remove any bitterness (there is always a little bitterness in foie gras). You may then soak it in a sweet wine or a stronger alcoholic beverage.

A foie gras terrine must be weighted down and cooked at about 175°F (80°C). The core temperature must reach 131°F (55°C). A terrine will keep no longer than a few days in the refrigerator.

CHEF'S NOTE

– Whether you prefer duck or goose foie gras, make sure that it is light colored, stain free, and firm. An average duck liver weighs between 1–1 lb. 2 oz. (450–500 g). An average goose liver is larger, between 1 ½–1 ¾ lb. (700–800 g).

DID YOU KNOW?

In ancient times, geese were force-fed with figs. Today, ducks are force-fed for two weeks and geese for three weeks, mainly with corn.

RECIPE IDEA

Foie gras terrine 275

Tying up a roast ✳

Tying a roast makes the meat look attractive and ensures that it cooks evenly.

Separate ties

This method is usually used for individual pieces of meat, such as medallions, tournedos, and chateaubriand steak.

Prepare pieces of kitchen twine sufficiently long to go round the piece of meat and tie a knot.

Slide each length of kitchen twine under the meat, bring the ends round to the top and tie a knot.

Trim the excess twine closely.

With one piece of string

This method is used for large pieces of meat, such as a shoulder or leg of lamb, and loin.

Make a loop around one end of the meat and tie a knot. Do not cut the twine (**1**).

Loop the string around your hand and slip the loop around the meat at about 1 ¼ in. (3 cm) from the first loop (**2**). Tighten as necessary.

Repeat the procedure until you reach the other end of the piece of meat. Then tie the last loop to the first by looping the string under the meat to tie it on top (**3**).

RECIPE IDEA

Provençal shoulder of lamb and vegetable *tian* **379**

Dressing and trussing poultry ✳✳✳

This involves all the procedures that transform a raw product into a ready-to-cook ingredient.

To dress a fowl, stretch it out and burn off any remaining traces of feathers **(1)**.

Cut the legs at the "knee" articulation, remove the tips of the wings and the gland located above the rump (parson's nose). Remove the neck and set it aside to use for stocks and/or a roasting gravy **(2)**.

Remove the wishbone at the base of the neck **(3)**.

Check that there are no giblets or other innards left. Season and stuff the cavity if your recipe calls for it.

Place the bird breast side down and thread twine—leaving about 4 in. (10 cm) loose at the entry point—through the wing, between the two bones, using a trussing needle. Continue through the skin of the neck and under the backbone **(4)**.

Repeat the operation in the reverse order on the other side. Turn the fowl onto its back and pull the needle through the leg, between the drumstick and the thigh **(5, 6)**.

Knot the two ends of twine together **(7)**. Pierce the belly skin and thread the twine above the two legs. Make a loop around them.

Hold the legs firmly and make a knot so that the cavity is tightly closed **(8)**.

CHEF'S NOTES

– You may place a strip of bard on the escalopes of some poultry (squab [pigeon], guinea hens, and game birds) before trussing them. This will ensure that they do not dry out during cooking.
– You can also insert an aromatic ingredient under the skin before trussing (see p. 78).
– Baste the poultry regularly while it cooks so that it does not dry out.

DID YOU KNOW?

Poultry from the Bresse region is famous, and is the only kind to have its own AOC (Appellation d'Origine Contrôlée, see p. 224). Turkeys, chickens, and capons (a fattened, castrated cock traditionally eaten during the festive season) are raised there. Fine restaurants often serve poultry from Bresse, and will specify its origin on their menus.

Mincing meat ✳

This involves cutting meat more or less finely with a knife or a mincing machine. When meat is minced, it can be mixed with other types of meat, shaped, and seasoned throughout.

Preparing a rack (pork, veal, lamb) ✳ ✳ ✳

This preparation involves removing the vertebrae and removing the fat (and any meat) from the tips of the rib bones so that cutting the meat after it is cooked becomes easy. It is known as frenching a rack. When preparing lamb, allow two chops per person. For pork and veal, one chop or sirloin steak is enough.

Remove the fat and, if necessary, trim the top of the rack.

Make a few incisions so that the meat does not shrink too much during cooking.

Trim the meat and fat between the tips of the ribs, about 1 ¼–1 ½ in. down (3–4 cm), leaving them clear. Scrape all remains off the rib tips with a boning knife so that they do not color during cooking (1, 2).

Remove the meat by cutting along the flat side of the vertebrae until you reach the backbone (3).

Turn the rack over and separate the vertebrae one by one, cutting round each one. Pull on the base of each vertebra (4). Cut off the backbone. Only the ribs will remain joined to the loin. Tie the ribs together with the backbone to hold the rack.

The rack may be covered with a crust, such as herbs, garlic and parsley breadcrumbs, gingerbread crumbs, and so on, and then browned.

To reach a pale pink color, a rack of veal must be cooked gently until a drop—or "pearl"—of exuded juice appears when it is cut after its post-cooking resting time.

RECIPE IDEA

Roasted rack of lamb with garden vegetables **389**

Preparing a leg of lamb ✳✳

The US and UK equivalent of a French *gigot d'agneau* is the leg. To serve 8, allow 2 lb. 10 oz.–3 lb. (1.2–1.4 kg) of meat with the bone.

Remove the thin membrane on the outside of the leg and trim any fat (1).

If the pelvic bone is still there, remove it by cutting round it and sectioning off the joint.

Sever the tendons at the knee, making as small a hole as possible, to remove the hip bone (2, 3). All that will remain is the shank bone.

In France, lamb is often combined with typically Mediterranean flavors and studded with garlic cloves.

A slow-roasted leg of lamb, known in French as a *gigot de sept heures*, a seven-hour leg of lamb, is first slowly braised and then cooked in a luted (sealed with dough) cooking pot. The meat is so tender that it can be removed with a fork. Lamb is widely available at Easter time, and has a particularly tender, tasty meat.

The meat of the foreleg around the shank is considered a morsel of choice. In French, it is known as the *souris*, literally, the mouse.

The term "leg" is reserved for lamb and mutton. The equivalent on a game animal is known as a "haunch."

RECIPE IDEA

Breton-style braised leg of lamb **398**

Preparing chops ✳

Let us take the example of a rib roast, with an average weight of 2 lb. 10 oz.–3 ½ lb. (1.2–1.6 kg). Veal and pork chops constitute individual portions, while it takes two or three lamb chops to make one serving.

Cut the meat away from the top of the rib bone, down about ½ in. (3–4 cm), leaving it visible. Scrape away any remains so that it does not color during cooking. Remove any excess fat.

Remove the vertebrae with the boning knife. If you are preparing a rib-eye roast, it is easier to saw the bone.

Make a small incision (⅛ in./3–4 mm) on the nerve on the outside (curved side) so that the meat does not shrink during cooking.

If your chop is very thick, tie it: start with a knot at the trimmed bone. Loop the string around and tie it at the starting point. Wrap the tip of the bone in foil so that it does not burn.

For chops, it is best to use high heat (grill, roast, or sauté), and it is important to let the meat rest once it has been cooked. This enables the juices to penetrate the meat, which becomes more tender.

Use high, dry heat (grilling, roasting, or sautéing) and allow your meat to rest after cooking so that the juices can reabsorb into the meat, thereby making it tender.

DID YOU KNOW?

The entrecôte is a piece of meat located between two ribs. It is usually cut off a rack of boned ribs.

RECIPE IDEAS

Normandy-style veal chops **393**
Grilled rib roast and béarnaise sauce **376**

Preparing escalopes ✳

Cut thin slices of meat in a prime cut. The best pieces to use for veal escalopes are the leg and hind shank (UK silverside, topside, and hind shank).

Place them between two sheets of plastic wrap and flatten them by bashing on them with a mallet or meat tenderizer. If you don't have one, use the bottom of a clean saucepan.

Trim the edges of the escalopes with a kitchen knife.

DID YOU KNOW?

Piccatas are thin slices (just under ½ in./1 cm) cut from the fillet. Allow three pieces, each weighing about 2 ½ oz. (40 g) per person.

A *paillarde* is a thin escalope of veal or beef that has been completely flattened and then grilled or fried.

RECIPE IDEA

Crumbed turkey escalopes with sautéed potatoes **357**

Preparing veal sweetbreads ✳✳

The sweetbread is the thymus gland of young animals. In fact, there are two glands, one near the heart and one near the throat. Sweetbreads are one of the few animal foods to contain Vitamin C. Allow approximately 10–12 oz. (250–300 g) of unprepared sweetbread, either lamb or veal, per person.

Soak the sweetbreads in water in the refrigerator for 4–6 hours to rid them of all blood. Change the water at regular intervals.

Drain the sweetbreads and blanch them: place them in cold water (1) and bring to a boil. Allow to boil for 4–5 minutes. Skim the water frequently during this process.

Remove the sweetbreads from the water and refresh them briefly in cold water with ice cubes.

Drain carefully.

Using a paring knife, remove the skin, fat, and cartilage, if any (2).

Place the sweetbreads on a clean cloth (3) between two plates. Apply pressure with a weight for a minimum of 3 hours, overnight if possible.

CHEF'S NOTES

– Transferring the sweetbreads into very cold water after they have been blanched not only stops the cooking process, it also makes them firmer for trimming.
– The more pressure you apply to them, the more pink liquid they will exude. This will enable them to stay white.

RECIPE IDEA

Sweetbread vol-au-vents with cider and apples **283**

Preparing kidneys ✳✳

Allow approximately 10 oz. (250 g) of unprepared kidneys per person.

Remove the fat from the kidneys and pull off the fine, transparent membrane that adheres to them.

Remove all the white parts, blood vessels, and the urinary tract.

You may either leave the kidney whole or cut it into small lobes, depending on your recipe.

To prevent the kidneys from becoming rubbery or elastic, it is essential to cook them rapidly on high heat and to ensure they remain pink inside.

CHEF'S NOTES

– It is best to buy kidneys in their fat as this helps maintain freshness.
– They should not have a strong smell.

DID YOU KNOW?

Veal kidneys are considered to have the finest taste of all types of kidney.

RECIPE IDEA

Kidneys in mustard sauce **387**

Boning and stuffing a chicken leg ✳✳

This technique creates a small, plump-looking leg that is firm and easy to eat, since most of the bone is removed.

Using dressed thighs, remove the femur bone by scraping around it until you have freed it from the meat **(1)**.

Remove the knee cap and continue to scrape around the other bone, the tibia.

Halfway down, cut the tibia, making sure you do not leave any bone shards **(2)**. If you do not plan to stuff the leg, replace the remaining part of the tibia **(3, 4)** now, and season.

Otherwise, season the meat and fill it with a spoonful of mousseline stuffing (see p. 159) **(5)**.

Fold the meat over the stuffing **(6)** and sew up with a trussing needle **(7)**.

You may also wrap the legs in caul to hold the meat together and prevent it from drying out during cooking **(8)**.

RECIPE IDEA

Stuffed chicken legs with chestnuts **365**

Preparing terrines and pâtés (terrine stuffing) ✳✳✳

These stuffings or forcemeats can be used for vegetables, fish, and meat. The delicacy of your stuffing will be determined by how finely you chop your ingredients. However, meat chopped too finely will lose its distinctive taste and will tend to dry out, particularly if you have removed too much fat. Allow about 3 oz. (80 g) of terrine per person.

INGREDIENTS
(for 1 country-style terrine for 8 people)

14 oz. (400 g) pork side belly (*poitrine* cut in France)
7 oz. (200 g) pork picnic shoulder (hand [UK], *épaule* cut in France)
2 scant teaspoons (9–10g) salt
1 pinch (1 g) pepper
1 egg
1 generous pinch of fresh *herbes de Provence*
1 ⅓ tablespoons (20 ml) cognac
6 ½ tablespoons (40 g) flour
5 oz. (150 g) larding strips
3 oz. (80 g) caul
3 ½ oz. (100 g) strips smoked bacon
¾ cup (200 ml) prepared clear aspic (optional)

Special equipment: a meat thermometer

Trim the meat. Remove some of the fat and all the sinews and nerves. Cut into cubes or strips weighing about 2 oz. (50 g). Mince (1) and season the meat (2).

Mix with the remaining ingredients (for this recipe, use the egg, herbs, cognac, and flour).

Line the terrine mold with bard, caul, or dough, and fill it, pressing down regularly to eliminate any air. You may insert ingredients such as foie gras, fruit, or truffles. For this recipe, insert strips of smoked bacon (3).

Use whatever you have lined your mold with (in the photo, caul) to cover the terrine (4). Cook at 275°F–285°F (140°C), in a water bath, until the center of the terrine reaches 154°F–160°F (68°C–70°C).

When the terrine is done, pour the clear aspic over it so that it does not dry out. This will make it more tender and shiny.

CHEF'S NOTE

– Opt for curing salt to enhance the pinkish color of the meat and prevent oxidation.

– You may marinate the meat before preparing the terrine.
– If you prepare other terrines with different quantities of meat, bear in mind that you should use 3–3 ½ teaspoons (14–16 g) salt and 1 pinch (1 g) pepper for every 2.2 lb. (1 kg) of the total meat used.

DID YOU KNOW?

In the late Middle Ages, only the corporation of *chair-cuitiers saulcissiers* (cookers of meat and sausage) were authorized to prepare and cook pork in all its forms. The generic French term for products that use pork meat and offal as a base, *charcuterie*, derives from this.
The *pastissiers*, makers of pastry, were allowed to cook pâtés that were wrapped in pastry.

RECIPE IDEA

Rabbit and pistachio terrine with exotic fruit chutney **270**

Cutting medallions and noisettes ✳

Allow 3 × 2 oz. (50 g) small cuts per person.

Remove the sinews from the small end of the tenderloin (*filet mignon*).

Roll it up and tie with kitchen twine every 1 ½–2 in. (4–5 cm) **(1, 2)**.

Cut the medallions between each loop of twine **(3)**.

The best way to cook them is to sauté them; cooking time will be very short.

DID YOU KNOW?

If the cut is a well-rounded shape and not particularly thick, you will find it in French restaurants under the name "medallion." Medallions of beef are also known as "tournedos."

If you leave the filet mignon whole and tied, on the other hand, the cylindrical shape gives it its name of "canon."

RECIPE IDEA

Lamb medallions with licorice-infused foamed milk and duchess potatoes **407**

Cooking

Accompaniments, Fish, and Meat

Food preservation ✳

Food preservation methods allow us to make the most of seasonal produce so that we can enjoy it throughout the year. By preserving abundant harvests, we also reduce waste and save money. When carried out correctly, preserved foods make for a rich and varied pantry, year-round, help save time in the kitchen, and offer a wide range of possibilities for creativity.

You can preserve most foods that are ultra-fresh and well cleaned. There are many methods to choose from:

· Drying for several hours in a convection oven at 122°F (50°C): mushrooms, herbs, quartered tomatoes, etc.

· Curing with salt: ham, pork belly, cod, etc.

· Cooking in oil infused with herbs and/or spices (see slow cooking in oil or fat p. 98): duck confit, etc. Good quality oil is key.

· In flavored vinegar: vegetables cut into small pieces and blanched but still crisp.

· Cooking in sugar syrup (either for one long or several short cooking times): fruits, such as candied fruits poached several times in syrup that is increasingly more concentrated.

· In alcohol: fruits. The fruit's sweetness will influence the end result.

· Freezing at –4°F (–20°C) or below, to allow for quick freezing: Almost all foods can be frozen, but those containing less water freeze best. Small pieces are better as they freeze more quickly, and fatty foods keep for less time as the fats turn rancid. Vacuum sealing before freezing prevents browning. To defrost foods, place on a rack in the refrigerator to let the condensation and excess water drain off.

· Canning: well-cleaned fruits, vegetables, cooked foods, etc. After sealing jars airtight with lids or new seals, immerse them in a pot of water, bring to a boil, and let simmer for at least 30 minutes. Check for leaks and label the jars before storing.

Low-temperature cooking ✳✳

This is a recently developed cooking technique that is mainly used for meat and consists in cooking it either in direct contact —with a grill, oven grill, flat-top grill (*plancha*), etc.—or in indirect contact (vacuum packed or sous vide) at a temperature of 136°F (58°C). This method takes longer than traditional methods (about 20% longer), and requires impeccable hygiene— in the products used, the material, and on the part of the cooking staff. It results in tender, juicy food that has undergone very little color change and is hence slightly less flavorful. To compensate, the meat may be browned before or after cooking with the sous-vide method.

Browning quickly in hot fat before cooking

Dress the main ingredient (here, meat) and preheat the oven to 136°F (58°C). Rapidly brown the meat over high heat and season it. Place it on a rack with a dish below to catch the juices it exudes when cooked. Place in the oven. Insert a meat thermometer as near to the center of the meat as possible and set it to 136°F (58°C). *Do not exceed this temperature.*

Remove from the oven when the desired temperature is shown on the thermometer and serve.

Browning quickly in hot fat after cooking

Dress the main ingredient (here, meat) and preheat the oven to 136°F (58°C). Insert a meat thermometer as near to the center of the meat as possible and set it to 136°F (58°C). *Do not exceed this temperature.* Place in the oven on a rack with a dish below to catch the juices it exudes during cooking. Remove from the oven when the desired temperature is reached and rapidly brown the meat over high heat. Season it and serve.

CHEF'S NOTES

– It is essential to place the thermometer at the center of the meat to check for doneness.

– No resting time is required for this method, which results in little weight loss caused by evaporation. There is only about 15% shrinkage.

Brown braising (meat, poultry, offal) ✳✳

A large-sized piece of meat is browned in fat in a pan with a tight-fitting lid over an aromatic base. Cooking liquid, which may or may not be thickened, is added. If the cooking is done in the oven at a low temperature, it will take longer for the meat to be tenderized and the flavors of the cooking liquid and the product to meld. The cooking liquid, called a braising stock, is used to glaze the meat and as an accompanying sauce.

Dress and prepare the main ingredient.

Dice the aromatic base into a mirepoix. Prepare a bouquet garni.

Begin cooking in the braising pan and brown all sides evenly in the fat you are using (1).

Transfer the meat to a dish and discard the fat from the cooking pot. Add the aromatic base and sweat it (2). Pour in the marinade or wine (3). Reduce it by half over high heat.

Preheat the oven to 350°F–400°F (180°C–200°C). Return the meat to the braising dish and pour in enough cooking stock to half cover it.

Place the braising dish in the oven. Allow about 1 ½ hours for pieces of offal, at least 2 hours for poultry, and 3 hours for a large piece of meat. Halfway through, turn the meat and vegetables over. This is particularly important for smaller pieces such as vegetables and legs.

Make the sauce:
Remove the pieces of meat or offal and tent under aluminum foil. Reserve in a warm place.

Skim the fat off the braising stock. Return the braising pot to the stove top and, over high heat, reduce the stock until it reaches a thick consistency. Strain it through a fine-meshed sieve.

Adjust the seasoning and flavor it with ingredients of your choice, such as wine or other alcohols, extracts, strongly flavored jus, etc.

Pour the sauce over the dish and place it in the oven so the glaze can coat it (4).

CHEF'S NOTE

– To make sure that no moisture escapes, the braising pan or stew pot may be luted (see technique, p. 105). In this case, the meat will obviously not be turned over halfway through the cooking process.

DID YOU KNOW?

There is considerable loss of weight with the braising method. Some types of offal should be blanched before being braised. You may also marinate your ingredients prior to braising them. The term "braise" comes from when dishes of meat were cooked in a closed pot that was surrounded and covered by *braises*, or embers.

RECIPE IDEA

Boeuf bourguignon with fresh pasta **383**

Braising vegetables ✴

Use raw or blanched vegetables (1). Place over the aromatic base without browning. Fill three-quarters way up with cooking liquid, such as stock (see pp. 138, 140) (2).

Cover with the lid and cook slowly in the oven.

OTHER TYPES OF BRAISING

– Whole fish are placed raw over the aromatic base without being browned. Fill three-quarters way up with fish stock or velouté. Put the lid on and cook in the oven at 250°F (120°C). Small fish or fish pieces will take up to 30 minutes.
– For meat, sear it first without browning. Place over the aromatic base and pour in white stock. Cover with the lid and cook in the oven at 325°F–350°F (160°C–170°C). Meat may take 2–3 hours.

Slow cooking in oil or fat ✴

This involves slow cooking in fat at 136°F (58°C) as a method of preserving food. In French, the process is known as *confire*, and the final result is a confit (such as duck confit, a popular French dish). Cooking time will depend on the size of the piece you are preparing. This method takes some time (from 20 minutes for unpeeled garlic cloves to about 2 hours for duck thighs). Hygiene is all-important.

If you wish, you may start by pickling or brining the main ingredient. If you have done so, rinse it well and dry it. Dress and prepare the main ingredient. Place it in a bath of liquid fat (oil or clarified butter).

Bring the temperature of the ingredients very slowly up to a core temperature of 136°F (58°C). The temperature of the fat should also not exceed 136°F (58°C), and must be checked with a thermometer. Drain if necessary.

If a dish or foodstuff has not been sterilized, it is fragile and must be consumed quickly. Use various types of oil or fat, and flavor them if you wish: see chapter on Basic preparations and sauces p. 126. See also the table of fats p. 236.

RECIPE IDEA

Duck confit and potatoes sarladaises **358**

Candying (crystallizing)

This involves cooking a food in a sugar and water syrup, whose sugar concentration is progressively increased. It is traditionally used for fruit and vegetables.

Prepare the fruit or vegetables (1). If using products like citrus fruit or chestnuts, they will need to be blanched at this stage.

Prepare a sugar syrup with an equal weight of water and sugar and bring it to 225°F (107°C).

Immerse the ingredients into the hot syrup (2) (you may want to lower them in using a metal basket), leave to simmer for 10 minutes, and remove from the heat. Strain the syrup into another receptacle and add 25% more sugar than you used initially (first sugar bath) to this syrup and return the ingredients to be candied. Repeat the procedure three to seven times, adding 25% of the original weight of sugar to each sugar bath, bringing the syrup to a boil each time and leaving to simmer for about 10 minutes. The more sugar baths you candy your fruit in, the longer it will be preserved.

Drain the fruit and dust with confectioners' sugar.

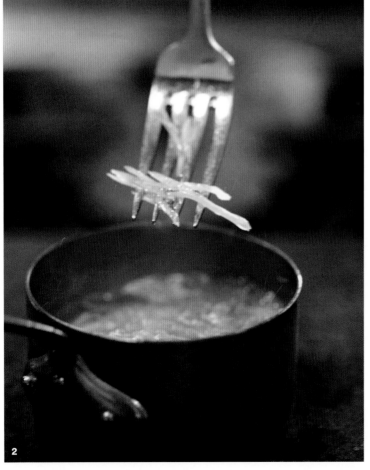

Gentle stewing ✳

This is a method of cooking without browning that uses low heat and requires a tight-fitting lid. Little or no fat or cooking liquid is required. It is mainly used for vegetables, with the vegetables cooking in their own liquid.

Peel, wash, and finely slice the vegetables.

Heat any fat you may be using over a low heat (**1**) and add the vegetables (**2**).

If using cooking liquid, such as water, fumet, or stock, pour it in now to create steam. Cover with a parchment paper lid (**3**), which will allow you to keep an eye on the cooking, and simmer over low heat until done (**4**).

DID YOU KNOW?

A vegetable fondue involves similar preparation.

Sweating means softening a vegetable in its own liquid. The pan is covered and placed over low heat. Very little fat is used. Cooking time is brief (2–3 minutes), and the vegetable retains its crunch.

Stewing to make a *compotée* is a variation on this technique; the cooking time is extended until the ingredients are particularly soft.

RECIPE IDEA

Fish papillotes with vegetable scoops **311**

Cooking in a crust ✳✳

This involves cooking an ingredient in an oven, totally or partially covered in a crust, which may be of varying thickness. The coating may be a dough (brioche, puff pastry, bread, etc.), a crust (herb mixture, flavored breadcrumbs, salt, gingerbread, flavored butter, etc.), or other foodstuffs. This cooking method results in the flavors blending between the main ingredient and the coating. It also keeps the main ingredient moist, and, in certain cases, such as a salt crust, results in cooking by steaming. This is what occurs when the ingredient is coated in kosher or other coarse salt.

Prepare the coating as required (crust, dough, flavored butter, etc.) and set aside.

Dress and trim the main ingredient. If necessary, pre-cook it and allow it to cool completely. (This is particularly important if you are using dough, which must not be softened or partially baked before it goes into the oven.) Season with salt and pepper.

If using dough, roll it out and place the accompanying ingredients of your choice on it. Wrap the main ingredient partially or wholly.

If you are using a yeast dough, allow it to rise, decorate it if necessary, and baste with egg.

Preheat the oven as required. Place on a baking tray and cook until the crust is nicely colored.

CHEF'S NOTES

– To intensify flavors, we recommend you pre-cook your main ingredient. If you are preparing a fillet of beef in a pastry case, for example, brown the beef. For sausage in brioche pastry, poach the sausage.
– Use this technique for both small and large pieces of meat or fish, and give free rein to your imagination when it comes to the coating.

RECIPE IDEAS

Glazing vegetables ✳

Glazing vegetables gives them a shine thanks to a cooking method that uses butter, water, and sugar. Vegetables such as turnips may be blanched, and carrots may be pre-cooked. Baby vegetables are particularly well suited for this cooking technique. Instead of water, try using stock.

Cut the vegetables into regular shapes. For pearl onions, this step is not necessary.

Place the vegetables, butter, sugar, and fine salt in a sauté pan and cover with water (1).

Cut out a circle of parchment paper the size of the pan and cover the vegetables (2). Cook over low heat.

As soon as all the water has evaporated, hold the pan with both hands and whirl the contents around to coat the vegetables in a shiny glaze.

"White" glazing is the result of cooking the vegetables without browning them. If you cook them further so that they caramelize, the glaze will at first be light colored and then brown.

DID YOU KNOW?

White sauce = white glazing (for blanquette)

Blond (straw-colored) sauce = blond glazing (for fricassee)

Brown sauce = brown glazing (for boeuf bourguignon)

RECIPE IDEA

Boeuf bourguignon with fresh pasta **383**

1

2

Frying ✳

Frying involves immersing an ingredient in hot fat. It is essential to choose the appropriate fat for your recipe (see table of fats p. 236). Fragile products such as fish should be dipped in milk and then in flour to form a thin surrounding crust. This will prevent the flesh from falling apart. You may also make a crumb preparation (see p. 124), frying batter (see p. 25), crêpe batter (see p. 20), or choux pastry (see p. 22).

Certain varieties of potato need to be fried in two stages. The first stage, at 300°F (150°C) cooks them; the second stage, at 350°F (180°C), browns them. Only souffléd potatoes require three successive immersions.

Prepare the ingredients and preheat the fryer to 350°F (180°C).

Make sure the food is carefully dried.

Immerse the food into the deep fryer or oil bath.

Turn until all the sides are evenly colored.

Remove from the fryer, drain, and use a paper towel to absorb any excess fat.

CHEF'S NOTES

– It is important to stir whatever you are cooking, particularly if you are preparing fritters.
– It is preferable to season your ingredients before cooking them, as seasoning will not penetrate the crust formed during frying. Potatoes are the exception to this rule.
– Never sprinkle salt over the deep fryer.
– Don't fry different types of food, such as meat, fish, vegetables, and fruit, in the same oil, and discard your oil after it has been used ten times.
– When not using your deep fryer, protect it from air and light so that the fat does not oxidize.

RECIPE IDEAS

Brie fritters with spicy stewed black cherries **434**
Apple fritters with apricot coulis **474**

Gratin ✳

When preparing a gratin, the surface of the dish is browned and acquires a crusty texture. This develops as the dish cooks or can be done afterwards.

There are three types of gratins:
· Glazing: superficial color formed under high heat (oven broiler, salamander, caramelizing blowtorch).
· Blond gratin: a crust of cheese, breadcrumbs, flavored butter, and so on, placed on already cooked foods to brown and become crisp.
· Full gratin: the dish is cooked in the oven from beginning to end. The crust forms on the surface and is browned.

CHEF'S NOTE

– Browning the crust of a blond gratin won't be enough to reheat an entire dish. To reheat, you will have to bring the various elements to a suitable temperature.

DID YOU KNOW?

The term "gratin" originates from the term for the crust that formed on the cooking pot, which was then scratched (*gratter*) off to be eaten.

RECIPE IDEAS

Onion soup **294**
Florentine-style gnocchi **412**
Rolled Picardy crêpes **428**
Hot oyster gratin **266**

Grilling ✳

Grilling involves cooking a food in contact with a grilling rack or a very hot grill pan heated from below. The term also applies to food that is rapidly exposed to high, dry heat, and this is actually more like the roasting one does for almonds, hazelnuts, coffee beans, and so on.

If using an electric grill pan, turn it on; otherwise heat your pan on the stove top or the barbecue.

Rub the ridges with a slightly oiled cloth.

Dry, and apply a little oil to the food you are preparing.

To obtain a regular diamond pattern—this is called branding—(see photo, below), put the pieces you are grilling at an angle to the grill bars, and turn through 90 degrees halfway through the cooking process.

Season when done.

Remove from the heat.

CHEF'S NOTES

– Dust sole with flour before cooking for better browning.
– When cooking red meat, allow the same amount of resting time as cooking time.
– If you are cooking a thick item that is not done to your satisfaction after grilling, finish cooking in the oven.
– The crisscross design is more attractive in a diamond shape than a square shape and, more importantly, easier to achieve.
– Use an instant marinade prior to grilling (see p. 143) to tenderize and flavor the meat or fish.

RECIPE IDEAS

Grilled salmon steaks with braised fennel **325**
Grilled rib roast and béarnaise sauce **376**

Luting ✳

Luting is a method providing a hermetic seal between a cooking receptacle and its lid. It is made of a mixture of water and flour and rolled out to a strip or cord shape, which is placed around the cooking receptacle and overlaps both the lid and the container. Luting is a technique mainly used for dishes with sauces, as it prevents too-rapid evaporation of the cooking liquid and allows the food to remain tender.

Sift 2 cups (200 g) all-purpose flour and make a well in the center. Pour in a scant ½ cup (100 ml) water and combine until the mixture has a smooth texture.

Cover in plastic wrap and chill for 20–30 minutes.

Roll out into a strip or cord shape about ¼–⅓ in. (5 mm–1 cm), depending on the size of the container.

Make sure that the lid and the container are cold so that the dough does not dissolve. Seal them with the dough and check that there are no gaps.

Begin cooking, following the recipe.

Remove the lute at the very last moment, unless you are braising. Discard it, as it is not meant to be eaten.

CHEF'S NOTES

– You can use leftover puff pastry for luting. If your dish requires no more than 30 minutes' cooking, baste it with egg yolk before putting it into the oven.
– Resting time for the dough depends on the quantity and elasticity of your paste (*détrempe*). Bear in mind that insufficient resting time results in an elastic pastry.

RECIPE IDEA

Luted scallops on a bed of vegetables **284**

Marinière ✳

This is used only for seafood, and involves cooking it with white wine and finely sliced shallots. It is often used for shellfish, particularly for mussels. Allow 2 cups (0.5 liters) of mussels per person. This works out to approximately 1 lb. (450 g) for a main dish. For an appetizer, prepare ¼ lb. (250 g) per person, as below.

INGREDIENTS
(serves 4)

2 lb. (1 kg) mussels
2 shallots
1 large sprig of parsley
2 plus 1 tablespoons (50 g)
   unsalted butter
6 cups (1.5 liters) white wine
Pepper

Scrape and clean the mussels. Finely dice the shallots and chop the parsley.

Sweat the shallots in 2 tablespoons (30 g) of the butter.

Add the mussels (1), white wine (2), and half the chopped parsley.

Cover and bring to a fast boil over high heat, stirring regularly (3).

Check that all the mussels have opened. Discard those that are still closed, and transfer the rest to a warm dish using a slotted spoon.

Filter the cooking liquid to remove any traces of sand.

Reduce the liquid by half and then whip in the remaining butter.

Adjust the seasoning and pour the liquid over the hot mussels.

TRADITIONAL MUSSEL RECIPES

– Different regions in France have their own regional specialties:
• Biarritz style (*à la biarrote*): with finely diced bell peppers
• Bonne femme (home-style cooking): with julienned mushrooms and celery
• Provençal: with garlic and tomatoes
• Normandy style (*à la normande*): with heavy cream and hard cider
• Poulette sauce (a light white sauce): with shallots and mushrooms. The lemony sauce is reduced and then bound with heavy cream and egg yolk.

• *Mouclade*: this is a specialty of the Poitou-Charentes region. The mussels are first cooked marinière style and, when they open, cream is added to the sauce, butter is whipped in, and it is thickened. Cultured mussels from this region are flavored with a hint of curry and saffron.

CHEF'S NOTE

– Never leave mussels for more than 15 minutes in their soaking water. Remove all those you find floating. Do not eat a mussel that remains shut after cooking.

DID YOU KNOW?

In 2006, the first appellation for a sea product was awarded to the cultured mussel of the bay of Mont Saint-Michel. A *bouchot* is a wooden post that stands on the seabed. Mussels are attached to these posts by the cultivators. In France, you will often find recipes for *moules de bouchot*.

RECIPE IDEA

Mussel *mouclade* 265

Cooking en papillote ✳

To cook en papillote is to wrap ingredients in a sheet of greased parchment paper. The aim is to blend the flavors of the aromatic ingredients and the main ingredient, ensuring all the while that they remain moist. The contents of a papillote are done when the parchment paper parcel has puffed up due to the steam that comes from the food inside. Open the papillote at the last moment; it is best to allow guests to do it themselves so that they can fully appreciate the aroma that will emerge from inside.

Dress and prepare the main ingredients (fish, crustaceans, poultry, fruit, vegetables, etc.) and finely slice the accompanying garnish.

Prepare the sheets of parchment paper (approximately notebook or foolscap sized). Grease one side with oil to prevent the contents sticking. If you wish, lightly beat an egg white with a pinch of salt and brush the edges of the paper with it (1).

Prepare the papillote: arrange the main ingredient and the garnish attractively on one half of the oiled side of the paper.

If you wish, drizzle over a little liquid such as fish stock, wine, syrup, or whatever complements your recipe, and season.

Fold over the other half of the paper (2) and press the edges together, then turn them over, making several tight folds. Press down hard on the edges and use paper clips to ensure that your papillote is properly closed.

Cook in an oven heated to a medium temperature. If the heat is too high, the paper will brown before the ingredients are cooked.

When the papillote has puffed up, allow an extra 5–6 minutes for cooking.

DID YOU KNOW?

Today, aluminum paper is not in favor for papillotes: it causes the food to oxidize if an acidifier like lemon juice or vinegar is used. It also tears more easily than parchment paper.

The bed of vegetables under the main ingredient should be pre-cooked or cut very finely—use a julienne or diced *brunoise* technique.

RECIPE IDEA

Fish papillotes with vegetable scoops **311**

1

2

Poaching (hot start) ✳

Shallow poaching

This cooking technique is reserved for vegetables such as button mushrooms or turned vegetables. They are cooked in water to which lemon juice has been added. This preserves their color and prevents oxidation.

INGREDIENTS

A scant ½ cup (100 ml) water
Juice of ½ lemon
Salt
About 1 ½ tablespoons (20 g) butter
¼ lb. (250 g) button mushrooms

Place the water, lemon juice, salt, and butter in a pot. Bring to a boil.

Prepare the mushrooms and put them in the water.

Cover the pot with a parchment paper lid.

Leave to boil until the vegetables are completely done. Allow 3–5 minutes, depending on the size.

Leave to cool in their cooking liquid.

Deep poaching

In a *blanc*

A *blanc* is a solution of water with salt, lemon juice, and flour added. The technique preserves the light color of certain foods, like artichoke bottoms or white offal.

INGREDIENTS

Main ingredient to be poached (e.g salsify, white asparagus)
1 lemon, or more if required
4 cups (1 liter) water, plus a little more to dilute the flour
Scant ¼ cup (50 ml) oil
Seasoning of your choice
½ cup (50 g) flour

Drizzle lemon juice all over the food you are about to cook. Bring the water, lemon juice, seasoning, and oil to a boil. Dilute the flour in a little cold water **(1)** and pour it into the boiling mixture. Allow the mixture to thicken until it reaches a light, velvety texture.

Place the food into the *blanc* **(2)** and cook. Depending on what you will be using it for, you may need it to cool in the liquid when it is done.

In water (pasta, rice, fruits, shellfish served in cooking liquid)

This is a way of cooking food in a large volume of boiling liquid (water, broth, fish stock, etc.). Pasta and rice should be cooked in ten times their volume of water.

Bring a large volume of liquid (water, syrup, court bouillon, etc.) to a boil.

Season according to the recipe and add a drizzle of oil if you are cooking a starchy food (1).

Add the food and quickly bring the liquid back to a boil (2). Cook for required time.

Check for doneness (al dente for pasta) (3). If preparing starches or other foods that must have the cooking process stopped, refresh immediately in cold water. Items such as pears, however, should be allowed to cool in the cooking liquid.

CHEF'S NOTE

– Drizzle a little oil over pasta after refreshing so that the pieces do not stick together.

RECIPE IDEA

Soft-boiled eggs on a bed of artichokes with eggplant caviar **424**

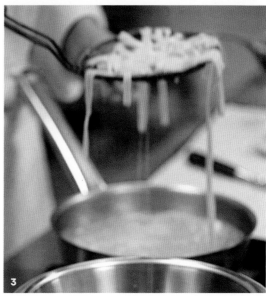

Poaching (cold start) ✳

Shallow poaching

This cooking method uses the least possible liquid. For vegetables, grains, pulses, and fish.

Greek-style vegetables

To prepare Greek-style vegetables, the cooking is carried out on the stove top. The flavors of the vegetables meld with those of the cooking liquid.

INGREDIENTS
(serves 6)

3 tablespoons (50 ml) olive oil
3 oz. (80 g) onion
½ cup (100 ml) white wine
2 lb. (900 g) button mushrooms
1 lemon
1 bouquet garni
Peppercorns, coriander seeds,
  and fennel seeds

Finely slice the onions and sweat them in the olive oil. Cut up vegetables into pieces of identical size and add them to the pot (1).

Fill to halfway with white wine and the juice of a lemon (2).

Add a bouquet garni (3) and a muslin bag containing peppercorns, coriander seeds, and fennel seeds.

Season with salt and leave to boil with the lid on.

Test the vegetables for doneness. The liquid exuded by the vegetables and the cooking liquid should have partially evaporated, as the lid is not hermetically sealed. Serve cold.

CHEF'S NOTES

– Even when preparing mixed vegetables cooked Greek-style, each vegetable should be cooked separately.
– As a variation, you may add chopped tomatoes.

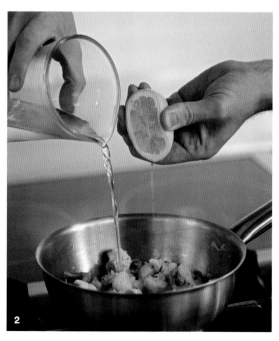

Rice and other grains

When it comes to cooking grains, allow all of the poaching liquid to evaporate. Rice pilaf is a classic preparation of cooked rice with sliced onions sweated in butter and covered with stock. It is often accompanied by a garnish.

Sweat a white aromatic base in butter. It is a good idea to use aromatic ingredients of the same color (leek whites, onions, shallots, etc.) as the grain you are preparing.

Coat the grains with the fat and cook until they become translucent (1).

If you are cooking long-grained white rice, add one and a half times its volume in cold liquid (water, stock, broth, etc.) (2).

Add the seasonings and the bouquet garni.

Preheat the oven to 250°F (120°C).

Bring to a boil and cover with parchment paper or aluminum foil (3).

Leave the rice in the oven until it is cooked and the liquid has evaporated (35–40 minutes).

Separate the grains of rice with the tines of a fork and serve.

DID YOU KNOW?

Rice is a grain of the Poaceae or Gramineae family. It is the main foodstuff of a large proportion of the world's population. It is found in various forms, long or round grains; the long grains stay separate when cooked while round grains tend to stick together. Its colors range from white through yellow and red to black and it may be fragrant, such as Basmati and Thai (also known as jasmine).

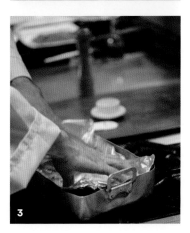

Pulses

Pulses should be cooked until practically all of the cooking liquid has evaporated (35–40 minutes).

Sweat the aromatic base (carrots, mushrooms, and celery). Add the pulses.

Pour in twice their volume of cold liquid, using water, stock, or broth.

Add the seasonings, except for the salt, which should only be added when cooking is completed.

Bring to a boil over the stove top and cover.

Simmer until the consistency of the pulse is sufficiently soft.

CHEF'S NOTE

– Soak the pulses for a few hours or overnight in cold water, except lentils and split peas, which might ferment if soaked.

DID YOU KNOW?

In France, two pulses carry the AOC label:
• AOC coco de Paimpol: a semi-dry white bean, originally from South America, which is grown in the Paimpol region of Brittany. It is harvested by hand.

• AOC lentille verte du Puy: green lentils of the Puy-en-Velay region in Auvergne. They are dark green, marbled lentils that are tasty and fine-textured.

Cooking Accompaniments, Fish, and Meat

Fish

For fish, a small quantity of the poaching liquid can be used after cooking to prepare an accompanying sauce.

Butter the base of a high-sided cooking dish. Arrange the appropriate aromatic base at the bottom **(1)**. Place the fish (whole or in fillets) on this, skin-side down to avoid shrinkage, and half cover with fumet and/or white wine **(2)**.

Preheat the oven to 250°F (120°C).

Place the dish on the stove top and bring to a boil. Cover with parchment paper **(3)** and transfer immediately to the oven for a few minutes to finish the cooking. Pour the cooking liquid into a saucepan and reduce it to make a sauce **(4)**. You may, for example, whip cubed butter into it.

CHEF'S NOTES

– Select firm-fleshed fish, such as pollack, sole, salmon, and plaice.
– Use your imagination when choosing the cooking liquid. Try hard cider, beer, or red wine, for example.

DID YOU KNOW?

Some well-known recipes:
• Turbot slices with Dugléré sauce (light butter sauce named for the revered nineteenth-century chef). Poach the fish briefly with a fish fumet, white wine, shallots, and paprika. Reduce the cooking liquid and whip in cubed butter.

• Lemon sole fillet *à la hongroise*. Briefly poach the fillets in fish fumet with white wine, shallots, and paprika. Reduce the cooking liquid and whip in cubed butter.

• Sole fillet Marguery. Marguery (1834–1910) was another famous chef whose signature dish this was: poach fillets of sole briefly with fish fumet, white wine, and shallots. Garnish with shelled shrimp and mussels prepared marinière style. Reduce the cooking liquid and whip in cubed butter. Pour the sauce over the sole fillets and broil them briefly. Garnish with puff pastry cut in the shape of flowers.

RECIPE IDEAS

Pollack fillets bonne femme **319**
Monkfish medallions
à l'américaine and rice pilaf **338**
Langoustine and pineapple skewers **314**

Poaching (cold start) ✳

Deep poaching

This method is mainly used for meats and fish, and involves completely covering the ingredient with cold water to which aromatic ingredients have been added. (In some cases, an even greater volume of liquid is required.) The flavors of the food and the aromatics blend.

Peel, wash, and roughly cut the vegetables used for the aromatic base.

Place them with the main ingredient in a suitably sized cooking pot and cover with the cold cooking liquid (water, court bouillon, stock, etc.). Bring to a boil over high heat and then reduce to a simmer.

Remove the cooked food, and reserve the cooking liquid to make an accompanying sauce for your recipe.

CHEF'S NOTE

– If you are making a ragout or stew in a white stock, blanch the pieces of meat before poaching.

USE THIS METHOD FOR:

Pot-au-feu, poached salmon in aspic, poached ham Parisian-style, poached hen, etc.

RECIPE IDEA

Pot-au-feu **401**

Thickened soups (*potages liés*) ✳

A liquid preparation made from raw or cooked ingredients, served hot or cold.

Names of the main consommés

Name	Cooking liquid	Main ingredients
Hochepot	Clear brown stock	Oxtail and aromatic garnish
Brunoise	Clear brown stock	Vegetable *brunoise*
Printanier	Clear brown stock	Carrot and turnip scoops and garden peas
Jacobine	Clear brown chicken stock	Diced potatoes, green beans, turnips, peas, julienned truffles
Chasseur	Clear brown game stock	Port wine, julienned mushrooms, chervil leaves
Vatel	Fish fumet	Crayfish flans, small sole fillet shapes

Names of the main soups

Name	Cooking liquid	Main ingredients
Parmentier	*Blanc* or water	Leek, potatoes
Champenoise	*Blanc* or water	Creamed potatoes plus celery root and carrot and celery *brunoise*
Julienne Darblay	*Blanc* or water	Creamed potatoes plus julienned vegetables
Freneuse	*Blanc* or water	Creamed potatoes plus turnips
Crécy	*Blanc* or water	Creamed potatoes plus carrots

Creamed soup

This is a soup made from a thickened white stock. It is thickened again with crème fraîche or heavy cream just before serving, which makes it even more creamy and smooth.

Peel, wash, and cut your chosen vegetables (aromatic base and main ingredients).

Sweat the aromatic base (**1**).

Cover it with some thickened white stock and bring to a boil.

Add the main vegetables (**3**).

Cook about 30 minutes, checking from time to time for doneness.

Blend and strain.

Add some crème fraîche. Return to the pot, bring to a simmer, and season.

CHEF'S NOTE

– If you are using a clear white stock, sprinkle flour over the aromatic base once it has been sweated and before it is covered with liquid (**2**).

Velouté soup

A velouté (literally, velvety) soup is a creamed soup that is thickened a second time with a mixture of crème fraîche and egg yolk.

Make a creamed soup (see facing page).

Remove from the heat. Combine crème fraîche and egg yolks and pour the mixture into the creamed soup. Do not bring the velouté back to a boil once you have bound it with egg yolk.

Mix and serve immediately.

CHEF'S NOTE

– As for the creamed soup, if you are using a light white stock, sprinkle flour over the aromatic base once it has been sweated and before it is covered with liquid (**2**).

RECIPE IDEA

Creamed lettuce soup (*velouté Choisy*) **299**

Bisque

A bisque is a shellfish soup based on the *sauce américaine* (sautéed live lobster, flambéed in cognac, and simmered with wine, aromatic ingredients, and tomatoes) and bound with rice. Allow 1 cup (¼ liter) of soup per person.

Rinse some small crabs under running water. Rinse the shells of shellfish.

Peel, wash, and finely dice (make a mirepoix) of aromatic vegetable ingredients.

Color the small crabs and the shells in olive oil. Crush them finely using a pestle. Add the aromatic ingredients and flambé with cognac.

Deglaze with white wine and allow to reduce a little, about 10%.

Cover with fish fumet.

Add tomato paste, a bouquet garni, and garlic cloves from which the shoot has been removed.

Cook, uncovered, and skim regularly.

Blend (if possible in a food processor with a lid, so that the shells do not splatter) and strain through a sieve.

Mix rice flour with the fumet or cold water and pour the liquid into the boiling bisque.

Bind using a whisk and thin with a little crème fraîche.

Adjust the seasoning.

See p. 135 for the full recipe for a crayfish bisque.

DID YOU KNOW?

To use the classic method, cook some round-grain rice in the cooking liquid.

Use the flesh of the shellfish to make a side dish of a *salpicon*, a medallion, flaked crab, or in a mini-raviole (tiny filled pasta).

Be creative and concoct a poultry or game bisque using the same technique.

115

Soups and consommés ✳✳

Soup

This is a hot or cold liquid made of vegetables, fish, or meat, and classically thickened with bread.

Peel, wash, and cut the vegetables for the aromatic base and the main ingredients.

Sweat the vegetables in oil or fat.

Add fish or meat, depending on the recipe you are preparing.

Cover with stock, water, wine, or beer, and simmer.

Season and skim if necessary.

Prepare the ingredients for the garnish.

Blend the soup, particularly if you are making a fish soup, or leave as is.

Serve very hot accompanied by bread (fresh, or as croûtons, toast, grissini, etc.).

CHEF'S NOTE

– Drizzle a little olive oil over the bread and/or rub it with a garlic clove.

FISH SOUPS

· Bouillabaisse: older books on cooking define it as a fish soup served as a main dish. Found on the Mediterranean coast from Marseille to Toulon using many different species of local fish, such as scorpion fish, conger or sea eel, and red gurnard, it is made in two stages. First the stock is made and then the bouillabaisse itself. A rouille, a sauce made of red chilies, garlic, and saffron, always accompanies it.

· *Cotriade.* This is a pot-au-feu with pieces of fish, potatoes, and herbs to which a dash of vinegar is added. Examples of the name are found from 1877 onward. It is thought to derive from the Breton word "*kaoter*" meaning a cauldron, or else from the Provençal.

· *Chaudrée.* A popular seafood pot-au-feu in the Charentes region. The word has the same origin as the *cotriade.*

DID YOU KNOW?

In the southwest of France, a major wine-producing area, it was customary to pour some red wine into the last of the soup to finish it; this was known as "*faire chabrot.*"

In the Middle Ages, "soup" meant the thick slices of bread on which broths were poured.

Consommé

A consommé is a broth made of vegetables, poultry, or meat that has not been thickened and is clarified. It is clear and the color—usually brown—is determined by the main ingredient.

Peel, wash, and cut the vegetables for the aromatic base and the main ingredients.

Blanch the meat and the bones, if using. Skim the top.

Place all the ingredients in a pot of cold water.

Add kosher salt and bring to a simmer. Leave to simmer for a long time, a minimum of 2 hours, for instance, for poultry or beef.

Prepare the garnish.
Strain the soup through a fine-mesh sieve and allow the broth to cool.

Clarification

Clarifying eliminates the particles in suspension in a broth or consommé and makes it clear. The method here is actually a double clarification.

Chop the meat or fish.

Finely slice the aromatic base (carrots, leeks, celery, and so on). In a pot, mix the chopped meat, the aromatic base, and the egg whites. Use 4 egg whites and 5 oz. (150 g) in total of aromatic vegetables and meat for every 4 cups (1 liter) of liquid.

Pour the cold broth over the mixture and combine thoroughly. The aromatic base adds taste to the broth that is to be clarified.

Bring slowly to a simmer until a thick layer forms on the surface. This will take roughly 45 minutes.

Make a hole in the center.

Carefully remove the coagulated matter with a slotted spoon.

Ladle out the broth and strain it through cheesecloth (muslin) to remove all suspended matter.

RECIPE IDEAS

Rockfish soup **278**
Onion soup **294**

Fricassee ✳✳

This is chiefly used for cut meat, such as rabbit, chicken, and veal; firm fish, such as conger or sea eel, John Dory, and monkfish; and vegetables. The pieces are cooked slowly in a thickened, creamed white liquid with the lid on. It is usual to serve a side dish with it. Let us take the example of meat here.

Prepare and cut the meat, and prepare a white aromatic garnish of onions, leek whites, and celery.

Quickly sauté the pieces of meat in butter over a low heat, making sure they do not brown (1). If you are cooking delicate fish, lightly sauté them so they do not brown and coat them in a velouté sauce.

Place the aromatic base in the pot and leave to sweat (2).

Sprinkle some flour over and cover with a cold white stock. Season and add a bouquet garni if you wish.

Simmer gently with the lid on, or place in the oven at 350°F (180°C). If you are cooking small or delicate pieces, finish the cooking with the lid on, either on low heat or in a moderate oven, at 250°F (120°C).

Remove the pieces of meat when they are cooked and keep warm under aluminum foil or plastic wrap so they do not dry out.

Stir in the cream (3), and reduce the sauce until it is thick enough to coat the back of a spoon.

Adjust the seasoning and strain the sauce through a sieve.

Return the pieces of meat to the cooking dishes, along with other ingredients, if the recipe calls for them, such as glazed pearl onions, thinly sliced mushrooms, bacon bits, and so on.

CHEF'S NOTES

– Searing the meat (in the case of chicken) prevents it from sticking to the pot.
– The pieces of meat may be removed from the pot before the flour is added. In this case, a white roux is made.

DID YOU KNOW?

Some regional specialties, like eel fricassee and Limoux pork fricassee, call for white wine to be added in addition to the white stock.

A rabbit stew cooked in white wine is known as a *gibelotte*.

RECIPE IDEAS

Squab fricassee and garden peas *à la française* **366**
Chicken breasts with baby vegetables **370**
Rabbit stew with puréed Golden Hubbard squash **361**

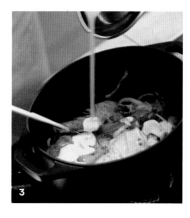

Browned stews (sautéed dishes in sauce) ✳✳

Preparing stews is comparable to braising, but the pieces of meat are smaller and there is more sauce.

Dress, prepare, and cut the pieces of meat.

Cut the aromatic base into a mirepoix.

Prepare a bouquet garni.

Sauté the meat evenly on all sides **(1)**.

Remove the excess fat from the cooking pot and add the aromatic base.

If you wish, add tomato paste and garlic cloves with the shoot removed.

Heat the oven to 350°F–400°F (180°C–200°C).

Cover with wine **(2)**. Reduce by half over high heat. Cover with stock **(3)**.

Add the bouquet garni.

Place in the oven with the lid on.

Make the sauce:
Remove the pieces of meat from the pot and spoon off any fat from the surface of the sauce.

Place the pot over high heat and reduce until the sauce is thick enough to coat the back of a spoon.

Strain through a fine-mesh sieve and adjust the seasoning.

Put the meat back in the pot and pour the sauce over. Bring back to a boil quickly to dissolve the salt just added.

Add the garnish and serve.

CHEF'S NOTES

– To make a game stew (a browned stew), use the animal's blood to bind the sauce. Once you have added this, it must not boil again.
– Do not sprinkle flour over your ingredients if you are using a thickened stock.
– When making lamb stew, add the potatoes 30 minutes before the cooking process is finished.

DID YOU KNOW?

The word for ragout, a stew, comes from the French verb *ragoûter*, which means to give taste (*goût*) to small sautéed pieces by placing them in a sauce that will tenderize them. The first known recipes for ragout in France were used for mutton. In Old French, an *estouffade* referred to a slow cooking process in a hermetically sealed pot. It is now the name of a type of stew, usually beef. To make a daube, a traditional braised joint of beef, the pieces are cooked in their marinade. Curry, matelote (fish stew with wine), and navarin (a lamb stew) all call for a brown sauce to be used.

RECIPE IDEA

Boeuf bourguignon with fresh pasta **383**

Roasting ✳

To roast is to cook in a dry oven or rotisserie, or on a spit, adding a little fat to the food so that it browns evenly to the desired color. You may, if you wish, brown your meat over high heat before placing it in the oven.

Dress and prepare your main ingredient (**1**). Preheat the oven to about 400°F (200°C).

Brown all the sides over high heat using a little fat (oil and/ or clarified butter).

Place in the oven.

Baste regularly during cooking with the fat and juices that exude from the meat. This prevents it from drying out and gives it a good color.

Check for doneness and transfer to a rack to drain. Season and tent under aluminum foil.

Prepare the gravy:
Reduce the juices remaining in the pan over high heat to caramelize them. Remove the excess fat from the roasting dish.

Sweat the aromatic base (onions, carrots, mushrooms, celery, and so on) in the roasting dish.

Deglaze the dish with wine (optional) and/or water (**2**). Strain through a fine-meshed sieve and adjust the seasoning. Serve while still very hot.

CHEF'S NOTES

– To give a personal touch to your gravy, add an aromatic base and a bouquet garni to the liquid in the roasting dish just before the estimated end of cooking time.
– Red meats should be allowed to rest a few minutes before serving. This makes the flesh tender because it allows the juices to return to and penetrate the muscle fiber.
– Season all your ingredients when cooking is done.

RECIPE IDEAS

Aniseed-flambéed sea bream **308**
Roasted rack of lamb with garden vegetables **389**
Provençal shoulder of lamb and vegetable *tian* **379**

Internal temperatures for doneness for beef and lamb	
Very rare	113°F (45°C)
Rare	118°F (48°C)
Medium	136°F (58°C)
Well done	149°F (65°C) and higher

Average roasting times in an oven at 400°F (200°C)	
White meats (pork, veal)	35 min./lb., 60–70 min./kg
Red meats (beef, lamb)	15–17 min./lb., 25–35 min./kg
Poultry (chicken, turkey, capon)	30 min./lb., 45–60 min./kg

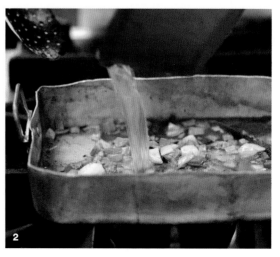

Game stews (salmis) ✳ ✳ ✳

This involves two stages of cooking and is used for feathered game. They are initially roasted whole, and then cut up and stewed in brown stock.

Dress and prepare the bird. Preheat the oven to about 400°F (200°C).

Brown the bird on all sides in oil and/or clarified butter over high heat.

Place in the oven immediately.

Baste regularly with the fat and juices from the bird to moisturize the meat and ensure a good color.

Halfway through the cooking process, cut up the bird and set aside the carcass to prepare a thickened brown stock (see p. 140) (1).

Flambé the pieces and cover with the thickened brown stock (2).

Lower the oven temperature to 325°F–350°F (160°C–180°C) and place the dish in the oven with the lid on. Alternatively, cook over low heat.
Add the garnish required for the recipe and serve.

CHEF'S NOTE

– In French, this is called a salmis. It is made using wild duck, pheasant, and partridge, but you will also find guinea fowl and squab (pigeon) salmis.

RECIPE IDEA

Quail stew and potatoes
à la boulangère **354**

Sautéing ✳

This means cooking food in direct contact with a smooth, flat, hot pan using fat. It is a cooking method to be used at the last minute.

Prepare, dress, and cut up the food to be sautéed.

Preheat the sauté pan or cast-iron flat-top grill (*plancha*) with a little oil or butter.

Sear the food, browning it.

Turn it over and season.

Transfer to a rack to allow the juices to flow out.

Prepare a sauce by deglazing the pan according to your recipe.

CHEF'S NOTES

– It is best to salt smaller pieces after they have been cooked because salt dries out the meat.
– Avoid pricking red meat so that the juice remains within the pieces.

RECIPE IDEA

Sesame-coated rabbit liver salad **286**

Sauté meunière ✳

The food is kept whole or cut up, dusted in flour, and cooked by exposing it to high heat with fat. This cooking method is used at the last minute, and is most suitable for fragile fish, as it forms a crust that protects the flesh and holds it in place.

Prepare, dress, and cut up (if necessary) the food that is to be sautéed.

Use paper towel to dry it, ensuring there is no moisture left. Season with salt and pepper (1).

Quickly dip the pieces in flour and tap them to remove the excess (2).

Preheat the sauté pan with a little oil and/or butter.

Sear the fish with the skin side downward. Brown evenly.

Turn over and finish cooking (3).

Make the sauce for your recipe.

DID YOU KNOW?

It is the flouring of the fish that gives the dish its name meunière, which is French for "miller's wife." Confusingly, *beurre meunière* does not contain flour but is browned butter to which lemon juice and chopped parsley have been added.

RECIPE IDEAS

Sole meunière and potatoes cocotte **336**
Trout with almonds **306**

Crumbed sauté ✴✴

The food is dusted with flour, dipped in egg, and then coated in crumbs. The cooking is identical to simple sautéing. Use the technique at the last moment to ensure that the crumbed coating remains crisp.

Prepare, dress, and cut up the food to sauté.

Remove any remaining moisture with paper towel.

Dust the pieces with flour and tap them to remove the excess (1).

Dip them in a mixture of beaten egg, salt, and oil (2).

Coat in crumbs, such as breadcrumbs, ground hazelnuts, sesame seeds, and so on (3).

To decorate, make a grid pattern using the back of a slicing knife.

Sear and brown evenly (4). Turn over and finish cooking.

Make the sauce for your recipe.

CHEF'S NOTES

– If you use the same sauté pan several times, wipe it off and change the oil and/or butter.
– Use a dry bread of your choice to make your own tasty breadcrumbs in a food processor.

RECIPE IDEAS

Plaice *goujonnettes* with tartare sauce 330
Crumbed turkey escalopes with sautéed potatoes 357

Steaming ✳

The food is cooked in air moistened by the steam given off by boiling liquid. This cooking method preserves the taste, texture, and aroma of the food. A fat-free sauce is an ideal accompaniment to food that is steamed. Steam cooking involves either high or low pressure.

Place a small piece of food in a steaming basket or on a rack.

Place it in a pot holding a liquid (usually water), which you may flavor if you wish.

Close the steam cooker and heat.

Check for doneness and serve immediately.

CHEF'S NOTES

– This cooking technique is principally used for vegetables and fish.
– Since they are not soaked in water, they maintain their taste, smell, and texture.

RECIPE IDEA

Steamed pout fillets in lettuce leaves **320**

Savory Sauces, Condiments, and Stuffings

Emulsified sauces

These sauces combine two ingredients, a watery substance and a fatty substance, which do not naturally mix. The emulsion may be stabilized for a certain time by adding an emulsifying ingredient. The resulting taste depends on the choice of basic components. Try flavored vinegars, for example, and vary the oils—think of walnut or olive.

Unstable emulsions

Basic recipe	Additional ingredients	Name
Vinaigrette (Salad dressing) (see p. 152) 1 part vinegar 2 parts oil salt freshly ground pepper	+ mustard	= mustard vinaigrette
	+ sliced onion, capers, chopped herbs	= *ravigote* sauce
	+ crème fraîche or heavy cream (no oil)	
	+ verjuice (no vinegar)	= *aigrelette*/sharp sauce
Uses	Salad seasoning. Serve cold or warm.	
Fresh tomato coulis (see p. 136) peeled fresh tomatoes vinegar or lemon juice oil + salt freshly ground pepper chopped fresh herbs	+ locally produced honey	= sweet-sour tomato sauce
	+ whipped cream and cubed tomatoes	= sauce aurore
	+ slow-roasted pink garlic and rosemary	= sauce *à la Gasconne*
Uses	Ideal condiment for fish, shellfish, and summer crustaceans. Good with terrines, salads, mousses, and so on. N.B. Use tomatoes when they are in season and choose the tastiest varieties.	
Raw, crushed ingredients (condiments) basic components (olives, anchovies, bell peppers, etc.) aromatics (basil) garlic + oil + vinegar or lemon juice + salt freshly ground pepper	+ salted anchovies	= *anchoïade*
	+ basil, grated Parmesan and pine nuts	= pesto (see p. 146)
	+ basil	= *pistou* (see p. 146)
	+ puréed anchovies, cloves, thyme	= *pissalat*
	+ olives	= tapenade
Uses	Mainly used for Provençal dishes (carpaccio, croutons, and so on) and to accompany grilled fish and meat, or in crusts.	
Melted butter (see p. 134) butter water lemon juice salt freshly ground pepper	+ saffron threads	= saffron sauce
	+ julienned smoked bacon	= smoked sauce
	+ Roquefort cheese	= Roquefort butter
	+ browned butter	= *beurre meunière*
	+ reduced citrus juice	= citrus butter
Uses	These sauces enhance steamed, poached, and sautéed fish, and vegetables	
Beurre blanc (see p. 134) butter shallot white wine (to be reduced) wine vinegar	+ cream	= *Nantais* butter
	+ softened sorrel	= beurre blanc with with sorrel
	+ dill	= beurre blanc with dill
Uses	Replace white wine with beer, red wine, or hard cider. N.B. If you use an electric blender, the emulsion will take longer to prepare.	

Stable emulsions

	Basic recipe	Additional ingredients	Name
Raw egg yolk (lecithin)		+ tomatoes, finely cubed sweet bell peppers	= Andalusian sauce
		+ olive oil, garlic, chopped cilantro, chervil, and parsley	= Antibes sauce
		+ whipped cream	= Chantilly sauce
		+ cognac, ketchup, Worcestershire sauce	= cocktail sauce
		+ gelatin	= aspic
	Mayonnaise (see p. 145)	+ puréed herbs and pistachios	= genoise sauce
	Egg yolk	+ sour cream, lemon juice, chopped fennel	= Gloucester sauce
	+ mustard*	+ reduction of white wine and shallots, chives, chili	= mousquetaire sauce
	+ sunflower seed oil	+ mustard, gherkins, capers, chopped fine herbs, anchovy extract	= *rémoulade*
	+ salt	+ puréed lobster, caviar, mustard	= Russian sauce
	+ freshly ground pepper	+ apple and white wine condiment, shredded horseradish	= Swedish sauce
		+ reduced red wine and shallot	= *vendangeur* sauce
		+ jus of herbs	= green sauce
		+ puréed herbs and boiled egg yolks	= Vincent sauce
	Uses	Serve with cold fish and crustaceans (chauds-froids, aspics, seafood platters), meat, cold poultry, vegetable sticks, and so on	
	Mashed potato + egg yolk + oil + salt + freshly ground pepper	+ puréed garlic	= aioli
		+ puréed garlic, soft bread, saffron, red chili	= rouille
	Uses	Traditionally accompanies soups and fish soups	
Hard-boiled egg yolk (lecithin)	Hard-boiled egg yolk + mustard + oil + vinegar + salt + freshly ground pepper	+ anchovy fillets, capers, chervil, tarragon, chives	= Cambridge sauce
		+ puréed chives and spiced onion	= tartare sauce (see p. 151)
		+ chopped gherkins, capers, parsley, chervil, tarragon, and julienned hard egg white	= *gribiche* sauce
	Uses	Mainly used with fried and grilled foods	

	Basic recipe	Additional ingredients	Name
Semi-coagulated egg yolk (lecithin)		+ reduction of white wine and vinegar, shallot, mignonette pepper, tarragon, and chervil	= béarnaise sauce (see p. 149)
		+ juice and zest of blood orange	= Maltese sauce
		+ juice and zest of mandarin	= Mikado sauce
	Hollandaise sauce (see p. 150)	+ whipped cream	= mousseline sauce
		+ mustard	= mustard sauce
	Water	+ browned butter	= noisette sauce
	+ butter	+ reduced fumet and white wine, crayfish coulis, and anchovy sauce	= Rubens sauce
	+ lemon juice	+ reduced fumet	= white wine sauce
	+ salt	+ tomato (no chervil or tarragon)	= Choron sauce
	+ Cayenne pepper	+ crustacean coral	= coral sauce
		+ meat glaze	= Foyot sauce
	Béarnaise sauce (see p. 149)	+ mint (no tarragon)	= *paloise* sauce
		+ tomato whisked with oil over heat	= Tyrolean sauce
	Uses	Fish, shellfish, meat, poached and grilled poultry, terrines, and so on	

Thickened sauces

Thickened sauces are liquids whose stable, coating consistency is achieved through the use of one or several binding ingredients—stabilizers, thickeners, and jelling agents. The texture (liquefied or solidified) depends on the temperature at which they are used. The thickeners or liaison agents are either starches or proteins.

Protein liaisons

Base	**Eggs**
Technique	Whole or with egg yolks, cream, milk, and so on
Name	Seafood quiche Hot eel pâté Pike quenelles with Nantua sauce Seafood timbale Layered fish dishes Sole soufflé Paupiettes of sole
Uses	Flans, stuffing, creamed batter for baking, pâtés, quenelles, veloutés, soufflés, and so on

Base	**Coral: crustaceans, sea urchins, scallops**
Technique	Reduce to a paste, thin with a hot liquid, and add gradually to the preparation. Do not bring to a boil unless combined with a starch.
Name	Scrambled eggs with sea urchin coral Lobster stew
Uses	Dishes with sauce, accompanying sauces

Base	**Lamprey blood** N.B. The blood of eel and conger or sea eel is toxic if it comes in contact with open wounds or the eyes.
Technique	Mix immediately with a little vinegar. Do not bring to a boil unless combined with a starch.
Name	Sturgeon stew Bordelaise-style conger eel Tuna stew
Uses	Dishes with sauce

Base	**Liver: red mullet, monkfish, cod**
Technique	Reduce to a paste, thin with a hot liquid, and add gradually to the preparation. Do not bring to a boil unless combined with a starch.
Name	Red mullet soup with fennel Sea casserole Sauce with red mullet liver Cod and tomato soup
Uses	Sauces, soups, stuffing, and so on

Starch liaisons

Base	Dry starch
Technique	Sprinkling with flour
Name	Tomato sauce. Aromatic base and smoked bacon are browned, flour is sprinkled over. Add fresh tomato or tomato concentrate and cover with liquid. Simmer (p. 151).
Uses	Stews and ragouts, not frequently used for fish and other seafood

Base	Starch and fat
Technique	**Roux**: white, blond (straw-colored), and brown (identical quantities of butter and flour, cooked depending on the desired color and taste) (see p. 152)
Name	Velouté fumet or white wine sauce and white roux: seafood stew (see p. 152). Béchamel sauce and derived sauces: milk and white roux (p. 133). Nantua sauce: béchamel sauce or velouté with cream, crayfish butter whipped in. Soubise sauce: béchamel sauce or velouté with blanched, chopped onions. *Sauce américaine*: crustacean coulis and blond roux (see p. 148). Oriental sauce: *sauce américaine* with curry. Livonienne sauce: julienned vegetables and a fumet velouté with butter whipped in. Sauce normande: velouté with sole fumet, oyster jus, and mushrooms. Diplomat sauce: normande sauce with lobster butter whipped in. Joinville sauce: normande sauce with crayfish and shrimp butter whipped in.
Uses	Poached, sautéed fish and shellfish, whole or cut. Glazed or gratin fish and shellfish. To make creams and veloutés.
Technique	**Beurre manié** (paste): identical quantities of softened raw butter and flour (see p. 155)
Name	Cardinale sauce: béchamel sauce + fumet, truffle essence, and lobster butter
Uses	Enables the creamy texture of sauces to be adjusted: fish stew

Base	Starch and cold liquid
Technique	Cornstarch, potato starch, arrowroot, rice flour, etc., diluted in cold liquid before being used for a cold liquid (water, fumet, wine, etc.)
Name	Shellfish bisque: shellfish coulis with a rice liaison. Soubise: same technique as above, but replace the béchamel sauce with a consommé thickened with rice flour.
Uses	Dishes in sauce, creams, and veloutés. Thickened sauces.

Base	Polysaccharides
Technique	Pectin, alginates, agar-agar, and carrageen (seaweed extract)
Name	Mousses
Uses	Bavarian cream, seafood terrine, aspic, and so on

131

Savory custard base for baking ✳

This mixture, which contains milk and egg, sets when baked and is used for quiches, pies, and flans.

INGREDIENTS
(for 1 quiche)

Scant ½ cup (100 ml) milk
Scant ½ cup (100 ml) whipping
  cream
2 eggs
1 egg yolk
Pinch grated nutmeg
Salt, freshly ground pepper

Whisk all the ingredients together lightly, ensuring that the mixture does not form bubbles.

Strain through a chinois or sieve, cover with plastic wrap, and chill until needed.

CHEF'S NOTES

– Use moderate heat to bake this mixture. If the oven is too hot, a brown, dry crust will form on the surface.
– Increase the number of eggs if using a garnish of vegetables that produce water.

RECIPE IDEAS

Quiche Lorraine **280**

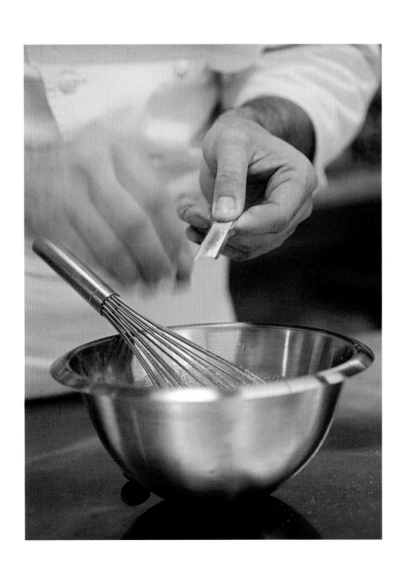

Béchamel or white sauce ✳

The béchamel is a velouté sauce with a milk base (a thickened sauce).

INGREDIENTS
(for 4 cups or 1 liter)

4 tablespoons (60 g) butter
²/₃ cup (60 g) flour
4 cups (1 liter) milk, divided
Pinch grated nutmeg
Scant ½ cup (100 ml) crème fraîche or heavy cream (optional)
Salt, freshly ground pepper, to taste

Make a white roux with the butter and flour (see p. 152) **(1, 2, 3)**.

Add 2 cups (½ liter) milk and the grated nutmeg **(4)**.

Bring the mixture to boil over high heat, whisking constantly.

Pour in the remaining milk, bring to a simmer again, and season. Check the consistency, which should be thick enough to coat the back of a spoon **(5)**.

Stir in the cream, if using.

Transfer to a bowl and cover with plastic wrap flush with the surface. This will prevent a film from forming.

CHEF'S NOTES

– Use a whisk to prepare your sauce to prevent lumps from forming.
– This sauce forms the basis for other sauces such as Mornay (egg yolk and grated Emmental cheese); half-milk and half-cream (very creamy béchamel); soubise (softened onions and béchamel sauce), or Scottish sauce (light béchamel with chopped hard-boiled eggs).

DID YOU KNOW?

Traditionally, a béchamel is seasoned with fine salt, white pepper, and nutmeg. If you wish, replace the nutmeg with other spices like four-spice powder (pepper, nutmeg, cloves, and ginger), paprika, or old-fashioned French mustard with seeds.

This sauce comes to us from Marquis Louis de Béchameil, maître d'hôtel to King Louis XIV.

RECIPE IDEAS

Rolled Picardy crêpes **428**
Florentine-style gnocchi **412**

Beurre blanc ✳✳

An unstable emulsified sauce used cold.

INGREDIENTS
(serves 4)

1 average-sized shallot (about 1 oz. [30 g])
1 ½ tablespoons (25 ml) dry white wine
2 teaspoons (10 ml) white wine vinegar and/or lemon juice
1 stick (125 g) good quality unsalted butter, very cold and cubed
Salt, white pepper or Cayenne pepper

Peel, wash, and finely dice the shallots.

Combine the white wine, vinegar, and shallots in a saucepan **(1)**. Place on low to medium heat and reduce.

Do not allow the mixture to go completely dry. There should be 2–3 tablespoons of liquid left in the saucepan, and the shallots will be nice and moist. The alcohol will have evaporated and much of the acidity is removed.

Add the cubes of butter **(2)**. Whisk in briskly to form the emulsion **(3)**. Too high a temperature will cause the sauce to separate so it is best to leave it over a hot water bath at 122°F (50°C). Season.

If you wish, strain the sauce through a chinois or fine-mesh sieve.

CHEF'S NOTES

– To obtain a nice, airy texture that will coat your dish attractively without masking it, use an electric blender.
– When re-heating the sauce, do not bring it to a boil.
– It is best to prepare the sauce at the last minute.
– The quality of the butter is all-important, for it determines the taste of your sauce. For a balance of the salt seasoning, you may use half unsalted butter and half salted butter.
– As with all butter sauces, allow around 1 oz. (25–30 g) butter per person when calculating the quantities for your guests.

RECIPE IDEA

Fish terrine with beurre blanc **292**

Melted butter ✳

An unstable emulsified sauce used hot.

INGREDIENTS
(serves 4)

1 ½ tablespoons (25 ml) lemon juice
2 teaspoons (10 ml) water
1 stick (125 g) good quality unsalted butter, cold and cubed
Pinch ground *piment d'Espelette*
Salt

CHEF'S NOTE

Even if the sauce is to be served hot (about 130°F or 55°C), make sure that your butter cubes are well chilled. This will facilitate the emulsion process.

Place the lemon juice and water in a saucepan and reduce by half.

Whip the cubes of butter in until completely combined.

Season.

DID YOU KNOW?

You can vary this butter with other citrus fruits: use grapefruit, lime, or orange juice. Reduce it by half and make an emulsion with the butter.

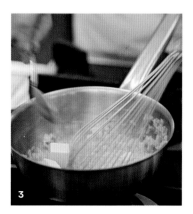

Bisque ✳ ✳

This uses crustaceans as a base, and is a thickened sauce. The following recipe is for a crayfish bisque.

INGREDIENTS
(serves 4)

1 ¾ lb. (800 g) crayfish shells
2 teaspoons (10 ml) olive oil
1 large onion
2 small shallots (40 g), finely diced
1 carrot (80 g), finely diced
14 oz. (400 g) chopped tomatoes
3 ½ tablespoons (50 ml) cognac
6 cups (1.5 liters) white wine
6 cups (1.5 liters) fish fumet
2 cloves garlic
1 bouquet garni
2 tablespoons or 1 oz. (30 g) tomato paste
¾ cup (125 g) rice flour
¾ cup (200 ml) cream
Salt, peppercorns

Sauté the shells over high heat in olive oil. They will turn a red-orange color.

Finely dice the onion, shallot, and carrots (make a mirepoix).

Sweat the ingredients.

Remove the gut from the crustaceans before you start cooking. Crush the carcasses.

Add the chopped tomatoes. Deglaze with cognac and add the white wine.

Reduce by half and pour in the fish fumet, reserving a little to dilute the rice flour.

Add the garlic, bouquet garni, and tomato paste.

Simmer for 30 minutes, skimming if necessary.

Blend and strain through a chinois.

Dilute the rice flour in the cold fish fumet you have reserved.

Add it to the crayfish coulis together with the cream. Return to the stove top and bring to a simmer so that it thickens.

Blend again and strain through cheesecloth (muslin).

Adjust the seasoning.

DID YOU KNOW?

This bisque has been known since 1651, when it was mentioned in *Le Cuisinier François* (*The French Cook*) by La Varenne, a distinguished chef who authored the first rigorous works on cooking. In 1742, François Marin, who was chef to both Mme de Pompadour and the Marquis de Soubise (who gave his name to the sauce) and also the author of a well-known book on food, published it as a crayfish soup.

Today, the bisque is a coulis of crustaceans usually thickened with rice flour.

Shellfish coulis (or cream) ✳✳

This is a crustacean fumet enriched with cream and/or butter.

INGREDIENTS
(serves 8)

2 shallots (50 g)
¼ large onion (50 g)
14 oz. (400 g) crustacean shells or whole small
　crustaceans
3 tablespoons (40 ml) olive oil
Scant ½ cup (100 ml) white wine
4 cups (1 liter) water
1 bouquet garni
1 slightly heaped tablespoon (20 g) tomato paste
Peppercorns

Peel, wash, and finely slice the vegetables.

Crush the crustacean shells.

Heat the olive oil in a pot. Brown the aromatic base and add the shells.

Pour in the white wine and water. Add the bouquet garni, a few peppercorns, and the tomato paste.

Bring to a boil and simmer for 30 minutes, skimming whenever necessary.

Filter, refresh over ice, and use within three days.

CHEF'S NOTE

All crustacean shells (langoustine, shrimps, crayfish, etc.) as well as whole crustaceans, like small crabs, may be used.

RECIPE IDEA

Pike quenelles and
　crayfish sauce **272**

Fresh tomato coulis ✳

An unstable emulsified sauce used cold.

INGREDIENTS
(serves 4)

7 oz. (200 g) fresh ripe tomatoes
2 level teaspoons (10 g) tomato paste (optional)
½ tablespoon wine vinegar or lemon juice
Fresh herbs (basil, tarragon, chervil, chives)
Salt, freshly ground pepper
3 tablespoons (40 ml) olive oil

Wash the tomatoes and peel them by plunging them in boiling water (see p. 63). If you wish, you may remove the seeds. Process or blend with the tomato paste, vinegar, herbs, salt, and pepper, until the mixture is liquid **(1)**. Use an immersion blender to incorporate the olive oil. Strain through a fine-mesh sieve **(2)**. Cover with plastic wrap and chill.

CHEF'S NOTE

– This sauce does not remain stable for long—just a few minutes, in fact. It will need to be mixed again just before serving. For best results, make this sauce at the height of the tomato season.

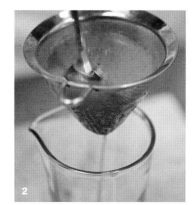

Simple court bouillon ✳

"*Court bouillon*" literally means "short boil" in French. It must only be simmered briefly with the cooking ingredients. Make sure you have enough liquid to cover all the pieces you are cooking. A simple court bouillon is made by brewing—it is a decoction. It is basically salted water with an acidic ingredient, like white wine, vinegar, or lemon juice. However, it is best not to use an acidic ingredient if you are cooking fish that is not white, such as salmon, because that would whiten it.

INGREDIENTS
(for 4 servings)

5 cups (1.25 liters) water
2 cups (0.5 liters) white wine
1 oz. (25 g) kosher salt
Scant ½ cup (100 ml) vinegar or lemon juice
1 bouquet garni
5–6 peppercorns

Bring the water to boil with the white wine, kosher salt, and vinegar or lemon juice.

Simmer for 5 minutes and add the bouquet garni and peppercorns. Simmer for a few more minutes. Cool over ice if not using immediately. Keeps, chilled, for 2 days.

CHEF'S NOTES

– You may also make a simple court bouillon, from cold, with fish included. Fragile pieces of fish should be tied with twine so that they hold their shape during cooking.
– For some shellfish and crustaceans, like shrimp and winkles, try recreating sea water with water and coarse sea salt (1 oz. per 4 cups or 30 g per liter) to use as a cooking base.

Vegetable court bouillon ✳✳

This is a simple court bouillon to which an aromatic base has been added.

INGREDIENTS
(for 4 cups or 1 liter)

1 large carrot (3 ½ oz. or 100 g)
1 large onion (3 ½ oz. or 100 g)
3 ½ cups (800ml) water
¾ cup (200 ml) white wine
½ oz. (15 g) kosher salt
1 bouquet garni
1 teaspoon (5 g) peppercorns

Peel, wash, and finely chop the vegetables.

Bring the water and white wine to a boil with the kosher salt.

Add the onion, and then the carrots.

Simmer for 15 minutes, then add the bouquet garni and the peppercorns. Simmer for a further few minutes.

Chill over an ice bath and use within 2 days.

CHEF'S NOTE

– Most aromatic vegetables, as well as various kinds of seaweed and whole spices, are a tasty addition to this type of court bouillon.

White stock ✳

This is a flavorsome liquid used as a base for many sauces and cooking methods. White stocks may be clear or thickened, and use bones, an aromatic base, and water. The solid ingredients are not browned.

INGREDIENTS
(for 4 cups or 1 liter)

1 lb. (500 g) veal, poultry, or game bones
½ carrot (2 oz./50 g)
½ onion (2 oz./50 g)
½ leek , white only (2 oz./50 g)
½ celery stalk (1 oz./30 g)
1 bouquet garni
2 cloves
6 cups (1.5 liters) water

Slightly crush the bones and blanch them. Rinse well.

Peel, wash, and cut the vegetables into chunks.

Place the bones in a cooking pot and cover with water. Add the vegetables, bouquet garni, and cloves. Bring to a boil.

Cook with the lid off, skimming regularly. Cooking time (the time necessary to extract the flavors) will depend on the size of the bones (1 to 3 hours). Here is a rough guide: small poultry bones: roughly 1 hour; chicken: 1 ½ hours; veal: 2 hours; beef: 3 hours.

Strain through a cheesecloth (muslin), skim the fat off, and chill over an ice bath. Chilled, this keeps for a maximum of 2 days.

CHEF'S NOTES

– Never season a white stock. If you reduce it, the concentration of salt will increase.

– To thicken it, make a roux liaison ½ cup [50 g] flour for 3 tablespoons plus 1 teaspoon [50 g] butter), or use starch (3 tablespoons cornstarch or 2 tablespoons potato starch [50 g], diluted in cold water).
– Freeze-dried stocks or cubes are widely available and can be used to reduce preparation time.

DID YOU KNOW?

A sauce allemande (literally, German sauce), which is a basic white sauce, comprises a white veal or poultry stock that is thickened and enriched with an aromatic base.

RECIPE IDEAS

Squab fricassee and garden peas *à la française* 366
Rabbit stew with puréed Golden Hubbard squash 361

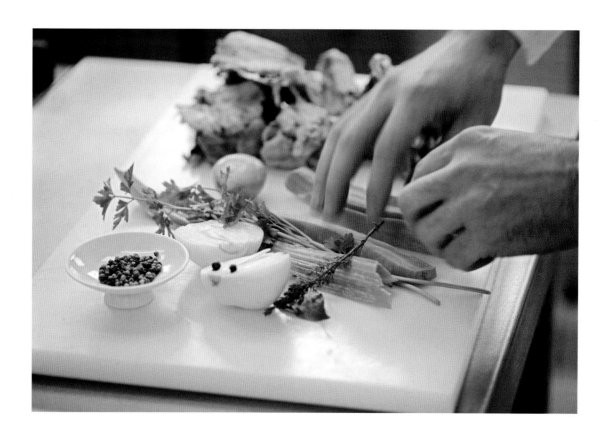

Spiced or creamy court bouillon (*à la nage*) ✳✳

À la nage means "swimming"; here the main ingredient is served bathed in the liquid, to which a condiment and/or cream has been added. This is a vegetable court bouillon whose aromatic base is served with the main ingredient. Depending on the recipe, fish fumet and vinegar may also be added.

CHEF'S NOTES

– Small pieces of fish and whole shellfish lend themselves particularly well to this court bouillon. The liquid, which is often very spicy, works as a marinade.
– To prepare a fish *au bleu*, pour hot vinegar on very fresh fish to turn the mucus covering the scales a blue color.

DID YOU KNOW?

An *escabèche* is the name of a fish dish in which boiling court bouillon is poured over small fish or fish fillets and then slowly cooled. *Escabèche* literally means "without a head" (head is *cabeza* in Spanish; the marinade originated there), as the heads are removed from the fish.

RECIPE IDEA

Mackerel in *escabèche* 332

Court bouillon with milk ✳

This is used to preserve the natural color of certain white fish, such as turbot, halibut, and brill, or to tone down the intense smoked taste of herring and haddock, for example. Its components are salted water, milk, lemon, and sometimes a bouquet garni.

INGREDIENTS
(for 4 cups or 1 liter)

1 lemon, preferably unsprayed or organic
3 ¼ cups (800 ml) water
¾ cup (200 ml) milk
1 bouquet garni
½ oz. (15 g) kosher salt

Slice the lemon. Place all the ingredients in a pot to boil.

Chill rapidly over an ice bath, skim, and use within 24–36 hours.

CHEF'S NOTE

– There is not much milk in this preparation because of the lemon, which causes it to curdle. This court bouillon is particularly good for pieces of large, flat fish such as turbot and halibut.

RECIPE IDEA

Turbot poached in cardamom-infused milk, with hollandaise sauce 335

Brown stock ✳✳

This flavorsome liquid is used as a base for many sauces and types of cooking. Brown stocks may be clear or thickened. They are made with bones, an aromatic base, and water. The ingredients are browned, unlike the method for a white stock, and this is what makes for a tastier stock.

INGREDIENTS
(for 4 cups or 1 liter)

1 lb. (500 g) bones
½ carrot (2 oz./50 g)
½ onion (2 oz./50 g)
½ leek (2 oz./50 g)
4 oz. (100 g) fresh tomato
½ celery stalk (1 oz./30 g)
1 bouquet garni
2 cloves
6 cups (1.5 liters) water

Crush the bones, or ask your butcher to do so. Brown them in a very hot oven (425°F [220°C]) **(1)**.

Peel, wash, and cut the vegetables into chunks **(2)**.

Place the bones in a large pot and cover with water.

Add the vegetables, bouquet garni, and cloves.

Bring to a boil.

Cook with the lid off, skimming regularly. Cooking time (the time necessary to extract the flavors) will depend on the size of the bones (1 to 3 hours). A rough guide is small poultry bones: 1 hour; chicken: 1 ½ hours; veal: 2 hours; beef: at least 3 hours.

Strain through a fine-meshed sieve, remove the fat, and cool down quickly.

CHEF'S NOTE

– Do not confuse the jus of a roast, made from the juices remaining after cooking, and a brown stock, which uses bones as a base.

DID YOU KNOW?

Sauce espagnole (basic brown sauce) is a veal stock, thickened and enriched with aromatic ingredients.

Demi-glace is a rich sauce made with *sauce espagnole* and reduced by half.

Glace is a clear cooking jus without a liaison (brown stock, reduced court bouillon, fumet) slowly reduced to a syrupy consistency. Used like this, it is strongly flavored. When cold, it takes on a jelly-like consistency.

RECIPE IDEAS

Boeuf bourguignon with fresh pasta **383**
Normandy-style veal chops **393**
Kidneys in mustard sauce **387**

Fumet ✳✳

This is a clear stock that is used to cook fish. It is also the base for aspic, the chaud-froid, and consommé, and can be clarified. However, it is not recommended for fatty fish like sardines, eel, and herring, and freshwater fish. Some fish are cooked in a fumet with red wine, and this makes a stew called a matelote.

INGREDIENTS
(for 4 cups or 1 liter)

1 ½ lb. (600 g) fish bones
2 small shallots (2 oz./50 g)
½ large onion (2 oz./50 g)
½ leek (2 oz./50 g), white only
½ carrot (2 oz./50 g)
1 oz. (30 g) button mushrooms
1 bouquet garni
4 cups (1 liter) water
²/₃ cup (150 ml) white wine
Peppercorns

Crush the fish bones. Leave them to soak in cold water until all traces of blood are removed.

Peel, wash, and finely slice the vegetables. Sweat these gently and add liquid in two stages, or just put straight into a large pot with all the other ingredients and bring to a boil (1, 2).

Skim when necessary (3).

Simmer for 25–30 minutes. Do not stir, as this will cloud the liquid.

Strain through a sieve, cool down rapidly, and use within 3 days.

DID YOU KNOW?

Essences are obtained by reducing liquids, stocks, or infusions to produce a concentrate of flavors.

RECIPE IDEA

Pollack fillets bonne femme **319**

Boiled vinegar and sugar (*gastrique*) ✳

This is the base for a thickened sweet-and-sour sauce obtained by reduction.

INGREDIENTS
(for 1 cup or ¼ liter of sauce)

Scant ½ cup (100 ml) vinegar
Scant ½ cup (80 g) sugar
1 scant cup (200 ml) liquid (juice, water, or stock) to bring the temperature down

Place the vinegar and the sugar in a saucepan (1).

Slowly bring to a boil and reduce until it reaches a syrupy consistency. (This is the stage before it caramelizes.)

Deglaze with the liquid you have chosen (2) and stir until thoroughly mixed.

CHEF'S NOTES

– The liquid you use to reduce the temperature can be as varied as you wish. Try fruit juice, wine, coconut milk, soy sauce, and so on.
– Substitute honey or maple syrup for the sugar. With its sweet-and-sour taste, sauces that use *gastrique* show the influence of the cooking of both the English-speaking world and Asia on French cuisine.

RECIPE IDEA

Duckling à l'orange with sautéed potatoes and artichokes **353**

Marinades

These are flavorful, liquid preparations used to tenderize and enhance food, or, in the case of strong flavors (game and freshwater fish), tone them down. A marinade may also work as a preservative for certain foods. Marinades always include an acidic ingredient that acts on the proteins to tenderize the product. Some or all of the marinade liquid may be used to make sauces or cooking liquids. The food you marinate is always raw, so hygiene must be scrupulous. Check that the storage temperature is appropriately cold, and that the food is covered with plastic wrap or vacuum packed.

The length of time a product is marinated depends on its size and type. A marinade will penetrate about ½ in. (1 cm) of a food every 24 hours. Marinades, like stocks, should not be seasoned with salt.

Instant marinade ✴

This is used for small pieces, like fish steaks or fillets, steaks, and vegetables, usually before grilling. The base is a flavored oil to which an acidic ingredient like lemon juice is added. The food is left to marinate for 1–2 hours.

INGREDIENTS
(to marinate 8 pieces)

1 ½ cups (300 ml) olive oil
½ bunch fresh or dried herbs
1 sprig of thyme
Bay leaf (1 per piece)
2 lemons
Mignonette pepper

Pour half of the oil into a pan. Add the dried or fresh herbs, the thyme, and the bay leaves.

Arrange the pieces to be marinated in the pan and pour over the rest of the olive oil.

Peel the lemons, removing all the white pith, and slice them. Place the lemon slices over the pieces and sprinkle with mignonette pepper.

Cover with plastic wrap and chill.

Turn the pieces over halfway through the process (allow 1–2 hours total).

CHEF'S NOTE

– To marinate thick pieces, make incisions or prick them with a needle. This will enable the marinade to better penetrate the food and will result in improved flavor.

DID YOU KNOW?

Fish used to be preserved in a brine called *eau marine* (marine water) which gave rise to the word "marinade." The aim of the process was not to improve flavor, but merely to help preserve freshness in the days before it was possible to chill food.

RECIPE IDEA

Grilled salmon steaks with braised fennel **325**

Raw marinade ✳

This marinade uses wine, coconut milk, or beer, and a raw aromatic base comprising ingredients such as carrots, celery, onions, and seaweed. Add spices to intensify the basic flavors. Marinade the food from between 1 to 3 days.

INGREDIENTS
(for 8 servings of a raw red wine marinade)

½ carrot (2 oz./50 g)
½ celery stalk (2 oz./50 g)
½ fennel bulb (2 oz./50 g)
½ bunch dried or fresh herbs
A sprig of thyme
Bay leaves (one per piece)
A pinch of peppercorns
6 cups (1.5 liters) red wine
Scant ½ cup (100 ml) wine vinegar
3 ½ tablespoons (50 ml) oil

Finely slice the vegetables for the aromatic base.

Place half of them at the bottom of a mixing bowl.

Place the pieces to be marinated over them.

Add the other half of the vegetables, the fresh or dried herbs, thyme, bay leaves, and peppercorns.

Cover with wine and vinegar and drizzle the olive oil over.

Cover with plastic wrap and chill.

CHEF'S NOTES

– Depending on your recipe, you may use cognac or Armagnac as well as wine and vinegar.
– To make foie gras, soak it in milk to reduce any bitterness and then marinate it in a strong alcohol such as port, cognac, or Armagnac.
– You can omit the oil poured over the surface if—when covering the container—you ensure the plastic wrap lies flush with the marinade.

Cooked marinade ✳

Cooked marinade contains the same ingredients as raw marinade. Sweat the aromatic base, add the wine, and simmer for 30 minutes. Cool before using.

INGREDIENTS
(for 8 servings of a cooked white wine marinade)

½ carrot (2 oz./50 g)
½ celery stalk (2 oz./50 g)
½ onion (2 oz./50 g)
3 ½ tablespoons (50 ml) oil
6 cups (1.5 litres) white wine
Scant ½ cup (100 ml) wine vinegar
3 ½ tablespoons (50 ml) cognac or Armagnac
4 garlic cloves (20 g)
½ bunch dried or fresh herbs
A sprig of thyme
Bay leaves (1 per piece)
Peppercorns

Finely slice the vegetables for the aromatic base. Sweat them in oil, or brown them just slightly. Cover them with all the liquid ingredients. Add the garlic, dried or fresh herbs, thyme, bay leaves, and a few peppercorns.

Bring to a simmer and cook for about 30 minutes. Allow to cool, then cover with plastic wrap and chill.

CHEF'S NOTE

– If you are using your marinade as a stock, choose a good-quality wine, as it will determine the final taste.

Mayonnaise ✳

A stable emulsified sauce used cold.

INGREDIENTS
(serves 4)

1 egg yolk
1 heaped teaspoon (15 g) French
  mustard
1 teaspoon (5 ml) wine vinegar
Salt, white pepper or Cayenne
  pepper
⅔ cup (150 ml) sunflower seed
  oil

Combine the egg yolk, mustard, vinegar, salt, and pepper **(1)**.

Pour the oil in gradually, whisking energetically all the while, (or use an electric beater) **(2)**.

Check that the texture is firm **(3)**, scrape down the sides so that it forms a compact mass, cover with plastic wrap, and chill.

CHEF'S NOTES

– If your mayonnaise separates (i.e. the emulsion disaggregates), add a little water, 1 tablespoon maximum, and/or some egg yolk. Beat together again so that the emulsion re-forms.
– Never season with salt when the mayonnaise is ready, as this might form white spots.
– If you add a drop of vinegar when you have finished whipping the mayonnaise, this will give it a slightly paler color, intensify the taste a little, and reduce the risk of contamination by salmonella.
– Fresh mayonnaise, covered and chilled, keeps no longer than 48 hours.

RECIPE IDEA

Plaice *goujonnettes* with tartare sauce **330**

Pesto and *pistou* ✳

An unstable emulsified sauce used cold.

PESTO INGREDIENTS
(serves 4)

3 cloves of new garlic (15 g)
3 tablespoons (25 g) pine nuts
¾ cup (200 ml) fresh basil leaves
¼ cup (40 g) finely grated
  Parmesan cheese
⅓ cup (75 ml) olive oil
Salt, freshly ground pepper

Remove the leaves from the basil. Wash them and dry well. Remove the shoots from the garlic cloves. Lightly roast the pine nuts. Crush them all together with a mortar and pestle (**1, 2**).

Add the basil and Parmesan cheese. Crush again and whisk in the olive oil (**3**).

Season with salt and pepper.

DID YOU KNOW?

Pesto comes from Italy—from Genoa, to be precise.

Pistou is from Provence, and is made of fresh crushed basil with garlic cloves and olive oil.

Pesto and *pistou* both work well with pasta.

Both words derive from the Latin "*pistare*," which means to crush or pound.

RECIPE IDEA

Beef carpaccio, Parmesan, and *pistou* **262**

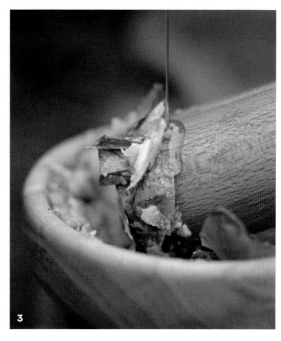

Rouille ✳

A stable emulsified sauce used cold.

INGREDIENTS
(serves 4)

2 ½ oz. (75 g) mealy potatoes
2–3 garlic cloves (15 g), peeled, shoots removed
1 egg yolk
⅓ cup (75 ml) olive oil
1 ½ tablespoons (25 ml) peanut oil
Saffron, ground or threads
Salt, freshly ground pepper

Boil the potatoes in their jackets. When cooked, peel and mash them, and place them in a mixing bowl.

Crush the garlic cloves and mix with the potatoes.

Mix in the egg yolk **(2)** and whisk in the oils **(3)**.

Add a little saffron **(4)** and adjust the seasoning.

Scrape down the sides of the bowl, cover with plastic wrap so it lies flush with the surface, and chill.

CHEF'S NOTE

– This sauce is the perfect accompaniment to fish soup.

DID YOU KNOW?

The name of the sauce comes from its color (*rouille* means rust), since it includes orange-yellow saffron.

RECIPE IDEA

Rockfish soup **278**

Sauce américaine ✳✳

This sauce is traditionally made using velvet swimming crabs, but you may also use lobster (which makes a Newburg sauce) or crayfish, which makes a Nantua sauce. It is a thickened sauce.

Savory Sauces, Condiments, and Stuffings

INGREDIENTS
(serves 8)

1 ¾ lb. (800 g) small crabs
Scant ½ cup (100 ml) olive oil
1 large onion (3 ½ oz./100 g)
3–4 shallots (3 oz./80 g)
1 large carrot (3 ½ oz./100 g)
7 oz. (200 g) chopped tomatoes
3 tablespoons (40 g) tomato paste
3 ½ tablespoons (50 ml) cognac
¾ cup (200 ml) white wine
6 cups (1.5 liters) fish fumet
2 garlic cloves
1 bouquet garni
1 sprig tarragon
1 pinch *piment d'Espelette*
Salt, freshly ground pepper

For the blond (straw-colored) roux (see p. 152)
2 tablespoons (1 oz. or 30 g) butter
⅓ cup (30 g) flour

Prepare the roux with the butter and flour.

Set aside to cool.

Roughly slice the crabs (**1**). Heat the olive oil and begin cooking them (**2**). Finely dice the onions, shallots, and carrots to make a mirepoix. Add the vegetables to the pot and sweat them (**3**).

Chop up the carcasses into small pieces. Add the chopped tomatoes and tomato paste. Deglaze with Cognac and flambé. Then add the white wine (**4**). Reduce by half and pour in the fish fumet. Add the garlic, bouquet garni, and tarragon leaves. Simmer for 30 minutes, skimming when necessary.

Blend in a food processor and strain through a chinois.

Pour the strained liquid over the cooled roux and bring it all to a simmer, stirring all the time so that it thickens (**5**).

Adjust the seasoning and reserve until needed.

DID YOU KNOW?

No one quite knows where this sauce originated, despite its name. It is also known as a *sauce à l'armoricaine* (Armorica is an old Gaulish name for an area including Brittany). However it's likely that it was the invention of Pierre Fraisse, a French cook who had worked in the United States of America before returning to Paris and setting up Peters Restaurant in Paris.

RECIPE IDEA

Monkfish medallions *à l'américaine* and rice pilaf **338**

Béarnaise sauce ✳ ✳ ✳

A hot, stable emulsified sauce.

INGREDIENTS
(serves 4)

1 gray shallot
3 tablespoons (40 ml) dry white
  wine
3 tablespoons (40 ml) tarragon
  vinegar
1 sprig tarragon
3 egg yolks
½ cup (120 g) good quality
  unsalted butter, cubed and
  softened
A few chervil sprigs
8 peppercorns, crushed
Fine sea salt

Peel, wash, and finely slice
the shallot.

Put the white wine, vinegar,
shallots, and some of the
tarragon leaves into a
saucepan and prepare the
reduction over low heat (**1**).

Do not reduce until dry; there
should be a few tablespoons
of liquid left and the shallots
will be moist. Most of the
acidity will have disappeared.

Allow to cool while the flavors
blend.

Add the egg yolks and place
the pot over hot water
(bain-marie) or very low heat
and whisk until the
consistency is nice and
thick—it should resemble a
sabayon (**2**).

Add the softened butter,
continuing to whisk (**3**).

Strain through a fine-mesh
sieve.

Chop the rest of the tarragon
and the chervil. Adjust the
seasoning and add the
chopped herbs.

DID YOU KNOW?

The French term fines herbes is
used for the following herbs only:
parsley, chervil, chives, and
tarragon. Tarragon has the
strongest flavor of the four, with a
pronounced aniseed-type taste.

RECIPE IDEA

Grilled rib roast and
  béarnaise sauce **376**

Hollandaise sauce ✳ ✳

A stable emulsified sauce used hot.

INGREDIENTS
(serves 4)

3 egg yolks
3 teaspoons water
1 stick (120 g) good quality
   unsalted butter, clarified
4 teaspoons (20 ml) lemon juice
Salt
Cayenne pepper or *piment
   d'Espelette*

Whisk the egg yolks with the water **(1)**. Place over a bain-marie or over very low heat and continue whisking until the mixture is nice
and thick. Remove from the heat and whip in the melted butter **(2)**.

Season and add the lemon juice.

CHEF'S NOTES

– If your egg yolks become grainy because the mixture is overcooked, add a little water and whip. However, if you have really overcooked the sauce, start again from the beginning.
– If the sauce separates into watery liquid and fatty matter, add a small amount of cold water or an ice cube and work into an emulsion again.
– Hollandaise sauce, just like béarnaise sauce, cools down rapidly. It is therefore important to make these sauces at the last moment or to keep them warm over a hot water bath.

DID YOU KNOW?

The recipe is a tribute to the quality of the dairy products of the Netherlands.

RECIPE IDEA

Turbot poached in cardamom-infused milk, with hollandaise sauce **335**

Tartare sauce ✳

A stable emulsified sauce used cold.

INGREDIENTS
(serves 4)

2 hard-boiled egg yolks
1 tablespoon (15 ml) French mustard
1 teaspoon (5 ml) wine vinegar
²/₃ cup (150 ml) sunflower seed oil
A few sprigs chives
2 new onions (2 oz./50 g)
Salt, white pepper, or Cayenne pepper or *piment d'Espelette*

Prepare a mayonnaise (p. 145), replacing the raw egg yolk with finely chopped or well crushed hard-boiled yolks.

Finely slice the chives and onions and add them to the sauce.

Season with salt and pepper.

Scrape down the sides of the bowl, cover with plastic wrap flush with the surface, and chill.

RECIPE IDEA

Plaice *goujonnettes* with tartare sauce **330**

Tomato sauce ✳✳

Published recipes for thickened tomato date to the early nineteenth century.

INGREDIENTS
(serves 8)

3 ½ oz. (100 g) smoked bacon
3 tablespoons (40 g) butter
1 carrot (3 oz./80 g)
1 onion (3 oz./80 g)
Scant ²/₃ cup (60 g) flour
3 lb. (1.5 kg) ripe tomatoes
2 cloves garlic
1 bouquet garni
3 tablespoons (40 g) tomato paste (optional)
4 cups (1 liter) water
2 teaspoons (10 g) sugar (optional)
Salt, freshly ground pepper

Special equipment: ovenproof pan

Preheat the oven to 350°F (180°C). Cut the smoked bacon into small cubes and blanch.

Peel, wash, and finely dice the carrots and onions to make a mirepoix. Sauté the bacon bits in butter in an ovenproof pan and add the diced vegetables. Allow to brown a little and sprinkle with flour **(1)**. Mix in the flour and place the dish in the oven for a few minutes.

Remove from the oven and lower the heat to 285°F (140°C).

Wash, peel, seed, and chop the tomatoes and add them to the other ingredients. Remove the shoot from the garlic cloves and crush. Add the garlic, bouquet garni, and tomato paste **(2)**. Pour in the water and season. Cover and cook in the oven for 1 hour.

Strain through a sieve or chinois, check the consistency and seasoning, adding sugar if necessary.

CHEF'S NOTE

– If serving with pasta, allow 2 cups of sauce for 10 servings. This base recipe can be enriched with flavorings, such as basil or celery, and meat, such as ham.

DID YOU KNOW?

Tomato sauce is used in many preparations, such as bolognese sauce, with sautéed minced meat, deviled sauce, zingara sauce, tomato chaud-froid, and the hussard, which contains finely sliced onions and shallots, and is deglazed with white wine and covered with a *demi-glace* to which tomatoes have been added.

151

Velouté ✳

A velouté is a cooking liquid (such as a stock or a fumet) that is thickened with a roux. It has a creamy consistency, and is considered a basic liquid, with fish, poultry, and veal velouté.

INGREDIENTS
(for 4 cups or 1 liter)

4 tablespoons (60 g) butter
Scant ²/₃ cup (60 g) flour
4 cups (1 liter) liquid, such as a white stock or fumet
Scant ½ cup (100 ml) crème fraîche (optional)
A pinch of grated nutmeg (optional)
Salt, freshly ground pepper

Make a white roux: melt the butter over low heat. Remove from the heat and add the flour. Mix in well and whisk over very low heat for a few minutes without letting it brown.

Stir in 2 cups (0.5 liter) of the cold cooking liquid. Bring to a boil over high heat, whisking constantly. Pour in the rest of the cooking liquid and the cream and bring to a boil again, stirring constantly. Boil for 2 minutes. Remove from the heat and season.

Transfer to a dish and cover with plastic wrap flush with the surface. This will prevent a skin from forming.

CHEF'S NOTES

– If you follow all the steps carefully, whisking well, you should not have any lumps.
– If you have a cold roux, use a hot liquid (and vice versa). Use this method if you are making large quantities.
– This sauce forms the basis for other sauces such as Cardinal (fish velouté, truffles, lobster coulis); Allemande (ordinary velouté thickened with egg yolks); aurore (chicken velouté with tomatoes); Chivry (chicken velouté with herbs); curry (onions, apples, curry, coconut milk, velouté); or normande (sole velouté, mushrooms essence and oyster jus).

DID YOU KNOW?

A blond roux is a white roux that has been cooked just a few minutes longer, until it turns a nice straw color. It is more digestible because the starch in the flour is cooked.

Vinaigrette ✳

This is a cold, unstable emulsified sauce, used as a salad dressing.

INGREDIENTS
(serves 4)

2 ½ tablespoons (40 ml) vinegar
½ cup (125 ml) oil
Salt, freshly ground pepper

Dissolve a little salt in the vinegar. Grind in the pepper. Whisk the mixture with the oil until it emulsifies.

CHEF'S NOTES

– Adding mustard to your vinaigrette will give it a stronger taste and stabilize it too.
– You can vary this basic recipe by using a flavored oil (see p. 157).

DID YOU KNOW?

It goes almost without saying that vinegar is the most important ingredient in a vinaigrette. It is produced through the fermentation of wine or other alcohol and contains a minimum of 6% acetic acid. In France, wine vinegar is the type most widely used, and it is also used in recipes for deglazing.

Balsamic vinegar comes from the Modena and Reggio Emilia regions of Italy. The traditional vinegar is produced by cooking/reducing grape juice must, which is then aged in oak casks.

RECIPE IDEAS

Mixed garden vegetables **416**
Sesame-coated rabbit liver salad **286**

Flavored butters

The quality of butter and flavoring you choose will determine the taste of your final ingredient. Bear in mind that butter takes on other tastes and must be carefully stored. Cover it well after each use and return to the refrigerator, where it should be kept at between 35.6°F–39.2°F (2°C–4°C). Once butter has been worked with, it goes rancid more quickly.

Butter

Butter is made from the milk or cream of cow's milk. The minimum fat content of butter is 80%. Butter usually contains 18% water and 2% dry matters, including casein proteins and mineral salts. It should not contain any additives besides salt. France has a number of AOC butters, and the flavor of any particular butter is a result of the fodder given to the cows, their region and breed, and even of the seasons.

The first known written mention of butter goes back to 2500 BCE. It was not a foodstuff that the Romans and Greeks liked much, using it mainly for medicinal purposes (to heal wounds). In the Western world, butter is made from cows' milk, but in Africa and Asia other types of milk may be used.

Until the end of the Middle Ages, butter in Europe was considered to be a poor man's fat. After this period, however, demand for butter as a foodstuff increased. As it climbed the ladder of culinary respectability, the concept of terroir gradually came into play. Normandy and Brittany, particularly fertile regions with significant dairy production, are renowned for the quality of their butter. Farm production in France was widespread until the 1960s, when industrial production took over to the detriment of small producers.

Today, France is Europe's largest butter-producing country, and has the highest per capita consumption in the world: the average French person consumes just over 17 lb. (8 kg) a year.

Hot prepared butters

Name	Ingredients (for 2 sticks or 250 g butter)
Lobster Butter	½ lb. (250 g) flesh (head, antenna, appendages) of lobster + coral + salt, freshly ground pepper
Red Butter (*beurre rouge*) (see p. 156)	½ lb. (250 g) crustacean shells, (crayfish, small crabs, langoustes, etc.) + salt, freshly ground pepper

Flavored butters (cold and raw)

Name	Ingredients (for 2 sticks or 250 g butter)
Nut butters (almond, hazelnut, pistachio, etc.)	1 ¾ cup (150 g) ground almonds, hazelnuts, or pistachios
Anchovy butter	3 ½ oz. (100 g) anchovies in oil or salt
Snail butter (*beurre d'escargot*) (see p. 155)	1 chopped shallot (25 g) + 1 clove garlic, shoot removed and crushed 2 tablespoons (20 g) chopped parsley + fine sea salt, freshly ground pepper
Maître d'hôtel butter	1 tablespoon (10 g) chopped parsley + ¼ cup (60 ml) lemon juice + salt, freshly ground pepper
Horseradish butter	2 tablespoons (50 g) shredded horseradish + salt, freshly ground pepper
Smoked salmon butter (and other fish)	3 ½ oz. (100 g) smoked salmon (or trout, sturgeon, eel, smoked herring) + salt, freshly ground pepper
Mustard* butter	2 heaped tablespoons (80 g) Meaux mustard (with seeds) + salt, freshly ground pepper
Cheese butters (Roquefort, cream cheeses, etc.)	3–4 oz. (100–125 g) cheese, depending on strength + salt, freshly ground pepper
Sea urchin butter	1 teaspoon (25 g) sea urchin coral + 1 teaspoon (5 ml) lemon juice + salt, freshly ground pepper
Seaweed butter	2 oz. (50 g) fresh nori and/or dulse and/or sea lettuce
Shellfish butter (oyster, cockles, clams, etc.)	3 ½ oz. (100 g) raw, shelled shellfish with their liquid + 1 ⅓ tablespoons (20 ml) lemon juice + fine sea salt, freshly ground pepper

Cold flavored butters with cooked ingredients

Name	Ingredients (for 2 sticks or 250 g butter)
Bercy butter	3 small shallots (80 g), finely sliced, reduced with ⅓ cup (80 ml) dry white wine + 1 teaspoon (5 g) chopped parsley + 3 ⅓ tablespoons (50 ml) lemon juice + 1 oz. (25 g) poached, diced spinal marrow of sturgeon + salt, freshly ground pepper
Chivry butter	¾ cup (200 g) herbs (salad burnet, chervil, parsley, tarragon, chives), blanched and squeezed to drain + 2 shallots (50 g), sliced and blanched + salt, freshly ground pepper
Shrimp butter	10 oz. (250 g) brown shrimp, poached in salt water and shelled + salt, freshly ground pepper
Roe butter	4 ½ oz. (125 g) poached roe (herring, carp, mackerel) + 1 teaspoon (10 g) French mustard + salt, freshly ground pepper
Herb butter (tarragon, parsley, shallot, etc.)	⅓ cup or 4 ½ oz. (125 g) tarragon or parsley or shallot, blanched and chopped + salt, freshly ground pepper
Montpellier butter	Spinach leaves, watercress, parsley, chervil, chives, tarragon, shallots (⅙ oz. or 5 g of each). Blanch and reduce to a paste with: gherkins, capers, anchovy fillets (½ oz. or 15 g of each) + 1 garlic clove + 1 egg yolk, hard-boiled + 1 egg yolk, raw + salt, Cayenne pepper + scant ½ cup (100 ml) oil (to facilitate straining)
Paprika butter	3 shallots (80 g), chopped and sweated + 1 scant teaspoon (4 g) paprika + salt, freshly ground pepper
Hôtelier butter*	6 oz. (170 g) maître d'hôtel butter + dry duxelles (4 oz./125 g button mushrooms + 1 small shallot [20 g] + 2 teaspoons/10 g butter)
Marseillaise butter*	6 oz. (170 g) maître d'hôtel butter + ¼ cup or 2 ¾ oz. (80 g) chopped, cooked tomato fondue + 3 garlic cloves + 2 pinches (1 g) fennel or anise seeds
Crustacean butter	7 oz. (200 g) cooked crustacean meat + salt, freshly ground pepper

* no need to add 2 sticks (250 g) uncooked butter

Snail butter (*beurre d'escargot*) ✳

This is made cold using raw ingredients that are chopped or puréed and incorporated into softened butter. For this technique, it is advisable to use the blade knife of a food processor. Allow 1–1 ½ tablespoons (15–20 g) snail butter per person if you are serving individual portions.

INGREDIENTS
(serves 8)

2 sticks (250 g) softened butter
1 grey shallot (25 g), chopped
1 clove garlic (4 g), shoot
   removed, minced
2 tablespoons (20 g) chopped
   parsley
Salt, freshly ground pepper

Use a rubber spatula to combine all the ingredients, or use a food processor. Check that they are thoroughly mixed.

Scrape down the sides of the bowl, cover with plastic wrap, and chill until needed.

CHEF'S NOTE

If you can find butter with salt crystals, such as butter with *sel de Guérande*, it will give a pleasantly light crunch to your preparation.
When keeping the snail butter in the refrigerator or freezer, wrap it in plastic wrap so that it does not absorb any tastes and smells.

DID YOU KNOW?

You should not put aluminum foil in contact with butter, because it oxidizes in the presence of salt and acidic ingredients like lemon juice and vinegar, and imparts its metallic taste. Snail butter was initially only used with snails, but today it accompanies shellfish, crustaceans, and even frogs.

Beurre manié ✳

This butter will allow you to adjust the creaminess of sauces. It must be cooked sufficiently to avoid imparting a pasty, grainy texture to sauces, and to ensure that the flour is digestible.

INGREDIENTS

Equal quantities of softened
   butter and flour.

Combine the two using a fork until thoroughly blended.

CHEF'S NOTE

– This liaison butter can be made a few hours ahead of time, and even stored 2–3 days in the refrigerator if completely covered in plastic wrap. It is best to use unsalted butter.

RECIPE IDEA

Soft-boiled eggs on a bed of artichokes with eggplant caviar **424**

Shallot butter with red wine (*beurre marchand de vin*) ✳

This butter is prepared cold using cooked, cooled, and blended ingredients that are then incorporated into softened butter. For an even more refined butter, strain it through a sieve.

INGREDIENTS
(serves 8)

¾ cup (200 ml) red wine
2–3 shallots (80 g), finely sliced
2 sticks (250 g) unsalted butter, softened
Salt, freshly ground pepper

Place the red wine and sliced shallot in a saucepan over low heat.

Reduce gently until dry.

Allow to cool.

Mix in the softened butter and season.

Scrape down the sides of the bowl, cover with plastic wrap, and set to chill until needed.

CHEF'S NOTE

– The quality of the wine is decisive for the final taste. This sauce comes to us from the Bordeaux region, where it was made using only local red wine.

Red butter (*beurre rouge*) ✳ ✳

This is prepared hot. The cooked ingredients infuse slowly in the butter before being blended, strained, and cooled. This flavored butter is dry, and is mainly used to whip into sauces for crustaceans at the last minute.

INGREDIENTS
(serves 8)

2 sticks (250 g) unsalted butter, softened
10 oz. (300 g) crayfish shells
1 ⅓ tablespoons (20 ml) lemon juice
Salt
A little *piment d'Espelette*

Blend all the ingredients together.

Place on very low heat—maximum 140°F (60°C)—or over a hot water bath and infuse for 1 hour.

Strain through a fine-mesh sieve, cover with plastic wrap flush with the butter. Chill until firm.

CHEF'S NOTES

– A flavored butter made using the infusing technique loses some of its delicacy, and the taste of the main ingredient will predominate.
– A butter prepared in this way becomes a little dry and hard due to the loss of water and the addition of protein.
– If you wish, add other aromatic ingredients while the butter is infusing.

Flavored oils ✳

Flavored oils are used for seasoning, hot or cold, as well as to preserve food and cook it (frying, oil fondues, and slow cooking in oil). Select your oil (olive, sunflower seed, grape-seed, etc.) according to the use (cooking or seasoning), the taste (neutral or with a pronounced taste), and the consistency you require (fluid or thick).

For added taste, immerse one or several aromatic ingredients in the oil or mixture of oils and heat to a maximum of 140°F (60°C) to infuse. This will accelerate the blending of the soluble aromas.

Examples: truffle oil, dry or fresh herb oil, lobster shell oil, vanilla oil, chili oil, and cinnamon and star anise oil.

Make sure your oil containers are properly closed and out of the light so that they do not go rancid.

Oils are vegetable products and have many nutritional qualities, contributing to lowering cholesterol levels, prevention of heart disease, thinning the blood, etc.

Variety	Characteristics	Uses
Sweet almond	Delicate flavor with almond taste, clear	Cold seasoning
Peanut	Neutral, clear, multipurpose	Seasoning and cooking
Argan	Strongly flavored, dark red color, musk flavor	Cold seasoning
Hemp	Green, taste of fresh herbs and hay	Cold seasoning
Canola/rapeseed (refined)	Neutral with a slight herbal taste	Cold seasoning
Copra (coconut)	White concentrated oil with very little taste	Seasoning and cooking
Wheat germ	Neutral with a slight seed taste	Seasoning and cooking
Hazelnut, walnut	Distinctive flavor	Cold seasoning
Olive: may be virgin or extra virgin, depending on the percentage of oleic acid	More or less pronounced green color	Seasoning and cooking
Palm oil (from the fruit pulp)	Solid, red	Seasoning and cooking
Palm kernel (from the kernel of the fruit)	Solid, white	Seasoning and cooking
Grape-seed	Golden green, very little taste	Seasoning and cooking (fondues)
Sesame	Powerful taste, transparent, liquid	Cold seasoning
Soybean oil (most widely consumed in the world)	Neutral with a slight herbal taste, refined	Cold seasoning
Sunflower seed	Neutral, gold	Seasoning and cooking

Stuffings and forcemeats

A stuffing contains a mixture of ingredients—vegetable, meat, or fish, usually in a combination. It may be mixed to varying degrees of smoothness, cooked, and used to garnish a food. In fact, you can even serve them on their own. Stuffings are used to create a soft texture and combine flavors.

Duxelles for stuffing ✳

INGREDIENTS
(serves 8)

¼ lb. (250 g) dry duxelles (see recipe on right)
3 ½ tablespoons (50 ml) dry white wine
2 oz. (50 g) glaze (fish, meat, poultry consommé; prepare ahead of time or buy at specialty stores)
1 thin slice (1 oz. or 25 g) fresh sandwich loaf

Heat the dry duxelles and pour the white wine over. Reduce over low heat. Add the glaze. Push the bread through a sieve and combine it with the duxelles to bind it.

CHEF'S NOTE

– You can use the duxelles recipe to stuff vegetable side dishes, fish, poultry breasts, and legs.

DID YOU KNOW?

This mushroom stuffing is mentioned in the cooking treatise *Les dons de Comus* (*The Blessings of Comus*), a book by François Marin published in 1739. It was created by François Pierre de La Varenne, the greatest French chef of the seventeenth century, who developed many master techniques for lavish recipes.

Basic duxelles (mushroom) ✳

Instead of using shallots and onions, you may use one or the other.

Lemon juice squeezed over the mushrooms will prevent them from going black; do be careful to use very little so that the mixture does not become too sour.

A duxelles is used as a base for many different dishes. Enrich it with different flavors, such as ham, garlic, or parsley.

INGREDIENTS
(serves 8)

2 tablespoons (30 g) butter
1 ½ shallot (40 g), finely sliced
½ onion (40 g), finely sliced
½ lb. (250 g) button mushrooms, chopped
1 teaspoon (5 g) chopped parsley
Salt, freshly ground pepper

Sweat the shallots and onions in butter. When they are translucent, add the mushrooms and cook, uncovered, until all their water has evaporated.

Season and add the parsley.

CHEF'S NOTE

– Use the basic duxelles for hôtelier butter, stuffed vegetable side dishes, hot oysters, and more.

RECIPE IDEA

Rolled Picardy crêpes **428**

Mousseline stuffing (cream-based) ✳

A fine, light, smooth mixture used to stuff meats and fish.

INGREDIENTS
(serves 8)

¼ lb. (250 g) fish or meat
  (poultry, veal, whiting, sole)
1 egg white
Generous ⅔ cup (180 ml)
  whipping cream
Salt, pepper or chili pepper

Roughly chop and season the fish or meat **(1)**.

Place it in the food processor with the blade knife **(2)**, process, add the egg white, then process a little further. Transfer to a stainless steel bowl set over an ice bath. Gradually stir the cream in **(3)**. Push the mixture through a sieve **(4)**.

Adjust the seasoning.

Scrape down the sides of the bowl, cover with plastic wrap flush with the mousseline, and chill.

CHEF'S NOTES

– Whipping cream is less acidic than crème fraîche or heavy cream.
– If your fish has a high water content, reduce the quantity of cream. On the other hand, if you are using meats that are dry, like poultry and rabbit, increase the quantity of cream.
– The seasoning will intensify slightly during the cooking process.

– Add a personal touch to your stuffing with finely chopped aromatic ingredients (finely diced, julienned vegetables, vegetable sticks, shrimp *salpicon*) or spices. Let your culinary imagination inspire you.

DID YOU KNOW?

All the recipes that go under the name of "mousseline" (sauces, creams, and stuffings) designate preparations that are light and airy.

A purée of dried vegetables made using the same technique as this creamy mousseline gives a flan, when made with cream and eggs, or a mousse, when made using only egg whites.

You could put this technique into practice by making a colored terrine with layers of carrots, turnips, and green beans.

Mousseline stuffings are used for paupiettes, timbales, some *chartreuses* (layered dishes), souffléd or stuffed fish, and pastries with slatted pastry topping.

RECIPE IDEA

Stuffed chicken legs with
  chestnuts **365**

Mousseline stuffing (butter-based) ✳

A delicate stuffing that is creamy when sliced.

INGREDIENTS
(serves 8)

½ lb. (250 g) fish or meat (poultry, veal, whiting, sole)
2 eggs
1 egg yolk
Generous ¾ cup (200 g) unsalted butter, softened
Salt, pepper or chili pepper

Process the fish or meat with the blade attachment. Push through a sieve. Add the eggs and the yolk, and then the softened butter. Blend the ingredients thoroughly. Season.

Scrape down the sides of the bowl, cover with plastic wrap so that it is flush with the mousseline, and chill.

CHEF'S NOTES

– The delicacy of the mousseline depends on the meshing of your sieve—the finer the sieve, the finer the mousseline.
– Do not work the butter mousseline over ice because it will harden the butter too fast.
– This preparation is mainly used for meat and requires slow cooking.
– Play on the natural colors of your stuffing—salmon will give a pink hue and anything with chlorophyll will make it green. You can also use natural colorants to accentuate it.

Basic panada stuffing ✳✳

Panada stuffing uses a paste made with flour, bread, or another starch for thickening. It is particularly suitable for poaching.

INGREDIENTS
(serves 8)

½ lb. (250 g) meat, fish, or crustaceans
2 egg whites
¾ cup (200 ml) cream (optional)
1 generous pinch salt
1 pinch pepper

Panada
½ cup (125 ml) fumet, water, or milk
¾ stick (⅓ cup or 90 g) unsalted butter
1 ¼ cups (125 g) all-purpose flour
4 eggs

Make a panada using the same method as for choux pastry (see p. 22). Bring the liquid and butter to a boil, then pour in the flour. Mix with a spatula over a low heat until it dries out. Remove from the heat and add the eggs, one by one, mixing thoroughly each time. Allow to cool.

Process the meat, fish, or crustaceans in a food processor using the blade knife. Gradually pour in the egg whites, followed by the cold panada.

Adjust the seasoning and push through a sieve.

If necessary, thin your stuffing with cream.

DID YOU KNOW?

This recipe is also used to make quenelles (see p. 272). They are shaped into oval scoops with two spoons and poached. Quenelles are a typical dish from in and around Lyon.

RECIPE IDEA

Pike quenelles and crayfish sauce **272**

Gratin stuffing (*farce à gratin*) ✳

This delicately minced chicken liver can be served on canapés and as an accompaniment for poultry and game birds.

INGREDIENTS

3 ½ oz. (100 g) fatty bacon
10 oz. (300 g) poultry or game bird livers
2 oz. (50 g) shallots, finely sliced
2 tablespoons (30 ml) Cognac
Thyme flowers
Salt, freshly ground pepper

Sauté the fatty bacon so that it renders some of its fat. Clean the livers and remove the nerves. Add them to the pan (**1**).

When they are half-cooked, i.e. still very pink, add the finely sliced shallots (**2**) and flambé with the cognac (**3**).

Season and scatter with a few thyme flowers.

Process the stuffing and push it through a sieve.

Scrape down the sides of the bowl, cover with plastic wrap flush with the stuffing, and chill.

CHEF'S NOTE

– Make sure that the livers are browned outside but still pink inside. If they are overdone, your stuffing will be dry and grainy.

DID YOU KNOW?

This recipe was traditionally made with the livers of cooked poultry.

Today, it is often spread on canapés to accompany poultry.

RECIPE IDEA

Bay leaf-infused young guinea hen with canapés **350**

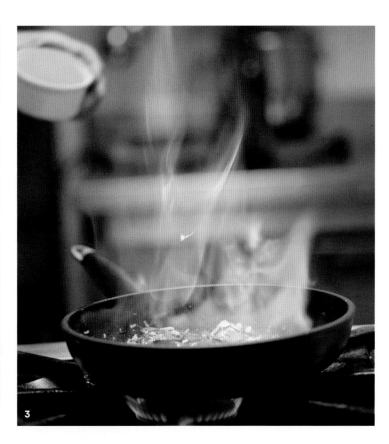

Varieties of potatoes and their uses

As soon as you have peeled your potatoes, cover them in cold water so they do not brown.

Depending on your recipe and the size of your potatoes, some varieties will need rinsing to eliminate their starch (potatoes cocotte, wafers, potato straws, etc.), while others will need to maintain their starch to stay firm during cooking (Dauphin, gratin, potatoes Anna, etc.) Do remove all traces of green, which contain a toxic substance (solanine).

Potatoes must be stored away from light and in a well-ventilated place so that they do not begin sprouting. If, despite your precautions, they do, remove the sprout and hollow out the potato a little around the eye.

Variety	Characteristics	Uses
Atlantic, Norwis etc. (Round Whites)	Smooth, thin, light skin with white flesh. Medium in starch level, creamy texture when cooked, hold shape well.	Particularly good for salads, sautéing, roasting, and boiling; generally good all-rounders.
Burbank, Norkotah etc. (Russets)	Netted brown skin, white flesh. High in starch, floury texture when cooked.	Ideal for baking and mashing; generally good all-rounders.
Chieftain, Dakota Rose etc. (Red Potatoes)	Rosy red skin, can have either white, yellow, or even red flesh. Firm, smooth, waxy texture.	Good for salads, roasting, and boiling.
Kennebec, White Rose etc. (Long Whites)	Oval-shaped, thin light tan skin. Medium in starch level, firm and creamy texture when cooked.	Excellent for sautéing and boiling; good all-rounders.
Red Thumb, Russian Blue, etc. (Fingerlings)	Narrow elongated shape. Come in a variety of colors, though most have yellow flesh. Firm waxy texture.	Ideal for salads, baking, and boiling.
Anya	Long oval shaped body. Distinctive nutty flavor.	Excellent for salads.
Charlotte	Long oval shape, white skin. Moist texture.	Good for salads, roasting, and boiling.
Desiree	Red skin, light yellow flesh. Medium in starch level.	Ideal for gratins and roasting, also good for chips, baking, boiling, and mashing.
Estima	White to yellow skin, light yellow flesh. Firm texture when cooked, mild taste.	Good for boiling, baking, and mashing.
King Edward	White skin with distinctive pink coloration, creamy colored flesh. Floury texture.	Excellent for gratins, chips, roasting, and mashing, good all-rounder.
Maris Piper	Creamy colored flesh, floury texture, medium in starch level.	Good for chips, baking, boiling, roasting, and mashing.
Rooster	Distinctive red skin, cream flesh. Very versatile.	Ideal for chips, mashing, and roasting.

☐ Common in US   ☐ Common in UK

Duchess potatoes ✳

A dried potato purée, thickened with butter and egg yolks. It is used as a garnish or vegetable stuffing.

INGREDIENTS

1 lb. (500 g) all-rounder potatoes
3 egg yolks
5 ½ tablespoons (80 g) butter
A pinch of grated nutmeg
Salt, freshly ground pepper

Boil the potatoes in their jackets.

Peel them and purée them in a food mill.

Dry out carefully, if necessary, over low heat. Combine them with the egg yolks and butter.

Season with salt and pepper.

RECIPE IDEA

Lamb medallions with licorice-infused foamed milk and duchess potatoes **407**

Sweet Sauces
and Decorations

Fruit coulis ✳

To make a fruit coulis, you will need to blend ripe fruit and add, if necessary, a little sugar and a squeeze of lemon juice. They are always very quick to prepare, but do not keep for more than a day as they ferment quickly. The following recipe is for raspberry coulis.

INGREDIENTS
(serves 8)

1 lb. (500 g) raspberries
Juice of 1 lemon
⅓ cup (50 g) confectioners' sugar

Wash (see Chef's notes) and prepare the fruit.

Blend it with the lemon juice and sugar **(1)**.

If necessary for your recipe, strain the coulis through a sieve **(2)**.

Cover with plastic wrap and chill.

CHEF'S NOTES

– Wash strawberries only after you have hulled them, otherwise they absorb the water. Be especially careful with slightly damaged fruit—dry it quickly so that no water gets in.
– Pour in the lemon juice as you blend the fruits to avoid its oxidizing rapidly.
– For the tastiest results, choose seasonal fruits when they are at their best (see fruit seasons table p. 225).
– If you find good-quality frozen fruits, they can of course be used at any time.

– When making a coulis with a fruit that has thick pulp, like banana, apricot, and peach, we recommend you thin it with a little cold sugar syrup.
– However, for a fruit that gives a lot of liquid, you will probably need to add a small quantity of preserves made from the same fruit.
– Add a liqueur to enhance the flavor or give it added complexity.
– For fresh tomato coulis, see p. 136.

RECIPE IDEA

Frozen nougat and raspberry coulis **535**

Plain printing paste ✳

Printing paste is really nothing more than a cookie paste, colored or plain, on which a sponge cake batter is poured before baking. Create your pattern using an icing comb, a paper cone, or a stencil.

INGREDIENTS

3 ½ tablespoons (50 g) butter
2 egg whites
⅓ cup (50 g) confectioners' sugar
Generous ½ cup (50 g) cake flour
A few drops of colored extract, such as coffee, or a colorant

Melt the butter and allow it to cool. Whisk the egg whites with the confectioner's sugar. Sift the flour and incorporate it into the mixture.

Pour in the cool melted butter and mix in until quite smooth.

If desired, add the colorant or extract.

Cover with plastic wrap and chill until the butter in the mixture has hardened.

Draw patterns using the paste on a sheet of parchment paper or on a silicone baking sheet.

Place in the freezer for 4–5 minutes, perfectly flat, until the patterns have hardened.

Remove the sheet and cover it with raw cake batter. Bake.

When the sponge cake is baked, remove the parchment paper or silicone sheet. The design will be printed on the base of the sponge which can then be turned upside-down to serve.

Chocolate printing paste ✳

INGREDIENTS

3 ½ tablespoons (50 g) butter
2 egg whites
⅓ cup (50 g) confectioners' sugar, sifted
Generous ⅓ cup (35 g) all-purpose flour
2 ⅓ tablespoons (15 g) cocoa powder, unsweetened
A few drops of colored extract, such as coffee, or a colorant

Melt the butter and allow it to cool. Whisk the egg whites with the confectioners' sugar. Sift the flour with the cocoa powder and incorporate it into the mixture. Pour in the cool melted butter and colorant and mix in until thoroughly combined and smooth. Cover with plastic wrap and chill until the butter in the mixture has hardened.

Draw raised patterns on a sheet of parchment paper or silicone baking sheet. Place in the freezer for 4–5 minutes, perfectly flat, until the patterns have hardened. Remove from the freezer and cover with cake batter. Bake in the oven. When the sponge cake is baked, remove the parchment or silicone sheet. The design will be printed on the base of your sponge.

CHEF'S NOTES

– You can use a paper cone, but remember to write backwards because it will be transposed onto the sponge. The most effective method is to make a design on the computer, print it out, and place it below the parchment paper or silicone sheet as a guide.
– Use this batter to make delicate cookies like *langues de chat*, cigarettes, and tulips.

167

1

Caramel sauce ✳ ✳

This is caramelized sugar with the cooking process stopped by the addition of cream and/or butter. Add your personal touch to the caramel sauce by adding coffee or vanilla extract, filberts, or whatever else takes your fancy.

INGREDIENTS
(serves 8)

⅔ cup (125 g) granulated sugar
Scant ½ cup (100 ml) whipping cream, minimum 30% butterfat
3 ½ tablespoons (50 g) butter (salted, if you wish)

Special equipment: candy thermometer

Make a dry caramel: cook the sugar on high heat in a nonstick or copper pan until it becomes a mahogany color—about 350°F (180°C) on a candy thermometer. Remove from the heat.

Slowly pour the cream on to stop the sugar cooking (1). Return the pan to the heat and whisk the caramel smooth.

The texture should be liquid but thick enough to coat the back of a spoon. Whisk in the butter (2).

CHEF'S NOTES

– You can also stop the cooking with the butter, which should be added once the pan is off the heat, and which takes on a light hazelnut flavor. Use unsalted, salted, or butter with salt crystals.
– Check the color of your caramel by dipping a piece of white parchment paper into it.
– Adding fruit juice is another way of halting the cooking process of the caramel.

DID YOU KNOW?

Caramel sauce made with salty butter is an excellent accompaniment to crêpes and the sweet specialties of northwest France, like waffles.

2

Chocolate sauce ✳

Chocolate sauce will be thick or runny, depending on how much liquid you add. Serve it on the side or over desserts like profiteroles (see p. 524), ice cream, poached fruits, and tarts, and use it as a suave complement to Bavarian creams and charlottes. The type of chocolate can equally determine the texture of the sauce.

INGREDIENTS
(serves 8)

1 cup total (250 ml) milk and/or
    cream
6 ½–7 oz. (180 g–200 g) dark
    chocolate, preferably
    64% cocoa

Special equipment: candy
    thermometer

Chop the chocolate. Heat the milk and/or cream over low heat. Do not let the temperature exceed 130°F–140°F (55°C–60°C). Remove the pan from the heat and add the chopped chocolate (1). Mix in with a rubber spatula or whisk (2, 3).

Set aside, either over a bain-marie if you need to keep it warm, or in the refrigerator.

CHEF'S NOTES

– Flavor your chocolate sauce with instant coffee, vanilla extract, spices, honey, or nuts.
– If you plan to serve it hot, you may whip in a little butter or add a cooked sugar syrup.

Fruit sauce ✳

A fruit sauce differs from a coulis in that it is cooked with a little sugar and lemon juice. Here, we give a recipe for apricot sauce.

INGREDIENTS
(serves 8)

1 ½ lb. (650 g) apricots
Scant ½ cup (80 g) sugar
Juice of 1 lemon
1 vanilla bean

Peel the apricots and remove the pits. Cut them into segments and put into a saucepan (1). Slit the vanilla bean lengthways. Stew the apricots gently, with the lid on, together with the sugar, vanilla bean, and lemon juice (or water) until the mixture starts steaming (2). When the apricots are soft, blend them in a food processor and strain (3). Chill if necessary until needed.

CHEF'S NOTES

– Add a personal touch to your fruit sauce with spices like vanilla, cinnamon, ginger, or others, or fresh herbs like verbena, lemon thyme, or lemon balm.
– For a more rustic texture, crush the stewed fruits with a fork.

Sugar

This is a liquid preparation with varying degrees of sugar concentration. Depending on the stage of cooking reached, it will be used for specific applications, such as saturating sponge layers, soaking, or making meringues or *pâte à bombe* (see p. 212).

Syrup ✳

Types of syrup

Syrups are classified by the use for which they are destined.

Syrup	Proportions	Uses
For soaking, poaching	4 cups (1 liter) water + 1 ½–2 ⅔ cups (300–500 g) sugar + flavoring.	Savarins, babas, fruits in syrup
For soaking pastry (punch)	4 cups (1 liter) water + 5 ½ lb. (2.5 kg) sugar + flavoring.	Desserts, sponge cakes, cookies
Candy syrup	4 cups (1 liter) water + 5 ½ lb. (2.5 kg) sugar. Cool the syrup in a closed container to 77°F (25°C), until lukewarm. Pour over candies or fruit placed on a candy rack. Allow to stand for 16 hours to coat in syrup.	Dried fruit stuffed with marzipan, cake decorations, molded marzipan pieces

Cooking sugar

It is best to use an electronic or candy thermometer for precision and to avoid burns.

Stage	Temperatures	Uses
Coated	223°F (106°C)	*Pâte de fruit* (fruit jellies)
Small thread or small gloss	230°F (110°C)	Florentine cookies
Large thread or large gloss	235°F–239°F (113°C–115°C)	Soft caramels
Soft-ball	244°F (118°C)	Soft fondant/almond paste
Hard-ball	250°F (121°C)	Italian meringue /butter cream/hard fondant
Light or soft crack	275°F –293°F (135°C–145°C)	White nougat /marshmallow
Hard crack	293°F–311°F (145°C–155°C)	Thread stage/poured or pulled sugar/soufflé or blown
Light caramel	329°F (165°C)	Croquembouche, etc. /poured or pulled sugar, soufflé, blown sugar
Caramel	350°F (180°C)	Caramel sauce with salted butter
Dark caramel or blackjack	370°F–400°F (190°C–200°C)	Dark caramel or blackjack

Cooking sugar ✳✳

INGREDIENTS

1 ⅓ cup water (330 ml)
2 lb. (1 kg) sugar cubes

Pour the water into a perfectly clean copper pan or a pot and bring to a simmer.

Add the sugar cubes.

Check the temperature with a thermometer, and stop cooking when it reaches the desired stage and temperature for your recipe.

CHEF'S NOTES

– If your sugar forms crystals while cooking, add a few drops of lemon juice or vinegar.
– Using a copper pan or pot ensures the best heat conduction, and prevents the sugar from forming unwanted crystals.
– Do not use high heat—this will darken the sides of the pot or pan. Use a wet pastry brush to keep the sides of the pan clean.
– Sugar may also be cooked without the addition of water. In this case, high heat is required.

Sweet Creams

Cream

There is no substitute for cream—the fat-rich part of non-homogenized milk. A key ingredient in many recipes in this book, cream lends moisture to baked goods and a silky, smooth consistency to sauces, mousses, and more. Creams are categorized according to their fat content, consistency (liquid or thick), and whether they have been pasteurized or not. In France, anything called "*crème*" must be made from dairy milk and contain at least 30% fat by law. Milks containing a minimum of 12% fat can be called *crème légère*. *Crème d'Isigny*—a crème fraîche—is France's only AOC cream.

For best results, it is important to use the type of cream specified in the ingredients list. Creams with a high fat content are easier to whip, and they are less likely to curdle when added to hot ingredients. Using well-chilled cream and a well-chilled bowl and whisk also help to ensure successful whipping. When a minimum fat content is required for a recipe to work, the recommended percentage is noted. The table below will help you determine the most suitable cream for your dishes.

Name	Characteristics	Fat content	Uses
Clotted cream	Thick, rich, yellow cream, made by heating unpasteurized milk.	Min. 55% (55–60%)	Serve as it is, with scones and jam (English "cream tea"). Mainly produced in Cornwall and Devon, in southwest England.
Double cream (UK)	Rich cream that whips easily and holds its shape. A little thicker than heavy cream. Can be over-whipped and become too thick.	48%	For pouring over desserts; in cooking; for whipping. When whipped can be piped or spooned on to desserts and cakes.
Heavy cream (US)	Denser than whipping cream and doubles in volume when whipped; whips well and holds its shape.	36–40%	As above.
Whipping cream	Thickens when whipped but lighter than double/heavy cream (does not whip or hold its shape quite as well). Sometimes contains stabilizers or emulsifiers to help hold shape when whipped.	30–38%	For whipping: toppings, cake fillings, mousses etc.
Crème fraîche	Rich, matured, thickened cream with tangy, nutty flavor.	Min. 30%	Serve with fruit and desserts; for salad dressings and dips; in cooking (sauces, soups, casseroles etc.).
Sour cream	Smooth and tangy cream, made by adding a bacterial culture + incubation until lactose turns to lactic acid.	18–20%	In cooking, particularly sauces and soups; in baking; for dips and dressings.
Light cream (US)	Pouring cream. Does not whip if less than 30%.	18–30%, generally 20%	In coffee; for pouring over desserts; in cooking, soups, sauces, or casseroles (although risk of separation when heated).
Single cream (UK)	Pouring cream. Does not whip or thicken when beaten.	Min. 18%, generally 20%	In coffee; for pouring over desserts; in cooking, in soups, sauces, or casseroles, (although risk of separation when heated).
Half-and-half (US)	Mixture of half cream and half milk. Can't be whipped.	10.5-18%, generally 12%	In coffee, pouring cream (over desserts).

Pouring custard (*crème anglaise*) ✳✳

Custard is a sauce that is served cold or warm to accompany a great many desserts. It is also used as a base for a number of more complex recipes, such as Bavarian cream desserts, ice creams, and charlottes.

INGREDIENTS

4 cups (1 liter) milk
1 vanilla bean
10 egg yolks
1 ¼ cup (250 g) granulated sugar

Slit the vanilla bean lengthwise and scrape the seeds out into the milk. Pour the milk into a saucepan and add the vanilla bean. Bring the milk to a simmer.

Whisk the egg yolks and sugar vigorously until the mixture becomes pale and thick.

When the milk is simmering, remove it from the heat and pour half of it over the beaten egg yolks **(1)**. Combine thoroughly and pour in the remaining milk, mixing again. Return the mixture to the saucepan, straining through a chinois and bring to a simmer again, stirring constantly, making figure-of-eight patterns with your spoon. While the mixture is cooking, remove it from the heat from time to time so that the yolks do not coagulate.

When the custard is done, it should coat the back of a spoon **(2)**, and a line drawn with your finger along the back of the spoon should stay clear. If you have a candy thermometer, the desired temperature is 185°F (85°C). Cover with plastic wrap and allow to cool, preferably over an ice bath.

CHEF'S NOTES

– It's essential to cool the custard down rapidly after it is cooked to avoid any risk of bacteria developing.
– The custard must not boil. If the temperature is too high, the yolks will coagulate and separate from the milk. This will cause the custard to split. Should this happen, mix it immediately with an immersion blender in a chilled metal bowl.
– When the bubbles on the surface of the custard start to disappear during the cooking process, you have an indication that it is practically cooked.

DID YOU KNOW?

The traditional flavor for custard is vanilla, but you can enhance it with other flavors of your choice: chocolate, liqueurs, caramel, praline, or orange and lemon zest. In this case, omit the vanilla and add your selected flavor when the custard is cooked.

RECIPE IDEAS

Floating islands with spun caramel **488**
Opéra **508**

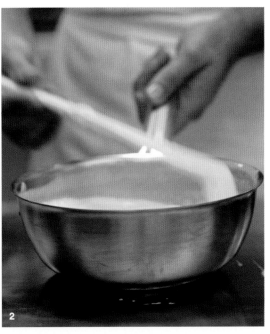

Butter cream (with cooked sugar) ✳ ✳ ✳

Butter cream is prepared by emulsifying butter on a mixture of egg and cooked sugar (as for a *pâte à bombe*, see p. 212). There are numerous variations on the basic technique used here, including Genoese sponge and Italian meringue.

INGREDIENTS

1 cup (200 g) sugar
Scant ⅓ cup (70 ml) water
2 egg yolks
2 eggs
2 sticks (250 g) unsalted butter, room temperature, cubed
A few drops of flavoring (coffee, rose, bitter almond, caramel, praline, chocolate, etc.)

Prepare a sugar syrup and cook until it reaches a temperature of 243°F (117°C). With an electric beater, whisk the eggs and additional yolks until foamy.

Pour the sugar syrup over the eggs, and continue beating for a few minutes to lower the temperature of the mixture.

Incorporate the cubed butter using a whisk **(1)** or an electric beater (medium speed) **(2)**.

Add your chosen flavoring.

CHEF'S NOTES

– For a more delicate taste, prepare the butter cream using only egg yolks (as for a *pâte à bombe*). For this recipe, you will need 5 egg yolks.
– Spread the butter cream onto the cake while it is still soft— approximate temperature 68°F (20°C).

DID YOU KNOW?

This is the perfect cream for the traditional French Christmas cake, a Christmas log (*buche de Noël*), a jelly roll garnished with flavored butter cream that represents the logs we burn in our fireplaces during year-end festivities. Butter cream is also used in the moka cake, created in the mid-nineteenth century. Butter cream was developed shortly before this. Moka is a variety of coffee exported from the port of Moka in the Yemen.

RECIPE IDEAS

Opéra **508**
Chestnut cream, nougatine, and walnut Succès **497**

Chantilly cream ✳

Chantilly cream is used to fill, garnish, cover, decorate, and accompany numerous pastries, desserts, and ice creams.

INGREDIENTS

2 cups (500 ml) whipping cream, min. 35% fat, well chilled
Generous ½ cup (75 g) confectioners' sugar
A few drops of natural vanilla extract

Pour the cold cream into a cold mixing bowl or the cold bowl of a food processor **(1)**.

Whisk briskly or beat at medium speed with the whisk of the food processor until the cream begins to thicken **(2)**.

Sift the confectioners' sugar into the cream **(3)** and then add the vanilla extract.

Whisk the cream briskly for a few moments until it forms stiff peaks.

CHEF'S NOTES

– For best results, it is essential that the cream be very cold, or chilled over ice. A minimum butterfat content of 30% is required. It is advisable to place the mixing bowl in the refrigerator before you use it. If you are using granulated or caster sugar, make sure it dissolves in the cream. Confectioners' sugar is preferable, however.
– Store Chantilly cream no longer than 24 hours in the refrigerator. It is best made at the last moment so that it does not deflate prior to being used.

DID YOU KNOW?

The term "Chantilly cream" is reserved for whipped cream with a minimum of 30% dairy fat, sucrose, and natural vanilla flavor. Chantilly cream is the ideal cream for pastry chefs. The intense whipping it undergoes increases its volume. It contains between 15 and 20% sugar. It is thought to have been created by François Vatel, chef to the Prince of Condé at the Château de Chantilly, just north of Paris, during the reign of Louis XIV.
"Whipped cream" refers to cream that is whipped without sugar or flavoring, and it is a component of other recipes.

RECIPE IDEAS

Tutti-frutti waffles **490**
Frozen blackberry vacherin **528**

Chiboust cream ✳✳

This cream is used with a Saint-Honoré, a grand cake often served on festive occasions. It is a derivation of pastry cream to which gelatin is added, together with Italian meringue.

INGREDIENTS

5 sheets gelatin (10 g)
2 cups (500 ml) milk
1 vanilla bean
3 eggs, separated
5 egg whites
²/₃ cup (125 g) plus 2 ²/₃ cups (500g) sugar
¹/₃ cup (2 oz./55 g) cornstarch
A few drops of flavors or extracts of your choice (coffee, rose, bitter almond, caramel, praline, chocolate, etc.)
1 pinch salt

Special equipment: candy thermometer

Soak the gelatin sheets in a bowl of very cold water. Slit the vanilla bean lengthwise and scrape the seeds into the milk. Add the vanilla bean to the milk and begin to heat.

Whisk the 3 egg yolks, ²/₃ cup (125 g) sugar, and the cornstarch until the mixture is pale and thick.

When the milk begins to simmer, remove it from the heat and pour half of it over the beaten egg yolks. Combine thoroughly. Add flavorings at this stage, unless you are using a liqueur, in which case you should add it when the mixture has cooled.

Pour the egg and milk combination over the rest of the milk and return to the heat. Bring it back to a simmer and leave to simmer for 2 to 3 minutes, whisking continuously.

Remove from the heat. Drain the gelatin sheets, squeezing out all their water, and fold into the milk-and-egg mixture. Mix thoroughly with a whisk until there are no visible traces of gelatin.

Transfer to a bowl and cover with plastic wrap flush with the cream. Cool until it reaches a temperature of about 60°F (15°C).

Prepare the Italian meringue. Begin by heating ²/₃ cup (165 ml) water with the remaining 2 ²/₃ cups (500 g) sugar. When the syrup reaches 230°F (110°C), begin beating the 8 egg whites with a pinch of salt in the bowl of a stand mixer.

When the temperature of the cooked sugar reaches 243°F–250°F (117°C–120°C), pour it in a steady stream over the beaten egg whites. Continue to beat the meringue until the mixture is lukewarm. It will be dense and shiny, and will form small firm peaks.

When the pastry cream has cooled but not yet set, mix it to smooth it well. Use a flexible rubber spatula to fold it delicately into the Italian meringue (see p. 51).

CHEF'S NOTES

– Leave the gelatin leaves to soften completely in very cold water. Squeeze out the excess water before you using. Once you have finished making the cream, add very quickly to your recipe (Saint-Honoré, for example) before it thickens. Chill immediately.
– The Italian meringue must be no hotter than lukewarm when it is incorporated into the pastry cream.
– With the use of Italian meringue, the risk of contamination is considerably reduced. The meringue has the added advantage of imparting a fine consistency, texture, and shine to your cream.

DID YOU KNOW?

Chiboust was a pastry chef in Paris, where he set up shop in 1840. He is thought to have created the Gâteau Saint-Honoré as a tribute both to the street where he worked (the still famous rue Saint-Honoré) and to the patron saint of bakers. This delicious cake, made with choux pastry, is garnished with the cream that bears his name.

RECIPE IDEA

Gâteau Saint-Honoré **477**

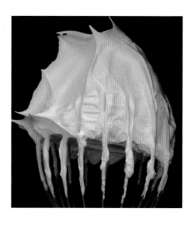

Almond cream ✳

This cream is prepared without cooking and uses equal quantities of blanched ground almonds (almond meal), eggs, butter, and sugar. Adding flour is optional. Almond cream is used in many classic French tarts, like the Kings' cake (*galette des rois*), traditionally eaten on Epiphany; the pithiviers, two layers of puff pastry filled with the cream; and the bourdaloue tart, where pears are placed on a bed of almond cream.

INGREDIENTS

7 tablespoons (100 g) unsalted butter, softened
½ cup (3 ½ oz./100 g) granulated sugar
1 generous cup (100 g) blanched ground almonds or almond meal
2 eggs
A few drops of vanilla extract
1 tablespoon (15 ml) rum

Cream the softened butter well with the sugar.

Add the ground almonds, and then the eggs, mixing them in one by one.

Add the flavorings and whisk until smooth.

CHEF'S NOTE

– Almond cream must always be baked in a pastry base.

RECIPE IDEA

Apricot tartlets **455**

Frangipane cream ✳

Frangipane cream comprises half pastry cream and half almond cream.

INGREDIENTS

Pastry cream
1 cup (250 ml) milk
½ vanilla bean
2 egg yolks
⅓ cup (65 g) granulated sugar
3 ¼ tablespoons (30 g) cornstarch
A few drops of bitter almond extract or Amaretto

Almond cream
1 generous cup (3 ½ oz./100 g) blanched ground almonds or almond meal
7 tablespoons (3 ½ oz./100 g) unsalted butter, softened
2 eggs
½ cup (100 g) granulated sugar

Make a pastry cream (see p. 185) and cool it down rapidly. While it cools, prepare the almond cream (see left).

Add the almond extract or Amaretto to soften the pastry cream.

Pour in the almond cream and whisk energetically to combine.

DID YOU KNOW?

Frangipane cream owes its name to the Italian perfumer, Don Cesare Frangipani, who worked in Paris in the seventeenth century. The French term *crème frangipane* appears in the 1732 dictionary of Trévoux with its current meaning. Frequent mention of a pastry cream to which almonds have been added are found; a variation called *franchipane* (a pie with almond cream and ground pistachios) is recorded in 1674. There are also records of a pastry cream with broken almond macarons.

RECIPE IDEA

Kings' cake (*galette des rois*) **471**

181

Diplomat cream ✳

Diplomat cream is a variation on pastry cream. Gelatin is added to it, and it is enriched with whipped cream. It is used for diplomat pudding (a dessert made with ladyfingers or brioche), mille-feuilles, filled crêpes, and fruit tarts.

INGREDIENTS

5 sheets gelatin (10 g)
2 cups (500 ml) milk
1 vanilla bean
3 egg yolks
⅔ cup (125 g) granulated sugar
⅓ cup (55 g) cornstarch
A few drops of flavor or flavors
  of your choice (coffee, rose,
  bitter almond, caramel,
  praline, chocolate, etc.)
3 cups (750 ml) whipping cream,
  min. 35% fat

Place the gelatin sheets in a bowl of very cold water to soften. Slit a vanilla bean lengthwise and scrape out the seeds. Place them in the milk, together with the vanilla bean, and bring to a simmer.

Whisk the egg yolks, sugar, and cornstarch briskly together until the mixture thickens and becomes pale.

When the milk is simmering, remove it from the heat and pour half of it over the egg yolk mixture. Whisk together. Incorporate the flavoring, except if you are using a liqueur, which should be added when the mixture is cold.

Pour this back onto the remaining milk, return to the heat, and bring back to a boil. Leave to simmer for 2–3 minutes, whisking constantly.

Remove from the heat. Wring the water out of the gelatin sheets with your hands. Mix the gelatin in with a whisk until the mixture is smooth, with no visible traces of gelatin.

Transfer to a bowl. Cover with plastic wrap flush with the cream. Refresh to about 60°F (15°C).

Using a stand mixer or hand beater, whip the 3 cups (750 ml) cream until it is the same consistency as a Chantilly cream.

When the pastry cream is cold but not yet set, mix it again. Delicately fold in the cold whipped cream with a rubber spatula.

CHEF'S NOTES

– Leave the gelatin leaves to soften completely in very cold water. Squeeze the excess water out with your hands before you use them.
– The whipped cream must be firm and smooth.
– To fold the pastry cream into the whipped cream, carefully lift it with the spatula so that it does not turn or separate.
– If you begin cooking the diplomat cream with boiling milk, it thickens immediately. There is also less risk that it will stick.
– If your pastry cream is too hot when you fold in the whipped cream, it will melt instead of giving an airy dimension to the preparation.
– This cream keeps for no longer than 24 hours in the refrigerator, but can be frozen.
– When it is ready, add it to your cake or dessert rapidly before it sets, and chill.

DID YOU KNOW?

"Light" diplomat cream is a diplomat that does not have gelatin added (and therefore will not set).

RECIPE IDEA

Diplomat cream mille-feuille **507**

Ganache ✳

Ordinary ganache refers to a mixture of chocolate and cream only. However, there are also buttered ganaches and ganaches with milk. Ganache is used for truffles and in desserts, tarts, and mousses.

INGREDIENTS

For ordinary ganache (for candies)
1 cup (250 ml) whipping cream, min. 35% fat
½ lb. (250 g) dark chocolate, 64% cacao

For buttered ganache (for tarts)
1 scant cup (230 ml) whipping cream, min. 35% fat
½ lb. (250 g) dark chocolate, 64% cacao
6 tablespoons (90 g) unsalted butter

For ganache with milk (soft)
½ cup (125 ml) whipping cream, min. 35% fat
½ cup (125 ml) milk
½ lb. (250 g) dark chocolate, 64% cacao

Bring the cream and/or the milk to a boil.

Chop the chocolate (1). Pour the boiling cream and/or butter over it and whisk until the chocolate has melted.

Do not return to the heat. If using butter, whip it in until the ganache is smooth (2).

Allow the cream to cool, stirring from time to time. You may flavor it if you wish.

CHEF'S NOTES

– To customize your ganache cream, infuse your cream/and or milk with spices or fresh or dried herbs. If you choose to do this, strain it through a chinois before pouring it over the chopped chocolate.
– The higher the proportion of liquid, the softer and more easily the ganache will spread.
– The quality of the chocolate (dark, milk, or white) and its percentage of cacao are decisive in giving your cream its flavor.

– Flavored pastes, like hazelnut, may also be added.
– Unsweetened condensed milk can be substituted for cream.

DID YOU KNOW?

Siraudin, a pastry chef in Paris, invented the ganache in 1850.

RECIPE IDEAS

Opéra **508**
Raspberry ganache tart **487**

Mousseline cream ✳

As its name indicates, mousseline cream is airy and light, somewhat like a mousse. It is made from pastry cream to which butter has been added. For the Paris-Brest cake, a round choux pastry that represents a bicycle wheel, praline paste is added to pastry cream for the filling. The fraisier, a type of strawberry shortcake, also has a good helping of mousseline cream to cushion the strawberries between two layer of Genoese sponge.

INGREDIENTS

2 cups (500 ml) milk
1 vanilla bean
3 egg yolks
²/₃ cup (125 g) sugar
¹/₃ cup (55 g) cornstarch
2 sticks (250 g) unsalted butter

Scrape the seeds of the vanilla bean into the milk. Pour the milk into a saucepan with the bean and bring to a simmer.

In a mixing bowl, whisk the egg yolks with the cornstarch and sugar until the mixture thickens and becomes pale.

When the milk is simmering, remove it from the heat and pour half of it over the egg yolk mixture. Stir well. Pour in the rest of the milk, return to the heat, and bring back to a boil. Allow to simmer for 2–3 minutes, whisking continuously.

Remove from the heat. Whip in half the butter **(1)** until fully incorporated.

Transfer to a bowl and cover with plastic wrap flush with the cream. Cool rapidly.

Using an electric beater, beat the remaining half of the butter into the cooled pastry cream **(2)**. Whip at high speed so that the cream expands and becomes airy.

CHEF'S NOTES

– When you incorporate the softened butter at the last stage of the recipe, heat the bowl slightly so that the ingredients blend better.
– Add any flavoring right at the end. However, if you are using a flavored paste such as praline paste, work it into the softened butter before you incorporate them both into the cooled pastry cream.
– This cream will keep no longer than 24 hours in the refrigerator, but freezes well.
– It's particularly important to ensure that the plastic wrap is flush with the cream: since it contains butter, it easily absorbs tastes and smells.
– It is the quality of the butter used that is decisive for the delicacy and taste of a mousseline cream.

Pastry cream (*crème pâtissière*) ✳

Pastry cream is one of the most widely used creams in French pastry making. It fills éclairs, puff pastries, *religieuses*, and cream horns, and is a comfortable bed for fruit to nestle into in tarts.

INGREDIENTS

2 cups (500 ml) milk
1 vanilla bean
3 egg yolks
²/₃ cup (125 g) granulated sugar
¹/₃ cup (60 g) cornstarch
A few drops of extract or extracts of your choice (coffee, rose, bitter almond, caramel, chocolate, etc.)

Slit the vanilla bean lengthwise and scrape the seeds into the milk (1). Add the vanilla bean to the milk and begin to heat. In a mixing bowl, whisk the egg yolks and sugar briskly until the mixture turns pale and thickens. Add the cornstarch and whisk in (2).

When the milk begins to simmer, remove from the heat and pour half over the thickened egg mixture. Combine thoroughly.

Add your chosen flavoring, unless you are using a liqueur, in which case you should add it when the mixture has cooled. Strain the remaining milk through a sieve or chinois (3) into the egg mixture, return to the heat, and bring back to a boil. Allow to simmer for 2–3 minutes, whisking constantly.

Transfer to a bowl. Cover with plastic wrap flush with the cream so that a skin cannot form. Chill or refresh quickly.

CHEF'S NOTES

– If the cream is too liquid: the boiling period was too short, or too little thickener was used. The cream must be thick when removed from the heat.
– If pastry cream is cooked with boiling milk, it thickens immediately and the risk of sticking is lessened.
– Store this cream for no longer than 24 hours in the refrigerator.

DID YOU KNOW?

Pastry cream is a base for many sweet dishes. It is liable to spoil quickly, and is always made as and when needed in pastry shops. Some variations: mousseline cream, diplomat, Chiboust, light, frangipane, and Pont Neuf.

RECIPE IDEAS

Orange liqueur soufflé **464**
Mixed berry tart **472**

Cake Bases, Fillings, and Desserts

Sweet custard base for baking ✳

This recipe uses milk and eggs. Together, they coagulate when baked and form the filling for sweets such as creamy fruit tarts and the base for flans, and a specialty tart—the mirabelle plum tart—made in the Alsace region.

INGREDIENTS
(for 1 tart)

Scant ½ cup (100 ml) milk
Scant ½ cup (100 ml) whipping cream
Vanilla bean
2 eggs
2 egg yolks
3 ½ tablespoons (40 g) sugar
A little liqueur (optional)

Combine the milk and cream in a saucepan. Slit the vanilla bean lengthwise, scrape the seeds into the milk and cream, and add the bean. Bring to a simmer. Beat the eggs, egg yolks, and sugar, but do not beat so much that the mixture becomes foamy.

Pour the hot liquid over the egg mixture, whisking as you pour, and combine thoroughly.

Strain through a fine-mesh sieve or chinois. Cover with plastic wrap and chill until you need it.

CHEF'S NOTES

– Do not use high heat for the milk and cream mixture, as a dark, dry-ish film will form on the surface.
– If you are making a tart with fruits that have a high water content, you will probably need to increase the quantity of eggs.

RECIPE IDEAS

Alsatian mirabelle plum tart **504**
French brioche toast and vanilla stewed rhubarb **485**

Savoy sponge cake ✳

This soft sponge owes its attractive golden color to the use of eggs.

INGREDIENTS
(serves 8)

4 eggs, separated
²/₃ cup (125 g) granulated sugar
¾ cup (2 ½ oz./65 g) cake flour, plus a little extra for the pan
4 ½ tablespoons (45 g) cornstarch
A little butter and flour for greasing

Special equipment: loaf pan or special Savoy sponge pan

Preheat the oven to 325°F–350°F (160°C–170°C). Grease the baking pan and dust it with a smattering of flour. Rap it on the counter to shake off any excess.

Beat the egg yolks with the sugar until the mixture is pale and thick, and forms a ribbon.

Whisk the egg whites until they form stiff peaks. Fold carefully into the egg yolk and sugar mixture.

Sift the flour and cornstarch together. Fold gradually into the egg mixture using a rubber spatula.

Fill the baking pan two-thirds full and bake for 30–35 minutes, or until a cake tester comes out clean.

CHEF'S NOTES

– Be careful not to overbeat the egg whites as this results in a grainy texture.
– The sifted flour and cornstarch may also be added to the beaten egg yolk mixture before being incorporated into the beaten egg whites.

DID YOU KNOW?

In French, this type of pastry is known as a *biscuit*, which literally means "baked twice." This type of baking meant that the pastry would be so dry it could be preserved for lengthy periods, thereby making it useful for food supplies for troops on land or sea. The Savoy biscuit was first made for the ruler of the small kingdom of Savoy in the mid-fourteenth century.

Sponge bases and their uses

Name	Sponge base	Filling
Christmas log	Jelly roll	Flavored butter cream, preserves, pastry cream, etc.
Hot charlotte	Sandwich loaf	Sautéed fruit
Cold fruit charlotte	Ladyfingers (see p. 190)	Bavarian mousse
Black Forest	Cocoa Genoese sponge	Chantilly cream (see p. 179)
Fraisier (strawberry sponge)	Genoese sponge (see p. 195)	Mousseline cream (see p. 184)
Mascotte	Genoese sponge	Praline butter cream (see p. 178 for butter cream)
Moka	Genoese sponge	Coffee butter cream
Montmorency	Genoese sponge	Cherry butter cream
Baked Alaska	Genoese sponge	Ice cream and meringue
Opéra	Joconde (see p. 196)	Ganache (see p. 183), butter cream (see p. 178)
Diplomat pudding	Ladyfingers	Sweet custard base for baking (see p. 188)
Singapour	Genoese sponge	Pastry cream (see p. 185), stewed pineapple

Ladyfingers ✳

These are very light, airy sponge biscuits with a crisp crust. They tend to dry out rather easily.

INGREDIENTS
(serves 8)

3 eggs, separated, plus 1 egg white
½ cup (100 g) sugar
Generous ½ cup (50 g) cake flour
⅓ cup (50 g) cornstarch
Confectioners' sugar for dusting

Prepare a French meringue (see p. 51) using 4 egg whites and the sugar. Combine this with the egg yolks (1, 2). Sift the flour and the cornstarch directly into the egg mixture (3). Carefully fold in using a rubber spatula.

Pipe out the mixture (4), or spoon it onto a silicone baking sheet or parchment paper. Each ladyfinger should be about 3 ½–4 in. (8–10 cm) long and ⅔ in. (1.5 cm) wide.

Dust them with confectioners' sugar and allow it to penetrate.

Preheat the oven to 400°F (200°C). Sprinkle the ladyfingers again with confectioners' sugar (5) and bake for 10–15 minutes, until pale beige.

CHEF'S NOTES

– You can flavor the ladyfingers and/or use coloring.
– They are delicious alone or with creamy desserts, and you can pair them with sparkling wine or have them with tea or coffee.
– Pipe them out so that they are all the same size. This will give an even lining for Bavarian cream desserts. However, the ladyfingers should not go all the way to the top of your mold. That way, an attractive layer of your mousse or cream will be visible.

DID YOU KNOW?

Ladyfingers are known in French as *biscuits à la cuillère*, literally, spooned biscuits, and this is how they were made until 1840. Then Antonin Carême, French culinary genius and author of major works on gastronomy, followed by Lasne, a pastry chef, improved the method, using a piping bag. Ladyfingers currently enjoy less popularity than they used to. The pink ladyfinger of Reims, capital of the champagne-producing region, was created specially to be eaten with champagne. It is rectangular, has a vanilla taste, and its shell is particularly crisp. Another member of the "family" is the *boudoir*, which takes its name from the small salons or boudoirs to which the ladies of the Belle Époque would retire.

RECIPE IDEA

Raspberry charlotte **483**

Fruit-based Bavarian cream ✳✳

This is a fruit purée that is set with gelatin or another jellifying agent. Whipped cream and/or Italian meringue are added.

INGREDIENTS
(serves 10)

5 sheets gelatin (10 g)
14 oz. (400 g) puréed fruit
¼ cup (50 g) granulated sugar
1 ²/₃ cups (400 ml) whipping cream, min. 35% fat
1 scant teaspoon (4 ml) fruit brandy or liqueur

Soak the gelatin sheets in very cold water **(1)**.

Bring the fruit purée and sugar to a boil. Drain the gelatin, wringing out the water with your hands, and add it to the purée **(2)**. Combine thoroughly.

Allow the mixture to cool.

Whip the cream until it forms firm peaks.

When the fruit purée has cooled to about 68°F (20°C), whisk in the fruit brandy or liqueur. Carefully fold in the whipped cream, little by little, using a rubber spatula **(3)**, taking care not to deflate the mixture.

The Bavarian cream is now ready. Pour it into molds immediately to set and chill.

CHEF'S NOTES

– Strictly speaking, a Bavarian cream uses a custard cream that is set with gelatin and flavored. Some might call the particular recipe given here a fruit mousse.
– Add pieces of the same fruit as used in the fruit purée, or another type of fruit, for a variety of textures.

DID YOU KNOW?

Gelatin is a setting agent of animal origin (pork or beef). Vegetable setting agents made from seaweed are also available. The most widely used type of gelatin in France is available in firm, translucent sheets weighing 1–2 grams. In this book, sheets weighing 2 grams are used. They must be softened in very cold water for a few minutes and then dissolved in a lukewarm or hot mixture. Gelatin is less effective when combined with acidic fruits like kiwis, pineapple, and raspberries. If using this type of fruit, make sure the purée is boiled right through on its own.

RECIPE IDEA

Raspberry charlotte **483**

Egg-based Bavarian cream ✳✳

This is a flavored custard cream set with gelatin or other jelling agent. Whipped cream and/or Italian meringue are then added to the mixture.

INGREDIENTS
(serves 10)

5 sheets (10 g) gelatin
2 cups (500 ml) milk
½ vanilla bean
5 egg yolks
½ cup (100 g) granulated sugar
1 ²/₃ cups (400 ml) whipping
   cream, min. 35% fat,
   well chilled

Soak the gelatin sheets in very cold water to soften them.

Scrape out the seeds of the ½ vanilla bean into the milk. Heat the milk with the vanilla bean in a saucepan over low heat. While it heats, whisk the egg yolks and sugar in a mixing bowl until the mixture becomes thick and pale (ribbon stage).

When the milk begins simmering, pour half of it over the egg mixture, beating constantly.

Pour the rest of the milk into the mixture. Then return it all to the saucepan and heat until it is thick enough to coat the back of a spoon. If you have a thermometer, the temperature should be 185°F (85°C).

While it is cooking, remove the pan from the heat from time to time. Too high heat can cause the yolks to coagulate, something that should be avoided here.

Strain the custard through a chinois or fine-mesh sieve and transfer to a bowl. Wring all the water out of the gelatin sheets and incorporate them thoroughly into the custard mixture. Cover with plastic wrap and allow to cool, over ice if necessary.

Whip the cold cream until it forms stiff peaks.

When the custard has cooled to room temperature, about 68°F (20°C), whisk it to ensure it is smooth.

Gradually fold in the whipped cream, very carefully, using a rubber spatula.

The cream is now ready and should be poured into a mold immediately to set.

DID YOU KNOW?

In Carême's authoritative work of 1825, *Le Pâtissier royal parisien* (*The Royal Parisian Pastrycook and Confectioner*), Bavarian creams are referred to as Bavarian cheeses because of both their shape and their origin, the region of Bavaria in Germany. Use the same method to make savory Bavarian creams with fish, shellfish, or vegetables. Simply set a liquid such as fish soup or puréed vegetable with gelatin and add whipped cream.

RECIPE IDEA

Mint-chocolate entremets **456**

Blancmange ✳

This is a white, jellied dessert that has traditionally been made with almonds.

INGREDIENTS
(serves 8)

5 oz. (150 g) whole, blanched almonds
¾ cup (150 g) granulated sugar
3 ½ tablespoons (50 ml) whipping cream,
  well-chilled
6 sheets (12 g) gelatin
A few drops of bitter almond extract

Process the almonds and the sugar until finely ground.

Add half the whipping cream and bring the three ingredients to a boil in a saucepan.

Soak the gelatin sheets in cold water. When they are sufficiently softened, wring out all excess water and incorporate them into the almond-cream mixture. Strain the liquid through a fine-mesh sieve and cool rapidly.

Make sure the remaining cream is still very cold before whipping it. When it forms stiff peaks, fold in the bitter almond extract.

Carefully fold the whipped cream into the almond mixture.

Pour it into individual ramekins or a serving dish for 8. Chill.

CHEF'S NOTES

– Roast the almonds lightly in a hot oven to bring out their flavor.
– A fruit coulis is a delightful accompaniment to this blancmange.
– You can use coconut instead of all or some of the almonds. You might even substitute other nuts, such as walnuts, hazelnuts, or peanuts.
– This blancmange is a variation of the Italian pannacotta.

DID YOU KNOW?

Blancmange is known to have been eaten as early as the Middle Ages.

Custard tart ✳

The custard tart contains pastry cream made using a ready-made mix, cooked on a pastry base (puff, short, or sweet). It can be divided into the portions once cooled.

INGREDIENTS
(serves 10)

4 cups (1 liter) milk
5 egg yolks
1 cup (200 g) sugar
3 ⅓ oz. (95 g) custard flan mix (buy online or at specialty stores)

Preheat the oven to 350°F–400°F (180°C–200°C).

Heat the milk over medium heat in a saucepan.

Whisk the egg yolks, sugar, and powder briskly in a bowl until the mixture starts to thicken and become pale (ribbon stage). When the milk is simmering, pour half of it over the mixture, beating constantly. Ensure it is thoroughly mixed and pour it back over the remaining hot milk until it comes to a boil. Leave to boil for 2–3 minutes, whisking constantly.

Pour it over the pastry crust of your choice and bake for about 20 minutes, depending on how thick the mixture is. It should be set. Allow to cool.

CHEF'S NOTE

– Check the ingredients of your flan mix and follow the baking instructions. Alternatively, you may use 1 ¼ cups (125 g) of all-purpose flour or 1 ¼ cups (125 g) of cornstarch instead of custard flan mix.

Genoese sponge ✳

This is a simple, light sponge that is used as a base for many desserts and cakes. Genoese sponge may be topped, filled (when cut into layers), and/or soaked in flavored liquid or liqueur.

INGREDIENTS
(serves 8)

4 eggs
²/₃ cup (125 g) granulated sugar
1 ¹/₃ cups (125 g) cake flour, plus a little extra for the pan
A little butter and flour to grease the pan

Preheat the oven to 350°F (180°C).

Whisk the eggs and the sugar together in a round-bottomed mixing bowl over a hot water bath until the mixture reaches the ribbon stage (1). If you wish, use an electric beater instead.

Sift in the flour in stages (2), folding it in gently each time with a rubber spatula. Work carefully so as not to deflate the batter. Prepare the baking pan, if using: grease it and sprinkle it with flour. Rap the pan to shake off any excess flour (3). Pour the batter into the pan, filling it to three-quarters way up (4).

Bake for 15–20 minutes, until well risen and light brown. Test for doneness, remove from the oven, and turn out onto a rack.

If you need your Genoese sponge in thin layers, pour the batter onto a large rectangular baking sheet lined with parchment paper or a silicone sheet. Reduce baking time accordingly—it should be a nice golden brown color and the tip of a knife should come out clean.

CHEF'S NOTES

– You can add a little melted butter (3 tablespoons or 40 g) into the mixture before baking.
– Flavor your sponge with anything you fancy—spices, cocoa powder, or liqueur, for example.

DID YOU KNOW?

The Genoese sponge takes its name from the Italian town of Genoa.

RECIPE IDEAS

Passion fruit and orange mousse **467**
Baked Alaska **532**

Joconde sponge ✳

This almond-based sponge is light and delicate, and is used in many layered cakes including the Opéra.

INGREDIENTS
(serves 8)

¾ cup (140 g) plus ¼ cup (50 g) sugar
1 ²/₃ cups (5 oz./140 g) blanched ground almonds or almond meal
4 eggs plus 4 egg whites
8 tablespoons (45 g) cake flour
1 ¾ tablespoons (scant 1 oz./25 g) butter, melted

Preheat the oven to 350°F (180°C). Sift together ¾ cup (140 g) granulated sugar and the ground almonds **(1)**.

Beat this together with the 4 eggs until the mixture reaches the ribbon stage. Fold in the sifted flour, followed by the melted butter.

Beat the 4 egg whites until they form stiff peaks. Add the remaining sugar and beat until the mixture is firm and shiny (it forms a French meringue) **(2, 3)**.

Carefully fold the French meringue into the egg and butter mixture.

Line a baking sheet with parchment paper and spread the batter over it **(4)**. It should be very thin, about ¹/₅ in. (3–5 mm) thick. Bake for 8–10 minutes. As soon as it is done, turn it over onto a rack to cool.

CHEF'S NOTES

– You can add finely diced pieces of fruit to the batter before baking.
– Use printing paste (p. 167) for decoration. Prepare it as a base for your sponge for an eye-catching dessert casing.

RECIPE IDEAS

Mint-chocolate entremets **456**
Opéra **508**

Almond macarons ✳ ✳ ✳

This small round cake with a crisp shell and delectably chewy interior comes in many varied forms: smooth, crackled, with almond pieces, and the popular Parisian or Gerbet macarons with a filling.

INGREDIENTS
(for 16 large or 40 small, filled macarons)

1 ¾ cup (5 ¼ oz./150 g) blanched ground almonds
1 generous cup (5 ¼ oz./150 g) confectioners' sugar
2 oz. (55 g) egg whites, whipped
¾ cup (5 ¼ oz./150 g) sugar
1 ¾ oz. (50 g) egg whites, whipped

Special equipment: a candy thermometer

Process the ground almonds and confectioners' sugar very finely in a food processor (1). Add the 2 oz. (55 g) whipped egg white and stir until the mixture forms a firm paste with the texture of almond paste (2).

Begin cooking the sugar and 3 ½ tablespoons (50 ml) water to form a syrup. When it reaches 243°F–250°F (117°C–121°C) prepare an Italian meringue (see p. 51) using the 1 ¾ oz. (50 g) whipped egg white. Whip until cool.

Gradually fold the Italian meringue into the almond mixture, working carefully (3). Work the mixture until the consistency is somewhat firm but still runny.

Line a baking sheet with parchment paper or use a silicone baking sheet. Spoon the mixture into a piping bag and pipe out your shapes (just under 1 in. [2 cm] diameter for small macarons, about 2 ½ in. [6.5 cm] for larger ones). Leave to dry out for 20 minutes. They will form a light crust.

Ensure that the oven is completely dry (no residual steam from previous use) and preheat it to 300°F (150°C). Bake for 8–10 minutes. Remove from the oven and leave to cool, then detach from the baking sheet.

CHEF'S NOTE

– Fill the macarons with creams, ganaches or preserves.

DID YOU KNOW?

This petit four was imported from Italy by the court of Catherine de' Medici. The name comes from *macarone*, which means "fine paste" in the Venetian dialect.

RECIPE IDEA

Assorted almond macarons **468**

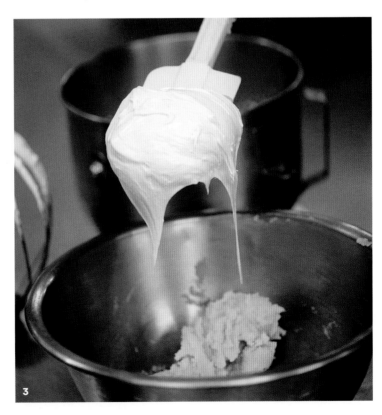

Chocolate mousse ✳

This is a rich, refined chocolate mousse, to be eaten as a dessert rather than used in layered cakes or desserts.

INGREDIENTS
(serves 8)

½ lb. (250 g) dark chocolate, 64% cacao
¾ stick (80 g) butter
3 eggs, separated, plus 3 egg whites
½ cup (100 g) granulated sugar

Special equipment: candy thermometer

Roughly chop the chocolate and dice the butter. Place in a container over a bain-marie (1), heated to 122°F (50°C), until melted.

Remove from the heat and stir in the 3 egg yolks until combined. Leave to cool down to about 83°F (28°C).

Stiffly beat the 6 egg whites. Add the sugar and beat until firm and shiny (see French meringue p. 51).

Carefully fold the meringue and chocolate mixtures together using a rubber spatula. Make sure you do not deflate the egg whites (2).

Spoon into a serving dish and leave to set for at least 1 hour.

CHEF'S NOTE

– It's best to eat this mousse soon after it has been prepared, preferably on the same day.

DID YOU KNOW?

To assemble layered desserts, a *pâte à bombe* is frequently used. Italian meringue and whipped cream are added to a ganache.

RECIPE IDEA

Mint-chocolate entremets **456**

Fruit mousse ✳ ✳

This light mousse is used to prepare many fruit desserts, and is often combined with a sponge layer.

INGREDIENTS
(serves 12)

7 sheets (14 g) gelatin
1 lb. 2 oz. (500 g) puréed fruit
10 egg whites
¾ cup (150 g) granulated sugar
2 cups (500 ml) water
2 cups (500 ml) whipping cream,
  30% fat content
A few drops of fruit brandy or
  liqueur, depending on the fruit

Soak the gelatin sheets in very cold water to soften them.

Bring the fruit purée to a boil. Wring the water from the gelatin and incorporate the sheets into the purée with a whisk until completely dissolved. Allow to cool.

Make an Italian meringue using the egg whites, the sugar, and water (see p. 51). Alternatively, if using an electric beater or stand mixer, you may incorporate the sugar directly into the eggs, without any water.

In a separate bowl, whip the cream until it forms stiff peaks.

When the fruit purée has cooled to 68°F (20°C), whisk in the fruit brandy if using.

When the Italian meringue has cooled, gradually and carefully fold it in to the fruit purée using a rubber spatula (1). Then carefully fold in the whipped cream until all the ingredients are blended (2).

Chill for 1–1 ½ hours to allow it to set.

CHEF'S NOTES

– If you use other gelling agents such as agar-agar, made from seaweed, make sure you change the quantities accordingly and follow the instructions carefully.
– For the best taste experience, use fruits that are in season.
– It is far quicker to add only whipped cream to a fruit purée with a gelling agent, but the taste will not be comparable.
– You can try making a dessert with different fruit mousses. You can layer them, insert one into another, or use one to line the others.

RECIPE IDEA

Passion fruit and orange
  mousse **467**

1

2

Genoa bread (*Pain de Gênes*) ✴

This dense cake, rich in ground almonds, can be eaten plain, or used to make petit fours or as a base for certain layered desserts.

INGREDIENTS
(serves 8)

2 whole eggs plus 3 eggs, separated
1 ½ cups (125 g) ground almonds
²/₃ cup (125 g) granulated sugar
Flavoring, such as vanilla or orange blossom water
¾ cup (75 g) all-purpose flour
5 ¼ tablespoons (75 g) unsalted butter, melted
  until brown and cooled

Preheat the oven to 350°F (170°C).

Whisk the 2 whole eggs together with the 3 egg yolks, the ground almonds, sugar, and flavoring until the mixture is light and foamy. Sift the flour and blend it in.

Whisk the 3 egg whites until they form stiff peaks. Fold them in to the batter.

Pour in the cooled melted brown butter and stir until combined.

Butter the cake pan and dust it with flour. Pour the batter in—it should be no higher than two-thirds of the way up the sides of the pan. Bake for 30 to 40 minutes, until a cake tester comes out dry and the edges start to pull away from the sides.

Turn out to a rack and allow to cool upside down. This cake is eaten when cooled.

CHEF'S NOTE

– There are many variations of this recipe, depending on the subtlety of the flavor desired or the use (coffee cake, petit-four base, etc.).

DID YOU KNOW?

Chiboust, the nineteenth-century pastry chef who created the cream that bears his name (see p. 180), made a variant of Genoa bread known as the Ambroisie.

Rice pudding ✴

Round-grain rice is cooked in milk, flavored with vanilla, and, if desired, thickened with egg yolk.

INGREDIENTS
(serves 6)

²/₃ cup (5 oz./140 g) Arborio or other round-grain
  rice
4 cups (1 liter) milk
1 vanilla bean
1 pinch fine salt
3 egg yolks
²/₃ cup (125 g) granulated sugar

Special equipment: an ovenproof pot with a lid

Preheat the oven to 325°F (160°C).

Rinse the rice. Begin cooking it in cold water. As soon as it starts to boil, remove the pot from the heat and refresh the rice under cold running water. Drain well.

Scrape out the seeds from the vanilla bean into the milk and bring to a boil (with the whole vanilla bean).

Pour in the rice and cover with a lid. Bake the rice for a good hour. Test for doneness by squeezing the rice between your fingers; the grains should be tender.

Beat the egg yolks with the sugar until the mixture become thick and pale (ribbon stage).

Pour the thickening mixture into the rice and combine. Return to the stove and bring back to a simmer.

Transfer to a serving dish and allow to cool.

CHEF'S NOTES

– Give a silky touch to your rice pudding by adding a little whipped cream when it has cooled.
– The advantage of round-grain rice is that it absorbs a great deal of liquid when cooked.

RECIPE IDEA

Cinnamon rice pudding **494**

Semolina pudding ✳

Semolina pudding is prepared in milk and flavored with vanilla. If you wish, you may bind it with egg yolks.

INGREDIENTS
(serves 8)

4 cups (800 ml) milk
1 vanilla bean
1 scant cup (5 oz./140 g) fine semolina
1 scant cup (180 g) sugar

Slit the vanilla bean lengthwise and scrape the seeds into the milk. Place the bean with the milk in a saucepan and bring to a simmer.

Pour the semolina into the simmering milk and turn the heat down to low.

Simmer gently for 7–10 minutes, whisking constantly.

When this is done, add the sugar and mix.

Transfer to individual ramekins or a serving dish. Cover with plastic wrap so that it is in direct contact with the pudding. Leave to cool.

CHEF'S NOTES

– Vary the quantity of semolina depending on how creamy a texture you want.
– Fine corn semolina (polenta) can also be used. The proportions are identical.
– Plump up a handful of raisins and add them to the pudding.

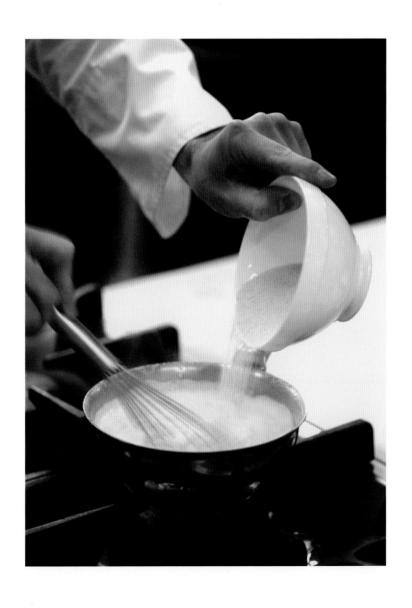

Almond rock cakes (*rochers*) ✳

Rocher **means "rock," and**
these small cakes get their
name from their irregular
shape. They can be made with
shredded coconut, or ground
almonds or hazelnuts.

INGREDIENTS
(makes about 25 rock cakes)

3 egg whites
1 cup (200 g) sugar
2 ⅔ cups (7 oz./200 g) shredded
    coconut

Preheat the oven to 200°F
(90°C). Line a baking tray
with parchment paper or a
silicone baking sheet.

Beat the egg whites and the
sugar in the bowl of a stand
mixer over a bain-marie **(1)**
heated to about 122°F–131°F
(50°C–55°C). Do not let the
mixture get too hot (test with
your finger). Remove from the
bain-marie and continue to
beat on the mixer for 5
minutes on medium speed

until you have a firm Swiss
meringue texture (see p. 52)
(2).

Add the shredded coconut **(3)**
and combine with a spatula.

Pipe or spoon heaps of the
mixture onto the sheet **(4)**,
forming small rock shapes.

Bake for about 1 hour until
the cakes are well browned.
Leave to cool.

Hot fruit soufflé ✳ ✳

This light, airy dessert is served hot and can be made with a range of fruit purées.

INGREDIENTS
(serves 8)

2 cups (390 g) sugar
½ cup (125 ml) water
6 egg whites
1 pinch of salt
¾ lb. (350 g) puréed fruit

For the soufflé mold
2 tablespoons (30 g) unsalted
 butter, melted
2 ½ tablespoons (1 oz./30 g)
 sugar

Special equipment: a candy
 thermometer

Grease the soufflé mold (or ramekins) with butter, using a pastry brush and making upward strokes to help your soufflé rise. Sprinkle it with sugar, ensuring that the coating is evenly distributed. Turn the dish upside down and give it a little rap to shake off excess sugar.

Prepare an Italian meringue (see p. 51). Place the water and sugar in a saucepan and bring to a boil. When the syrup reaches 230°F (110°C), begin beating the egg whites with the pinch of salt in the bowl of a stand mixer.

Place a baking tray in the oven and preheat to 400°F (200°C).

When the syrup reaches 243°F–250°F (117°C–120°C) and the egg whites form firm peaks, pour the syrup in. Continue beating until the mixture has cooled down. It will be dense and shiny, and form lots of small peaks.

Gently fold in the fruit purée **(1)**.

Fill the soufflé mold (or ramekins) to the top **(2)** and smooth the surface. Press your thumb lightly around the rim of the mold to create a "moat." This will help the soufflés to rise evenly.

Place the mold or ramekins on the hot baking tray and bake for about 20 minutes, depending on the size of your soufflés.

They are done when the top is nice and golden brown, but the inside is still soft.

Serve immediately.

1

2

1

Hot pastry cream soufflé ✳ ✳

This light, airy dessert rises significantly when baked, thanks to the egg whites.

INGREDIENTS
(serves 8)

Pastry cream base
1 vanilla bean
2 cups (500 ml) milk
4 egg yolks
²/₃ cup (125 g) sugar
⅓ cup (60 g) cornstarch
¼ cup (60 ml) of a liqueur or
   fruit brandy of your choice
6 egg whites plus 2 whole eggs,
   separated
1 pinch salt
⅓ cup (60 g) sugar

For the soufflé mold
2 tablespoons (30 g) unsalted
   butter, melted
2 ½ tablespoons (1 oz./30 g) sugar

Slit the vanilla bean lengthwise and scrape the seeds into the milk. Place the vanilla bean, seeds, and milk in a saucepan and place over medium heat.

Beat the egg yolks, sugar, and cornstarch until the mixture becomes thick and turns a pale color (ribbon stage).

When the milk begins to simmer, pour half of it over the egg yolk mixture and combine thoroughly.

Pour this mixture back onto the remaining milk and return to the heat. Bring back to a simmer. Simmer for 2–3 minutes, whisking constantly.

Transfer to a bowl, cover with plastic wrap, and cool rapidly.

Use a pastry brush to grease the ramekins or soufflé mold (1), making upward strokes as this will help the soufflé rise. Sprinkle the mold or ramekins with sugar, coating them evenly. Turn the ramekins upside down and give them a rap on the counter to remove any excess sugar (2).

Add the liqueur or brandy to the pastry cream.

Setting aside the 2 egg yolks, beat the 8 egg whites stiffly with the pinch of salt. Add the sugar and beat until the mixture is firm and shiny.

Place a baking tray in the oven and preheat to 400°F (200°C).

Add the 2 egg yolks to the pastry cream.

Use a rubber spatula to gently fold the beaten egg whites into the pastry cream, taking care not to deflate the mixture.

Fill the molds or ramekins to the top and smooth the surface. Press your thumb lightly around the rim of the mold to create a "moat." This will help the soufflés to rise evenly.

Place them on the hot baking tray and bake for about 20 minutes, depending on the size. Your soufflés should have a nice golden brown crust, and the inside must remain light and airy.

Serve immediately.

CHEF'S NOTES

– Some recipes call for ladyfingers soaked in liqueur, coffee, etc., to be placed horizontally in the center of the soufflé.
– Beat the egg whites at the last minute, just before you are ready to put the dishes in the oven.
– It's essential to serve a soufflé as soon as it comes out of the oven, for it falls very quickly.

RECIPE IDEA

Orange liqueur soufflé **464**

2

205

Succès ✳

This is a meringue batter that uses blanched ground almonds. It is used as a base that can be garnished with toppings, creams, etc.

INGREDIENTS
(serves 10)

5 egg whites
²/₃ cup (125 g) sugar, divided
¹/₃ cup (25 g) cake flour
1 ½ cups (125 g) ground almonds

Preheat the oven to 400°F (200°C).

Beat the egg whites until they form firm peaks. Add 1 generous tablespoon (15 g) sugar and beat until shiny.

Sift the remaining sugar, flour, and ground almonds together. Pour into the beaten egg whites and fold in carefully so that the mixture does not deflate.

Spoon into a piping bag immediately and pipe out onto a baking sheet. A close whirl pattern is the one most frequently used in French pastry making.

Bake for 8–10 minutes, depending on the size and shape.

Transfer immediately to a rack to cool.

CHEF'S NOTES

– Small, broken bits of macaron added to the batter will give your pastry a delightful crunch.
– The Succès bases may be prepared ahead of time, cut up if need be, and even frozen.
– Use a plain tip to pipe out your spirals.

DID YOU KNOW?

The Succès is a pastry comprising two disks of almond meringue filled with a praline butter cream (just like the small, filled macarons).

The dacquoise is a meringue specialty from the town of Dax in the southwest of France. It contains ground hazelnuts instead of ground almonds.

A Japonais simply contains less sugar.

A Progrès uses half ground almonds and half ground hazelnuts.

RECIPE IDEA

Chestnut cream, nougatine, and walnut Succès **497**

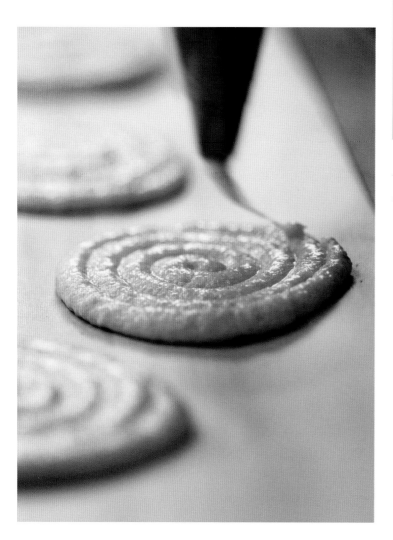

Almond tuiles ✳

A crisp, delicate round almond cookie traditionally served as a petit four with coffee. The French word *tuile* means "tile."

INGREDIENTS
(for about 30 tuiles)

3 egg whites
²/₃ cup (125 g) sugar
Scant ⅓ cup (25 g) cake flour
2 teaspoons (10 g) butter, melted
1 teaspoon (5 ml) vanilla extract
½ cup (2 oz./60 g) sliced blanched almonds

Special equipment: rolling pins or bottles to drape the cookies over

Preheat the oven to 350°F (180°C).

Whisk the egg whites **(1, 2)**. Add all the other ingredients except the sliced almonds.

Chill for about 20 minutes.

Drop the batter in teaspoonfuls onto a baking sheet (silicone or parchment paper), smoothing them out with the back of a spoon until thin and about 2 in. (5 cm) in diameter **(3)**.

Scatter the sliced almonds over the cookies.

Bake until they are a golden color, 5–8 minutes.

Remove them from the baking sheet and drape them immediately over a rolling pin so that they take on a curved shape. Allow to cool.

CHEF'S NOTE

– The mixture spreads, so leave enough space between your cookies when you prepare your baking sheets.

DID YOU KNOW?

There are many variations on this recipe. One of the finest is the lace tuile. It resembles open lace work and is particularly crisp. This requires ⅓ cup (80 g) butter, melted; ½ cup (100 g) sugar; 4 ½ tablespoons (50 ml) orange juice; 3 ½ oz. (100 g) chopped almonds; ⅓ cup (1 oz./30 g) flour; and 1 ⅓ tablespoons (20 ml) Cointreau or other orange liqueur.

RECIPE IDEA

Assorted tuiles **513**

Ice Creams, Sorbets, and Frozen Desserts

Some people will say it's not worth making your own: save yourself the effort and buy your ice cream at your favorite specialty store. But there's nothing quite like homemade ice cream, nothing quite so festive and gratifying. Even without an ice-cream maker, you can achieve astonishingly good results. And if you do have an ice-cream maker, well, your desserts will be just that much better.

Although ice cream is widely appreciated today, it is by no means a recent invention. At the court of Alexander the Great, in 350 BCE, cooks prepared mixtures of fruit and filtered juice, sweetened with honey, that they froze by burying the container in the snow. Marco Polo is said to have brought the method of cooling foods without ice from Asia to Europe, introducing water ices to Italy. From there, Catherine de' Medici brought frozen desserts to the French court. A seventeenth-century chef actually discovered how to make ices using milk, cream, and eggs, but it was only in the late eighteenth century that such desserts became popular.

The range of flavors eaten today—fruit, flowers, and spices—keeps widening. There are more and more reasons to invite ice creams to our tables.

Upside-down apple cake, in France known as a tarte Tatin, with its traditional scoop of vanilla ice cream, has inspired many other imaginative pairings. One could serve a melon sorbet to accompany cured ham, a dill and lemon sorbet with marinated salmon, and even a sweet wine sorbet with foie gras.

There are two types of ice cream: churned and unchurned frozen desserts.

Ice cream is best when served at a temperature between 9°F–14°F (-10°C–13°C), and so must be taken out of the freezer a few minutes before you serve it.

Churned frozen desserts

Churned desserts are recipes that require chilling accompanied by a paddle movement—preferably using an ice-cream maker.

These fall into three categories:
· sorbets
· egg-rich ice creams (custard-based)
· frozen creams

Ice-cream professionals juggle with their recipes in the manner of chemists, using specific ingredients like stabilizers, atomized glucose, and inverted sugar.

Here we merely give you a few recipes without delving into the complexities of the ice-cream making profession.

No stabilizers are required here, and our recipes are meant for immediate consumption, to be enjoyed at home within twenty-four hours.

Sugar is all-important in ice cream making; it has a key role in giving the right texture. Its antifreezing properties prevent ice cream from becoming excessively hard. The same is true of alcohol, which will considerably soften your frozen desserts.

Sorbet ✳

Sorbets are frozen preparations made with water, sugar, and fruit or wine or liqueur.

INGREDIENTS
(for strawberry sorbet)

1 ¼ cup (250 g) granulated sugar
Scant ½ cup (100 ml) water
1 ½ lb. (650 g) pureed
   strawberries

Prepare a syrup of cooked sugar (see p. 173) and leave it to cool to room temperature.

Add the puréed fruit. Chill for 4–6 hours and transfer to an ice-cream maker.

RECIPE IDEA

Frozen blackberry vacherin **528**

Custard-based ice cream ✳

INGREDIENTS
(for vanilla ice cream)

1 vanilla bean
1 ²/₃ cups (400 ml) full fat milk
Scant ½ cup (100 ml) whipping
   cream, min. 35% fat
6 egg yolks
½ cup (100 g) sugar

Slit the vanilla bean lengthwise. Bring the milk and cream to a boil with the vanilla bean.

Beat the yolks with the sugar in a mixing bowl until they are thick and pale (ribbon stage).

Pour the milk and cream mixture over the egg yolks, beating constantly, then return all the liquid to the saucepan.

Heat as you would to make a custard (see p. 177) to a temperature of 185°F (85°C).

Cool rapidly over ice and then transfer to an ice-cream maker for 2 ½–3 hours.

RECIPE IDEAS

Baked Alaska **532**
Rum and raisin profiteroles **524**

Egg-enriched ice cream ✳

This type of ice cream has a high egg-yolk content, and is often made with milk.

INGREDIENTS
(for coffee ice cream)

4 cups (1 liter) full cream milk
Scant ½ cup (100 ml) whipping
   cream, min. 35% fat
3 tablespoons (10 g) instant
   coffee
10 egg yolks (this should weigh
   7 ½ oz./200 g)
1 ½ cup (300 g) granulated sugar

Combine the milk with the cream and the coffee, making sure the coffee granules are dissolved.

Use the ingredients to make a custard (see p. 177). When the mixture has reached 185°F (85°C), remove from the heat and cool.

Chill for 4–6 hours in the refrigerator and transfer to an ice-cream maker.

CHEF'S NOTE

– For a more authentic coffee taste, infuse roughly chopped roasted coffee beans in the milk. However, it is instant coffee that will give the coffee color.

Unchurned frozen desserts

You do not need an ice-cream maker to prepare these frozen desserts. They are often rich and creamy, thanks to the high fat and sugar content, but whipped cream or meringue (or a *pâte à bombe*) can be added to provide airiness. Serve in small quantities in *verrines* or small bowls, or as an accompaniment to a non-frozen dessert (frozen vanilla parfait pairs beautifully with a strawberry tart, for instance).

Frozen parfait ✳

This parfait is made using a *pâte à bombe* (see following recipe) to which lightly whipped, unsweetened cream is added.

INGREDIENTS
(for a fruit parfait to serve 10)

10 egg yolks (these should weigh 7 ½ oz. or 200 g)
3 ¼ lb. (7 cups plus 1 scant cup or 1.5 kg) granulated sugar
3 ½ tablespoons (50 ml) water
3 cups (750 ml) whipping cream, whipped
8 oz. (250 g) fruit pulp

To make a fruit parfait, simmer the egg yolks and sugar over a hot water bath (poaching, see *pâte à bombe* recipe on this page) to a temperature of 185°F (85°C).

Whisk the mixture until it cools down. Carefully incorporate the whipped cream and the fruit pulp.

INGREDIENTS
(for a milk-based parfait to serve 8)

1 cup (250ml) milk
8 egg yolks (these should weigh 5 ½ oz. or 160 g)
1 ¼ cup (250 g) granulated sugar
1 ¾ cups (425 ml) whipping cream, whipped

Use the recipe for custard on p. 177, but simmer the ingredients over a hot water bath, which will take slightly longer. Allow to cool before carefully incorporating the whipped cream.

RECIPE IDEAS

Frozen nougat and raspberry coulis **535**
Frozen hazelnut parfait **526**

Pâte à bombe ✳

It is useful to master the technique for *pâte à bombe*. Here, we give you two methods, both of which involve cooking the egg yolks.

With cooked sugar
Prepare a sugar syrup and heat it to 244°F–250°F (118°C–121°C). Beat the egg yolks. Pour the syrup over the egg yolks, beating constantly. Continue whisking until the mixture has cooled down completely.

Poaching
Place the egg yolks and sugar in a bowl and beat together. Place the bowl over a hot water bath, stirring, until the yolks start to coagulate at the edges. The mixture will have reached a temperature of 131°F (55°C). Remove from heat. Whisk energetically until the mixture reaches the ribbon stage (see the method for Genoese sponge p. 195) and it cools down.

CHEF'S NOTE

– The *pâte à bombe* mixture is not the same thing as a *bombe glacée*! A *bombe glacée* is a domed frozen dessert. For the *pâte à bombe* mixture, whipped cream or Chantilly cream (sweetened) is added.

Frozen soufflé ✳

A frozen soufflé is basically a parfait to which Italian meringue has been added. It is just made to resemble the hot version.

INGREDIENTS
(for a frozen soufflé with liqueur to serve 10)

10 egg yolks (these should weigh 7 oz./200 g)
¾ cup (150 g) granulated sugar
2 ½ tablespoons (50 ml) water
3 cups (750 ml) whipping cream, whipped
4–5 tablespoons (60–75 ml) liqueur

Italian meringue
2 egg whites (these should weigh 2 oz./60 g)
⅔ cup (120 g) granulated sugar
2 tablespoons plus 2 teaspoons (40 ml) water

Prepare a *pâte à bombe* with cooked sugar (see p. 212).

Make up the Italian meringue (see p. 51).

Flavor your whipped cream with the liqueur of your choice and delicately fold it into the mixture.

DID YOU KNOW?

In the soufflé family of desserts, there is another category that uses fruits: frozen fruit soufflés. These use a mixture of fruit pulp or fruit juice, Italian meringue, and whipped cream. Fruit macerated in alcohol, candied fruit, or dried fruit may also be added.

RECIPE IDEA

Frozen banana soufflé 531

Frozen mousse ✳ ✳

Milk-based frozen mousse is made of custard and whipped cream. You may also add an Italian meringue. Fruit mousse comprises puréed fruit to which meringue and whipped cream are added.

INGREDIENTS
(for a frozen raspberry mousse to serve 8)

1 lb. (500 g) raspberry pulp
1 cup (250 ml) whipping cream, whipped

Italian meringues (makes 1 ¼ lb./550 g)
5 egg whites (these should weigh 5 oz. or 150 g)
1 ½ cups (11 oz./300 g) granulated sugar
Scant ½ cup (100 ml) water

Prepare the Italian meringue (see p. 51). Add the fruit pulp to it. Delicately fold in the whipped cream.

Freeze until set.

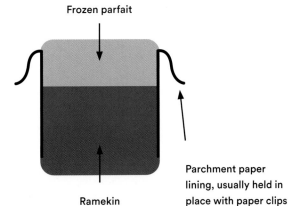

Frozen parfait

Ramekin

Parchment paper lining, usually held in place with paper clips

Other frozen desserts

Frozen vacherin

A frozen vacherin comprises a meringue base or shell that holds several flavors of ice cream and/or sorbets, covered by a layer of Chantilly cream—usually vanilla, but other flavorings that pair with the ice cream inside may be used.

Frozen log cakes

This is a frozen version of the log cake, traditionally served in France for Christmas—it resembles a log of wood. Various types of sponge base hold ice creams and/or sorbets. Today, ice-cream makers prepare their logs using an imaginative range of shapes, decorations, and flavors.

Ice cream profiteroles

Small choux puffs are filled with ice cream and topped with a hot or cold sauce or coulis. Profiteroles are most popularly to be found on menus teamed with vanilla ice cream and hot chocolate sauce, sometimes with Chantilly cream as well.

Frozen charlotte

Like the pastry version of a charlotte, the frozen charlotte is lined with ladyfingers and filled with ice cream, sorbet, or an unchurned frozen dessert, such as a parfait, soufflé, and mousse. Chantilly cream can add a delicious decorative touch.

Baked Alaska

A soaked sponge (usually a Genoese sponge) is the base for an ice cream, sorbet, or frozen dessert. This is covered all over in meringue and browned, either in the oven or using a caramelizing blow torch. Sometimes, the Baked Alaska is flambéed just before serving. In French it is known as a Norwegian omelet.

Frozen citrus fruit (*fruits givrés*)

Lemons and oranges are hollowed out and left whole and their flesh is used to make a sorbet or ice cream that then fills the skin. Other flavors may be added when the dessert is assembled.

Plombières

This name refers to an egg-based ice cream or ordinary ice cream made with vanilla or kirsch. Candied fruits soaked in syrup or kirsch are added to this, as is almond milk or almonds.

Sundaes

Name	What's in it?	The story behind it
Peach Melba	2 scoops of vanilla ice cream	The illustrious Auguste Escoffier was working at the London Savoy in 1893 when he created this dessert for the Australian opera singer Nelly Melba.
	Whole peaches poached in vanilla syrup	
	Red currant jelly	
	Chantilly cream	
	Sliced, toasted almonds	
Colonel	Lemon sorbet	
	Vodka	
Poire Belle-Hélène	2 scoops of vanilla ice cream	This dessert was created around 1864 in homage to Offenbach's popular comic opera, *La Belle Hélène*.
	Pear halves poached in syrup	
	Warm chocolate sauce	
	Chantilly cream	
	Sliced, toasted almonds	
Banana split	A split banana	
	3 scoops of ice cream, preferably vanilla or chocolate	
	Chocolate sauce or fruit coulis	
	Chantilly cream	
Café liégeois	2 scoops of soft coffee ice cream made with a coffee infusion	A frozen version of the Belgian coffee drink.
	Chantilly cream	
Dame blanche	2 scoops of vanilla or almond milk ice cream	This dessert probably takes its name from a successful opera by the French composer Boieldieu, published in 1825. The name means "white lady."
	Chocolate sauce	

PRACTICAL GUIDE

Basic equipment

BOWL SCRAPER
This unpretentious, half-moon-shaped plastic tool will ensure that every last little bit of batter is scraped out of the mixing bowl.

CHINOIS
A conical perforated metal sieve that is used to strain thicker sauces.

DUTCH OVEN
A large pot with a tight-fitting lid, ideal for stews as it can be used both on the stove top and in the oven.

FINE-MESH SIEVE OR STRAINER
For smooth sauces, mousselines, and coulis.

FLEXIBLE RUBBER SPATULA
Indispensable for mixing two or more ingredients gently, scooping, scraping, and spreading.

GRILL PAN
This will allow you to grill meat, sear it in attractive patterns, and ensure that it does not cook in its own fat.

HIGH-SIDED SAUTÉ PAN
Preferably with an ovenproof lid and handle so that you can finish cooking in the oven.

ICE-CREAM MAKER
This will enable you to make sorbets and ice creams by churning and freezing your preparations to well below freezing point.

MANDOLINE
To make attractive, paper-thin slices.

MIXING BOWLS
Two types of mixing bowls are useful, the flat-bottomed kind that serves most purposes, and the round-bottomed kind for whisking egg whites and cream and preparing your own mayonnaise. The latter is shaped so that a whisk can reach right to the lowest levels of the liquid.

SIPHON
A device that uses a gas cartridge to foam the liquid placed inside it. It is important to read the manufacturer's instructions carefully to ensure the equipment is correctly assembled and to avoid potential injuries.

STAND MIXER
Ideal for kneading dough, preparing Italian meringue, or generally preparing recipes in larger quantities.

STOCK POT
A high-sided pot for slow evaporation used to prepare stocks and soups.

WHISKS
There are two types of whisks, a balloon whisk for egg whites, short and rounded, and a sauce whisk, longer with more rigid wires.

Because precision is important:

SCALES AND MEASURING UTENSILS
An electric scale is useful, particularly if you have one that switches between the metric and imperial systems.

Measuring jugs, cups, and spoons will ensure your volumes are accurate.

THERMOMETERS
A meat or an instant-read thermometer to check on the progress of roasts and ensure that terrines do not overcook.

A candy thermometer, essential if preparing an Italian meringue to incorporate into a dessert. If it has a sufficiently large range, you may use it for both dairy and fat.

A fat thermometer will come in handy for deep frying.

1.	Dessert molds
2.	Dariole mold
3.	Tart rings
4.	Sauté pan
5.	Oyster knife
6.	Canelle knife
7.	Vegetable peeler
8.	Scoop or melon baller
9.	Turning knife
10.	Paring knife
11.	Boning knife
12.	Sole filleting knife
13.	Slicing knife
14.	Mandoline vegetable slicer
15.	Chinois
16.	Flexible rubber spatula
17.	Tip for piping bag

Meat cuts

Pork

FRANCE

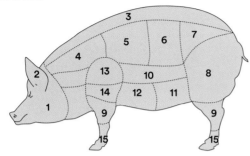

1. Tête 2. Oreille 3. Lard gras / gras dur / barde
4. Échine 5. Carré 6. Milieu de filet 7. Pointe de filet
8. Jambon 9. Jarret 10. Travers 11. Poitrine 12. Plat de côtes
13. Palette 14. Épaule 15. Pieds

USA

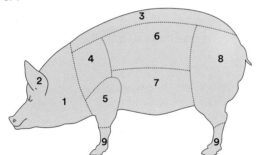

1. Head 2. Ear 3. Fatback 4. Shoulder Butt
5. Picnic Shoulder 6. Loin 7. Spare Ribs/Belly
8. Ham 9. Trotters

UK

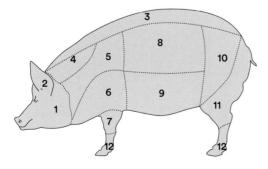

1. Head 2. Ear 3. Fatback 4. Spare Rib 5. Blade 6. Hand
7. Hock 8. Loin 9. Belly 10. Chump 11. Leg 12. Trotters

Lamb

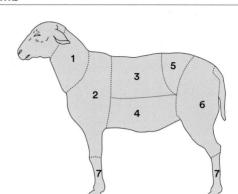

1. Collet 2. Épaule 3. Carré 4. Poitrine
5. Selle 6. Gigot 7. Pieds

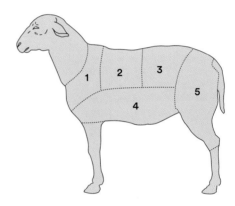

1. Shoulder 2. Rack 3. Loin
4. Foreshank and Breast 5. Leg

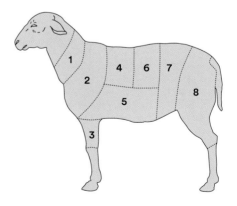

1. Scrag 2. Shoulder 3. Shank 4. Best end of neck
5. Breast 6. Loin 7. Chump 8. Leg

Veal

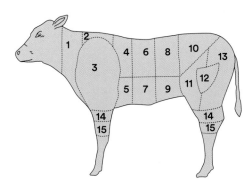

1. Collier 2. Côtes découvertes 3. Épaule
4. Côtes secondes 5. Poitrine 6. Côtes premières
7. Tendron 8. Longe 9. Flanchet 10. Quasi 11. Noix
patissière 12. Noix 13. Sous-noix 14. Jarret 15. Crosse

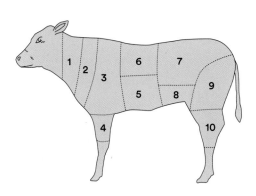

1. Neck 2. Chuck 3. Shoulder 4. Fore Shank 5. Breast
6. Ribs 7. Loin 8. Flank 9. Leg 10. Hind Shank

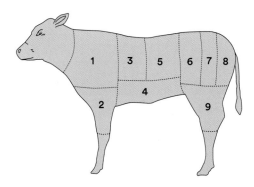

1. Shoulder 2. Fore Shank 3. Best End 4. Breast 5. Loin
6. Rump 7. Silverside 8. Topside 9. Hind Shank

Beef

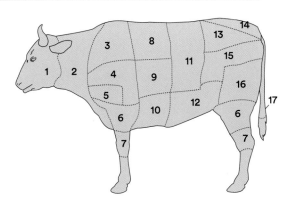

1. Joue 2. Collier 3. Paleron 4. Macreuse 5. Veine grasse
6. Gîte 7. Crosse 8. Côtes couvertes 9. Plat de côtes
10. Poitrine 11. Filet et aloyau 12. Flanchet 13. Culotte
14. Rumsteck 15. Tranche 16. Gîte à la noix 17. Queue de
bœuf

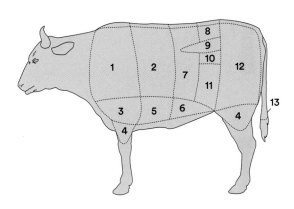

1. Chuck 2. Rib 3. Brisket 4. Shank 5. Plate
6. Flank 7. Short Loin 8. Sirloin 9. Tenderloin
10. Top Sirloin 11. Bottom Sirloin 12. Round 13. Oxtail

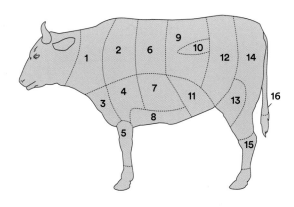

1. Neck 2. Chuck and Blade 3. Clod 4. Thick Rib
5. Shin 6. Fore Rib 7. Thin Rib 8. Brisket 9. Sirloin
10. Fillet 11. Thin Flank 12. Rump 13. Thick Flank
14. Topside and Silverside 15. Leg 16. Oxtail

Heirloom vegetables

1. Sunchoke or Jerusalem artichoke
2. Parsnip
3. Oriental radish
4. Crosne, Japanese or Chinese artichoke
5. White radish
6. Black salsify, scorzonera, or black oyster plant
7. Swede or rutabaga, also known as Swedish, yellow, Canadian, or Russian turnip

AOC and AOP

APPELLATION D'ORIGINE CONTRÔLÉE (AOC)

AOC, which means controlled designation of origin, is the French certification awarded by the governmental body L'Institut National des Appellations d'Origine (INAO) to certain regional agricultural products such as wines, cheeses, butters, and honey. All AOC products must adhere to clearly defined and strict standards, and be produced in a particular, traditional way, with ingredients from classified producers, within the region that holds the AOC status. These products are usually identified by a seal printed on the label, as with wines, or, in the case of cheese, on the rind.

APPELLATION D'ORIGINE PROTÉGÉE (AOP)

The European Union introduced a system of protected designation of origin in 1992, for products that are produced, processed, and prepared in a certain geographical area using a certified and recognized method. It is an extension of the AOC and is designed to protect locally produced butters, cheeses, and other agricultural products within the EU member states. It is also expanding globally and is recognized by more than 180 countries.

CHEESES

The first cheese to be given AOC status was Roquefort, in 1925; today, more than forty cheeses bear the AOC stamp. Most are made from cows' milk, as are the majority of cheeses in the world; however, many are produced using milk from goats and sheep.

Cheeses made from cows' milk: Abondance; Beaufort; Bleu d'Auvergne; Bleu de Gex Haut Jura; Bleu des Causses; Bleu du Vercors Sassenage; Brie de Meaux; Brie de Melun; Camembert de Normandie; Cantal; Chaource; Comté; Epoisses; Fourme d'Ambert; Fourme de Montbrison; Gruyère AOC; Laguiole; Langres; Livarot; Maroilles; Mont d'Or; Morbier; Munster; Neufchâtel; Pont-l'Evêque; Reblochon; Saint-Nectaire; Salers; Tome des Bauges.
Cheeses made from goats' milk: Banon; Brocciu; Chabichou du Poitou; Chavignol; Chevrotin; Mâconnais AOC; Pélardon; Picodon; Pouligny-Saint-Pierre; Rigotte de Condrieu AOC; Rocamadour; Sainte-Maure de Touraine; Selle-sur-Cher; Valençay.
Cheeses made from ewes' milk: Brocciu; Ossau-Iraty; Roquefort.

OTHER REGIONAL (AOC) PRODUCTS

Moules de bouchot de la baie du Mont-Saint-Michel (Bouchot mussels from the Bay of Mont-Saint-Michel)
These mussels, produced in the Bay of Mont-Saint-Michel, are classified AOC—the first seafood to be awarded the French label. The *moules de bouchot* are the most sought-after mussels in France, mainly due to their medium size and distinctly firm, orange-yellow flesh. They are grown on wooden pillars, or *bouchots*, which means they are underwater at high tide, yet exposed to the sea air when the water recedes, giving them their distinctive flavor.

Lentilles vertes du Puy (Green Puy lentils)
These lentils have been grown in the Auvergne region since Roman times; it is the area's volcanic soil free from fertilizer that gives them their unique, nutty, and mineral-rich flavor. The climate—a lack of humidity and plenty of sunshine due to the volcanic deposits and surrounding mountains—contributes to their unique texture, as the lentils are able to dry on the plants before being harvested. As a result, they have less starch than other lentils and are not as mushy.

Volaille de Bresse (Bresse poultry)
This is the only poultry to carry the AOC quality label. Bresse poultry is renowned for its quality of meat and unbeatable flavor, and is raised according to traditional local methods, free from any form of industrialization.

Piment d'Espelette (Ezpeletako Biperra)
The beloved chili pepper of the Basque region, the Espelette chili has become a culinary and cultural icon in this area, where it has gained controlled-name status. It has been grown in the small town of Espelette since the sixteenth century, and is noted for having a robust peppery and slightly smoked flavor.

Cocos de Paimpol (Breton semi-dried beans)
These beans originate from a seed brought back to the Paimpol region in 1928 by a sailor. They were marketed in 1948 and obtained AOC status in 1998. The pods are yellow, with purplish veins, and the beans are white and round.

Fruit seasons

Type of fruit	Southern Hemisphere season	Northern Hemisphere season
Apricot	November–March	May–September
Avocado	August–December	February–June
Banana	January–December	January–December
Blackberry (mulberry)	November–February	May–August
Black currant	December	June–August
Blood orange	November–May	December–March
Blueberry (bilberry)	November–March	May–September
Cape gooseberry	September–November	June–July
Cherry	October–February	June–August
Chestnut	March–April	November–January
Clementine	February–September	November–January
Coconut	October–December	Not usually grown
Cranberry	Not usually grown	October–February
Elder	July–September	September–November
Fig	December–May	June–September
Grape	December–May	September–October
Grapefruit	September–November	September–November
Guava	September–February	November–March
Kiwi	November–May	January–August
Kumquat	September–January	November–March
Lemon	All year round	January–March
Lime	March–September	September–December
Lychee	December–February	April–June
Mango	September–January	March–September
Melon	All year round	July–October
Orange	March–November	January–March
Papaya	All year round	Not usually grown
Passion fruit	February–July	July–March
Peach	December–February	June–August/September
Pear	March–November	September–January
Persimmon (Sharon fruit)	February–June	September–December
Pineapple	All year round	March–July
Plum	November–May	May–October
Pomegranate	March–May	October–January
Quince	December–May	October–December
Raspberry	November–February	June–September
Red currant	December	July–August
Rhubarb	November–February	January–May
Star fruit (carambola)	June–August	July–September
Strawberry	October–March	June–August
Tangerine	May–November	October–April
Tomato	March–July	June–September
Watermelon	December–March	August–October

Berries

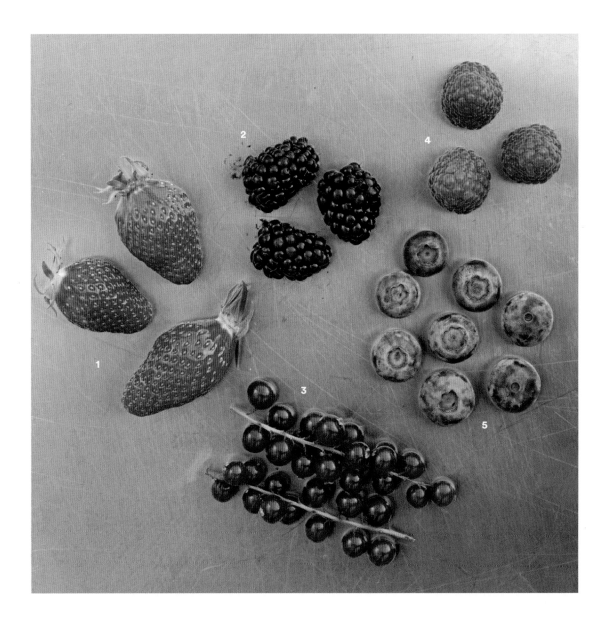

1. Strawberry
2. Blackberry (mulberry)
3. Red currant
4. Raspberry
5. Blueberry (bilberry)

Salad greens

1. Tetragonia or New Zealand ice plant or spinach (*Cryophytum cristallinum*)
2. Arugula (rocket)
3. Baby spinach
4. Beet leaf
5. Young Swiss chard
6. Miniature Japanese mustard
7. Mizuna
8. Purslane

227

Herbs

1. Chives
2. Rosemary
3. Mint
4. Basil
5. Frizzy-leaf (curly-leaf) parsley
6. Dill
7. Chervil
8. Bay leaf
9. Flat-leaf parsley
10. Tarragon
11. Thyme

French cheeses

Cheese, with bread and wine, symbolizes the gastronomy of France. The country produces some three hundred widely diverse varieties, and all of the regions and many small villages have their own unique specialty.

A slice of history

The word for cheese in French is *fromage*; its etymology is both Latin and Greek. *Forma* in Latin and *formos* in Greek both refer to a cheese mold. Dairy products were molded into shapes, and the origin of the word is still seen in the numerous regional cheese products that bear the name *fourme*.

Cheese-making goes back some 12,000 years, to the time when livestock farming began. Around 60 CE, Pliny the Elder mentioned what was certainly the forerunner to the eponymous hard cheese of the Cantal when describing the cheeses of the Arvernes and Gabales tribes of Gaul, much appreciated in Rome. Around 800 CE, monks began developing the first Roquefort (blue) cheeses and strong Munster cheeses.

What exactly is cheese?

Cheese is made by coagulating milk or other dairy products, such as cream, draining it in a mold, and then—in some cases— ripening. In French, these cheeses are known as *affinés*, and the professional whose task it is to bring cheese to maturity is known as an *affineur*. France counts a number of master specialists: *maîtres affineurs*.

Cheeses are categorized according to several criteria, one of which is their fat content:
· "Triple creams" contain at least 75% fat
· "Double creams" contain between 60% and 75% fat;
· "Fatty cheese" contains from 50% to 60% fat;
· "Light cheese," to which no sugar has been added, contains from 20% to 30% fat;
· "Low fat cheese" contains less than 20% fat.

Farmhouse cheeses (*fromages fermiers*) must be made only from the milk produced at their farm of origin. The label "*au lait cru*," made with unpasteurized milk, is used for cheeses made from milk that has not been heated to above 104°F (40°C).

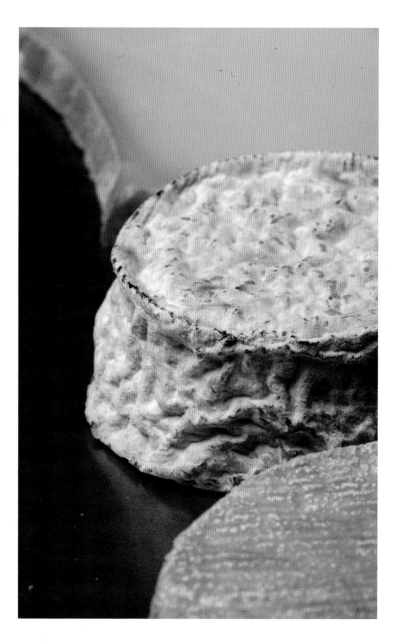

The eight types of cheese

FRESH CHEESES

Fresh soft cheeses are made by coagulation with lactic ferments. They are not ripened and have a high water content—between 60 and 80%. Salt may be added to them, or they may be enriched with crème fraîche.

Examples: *fromage blanc*, literally "white cheese," a soft cheese often sold in pots or jars that may be eaten as a dessert with sugar and fruit; *brousse*, made of ewe's milk, and fresh cheese spreads with herbs.

SOFT CHEESES WITH DOWNY RIND

These cheeses are generally not kneaded, and are never cooked. As they ripen, they are covered with a bacteria culture, giving them a more or less velvety appearance.

Examples: Camembert from Normandy, Brie from Meaux, and the rich Chaource made in the area between Champagne and Burgundy.

SOFT CHEESES WITH WASHED RIND

These cheeses are washed in salted water that sometimes has colorant added to it. The wax of annatto seeds, for example, imparts an orange color to the rind.

Examples: Munster (eastern France), Maroilles (northern France), Livarot (Normandy). Interestingly, all these cheeses were first developed in monasteries.

VEINED CHEESES

The curds are first cut up into small crumbs and then injected with culture before being shaped. As they ripen, blue-gray veins develop within the cavities, imparting a strong flavor to the cheese that can even be slightly piquant.

Examples: Roquefort, Vercors-Sassenage blue, Gex blue.

PRESSED CHEESES

These cheeses are ripened over a lengthy period. When the curds are cut, they are drained and then pressed. Finally, they are ripened. The texture of such cheeses is firm but not hard; in fact, they are also known as semi-hard cheeses.

Examples: Cantal, Saint-Nectaire, Reblochon, Tomme de Savoie.

PRESSED AND COOKED CHEESES

Such cheeses undergo a similar process to that of pressed cheeses, but the curds are heated for nearly an hour when they are cut and stirred. Maximum water content is drained from the curds by strong pressure to ensure that the cheese keeps well, so the resulting cheese is fairly dry.

Examples: Beaufort, Comté, Gruyère.

PROCESSED CHEESES

Such cheeses are made from pressed cheeses (semi-hard) and from pressed and cooked cheeses (hard). Flavors are often added to processed cheeses.

Examples: Cancoillote, walnut cheese, "La vache qui rit" (The Laughing Cow) cheese spread.

GOAT MILK CHEESES

Cheeses made from goat's milk are fresh or soft. They are often rolled in ash and may have a downy rind.

Examples: Sainte-Maure de Touraine, Crottin de Chavignol, Picodon de la Drôme.

Cheeses (AOC)

1. Beaufort
2. Comté
3. Selles-sur-Cher
4. Munster
5. Ossau-Iraty
6. Morbier
7. Camembert de Normandie
8. Valençay
9. Cantal
10. Roquefort
11. Bleu de Gex

Conversion tables

These conversion tables are meant as a guide and show the approximate equivalents. Exact conversions from metric to imperial measures do not generally give very convenient working quantities, and so the imperial measures in the recipes have often been rounded off into workable units. When making the recipes in this book, use either imperial or metric measurements (rather than a combination of the two) for best results.

Liquid measures (volume)

Cup/tbsp/tsp	Metric	Imperial
2 tbsp	30 ml	1 fl. oz.
4 tbsp	60 ml	2 fl. oz.
Scant ½ cup	100 ml	3 fl. oz.
Generous ½ cup	150 ml	5 fl. oz. (¼ pint)
Scant cup	215 ml	7 fl. oz.
1 cup	240 ml	8 fl. oz. (½ pint)
Generous cup	300 ml	10 fl. oz.
2 cups	475 ml	1 pint
3 cups	700 ml	1 ½ pint
3 ½ cups	830 ml	1 ¾ pint
4 cups	1 l	2 pints

Dry measures (weight)

Metric	Imperial
15 g	½ oz.
20 g	¾ oz.
30 g	1 oz.
45 g	1 ½ oz.
60 g	2 oz.
70 g	2 ½ oz.
85 g	3 oz.
100 g	3 ½ oz.
120 g	4 oz.
130 g	4 ½ oz.
140 g	5 oz.
170 g	6 oz.
200 g	7 oz.
215 g	7 ½ oz.
230 g	8 oz.
255 g	9 oz.
340 g	12 oz.
455 g	1 lb.
680 g	1 lb. 8 oz.
900 g	2 lb.

Fluid (volume)

	Teaspoons	Tablespoons	Fluid ounces	¼ cups	½ cups	Cups	Fluid pints	Milliliters	Liters
1 teaspoon	1	0.33	0.16	0.083	0.0416	0.0208	0.010416	5	0.005
1 tablespoon	3	1	0.5	0.25	0.125	0.0625	0.03125	15	0.015
1 fluid ounce	6	2	1	0.5	0.25	0.125	0.0625	29.56	0.030
¼ cup	12	4	2	1	0.5	0.25	0.125	59.125	0.059
½ cup	24	8	4	2	1	0.5	0.25	118.25	0.118
1 cup	48	16	8	4	2	1	0.5	236	0.236
1 fluid pint	96	32	16	8	4	2	1	473	0.473
1 milliliter	0.2	0.6	0.3	0.15	0.008	0.004	0.002	1	0.001
1 liter	203	68	34	17	8.5	4.2	2.113	1000	1

Mass (weight)

	Ounces	Pounds	Grams	Kilograms
1 ounce	1	0.0625	28.35	0.28
1 pound	16	1	454	0.454
1 gram	0.035	0.002	1	0.001
1 kilogram	35.2	2.2	1000	1

Conversions for common ingredients

The conversion of volume and weight varies somewhat depending on the ingredient; this table provides weight equivalents for some commonly-used ingredients.

Ingredient	1 tsp	1 tbsp	1 cup	1 stick (butter)
Flour	$^1/_{13}$ oz. (2 g)	$^1/_5$ oz. (6 g)	3 ½ oz. (100g)	
Sugar	$^1/_7$ oz. (4 g)	$^1/_{25}$ oz. (12 g)	7 oz. (195g)	
Brown sugar	$^1/_7$ oz. (4 g)	½ oz. (13 g)	7 oz. (200g)	
Confectioners' (icing) sugar	$^1/_{10}$ oz. (3 g)	½ oz. (8 g)	5 oz. (130g)	
Ground almonds	$^1/_{14}$ oz. (2 g)	$^1/_5$ oz. (5 g)	3 oz. (85g)	
Sultanas/raisins	$^1/_{10}$ oz. (3 g)	½ oz. (9 g)	5 ½ oz. (155g)	
Uncooked rice	$^1/_5$ oz. (4.5 g)	½ oz. (13 g)	7 ½ oz. (215g)	
Baking powder	$^1/_7$ oz. (4 g)	½ oz. (12 g)		
Salt	$^1/_5$ oz. (5 g)	½ oz. (15 g)		
Oil	$^1/_5$ fl. oz. (5 ml)	½ fl. oz. (15 ml)	8 fl. oz. (240 ml)	
Butter	$^1/_5$ oz. (5g)	½ oz. (15g)	8 oz. (230g)	4 oz. (125g)

Temperature

This table provides approximate temperature conversions between degrees Fahrenheit, degrees Celsius, and gas marks, to correspond with oven settings.

Temperature °F	240	265	290	310	335	355	380	400	425	450	470
Temperature °C	115	130	140	155	170	180	195	200	220	230	245
Gas mark	¼	½	1	2	3	4	5	6	7	8	9

Some useful temperatures

Room temperature: Approximately 68°F (20°C)

Optimal temperature for yeast dough to rise: 82°F (28°C)

Custard temperature (for pasteurization): 189°F (87°C)

Syrup (final temperature for Italian meringue): 244°F– 250°F (118°C–121°C)

Fats and oils

Fats & oils and their uses

Type	Used for
Butter	Cooking
Margarine	Cooking
Goose fat	Cooking
Copra (coconut oil)	Cooking
Lard	Cooking
Palm oil	Cooking
Sunflower seed oil	Cooking/seasoning
Canola (rapeseed) oil	Seasoning
Soy (soya) oil	Seasoning
Corn oil	Cooking/seasoning
Olive oil	Cooking/seasoning
Peanut oil	Cooking/seasoning
Grape-seed oil	Cooking/seasoning

Cooking temperatures for various fats & oils

◆ Melting Point
■ Maximum Temperature
● Smoke Point

Typical French products and aromatics

Bouquet garni

A French bouquet garni traditionally comprises the following aromatic plants: a bay leaf, a sprig of thyme (preferably fresh), two sprigs of parsley (preferably the more flavorful flat-leaf variety), one green leek leaf (about 5 in./12–15 cm), and optionally, a celery stalk of the same length as the leek leaf. These are all tied together so that they are easily removed just before serving, or whenever called for by your recipe. A bouquet garni of this size will flavor a dish of 4–6 servings.

This form of the bouquet garni goes back to the mid-seventeenth century, a time when culinary enthusiasm for exotic spices was waning, and was invented by the Breton Pierre de Lune, a disciple of La Varenne.

Caul

Caul or caul fat is the fat-laced membrane surrounding the stomach of animals. Pig's caul is frequently used to secure ingredients that would otherwise come apart during cooking, such as pâtés, stuffed cabbage leaves, and some sausage meats.

Crème fraîche

This cultured heavy cream with a tangy taste is similar to sour cream but can be heated without curdling or can be whipped. To make a substitute at home, stir 1 tablespoon buttermilk into 1 cup (250 ml) heavy cream, cover, and let sit at room temperature for up to 24 hours, until thickened, then refrigerate.

Fines herbes

This combination of aromatic herbs that includes parsley, chives, tarragon, and chervil is used to flavor sauces, omelets, cream cheeses, and other dishes. The mixture should be added just prior to serving as it loses its flavor rapidly.

Five-pepper mix

This attractive blend contains black, green, gray, and white peppercorns, and Jamaican pepper, also known as allspice.

Four-spice mix

This classic French blend contains ground black pepper, nutmeg, ginger, and cloves, and is frequently used in meat and poultry dishes.

Ground almonds

Sweet almonds are a staple in French patisserie. On supermarket shelves, the terms "almond flour" and "almond meal" are often used interchangeably to refer to ground almonds, but there can be differences, depending on the brand. Almond flour is typically made by grinding blanched (skinned) almonds very finely, while almond meal is produced by milling the nuts with their skins on, so is coarser. Almond flour produces finer results and is preferable in most recipes calling for ground almonds in this book. Almond paste, not to be confused with marzipan, is made with ground almonds and sugar in proportions that depend on their usage.

Hard cider

Cidre in France is the bubbly drink produced from fermented apple juice, principally in the regions of Brittany and Normandy, where it features in local cuisine. Like champagne, it is available both "sweet," with a minimum alcoholic content of 3%, and "dry," with a minimum of 5–5.5% alcohol. Regulations concerning cider production date back to Emperor Charlemagne's time.

Herbes de Provence

An assortment of dried herbs native to the region of Provence, this blend includes rosemary, thyme, fennel seeds, marjoram, and savory.

Mustards

A condiment firmly entrenched in French cooking traditions, it is made from the seeds of a herbaceous plant and sold in the form of a paste. Dijon mustard contains verjuice, wine must, or white wine, and powdered brown or black mustard seeds. *Moutarde à l'ancienne*, mustard in the old style that generally comes from Meaux, contains roughly crushed seeds. French mustards tend to be very tangy; they are a component of many sauces and dressings, and are used to coat poultry and meat for cooking.

Piment d'Espelette

The only native French chili pepper is grown exclusively in the village of Espelette and nine other villages in the Basque region in southwest France. Its relatively low grade on the Scoville chili heat scale means it adds piquancy rather than fire. It is sold ground or in paste form. See AOC p. 224.

Mushrooms

Mushrooms belong to the fungus kingdom. The numerous species have no chlorophyll and produce no flowers. They grow in fields and in forests, and some are cultivated. With their high water content, they are low in calories.

The mushrooms most commonly eaten in France are the button mushroom—which in French is known as a Paris mushroom—porcini (cèpes or *Boletus edulis*), chanterelles, morels, and the prized black truffle.

PREPARING MUSHROOMS

Cleaning
Remove the sandy base and any imperfections, and brush off any dirt. Cut mushrooms, including morels, in half lengthwise to ensure there are no insects inside.

Washing
Avoid washing mushrooms because they absorb water easily; it is preferable to clean them with a dry brush. If they are very dirty, you can gently rinse spongy mushrooms under running water or briefly immerse sliced mushrooms in cold water. Immediately pat them dry with paper towel.

Peeling
Some mushrooms with large caps can be peeled, including button mushrooms, Caesar's mushrooms, and certain members of the *Tricholoma* genus.

Cutting
Most mushrooms are cut using a knife, except for oyster and trumpet mushrooms, which must be torn apart or shredded using your hands. They can be quartered (technique p. 60), diced, sliced, or julienned (caps and meaty stems).

Cooking
Season mushrooms with salt only after cooking so that they do not release too much water. They are delicious with chopped herbs and shallots or garlic (see duxelles p. 158).

HOW TO USE MUSHROOMS
Cook them or eat them raw (except morels), on their own or as a side dish. Marinate them to serve in salads, stuff their caps, incorporate them into sauces, or prepare soups with them.

STORING MUSHROOMS
Most mushrooms can be kept for a few days in the refrigerator, wrapped in a slightly damp, clean cloth.

Various species of mushroom can be bought all year round; if they are not available fresh, you will find them dried, canned, or frozen.

A WORD OF CAUTION
Only eat mushrooms if you are certain that they are edible. Morels should not be eaten raw. Even if you have some knowledge about mushroom gathering already, double-check with an expert on your harvest if you have the slightest doubt.

DID YOU KNOW?
The black truffle that comes from Périgord (*Tuber melanosporum*), a region in southwest France, is the most prized in France. Truffles are subterranean fungi that grow beneath certain trees, notably the oak. With their distinctive, heady aroma, they are much appreciated by chefs; the flavor of truly fine truffles is so powerful that a little goes a long way. This is fortunate, as they are one of the most expensive foodstuffs in the world, partly because of the labor required to find them, and partly because of their scarcity. Black truffles can be bought fresh (they will keep for five to six days), canned, jarred, whole, puréed, and in the form of juice (jus), and their full aroma enjoyed by sprinkling shavings on scrambled eggs, omelets, mashed potatoes, and risotto.

Mushrooms

1.   Morels
2.   Chanterelles
3.   Black trumpets
4.   Black truffles
5.   Oyster mushrooms
6.   Girolles
7.   Button mushrooms

Spices

1. Green cardamom
2. Cayenne pepper
3. Curry powder
4. Green pepper
5. Saffron threads
6. Coriander seeds
7. Dried pink pepper berries
8. White pepper
9. Paprika
10. Black peppercorns
11. Cinnamon
12. Star anise

Pasta

1. Tagliatelle
2. *Diavolini*
3. *Graminia*
4. *Conchiglie*
5. Fusilli
6. *Chifferi*
7. *Serpentini*
8. Penne rigate
9. Farfalle
10. Spaghetti

Grains

1. Corn
2. Spelt
3. Husked oatmeal
4. Quinoa
5. Whole wheat
6. Round-grained rice
7. Long-grain Basmati rice
8. Semi-wholewheat long-
    grain rice

Pulses

1. Dried red beans
2. Green Puy lentils
3. Broad beans
4. Split peas
5. Brown lentils
6. Lingot beans
7. Red lentils
8. Chickpeas

Glossary

Bain-marie, or hot water bath
If you have a double boiler, you can easily melt chocolate and make delicate sauces in it without fear of burning. If not, place a heatproof bowl over a saucepan that is half filled with hot water (it should not be filled enough to risk bubbling over into your preparation). Depending on the recipe, this water may or may not have to simmer. A bain-marie may also be used to keep food warm. Certain recipes here specify the temperature of the bain-marie if it has to be lower than simmering, so a thermometer may come in handy.

Basting
Basting involves using a spoon or pastry brush to cover food with liquid, melted butter, or fat, generally to prevent it from drying out.

Beurre noisette, or browned butter
To brown butter, gently heat it until golden brown. The milk proteins and sugar in the whey will caramelize, thus giving beurre noisette its particular hazelnut aroma.

Blanching
This is a term that has two different meanings in cookery:
- To place a food in cold water and then bring it to a boil. This is done to remove excess salt (salted bacon, for example) or starch (potatoes); soften the outer skin of pulses; and eliminate impurities (in meat, perhaps).
- To briefly plunge fruits or vegetables into boiling water and then immerse them in cold water. This technique can be used to peel; remove bitterness (for example, spinach); and/or preserve color and texture for immediate consumption, canning, or freezing.

Blind baking
This refers to baking a pastry crust before it is filled, and is necessary for tarts with an unbaked filling, or for crusts that require a longer baking time than their filling and that would otherwise turn soggy.

To blind-bake, prick the pastry all over with a fork and leave to rest. Then line it with parchment paper and fill with dried beans or pie weights to keep it from rising. Remove them, along with the paper, a few minutes before baking time is up, so that the pastry can turn an even golden color.

Bulk fermentation and proofing
Both of these steps contribute to flavor and strength in yeasted doughs and are essential for well-risen pastries and breads. Bulk fermentation is the first rise, after all the ingredients have been mixed together. Proofing (also known as proving) is the second rise, after the dough has been shaped and before it is baked. The rising times in the recipes are general guidelines and depend on many factors, especially room temperature; for best results, look for signs of doneness before proceeding.

Clarified butter
To clarify butter, melt it slowly, either in a bain-marie or microwave, so that most of the water evaporates. The milk solids will sink to the bottom and the gold-colored liquid will remain at the top. Skim off the foam from the top and then pour the clear butter off to use for your cooking. Without the milk solids, the clarified butter now has a higher smoke point (350°F/180°C), thereby facilitating cooking. Note that when "clarified butter" is listed as an ingredient, the weight in grams is given after clarification, i.e., with about 20% water removed.

Clarifying
To clarify a liquid is to rid it of its impurities. A commonly used method involves the addition of egg whites, which attract particles floating in the liquid. The liquid is simmered, thus bringing the egg white with the impurities to the surface, cooled, and then strained, so that the egg white with the residue remains in the sieve or cheesecloth. Simple clarification may also be achieved just by straining the liquid through cheesecloth.

To clarify, or separate, an egg means to separate the white from the yolk.

Cream of tartar
Cream of tartar serves three purposes: it is an ingredient in baking powder, stabilizes beaten egg whites, and prevents sugar from crystallizing.

Creaming butter and sugar
This refers to the process of beating butter and sugar together until well blended, fluffy, and pale yellow. This creates small air pockets in the butter, which helps produce light-textured baked goods. For best results,

use room temperature butter (around 65°F/18°C).

Deglazing
An instruction to deglaze a pan means dissolving the congealed solids at the bottom of the pan by adding a liquid and then scraping and stirring to combine liquids and solids. This should generally be done over high heat and the liquid brought to a boil. It is then used as part of the sauce of the dish.

Dicing (vegetables, fruit, etc.)
Many recipes call for finely diced vegetables, particularly aromatics and garnishes. The sizes required are variable, depending on the purpose or the delicacy of the dish.

A *brunoise* calls for extremely finely diced ingredients: approximately $1/8$ in. (2–3 mm) cubes. *See* Cutting into fine dice (*brunoise*), p. 64.

A *salpicon* requires slightly larger dice, approximately $1/5$-in. (5-mm) cubes.

The size of cubes for a **mirepoix** depends on the cooking time, and ranges from $1/5$ to $2/5$ inch (5–10 mm), depending on whether it is for a stock or a sauce.

It is important to dice all ingredients to the same size; they will cook more evenly, and if used as a garnish, uniformly small cubes will make for a more attractive presentation.

Dressing (poultry, fish)
This is the preparation of these foods prior to cooking. Poultry must be plucked, gutted, and often trussed. Fish must have fins trimmed and be gutted. It is usually scaled before being washed.

Flambéing
This means pouring an alcoholic beverage (often cognac or liqueur) over a food and then setting a flame to it. The process intensifies the flavor of the dish and is often recommended when the juices in a pan are required to make a sauce. It is also a rather spectacular way to serve certain desserts. To flambé, warm brandy or liqueur in a deep dish, pour it over the hot food, and ignite using a long match set to the edge of the pan holding the food. Be careful, of course, not to lean over the dish. Allow to cook until all the flames have burned out.

Folding in (egg whites and cream)
Many recipes call for stiffly beaten egg whites or cream. Beating such ingredients means that they have incorporated a great deal of air, and this is what will help a cake or soufflé rise, and give it a light, airy texture. To incorporate whisked ingredients into the batter, chocolate, etc., proceed carefully so that you do not deflate all those minute bubbles you or your electric beater have worked so hard to create. Use a flexible rubber spatula to mix in the whisked ingredient, turning the bowl as you work, and take care not to apply pressure to the sides of the bowl.

Beaten egg whites are always incorporated into the heavier mixture, usually in several stages.

The same is true for whipped cream, but cream may only be folded into other cold ingredients. Stop folding in as soon as the color of the batter or other mixture is even throughout.

By extension, delicate "folding in" is also required for fragile ingredients that must be combined with a sturdier mixture.

Fumet
A clear stock used to cook fish. *See* Fumet, p. 141.

Glazing
Glazing literally means giving a shine to a food. There are many ways to glaze different types of food.
- Vegetables: these may be turned (*see* p. 66) and then cooked with a little sugar and butter. When the cooking liquid has evaporated, the vegetables are coated in the sugar and butter. You may leave them with a clear glaze or cook them further, leaving them with a light or dark coating.
- Meat: when cooked meat has sauce poured over it, it is left under the broiler until a shiny film forms. Cold fish and terrines may be glazed with aspic, which is not only decorative but also provides a protective casing.
- Pastries and cakes: covering the top (and in some cases, the sides) of a tart with a fondant icing, water icing, chocolate, sugar syrup, fruit glaze, etc. Some pastries (for example, the Kings' cake [*galette des rois*], p. 471) may also be glazed by dusting them with confectioners' sugar or basting with sugar syrup as soon as you remove them from the oven, and then returning them very briefly to the oven.

Jus
In addition to the meaning of "juice," this term refers to a gravy prepared with the pan juices, usually of a meat dish, diluted with

stock or water and then boiled until all the flavors have melded into the stock. Truffle jus, available in cans, will add a striking umami note to your dishes.

Kneading
Kneading dough by hand involves flattening down the ingredients using your palm and pushing it away from you. The procedure blends the ingredients together and smooths and strengthens the dough to give it the right texture.

Offal
The edible internal parts of an animal, as well as some external parts and extremities, are known as offal (variety meats). These include the liver, kidneys, sweetbreads, and brain. The edible internal parts of poultry are known as giblets.

Pans (cake or loaf), preparation of
To ensure that cakes do not stick, brush the pan with a little melted butter, making sure it is thoroughly coated. Allow the butter to harden (if you are in a hurry, chill it for a few moments) and then sprinkle a little flour into the pan. Shake it around so that it adheres to the entire surface of the cooled butter, turn the pan upside down, and give it a rap to remove any excess. You should have no more than a fine dusting of flour when this is done. To prepare molds for recipes such as charlottes, the recipe may call for the pan to be lined with sponge, ladyfingers, and so on. Pack your lining ingredients as tightly as possible, unless otherwise specified, for even, attractive results.

Reducing/reductions
Reducing liquids is an all-important stage in sauce preparation and involves boiling down a liquid to concentrate its taste. It is best to season with salt when the reduction is ready to serve to avoid the risk of over-salting. If reducing a sauce that has shallots in it, such as a beurre blanc, be careful not to reduce so much that all the liquid evaporates.

Refreshing (cooked food)
To refresh, or cool food down rapidly, prepare a large bowl with cold water and ice cubes, and place your sauce, purée, etc. in a smaller bowl over this.

To stop the cooking process of vegetables and pasta, cool down briefly under running water. This will prevent them from softening further and, in the case of vegetables, help maintain their color.

Ribbon stage
When you beat egg yolks and sugar together, the final result will be thick and pale yellow, and will have reached what is known as the ribbon stage. When a little of the mixture is lifted with the whisk or beater, it should slowly flow back down into the bowl in a ribbon shape. This is crucial in sponges that rely on eggs for leavening.

Sauce consistency (coating the back of a spoon)
This traditional test for the desired thickness of a sauce works best with a wooden spoon. The spoon is dipped into the mixture so that it is thoroughly coated in the sauce. When you draw a line with your finger across the back of it, the sauce stays in place, instead of filling the gap. However, in the modern kitchen it is far more reliable and hygienic to test the temperature of the sauce using a thermometer. A custard, for example, should reach a temperature of 185°F (85°C).

Scoring
This entails marking the top surface (of bread, pies, meat, etc.) with a knife, to create small slits. This is done for a variety of reasons: to render meat more tender; to create a nice browned crust; to allow steam or excess fat to escape; to allow for a better penetration of marinades or aromatics; or simply for decoration.

Searing (sealing)
Searing meat, poultry, or fish means to begin the cooking process at a high temperature in fat to brown the surface, enhancing the flavor.

Softened butter
This is butter brought to a temperature of close to 86°F (30°C), when it takes on a creamy consistency that makes it easier to incorporate with other ingredients and/or mold it.

Sous vide
The sous vide technique involves preparing food in vacuum-sealed containers. The method gives the cook complete control over time and temperature. It allows meat to remain tender and moist, and prevents fish from overcooking. *See* Grilling, p. 104.

Sweating (vegetables, fruit, etc.)
When it is important for vegetables, aromatic ingredients, or fruit not to change color, they must be cooked briefly, often

until just translucent (for onions and shallots) and slightly softened. They will exude their own liquid in the process.

Trussing
To truss poultry is to tie it up with trussing twine so that the wings and thighs stay in place. If the technique is well mastered, the twine is hardly visible. Trussing facilitates roasting and carving. The twine is removed when the bird is ready to serve.

General notes

Precision
French chefs—pastry chefs in particular—work with scientific precision, carefully weighing each ingredient to achieve their spectacular results. Scales are also a basic tool in many French home kitchens. It is therefore preferable, if possible, to use the metric measures and to weigh your ingredients.

The quantities in the recipes here have been converted into imperial measures and/ or into cups and spoons, or sticks for solid butter, and although every effort has been made to achieve as much accuracy as possible, this inevitably results in a little rounding up or down, to avoid awkward amounts. However, these small differences will not significantly change the end result. It is important, though, to stick to either imperial or metric measures in a recipe, and not mix the two.

A cooking thermometer is also a useful tool in the kitchen, to check cooking and baking temperatures.

Using gelatin sheets
Gelatin in transparent sheets (or leaves) weighing precisely 2 grams each is the form used in France, and we have opted to maintain this for the recipes in this book.

To use, soak them in a bowl of very cold water (unless otherwise specified), completely covered, until they are softened and very pliable, about 10 to 15 minutes. When they are ready for use, remove them from the water and squeeze out all the liquid with your hands. The texture will be rubbery but they will not break. Dissolve them in the quantity of warm liquid specified by your recipe, ensuring that there are no visible traces left. Follow the directions of the recipe for setting times. Gelatin is animal-derived; should you decide to use a plant-based setting agent (agar-agar is made from seaweed), carefully follow the directions for jelling quantities and times.

Cooking with chocolate
Chocolate comes in many forms. Couverture chocolate has long been used by professionals but is increasingly available to the general public; its high cocoa butter content (between 35% and 50%), not to be confused with its cacao content, makes it eminently suitable for baking and desserts, as it melts smoothly. Couverture chocolate is available as dark, semisweet (both with varying percentages of cacao), milk, and white chocolate. Unsweetened or baking chocolate consists of 100% cacao. Cocoa powder is made by extracting most of the cocoa butter from the pure chocolate liquor.

In France, the percentage of cacao is stipulated on the label, hence chefs' requirements in their recipes depending on just how chocolaty they wish the result to be.

Chocolate scorches easily, and scorching ruins its taste. This is why it is important to melt it gradually, preferably over a hot water bath (bain-marie). When it is combined with another ingredient, it should still be warm. If the other ingredient is also heated, check that both are at a similar temperature.

RECIPES

A few words of advice

Always read the recipe from start to finish before you begin cooking. This will ensure that:

· you understand all of the culinary terms;
· you have all the necessary equipment;
· you can preheat the oven or grill at the right moment;
· you can ask your butcher or fish seller to make certain preliminary preparations;
· if there are several stages or components to the recipe, or there are lengthy cooking procedures, you can clarify the order of approach and timings. Gauge what you can make ahead of time and what will need to be done at the last minute for an optimal result.

Other important considerations:
· Make sure you have a well-stocked pantry with a wide range of basic groceries, such as oils, condiments, and various types of flour. If, at the last minute, you realize that something is missing, you'll have a substitute.
· Select your recipes according to the seasons. Using products that are in season will guarantee a better-tasting result.

● Cleanliness and food safety
· Hands and cooking utensils must be spotlessly clean.
· Store raw and cooked food carefully. Practically all cooked foods must be covered in plastic wrap so that their smells do not permeate the refrigerator.
· Check the best-before/expiration dates on food packaging.

● A note on using these recipes
· Unless otherwise specified, the oils given in the lists of ingredients are neutral. Use canola, sunflower seed, grapeseed, or peanut oil interchangeably; their fluidity and cooking temperatures are practically identical.
· Unless otherwise specified, use whole milk, fine sea salt or table salt, and all-purpose flour.
· Eggs in the recipes refer to hens' eggs with an average weight of 2 oz. (55–57 g): "large" in the US and Canada, "medium" in the UK.
· Each oven has its own quirks, and this is why certain recipes indicate a range of temperatures. You will need to decide, based on past experience, whether your oven should be set at the lower or higher temperature given in the recipes.

● And always remember:
· A recipe involves subtle alchemy and calls for a handful of technique, a generous pinch of creativity, a goodly hint of practicality, and a soupçon of whimsy.

Appetizers

Anne-Sophie Pic

presents her recipe

For this book, I have selected an appetizer using as its main ingredients a vintage Gouda from Holland called Reypenaer VSOP, and black truffles. It comprises a hot soufflé with a melting truffled core and shredded vegetables with black truffle. I chose the soufflé because it is a classic of French cuisine and involves an interesting technique. My aim was to update it by varying its textures: the molten center is spiced up with a very creamy Gouda. I simply love to combine truffles and cheese. Since I work in France's major truffle-producing area, truffles are essential to my cuisine and a source of endless inspiration.

Appetizers always reflect the seasons. In winter, I like to create tasty, creamy appetizers, and in summer, they are fresher, with more piquancy. It is the appetizer that sets the tone and tempo of the meal, so it requires both lightness and precision, though it also allows a great freedom of expression. I can add original notes and pay attention to the appearance; I always find the visual side of my work fascinating.

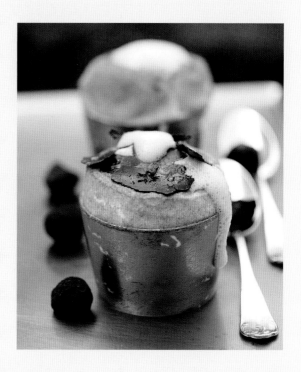

SERVES 4

Preparation:
45 minutes
Cooking: **11 minutes**

INGREDIENTS

Soufflé mixture
1 ¾ oz. (9 tablespoons or 50 g) cake flour
1 ¾ oz. (3 ½ tablespoons or 50 g) salted butter
2 cups (500 ml) milk
5 eggs, separated, plus 3 egg whites
1 pinch cumin
1 pinch grated nutmeg
3 ½ oz. (100 g) grated Gouda cheese
½ teaspoon cream of tartar
1 teaspoon (5 ml) potato starch

Creamed Gouda
2 ½ tablespoons (40 ml) milk
2 oz. (60 g) Gouda, finely diced

Gouda foam
2 oz. (55 g) egg yolks
2 tablespoons (30 ml) truffle juice
Scant ½ cup (100 g) melted butter
2 tablespoons (30 g) clarified butter, for greasing molds
¾ oz. (2 ½ tablespoons or 20 g) extremely finely ground breadcrumbs

⅐ oz. (4 g) black truffles, for garnish
Sea salt

Special equipment:
a siphon, 4 inserts, 4 small soufflé molds

Reypenaer VSOP vintage Gouda and black truffle soufflé, with a truffled molten center

Anne-Sophie Pic presents her recipe

Soufflé mixture

Prepare a béchamel sauce using the flour, salted butter, and milk. When it begins to boil, remove from the heat. Transfer to a mixing bowl and allow to cool to 150°F (65°C). Season the egg yolks with the cumin and nutmeg and incorporate into the béchamel.

To prepare the molds and inserts

Chill the molds. Using a pastry brush, grease them with some clarified butter. Be careful to make regular strokes from bottom to top as this facilitates the rising of the soufflés. Return to the refrigerator. When the butter has set, repeat the operation. After you have buttered them a third time, coat them with the fine breadcrumbs. Turn the molds upside down and rap them to remove any excess.

Chill the inserts just as you have done for the molds. Grease them on the outside with clarified butter from top to bottom, taking care not to leave any fingerprints on the butter. Wrap the inserts in parchment paper, which will stick to the butter. The paper should be hardly higher than the insert and should adhere well, without any creases. Then butter the parchment paper, working from top to bottom in the direction the soufflés will rise.

Creamed Gouda

Heat the milk and Gouda together. Blend and strain through a fine-mesh sieve. Chill until needed.

Gouda foam

Prepare a sabayon (see p. 52) with the 2 oz. (55 g) egg yolks and truffle juice. Gradually add the scant ½ cup (100 g) melted butter, and then 1 ½ oz. (40 g) strained, creamed Gouda. Adjust the seasoning. Pour into a siphon and keep in an oven preheated to 130°F (56°C).

To bake the soufflés

Pour the soufflé mixture into a round-bottomed mixing bowl. Add the grated Gouda and combine. Do not overmix.

Remove the four molds and inserts from the refrigerator. Place the inserts in the center of each mold, being careful not to touch them directly, and ensure that the buttered parchment paper is placed with the butter strokes upward (so that the soufflé will rise).

Preheat the oven to 400°F (200°C).

In another mixing bowl, beat the egg whites until they form very soft peaks. Add the ½ teaspoon (2.5 ml) cream of tartar and continue whisking. When they are firm, add the potato starch. Fold the beaten egg whites into the remaining creamed Gouda mixture, turning the bowl as you fold in carefully so as not to break the air bubbles.

When the mixture is thoroughly combined, spoon it into a piping bag. Fill the molds almost to the top. Make sure there is no direct contact between your fingers and the containers. Bake for 11 minutes.

To serve

Remove the soufflés from the oven and immediately and very carefully take out the inserts. Fill the cavity to the top with the gouda foam from the siphon. Carefully garnish with truffle slices and serve immediately.

Scandinavian canapés ✴

SERVES 8

Preparation: **40 minutes**
Cooking: **10 minutes**

INGREDIENTS

²/₃ cup (160 ml) heavy cream
8 slices smoked salmon
A little grated nutmeg
A little five-pepper mix
Juice of 1 lemon
1 tablespoon (15 ml) salmon roe;
 ½ red onion, sliced in fine rings;
 ¼ bunch dill; for garnish
Fleur de sel, freshly ground
 pepper
Optional: a few sprigs of chives

Blinis
1 ¼ cups (125 g) all-purpose
 flour
2 eggs, separated
1 cup (250 ml) milk
6 tablespoons butter, clarified, or
 ¹/₃ cup (80 g) clarified butter
1 pinch fine salt

To prepare the blinis, sift the flour with the salt and make a well. Pour the egg yolks in and dilute with the milk, whisking constantly.

Beat the egg whites until they form stiff peaks and fold them gently into the mixture.

Grease a small crêpe pan or crêpe maker with the clarified butter and pour out the batter to a thickness of about ¹/₅ in. (4–5 mm). Turn them over when they begin to color.

Beat the cream with a whisk or electric beater until it forms peaks. Season with *fleur de sel* and pepper.

Cut out the salmon slices to the same size as the blinis (use a cookie cutter or glass) and place a piece of salmon on each blini. Season with lemon juice and freshly ground pepper.

Top with some whipped cream and garnish with the salmon roe, a thin slice of onion, and a sprig of dill.

If you wish, tie each canapé with chives to make an easy-to-eat little "parcel."

Tuna rillettes with horseradish ✳

SERVES 6

Preparation: **30 minutes**

INGREDIENTS

1 lb. (480 g) tuna fillet
1 small pinch *piment d'Espelette*
Juice of 1 lemon
2 heaped tablespoons (40 g)
   tomato paste
1 ½ oz. (40 g) fresh horseradish,
   for garnish
A few sprigs of chervil,
   for garnish
Salt

CHEF'S NOTES

– Lemon juice or vinegar is
essential because the acidity
slows down the development of
germs.
– Other oily fish like salmon,
sardines, and mackerel work
well with the rillette recipe.

Trim the tuna and remove the bones.

Process the tuna with the seasonings and lemon juice in the
bowl of a food processor using the blade attachment. Add a
dash of tomato paste to heighten the color.

Arrange the tuna rillettes on canapés or in cocktail spoons,
garnished with a few shreds of horseradish and a chervil leaf.

DID YOU KNOW?

Rillettes were traditionally made with pork or goose. Contemporary
cuisine takes tried and tested preparations and transforms them with
quite different ingredients.

261

Beef carpaccio, Parmesan, and *pistou* ✳

SERVES 4

Preparation: **30 minutes**
Chilling: **30 minutes**

INGREDIENTS

10 oz. (300 g) beef fillet
½ cup (2 oz./35 g) Parmesan
  cheese, in shavings
A few leaves of basil, for garnish
4 pinches *fleur de sel*
Freshly ground pepper

Pistou
4 garlic cloves, peeled, shoots
  removed
½ bunch basil
3 ½ tablespoons (50 ml) olive oil
Juice of 1 lemon

TECHNIQUE

Pesto and *pistou* **146**

Prepare the *pistou*.
Crush the garlic cloves with the basil leaves using
a pestle and mortar.

Drizzle the olive oil in as you crush and then thin with the
lemon juice.

Trim the fillet of beef and remove all sinews. Cut into very thin
slices and arrange them attractively on a serving platter, as
regularly as possible.

Use a pastry brush to dab the beef here and there with the
pistou.

Chill for 30 minutes.

Scatter with the Parmesan shavings and *fleur de sel*. Give a few
turns of the pepper mill.

Garnish with basil leaves.

Allow between 30 minutes and two hours for the flavor of the
pistou to meld into the meat. Basil loses some of its taste and
smell after two hours and becomes slightly bitter.

Mussel *mouclade* ✳

SERVES 4

Preparation: **30 minutes**
Cooking: **30 minutes**

INGREDIENTS

2 lb. (1 kg) mussels
2 shallots
A few sprigs flat-leaf parsley
6 tablespoons (90 g) unsalted
  butter
Scant ½ cup (100 ml) dry white
  wine
1/3 cup (80 ml) heavy cream
2 teaspoons (10 g) curry powder
Freshly ground pepper

TECHNIQUES

Marinière **106**

CHEF'S NOTE

– Use the finest mussels you can
find for this tasty regional dish.
Allow about ½ lb. (250 g) of
mussels per person for an
appetizer.

Scrape off the dirt from the mussels and remove the beards.
Finely slice the shallots and chop the parsley. Sweat the shallots
in 3 ½ tablespoons (50 g) butter and then pour in the white
wine.

Add the mussels and half the chopped parsley.

Cover and cook over high heat, stirring regularly.

Check that all the mussels are open, discarding any that aren't,
and transfer them to a dish with a slotted spoon.

Filter the cooking liquid to remove any traces of sand. Reduce it
by half. Add the cream and reduce further, until it is thick
enough to coat the back of a spoon. Whisk in the remaining
butter.

Sprinkle half the curry powder into the sauce and leave it to
infuse. Season with pepper.

Serve the mussels on the half shell (remove one half of each
shell) and arrange them all in a serving dish or in soup plates.

Sprinkle the remaining the parsley over the dishes, and pour
over the hot sauce. Sprinkle with the remaining curry powder.

DID YOU KNOW?

This *mouclade* is a specialty of the Poitou-Charentes region, but other
coastal regions have their own variations.

Hot oyster gratin ✳ ✳

SERVES 6

Preparation: **45 minutes**
Cooking: **25 minutes**

INGREDIENTS

3 dozen medium-sized hollow
oysters
Equal quantities of the following
vegetables
1 large carrot (5 oz./150 g)
1 large slice celeriac or celery
root (5 oz./150 g)
1 leek, white only (5 oz./150 g)
4 tablespoons (60 g) unsalted
butter for the vegetables
1 stick (120 g) unsalted butter,
cubed, for the sauce
4 egg yolks
Scant ¼ cup (50 ml) dry white
sparkling wine
¾ cup (200 ml) fish velouté (see
p. 152)
Cayenne pepper
½ lb. (250 g) kosher salt, for
garnish
Fine sea salt, freshly ground
pepper

TECHNIQUES

Opening oysters and other
shellfish **74**
Cutting into julienne strips **61**
Sabayon (zabaglione) **52**

CHEF'S NOTES

– Use medium-sized oysters for
this recipe if you can.
– The velouté in this recipe gives
creaminess and stability to the
sabayon when it is broiled.

Open the oysters (see p. 74) and remove them from their shells, keeping their water.

Over high heat, bring them to a simmer in their water. Allow to simmer for no longer than 2–3 seconds. Remove immediately and leave to cool, preferably in a bowl on a stainless steel surface.

Carefully clean the hollow shells and poach them in boiling water to sterilize them.

Prepare the vegetable julienne. Peel and wash the carrots and the celery root (celeriac). Slit the leek whites in two and wash.

Cut the three vegetables into fine julienne strips (see p. 61).

Braise each one, separately if possible, in 4 tablespoons (60 g) butter with 4 ½ tablespoons (50 ml) water. This will preserve the taste of each one.

Season with salt and pepper.

To make the sauce, set the oven to broil. Place the egg yolks and the sparkling wine in a high-sided pan and whisk before placing on low heat or over a bain-marie. Continue whisking over the low heat until the mixture becomes foamy (a sabayon or zabaglione texture).

Remove from the heat and whisk in the remaining 1 stick (4 ½ oz./120 g) cubed butter. Season with salt and cayenne pepper.

Stir the fish velouté into the sabayon mixture.

Cover heat-resistant plates with a layer of kosher salt. Place 3 oyster shells on each plate.

Arrange the julienned vegetables in the shells, and then place 2 oysters in each one.

Drizzle the sauce over and place under the broiler for a few minutes.

Serve immediately.

Rolled mushroom omelet ✳

SERVES 6

Preparation: **30 minutes**
Cooking: **10 minutes**

INGREDIENTS

1 ½ cups (5 oz./150 g)
  button mushrooms
2 tablespoons (30 g)
  plus 4 tablespoons (60 g)
  clarified butter
15 eggs
½ bunch chives, snipped,
  for garnish
Fine sea salt, freshly ground
  pepper

TECHNIQUES

Quartering button
  mushrooms **60**

CHEF'S NOTES

– Contrary to popular belief, a
good omelet is barely browned
or golden. A pale color is a
guarantee that the texture will
be just right.
– Use a mixture of fresh, frozen,
and canned mushrooms if you
wish.

Wipe the mushrooms with a damp cloth, or brush with a dry brush (see p. 239), and cut them into quarters.

Melt 2 tablespoons (30 g) butter over high heat and, when it is sizzling, sauté the mushrooms. Season with salt and pepper.

Break the eggs into a mixing bowl. Season and beat, using a whisk or a fork.

Grease a nonstick pan with most of the remaining butter (set aside a little to clarify and brush over the omelet) and heat it. When it is hot, pour the eggs in and cook over high heat, constantly folding over the coagulated edges towards the center as the omelet cooks. It must be creamy and the omelet must not brown. Add some of the quartered button mushrooms.

Tilt the pan downward holding the handle upward. Roll the omelet over itself, from top to bottom, with a fork.

Give it a nice gloss with a little clarified butter.

Arrange the remaining mushrooms on the serving dish and scatter with snipped chives.

269

Rabbit and pistachio terrine with exotic fruit chutney ✳ ✳

SERVES 6

Preparation: **1 hour 30 minutes**
Cooking: **30 minutes**

INGREDIENTS

14 oz. (400 g) rabbit meat
5 oz. (150 g) fatty pork cut, such
 as blade shoulder (US) or spare
 rib (UK)
1 oz. (25 g) whole pistachios
1 ¹/₃ tablespoons (20 ml) cognac
1 egg
¹/₃ cup (1 oz./30 g) flour
2 oz. (60 g) caul fat
3 bay leaves
Scant ½ cup (100 ml) clear aspic,
 prepared using a mix
1 heaped teaspoon (7 g) fine sea
 salt
6 turns of the pepper mill (1 g)

Chutney
¼ pineapple
½ mango
¹/₃ cup (60 g) sugar
Juice of 1 orange

Special equipment: a meat
 thermometer

TECHNIQUES

Mincing meat **85**
Preparing terrines and pâté
 (terrine stuffing) **92**
Caramel sauce **169**

CHEF'S NOTES

– This recipe works very well
with almost all white meats.
– The terrine is best made a day
or at least 12 hours ahead. It will
keep for up to 4 days in the
refrigerator, in an airtight
container or plastic wrap.

Preheat the oven to 275°F (140°C).

Trim the rabbit by removing the transparent membrane and all
sinews. Cut the rabbit and pork meat into cubes or strips
weighing about 2 oz. (50 g) each. Grind the meat and season it
with the salt and pepper.

Combine the ground meats, whole pistachio nuts, cognac, egg,
and flour. Wrap the mixture in caul and fill the terrine mold.
Press down often to remove any air pockets. Arrange the 3 bay
leaves on top. Cook for 30–40 minutes until the core
temperature reaches 160°F (68–70°C).

As soon as you remove the terrine from the oven, pour the aspic
over it to prevent it from drying out. It will soften the texture
and give it an attractive shine.

Allow to chill for a minimum of 10 hours before serving.

Prepare the chutney.
Dice the pineapple and mango into very small (¹/₅ in. or 5 mm)
cubes.

Prepare a light caramel with the orange juice and sugar (see
pp. 168–69). Add the diced fruit as soon as the caramel reaches
the desired color to stop the cooking. Leave to stew for a few
minutes and then cool.

Cut the terrine into slices of about 3 oz. (70–90 g) each. Serve
with the chutney, a green salad, and sliced country bread.

DID YOU KNOW?

Traditionally, charcuterie (from the French *chair cuite*, cooked meat),
comprised only pork products, with sausages, cured meats, and pâtés and
terrines, but the range has widened to include other meats. A plate of
charcuterie products is a typical light dish served at cafés and restaurants
throughout France.

Pike quenelles and crayfish sauce ✳ ✳

SERVES 8

Preparation: **1 hour 15 minutes**
Cooking: **45 minutes**

INGREDIENTS

½ lb. (250 g) pike fillets
3 eggs plus 1 egg white
²/₃ cup (150 ml) whipping cream
1 cup (250 ml) water
6 tablespoons (90 g) butter
1 ½ cups (130 g) flour
A few sprigs flat-leaf parsley, for
    garnish
Fine sea salt, freshly ground pepper

Crayfish Sauce
1 ½ tablespoons (25 g) butter
¼ cup (25 g) flour
1 onion
1 shallot
½ carrot
2 ½ tablespoons (40 ml) olive oil
½ lb. (250 g) crayfish
1 tomato (3 ½ oz./100 g)
2 tablespoons (1 oz./30 g) tomato
    paste
2 ½ tablespoons (40 ml) cognac
Scant ½ cup (100 ml) white wine
2 cups (500 ml) water
Bouquet garni
Fine sea salt, freshly ground pepper

TECHNIQUES

Basic panada stuffing **160**

CHEF'S NOTE

– This is a very tasty dish if you
get the seasoning right, so do be
sure that both quenelles and
sauce are properly seasoned.

Prepare the finely ground pike forcemeat, which is the base for the quenelles. Process the fish using the blade attachment of a food processor. Add the egg white and mix in. Strain through a fine-mesh sieve. Transfer to a stainless steel bowl and place over an ice bath. Gradually stir in the cream. Season with salt and pepper, scraping down the sides. Cover with plastic wrap flush with the forcemeat so no skin forms on the surface. Chill.

Bring the water to boil with the butter. When the mixture comes to a boil, pour in the flour. Lower the heat and stir with a spatula to dry out the moisture. Remove from the heat, and stir in the three eggs, one by one. Incorporate this mixture into the minced pike.

Bring a pot of salted water to a boil. Use two soup spoons to form oval quenelles and drop them into the boiling water. Leave to boil for 4–5 minutes, then remove and drain.

For the crayfish sauce, prepare a blond roux with the butter and flour (see velouté recipe p. 152). Allow to cool.

Dice the onion, shallot, and carrot to make a mirepoix. Place the olive oil in a pan over high heat and sear the crayfish. Add the diced vegetables and allow to sweat. Chop the shells and the tomato. Add the shells, chopped tomato and tomato paste to the crayfish pan. Deglaze with the cognac and add the white wine. Reduce by half, then pour in the water. Add the bouquet garni. Simmer for 30 minutes, skimming the surface from time to time.

Blend the mixture and strain through a chinois. Be careful when blending the crayfish shells, particularly if using an immersion blender—it is best to crush them with a knife before you blend them to avoid splashes and decrease wear on the blade. Pour it over the cooled blond roux and bring all the liquid to a boil so that it thickens. Adjust the seasoning and set aside.

Arrange the quenelles in a serving dish or in soup plates and drizzle with sauce. Scatter chopped parsley over for garnish.

Foie gras terrine ✷ ✷

SERVES 6

Preparation: **1 hour**
Chilling: **12 hours**
Marinating: **2 hours**
Cooking: **15–25 minutes**

INGREDIENTS

1 lb. (500 g) raw foie gras,
   whole lobes
2 cups (500 ml) full cream milk
1 slightly heaped teaspoon (6 g)
   fine sea salt
½ teaspoon (2 g) granulated
   sugar
At least 6 turns of the pepper mill
   (1 g)
3 ⅓ tablespoons (50 ml)
   Armagnac
1 loaf of brioche sandwich loaf
Fleur de sel, freshly ground
   pepper

Special equipment: a terrine that
   fits the foie gras snugly and a
   meat thermometer

TECHNIQUE

Preparing foie gras **82**

CHEF'S NOTES

– This dish should preferably be
made a day ahead of serving.
– Duck foie gras is easier to find
than goose. It is also smaller,
weighing on average 1 lb (500 g),
and its taste is slightly more
pronounced.
– When buying, choose foie gras
without reddish or greenish
spots.

Remove the veins from the foie gras lobes (see p. 82). Place them in a deep dish and cover with milk. Cover the dish with plastic wrap and chill for 12 hours. This procedure is advisable as it removes some of the bitterness and makes any traces of blood paler.

Drain well, dabbing the lobes to remove excess moisture.

Combine the salt, sugar, and freshly ground pepper. The right seasoning at this stage is essential, so do pay attention to quantities—too little and your foie gras will be somewhat bland. Sprinkle the seasoning all over the foie gras. Return to a dish and pour in the Armagnac. Cover with plastic wrap and leave to soak for 2 hours, either in the refrigerator or at room temperature.

Preheat the oven to 175°F (85°C).

Place the foie gras in a terrine, pressing down to eliminate pockets of air. Cook for 15–25 minutes, depending on the size and type of your terrine. The core temperature must not exceed 135°F (57°C). Allow to cool for at least 4–5 hours.

To serve, slice the brioche sandwich loaf and toast. Keep the toast warm under a clean napkin. Slice the foie gras and sprinkle with crystals of *fleur de sel* and freshly ground pepper.

DID YOU KNOW?

Foie gras terrine is considered a great delicacy and is traditionally served at meals during the festive season, accompanied by a fine sweet white wine, such as Sauternes.

Snail ravioli and garlic cream ✳✳

SERVES 8

Preparation: **50 minutes**
Resting: **45 minutes**
Cooking: **15 minutes**

INGREDIENTS

2 eggs
2 tablespoons (30 ml) oil
2 ¼ cups (220 g) flour
½ bunch flat-leaf parsley
2 shallots
3 ½ tablespoons (50 g) butter
2 dozen snails (de-shelled)
A few sprigs of chervil for
 garnish
Fine sea salt, freshly ground
 pepper

Creamed garlic
5 oz. (150 g) garlic cloves,
 peeled, shoots removed
¾ cup (200 ml) milk
¾ cup (200 ml) cream
1 scant tablespoon (10 g) potato
 starch
Fine sea salt, freshly ground
 pepper

TECHNIQUE

Pasta and noodle dough **17**

CHEF'S NOTE

– Add an extra touch by
flavoring or coloring (or both)
your pasta dough. Try spices,
vegetable colorants, or
cuttlefish ink.

Prepare the pasta dough (see p. 17).
Beat the eggs with the oil and salt. Sift the flour and make a well in the center. Pour the egg mixture in and combine, working quickly so that the dough does not become too elastic. Shape it into a ball and chill, covered, for 30–45 minutes.

Roll it out roughly using a rolling pin and then work it through the pasta maker to make a fine sheet. Cut out twenty-four disks with a cookie cutter.

Chop the flat-leaf parsley and finely slice the shallots.

Heat the butter until it turns hazelnut brown (*beurre noisette*). Sauté the snails in the butter, and then add the parsley and shallots. Season with salt and pepper.

Place a snail on each dough circle. Fold over to form a half-circle, pinching around the edges to seal the dough.

Bring some salted water to a boil. Place the ravioli in the boiling water for 3 minutes. Drain carefully and serve immediately.

If you prepare the ravioli ahead of time, keep them well chilled and reheat briefly in the creamed garlic.

Prepare the creamed garlic.
Blanch the garlic cloves in cold milk, bringing it all to a boil. Discard the milk and repeat the procedure once more. Combine the cream, the potato starch, and the seasoning, and heat. Add the garlic and reduce, stirring constantly until the garlic cloves are soft. Blend in a food processor.

Serve in soup plates, miniature pots, or ramekins, and garnish with a few sprigs of chervil.

Rockfish soup ✷✷

Appetizers

SERVES 8

Preparation: **55 minutes**
Cooking: **50 minutes**

INGREDIENTS

4 lb. (2 kg) fish such as red
    gurnard, scorpion fish, weever
    fish, and conger or sea eel
1 large or 2 medium onions
    (7 oz./200 g)
1 large carrot (7 oz./200 g)
1 leek (5 oz./150 g), white only
4 tomatoes (10 oz./300 g)
½ celery stalk (3 ½ oz./100 g)
½ fennel bulb. (3 ½ oz./100 g)
Scant ½ cup (100 ml) olive oil or
    butter
1 ¼ cups (300 ml) dry white wine
1 bouquet garni
2 oz. (60 g) garlic cloves
3 tablespoons (50 g) tomato
    paste
8 threads saffron
½ French baguette
5 oz. (150 g) grated Gruyère
    cheese
7 oz. (200 g) rouille sauce (see
    recipe p. 147)
Fine sea salt, freshly ground
    pepper

TECHNIQUES

Rouille **147**
Cutting fish and shellfish into
    chunks **71**

CHEF'S NOTES

– Professionals fillet the fish
instead of slicing it. If you opt
for this technique, prepare a
fumet to cook the fish. This
method will take longer, but
there will be no solid residue
from the fish bones.

Prepare and trim the fish and rinse them under cold water. You
may leave them in the sink with the tap running until the water
is perfectly clear while you prepare your vegetables. Cut the fish
into chunks.

Dice the aromatic vegetables (onions, carrots, leeks, tomatoes,
celery, and fennel) finely to make a mirepoix. Sweat them in
olive oil or butter.

Add the chunks of fish. Pour in 8 cups (2 liters) of water and the
white wine. Add the bouquet garni, garlic, tomato paste, and
saffron and bring to a boil. Boil over high heat for 30–40 minutes,
skimming when necessary.

Remove the bouquet garni. Blend the soup with an immersion
blender or in a food processor and then process it through a
food mill. (This will take care of any fish bones, while leaving
the soup relatively thick.) Adjust the seasoning.

Prepare the accompanying garnishes: slices of bread or
croutons dabbed with olive oil, toasted and rubbed with a garlic
clove (shoot removed); grated cheese, and rouille sauce.

Serve in a soup tureen or individual bowls.

DID YOU KNOW?

From north to south, France offers many different types of fish soup.

Quiche Lorraine ✳

SERVES 8

Preparation: **40 minutes**
Baking: **30 minutes**

INGREDIENTS

Shortcrust pastry
2 ½ cups (250 g) all-purpose
   flour
1 egg yolk
1 stick (125 g) butter
Fine sea salt

¾ cup (200 ml) milk
¾ cup (200 ml) cream
2 eggs plus 1 egg yolk
A little grated nutmeg
7 oz. (200 g) bacon
4 oz. (120 g) grated Gruyère
   cheese or similar
Fine sea salt, freshly ground
   pepper

TECHNIQUES

Shortcrust pastry (*pâte brisée*)
   14
Savory custard base for baking
   132

CHEF'S NOTE

– Quiches can be made a day
ahead.

Prepare the shortcrust pastry (see p. 14).
Sift the flour and salt together. Make a well in the center and
incorporate the egg yolk, cubed butter, and 3 ⅓ tablespoons
(50 ml) water. Work rapidly with your fingertips to combine the
ingredients so that the dough does not become elastic. Form it
into a ball. Press it down with the palm of your hand so that it is
smooth. Chill for 30 minutes, covered in plastic wrap.

Roll out the dough very thinly, to a thickness of about ⅛ in.
(3 mm). Drape it over a rolling pin and transfer it to a tart dish.
Trim the edges, making a decorative border.

Combine the milk, cream, eggs, egg yolk, and nutmeg together
well, but make sure the mixture does not become foamy. Season
with salt and pepper. Strain through a chinois, cover with
plastic wrap, and chill.

Remove the hard rind from the bacon and dice it into small
pieces. Place the diced bacon bits in a pot with cold water and
blanch them. Allow to boil briefly and drain well.

Preheat the oven to 350°F (180°C).

Arrange the bacon pieces on the tart base. Fill the base with the
egg mixture. Spread out the grated Gruyère cheese over the
mixture. Bake immediately for 25–30 minutes, until the top just
starts to brown and the base is done.

It's best to cut the quiche at the table and to serve it warm.

DID YOU KNOW?

There are many variations on this recipe, which may call for vegetables,
meat, or fish.

Sweetbread vol-au-vents with cider and apples ✳✳

SERVES 8

Preparation: **55 minutes**
Cooking: **2 hours 10 minutes**

INGREDIENTS

1 ¾ lb. (800 g) sweetbreads
½ small carrot (1 ½ oz./40 g)
½ onion
½ small leek (1 oz./30 g), white only
1 bouquet garni
²/₃ cup (150 ml) hard cider
¾ cup (200 ml) brown veal stock, bound
10 oz. (300 g) Savoy cabbage
2 generous tablespoons (35 g) unsalted butter
2 apples (7 oz./200 g)
2 teaspoons (10 ml) calvados or other apple brandy
1 ½ tablespoons (20 g) sugar
½ lb. (250 g) puff pastry (see p. 19)
1 egg, beaten
Fine sea salt, freshly ground pepper

Special equipment: an ovenproof sauté pan with lid

TECHNIQUES

Brown stock **140**
Shredding (chiffonade) **58**
Scooping **62**
Puff pastry **19**

CHEF'S NOTE

– Vary the fillings: try sautéed mushrooms, fruit, or heirloom vegetables.

Place the sweetbreads in cold water and bring to a boil to blanch them. Allow to boil for 5 minutes. Remove the white membrane.

Preheat the oven to 350–400°F (180–200°C).

Finely dice the aromatic vegetables (carrots, onions, and leeks) to make a mirepoix. Allow the sweetbreads to color lightly in a pan, making sure that all sides are evenly done. Remove the sweetbreads and clean the pan of excess fat. Sweat the aromatic vegetables and the bouquet garni, and then cover with the cider. Turn the heat to high and reduce the liquid by half. Return the sweetbreads to the pan and pour in enough thickened brown veal stock to half cover the sweetbreads. Place the pan in the oven for 1 hour with the lid on. Turn the sweetbreads over after 30 minutes.

Remove the sweetbreads from the pan and tent under aluminum foil to keep them warm. Skim the fat from the braising liquid. Return the pot to the stove top and turn the heat to high. Reduce the braising liquid until it is thick enough to coat the back of a spoon. Strain through cheesecloth or a very fine-mesh sieve. Adjust the seasoning.

Pick the leaves off the cabbage and wash them. Roll them up and cut them into a chiffonade (see p. 58). Braise in butter with the seasoning. Scoop out small balls from the apples (see p. 62). Sauté the apple balls in hot butter. Flambé them with the calvados and sprinkle with a little sugar. Set aside.

Preheat the oven to 350°F (180°C). Cut out sixteen rounds of puff pastry, each with a diameter of about 3–3 ½ in. (8–9 cm). Using a smaller pastry cutter with a diameter of about 2–2 ½ in. (5–6 cm), cut out disks from the center of eight of the pastry rounds to make the tops of your vol-au-vents. Place the eight large disks on a baking tray and baste them with the beaten egg. Place the disks with the cut-out directly over them and baste these with the egg. Bake the puff pastry disks for 20 minutes. Then bake the smaller tops, which will be ready in less time.

Dice the sweetbreads and combine the cubes with the apple scoops. Place the cabbage at the bottom of each vol-au-vent and then fill with the sweetbread and apple scoop mixture. Drizzle with the braising stock.

283

Luted scallops on a bed of vegetables ✳✳

SERVES 6

Preparation: **45 minutes**
Cooking: **45 minutes**

INGREDIENTS

18 scallops in their shells
1 ½ leeks (7 oz./200 g), white
  part only
1 ½ large carrots (7 oz./200 g)
3 tablespoons (40 g) butter
2 oz. (60 g) canned salicornia
  (samphire) (buy online or at
  specialty stores)
7 oz. (200 g) strips of leftover
  puff pastry
1 egg, beaten
½ lb. (250 g) kosher salt
Fine sea salt, freshly ground pepper

Velouté
1 shallot
½ leek (80 g) , white part only
1 ½ tablespoons (20 g) plus
  1 ½ tablespoons (20 g) butter
1 lb. (500 g) fish bones
²⁄₃ cup (150 ml) dry white wine
1 bouquet garni
¼ cup (20 g) flour
Scant ½ cup (100 ml) heavy cream
Fine sea salt, freshly ground pepper

TECHNIQUES

Opening scallops **75**
Velouté **152**
Cutting into julienne strips **61**
Gentle stewing **100**
Luting **105**

CHEF'S NOTES

– Make this dish when scallops
are at the height of their season.
– The coral can also be added to
the scallop.

Open the shells (see p. 75).
Scrub the scallops and the beards. Wash several times,
particularly the beards, to rid them of all sand. Wash six shells
and place them in hot water for a few minutes.

Prepare the velouté (see p. 152).
Chop the shallot and finely slice the leek. Sweat them in
1 ½ tablespoons (20 g) butter. Add the scallop beards and the
fish bones. Pour in the white wine and reduce by half. Pour in
¾ cup (200 ml) water and add the bouquet garni. Simmer for
30 minutes, skimming whenever necessary. Strain the liquid
through a chinois. Reduce it until you have 1 cup (250 ml) of
fumet. Thicken with a roux (see p. 152) made with
1 ½ tablespoons (20 g) butter and ¼ cup (20 g) flour, add the
cream, and season.

Slit the white of the leek lengthwise and wash well. Peel and
wash the carrots. Slice them to make julienne strips (see p. 61).
Gently stew the julienne strips (see p. 100) in butter and season.
Add the salicornia (samphire).

Preheat the oven to 350°F (180°C).

Spread the softened vegetables out in the shells. Place three
scallops in each shell, slicing the larger ones if necessary, add
2 tablespoons of the velouté, and close.

Cut out strips of leftover puff pastry measuring 8 × 1 ¼ in. (20 ×
3 cm). Baste both sides of the strips with beaten egg and apply
tightly to seal the shells. Prepare small heaps of kosher salt on a
baking sheet. Place the scallop shells on the heaps of salt,
ensuring that they are perfectly horizontal—apply a little
pressure if necessary—so that they stay sealed. Cook for about
10 minutes.

Arrange them on flat plates. Your guests will cut open the
pastry seal themselves to savor the aromas.

Sesame-coated rabbit liver salad ✳

SERVES 4

Preparation: **40 minutes**
Cooking: **10 minutes**

INGREDIENTS

11 oz. (320 g) rabbit livers
¼ cup (1 ½ oz./40 g) sesame
  seeds
1 large sachet (for 4) mesclun
  (including, for example, Batavia
  lettuce hearts, oak leaf lettuce,
  raddichio, and lamb's lettuce)
⅓ cup (1 ½ oz./40 g) walnuts
1 ⅓ tablespoons (20 ml) aged
  wine vinegar
3 tablespoons (40 ml) oil
2 tablespoons (30 g) clarified
  butter
Fine sea salt, freshly ground
  pepper

TECHNIQUE

Vinaigrette **152**

CHEF'S NOTES

– Use the idea for this recipe as
a base for variations with
smoked duck breast, vegetable
sticks, croutons, and more.
– Rabbit liver is more delicate
than chicken liver, and has a
slightly sweet note.

Trim the rabbit livers and season them with salt and pepper. Coat them in sesame seeds.

Wash the green salad leaves, checking that there are no traces of sand and no wilted leaves. Dry well. Chop the nuts roughly and add them to the leaves.

Dissolve a little fine sea salt in the vinegar and season with the freshly ground pepper. Drizzle in the oil, whisking constantly.

Pour the clarified butter into a skillet and sauté the rabbit livers over high heat. Brown them, but do not overcook: they should be slightly pink inside.

Form little mounds with the salad leaves and arrange the warm livers over them. Drizzle with the vinaigrette.

Cheese straws ✳

SERVES 8

Preparation: **35 minutes**
Cooking: **45 minutes**

INGREDIENTS

14 oz. (400 g) puff pastry (see
   recipe p. 19)
7 oz. (200 g) Gruyère cheese,
   grated and then finely chopped
   (for a better texture)

Mornay sauce
2 tablespoons (30 g) butter
$^1/_3$ cup (1 oz./30 g) flour
1 ¼ cups (300 ml) milk
A little grated nutmeg
2 egg yolks
1 ½ oz. ($^1/_3$ cup/40 g) grated
   Gruyère cheese
Fine sea salt, freshly ground
   pepper

TECHNIQUE

Puff pastry **19**

Prepare a Mornay sauce.
Make a white roux with the butter and flour (see velouté recipe, p. 152). Add half of the cold milk and the grated nutmeg. Bring to a boil over high heat, whisking constantly. Pour in the remaining milk and bring back to a boil. Season. Remove from the heat and add the egg yolks, combining well. Stir in the grated Gruyère cheese. Cover with plastic wrap flush with the surface so that a skin does not form. Chill.

Preheat the oven to 375°F (190°C).

Roll out the puff pastry in a rectangle ⅛ in. (3 mm) thick. Spread the chilled Mornay sauce evenly over it. Sprinkle with grated, chopped Gruyère cheese. Cut out thin strips measuring 5 ½ in. × 1 ½ in. (14 cm × 4 cm). Allow 2 straws per person.

Bake for 25–30 minutes and serve immediately.

Mushroom *gougères* ✳ ✳

SERVES 8

Preparation: **40 minutes**
Cooking: **50 minutes**

INGREDIENTS

5 ½ oz. (160 g) button
  mushrooms
1 ⅓ tablespoons (20 g) butter
4 oz. (120 g) smoked bacon
3 ½ oz. (100 g) grated Gruyère
  cheese
Fine sea salt, freshly ground
  pepper

Choux pastry
1 ¾ cups (180 g) flour
²/₃ cup (150 ml) water
²/₃ cup (150 ml) milk
7 tablespoons (100 g) unsalted
  butter
4 eggs
Fine sea salt, freshly ground
  pepper

Béchamel sauce
1 tablespoon (15 g) butter
2 ½ tablespoons (15 g) flour
1 cup (250 ml) milk
A little grated nutmeg
Fine sea salt, freshly ground
  pepper

TECHNIQUES

Choux pastry **22**
Béchamel or white sauce **133**
Cutting into julienne strips **61**

Prepare the choux pastry (see p. 22).
Sift the flour. In a pot, bring the water, milk, salt, and cubed butter to a boil. Remove from the heat and add the flour all at once. Return to the heat and stir vigorously with a spatula to dry out the mixture. Transfer it to a bowl. When it is tepid, incorporate the eggs, one by one, mixing them in with the spatula. Season with pepper.

Prepare the béchamel sauce (see p. 133).
Make a white roux with the butter and flour. Add half of the cold milk and the grated nutmeg. Bring to a boil over high heat, whisking constantly. Pour in the other half of the milk and bring back to a boil. Remove from the heat and season.

Clean the mushrooms and cut them into julienne strips. Sauté them in sizzling butter and season them.

Remove the rind from the bacon and dice it finely.

Preheat the oven to 375°F (190°C). Lightly butter a baking sheet. Make sure there is no steam in the oven from previous use—the oven must be perfectly dry to bake the choux pastry. Combine the choux pastry, the béchamel sauce, the mushrooms, bacon bits, and Gruyère. Spoon the mixture into a piping bag without a nozzle. The hole should have a diameter of just under ½ in. (1 cm). Pipe out the mixture onto the baking sheet to form a crown shape. To make the task easier, trace out a circle on a piece of parchment paper. Pipe out the first circle. Just inside that circle, and touching it, pipe out a second circle of mixture. Pipe out a third circle just above them that overlaps the two others.

Bake for 25–30 minutes. As soon as it is done, place it on a round serving dish and cut slices as they are required. Alternatively, prepare individual *gougères* in buttered ramekins and reduce the cooking time accordingly. Be careful to fill the ramekins no more than two-thirds full as this mixture will rise.

DID YOU KNOW?

This recipe highlights the versatility of choux pastry, also used to make the cheese *gougères* that accompany wine-tasting in Burgundy.

Provençal-style sardine *tartes fines* ✳ ✳

SERVES 8

Preparation: **1 hour 45 minutes**
Resting: **1 hour**
Marinating: **1 hour**
Cooking: **45 minutes**

INGREDIENTS

8 fresh sardines
3 tablespoons (40 ml) olive oil
Juice of 1 lemon
1 teaspoon *herbes de Provence*
1 lemon, for garnish
Fleur de sel, freshly ground
    pepper

Puff pastry
3 cups (300 g) flour
Generous ½ cup (130 ml) water
7 ½ oz. (200 g) puff pastry
    margarine or 1 ¾ sticks (200 g)
    butter
1 teaspoon (5 g) salt

Chopped tomatoes
1 ¾ lb. (800 g) tomatoes (about
    eight)
1 shallot
3 tablespoons (40 ml) olive oil
2 garlic cloves
1 teaspoon *herbes de Provence*
Fine sea salt, freshly ground
    pepper

TECHNIQUES

Puff pastry **19**
Peeling using hot water **63**
Filleting a fish (two round, flat
    fillets) **72**

Prepare the puff pastry (see p. 19).
Sift the flour and salt together and make a well in the center. Add the water. Work rapidly to combine the ingredients into a smooth dough, the *détrempe*, which is the base for your puff pastry, and chill for about 20 minutes. Bring the butter to the same consistency as the dough mixture (see pp. 18–19). Now roll out the dough mixture to form a cross shape, leaving the center—where you will place the butter—about ¹/₅ in. or 5 mm thicker than the four other parts. Place the butter in the center of the dough and wrap it with the four other sections so that it is completely enclosed. Roll out the dough to form a rectangle whose length is three times greater than its width. Fold it in three, rotate it a quarter-turn and repeat the procedure five times—a total of six—chilling it for 20 minutes after you have rolled it out and folded twice.

Preheat the oven to 350°F (180°C).

Cut out eight ovals about 5 ½ in. (14–15 cm) long. Prick them with a fork and bake for 15 minutes.

Peel the tomatoes (see p. 63). Cut them in two, between the stem and the incision you have made. Squeeze the halves in the palm of your hand to eliminate the seeds and dice the flesh.

Finely chop the shallot and sweat it in the olive oil. Add the diced tomatoes. Remove the shoot from the garlic cloves and chop them. Add the cloves with the *herbes de Provence* to the tomatoes. Allow the mixture to stew gently over low heat for 30 minutes. Season with salt and pepper.

Clean and fillet the sardines (see p. 72). Season the fillets with *fleur de sel* and ground pepper. Marinate them in the olive oil, lemon juice, and *herbes de Provence* for 1 hour in the refrigerator.

Spread the chopped tomatoes over the puff pastry ovals. Drain the sardine fillets and arrange them over the chopped tomatoes. Garnish with a lemon wedge.

Fish terrine with beurre blanc ✳✳

SERVES 8

Preparation: **50 minutes**
Cooking: **50 minutes**

INGREDIENTS

10 oz. (300 g) whiting fillets
10 oz. (300 g) salmon fillets
2 egg whites
1 ½ cups (350 ml) whipping
  cream
Pinch of ground turmeric
1 ⅓ tablespoons (20 g) butter
1 lemon, for garnish
Fine sea salt, freshly ground
  white pepper

Beurre blanc
2 shallots
Scant ½ cup (100 ml) white wine
7 tablespoons (100 g) salted
  butter, well chilled and cubed

TECHNIQUES

Mousseline stuffing (cream-
  based) **159**
Beurre blanc **134**
Canelling **56**

Prepare the forcemeats of the two fish separately (see p. 159). Remember to use half the ingredients (egg white, cream, and butter) for the whiting and the other half for the salmon.

Process the fish fillets using the blade attachment of a food processor and strain the mixture through a fine-mesh sieve. Return it to the bowl of the food processor with the egg white and pulse very briefly (so that no air bubbles form) to incorporate it. Transfer to a stainless steel bowl over an ice bath. Gradually mix in the cream and then season. Add a pinch of ground turmeric to the salmon mixture to heighten its orangey color.

Preheat the oven to 250°F (120°C).

Butter a terrine and layer the two mixtures. You may make either two or four layers altogether. Cook for about 40 minutes; the terrine is done when the tip of a knife comes out clean.

Prepare the beurre blanc (see p. 134).
Finely chop the shallot and place in a small saucepan. Pour in the white wine and reduce over low heat until there is very little liquid left. Whisk in the cold cubed butter.

Arrange the terrine on flat plates. Place a slice of hot terrine on each plate and surround it with a ribbon of beurre blanc. Decorate it with a canelled lemon slice.

Scrambled eggs with a mini-ratatouille ✳

SERVES 4

Preparation: **35 minutes**
Cooking: **30 minutes**

INGREDIENTS

10 eggs
3 tablespoons (40 g) butter
3 tablespoons (40 ml) whipping
  cream
Salt, freshly ground pepper

Ratatouille
½ eggplant (aubergine)
  (3 oz./100 g)
1 medium-sized zucchini
  (courgette) (3 oz./100 g)
1 large onion
1 small red bell pepper
  (3 oz./100 g)
2 garlic cloves, peeled, shoots
  removed
3 oz. (100 g) tomatoes
3 tablespoons (40 ml) olive oil
A sprinkling of *herbes de Provence*
A pinch of ground *piment
  d'Espelette*

TECHNIQUES

Peeling using hot water **63**
Chopping tomatoes **57**
Scrambled eggs **44**

CHEF'S NOTE

– The mini-ratatouille may be
prepared a day ahead, or several
hours before serving.

Wash all the vegetables. Keeping them separate, dice the
eggplant, zucchini, large onion, and red bell peppers finely to
make ⅕ in. (5 mm) cubes. Chop the garlic cloves. Peel the
tomatoes, remove the seeds, and chop them (see p. 57). If you
wish, reserve the skins to fry for garnish.

Combine all the ingredients in a pot, add the oil and the *herbes
de Provence*, and leave to simmer on very low heat for about
30 minutes. Season with salt and *piment d'Espelette*.

Prepare the scrambled eggs (see p. 44).
Break the eggs into a round-bottomed mixing bowl. Season and
beat them with a fork or a whisk. Melt half of the butter in the
pan over low heat. Pour the eggs into the hot pan. Stir
constantly with a spatula or wooden spoon. The final texture
should be creamy. Remove from the heat and stir in the
remaining butter, and/or cream. Keep warm at a temperature of
122°F (50°C) maximum.

Serve in a dish or on individual plates.

Onion soup ✳

SERVES 8

Preparation: **10 minutes**
Cooking: **1 hour**

INGREDIENTS

1 ¼ lb. (600 g) large onions
3 tablespoons (50 g) butter
10 cups (2 liters) clear white
   stock (ready-to-use mix or
   recipe p. 138)
1 bouquet garni
16 slices of baguette, toasted
   to make croutons
5 oz. (140 g) grated Gruyère
   cheese
Kosher salt to taste
Fine salt, freshly ground pepper

TECHNIQUES

Cutting round slices **58**
White stock **138**

CHEF'S NOTE

– It's the quality of the clear
stock that will determine the
final taste of the soup. Adding a
slice of bacon when you begin
cooking will bring a pleasant
rustic taste to your dish.

Peel, wash, and slice the onions. Sweat them in butter.

Add the light white stock, the bouquet garni, and the kosher salt. Simmer for 45 minutes to 1 hour. Adjust the seasoning. Set your oven to broil.

Pour the broth into individual ovenproof bowls. Place two croutons in each bowl of soup and sprinkle with the grated cheese. Place in the oven until a gratin crust forms on top.

Pissaladière ✳ ✳

SERVES 8

Preparation: **30 minutes**
Resting: **about 2 hours**
Cooking: **1 hour 10 minutes**

INGREDIENTS

Bread dough with olive oil
2 cups (250 g) all-purpose flour
²/₃ cup (150 ml) lukewarm water
¹/₆ oz. (6 g) fresh (compressed)
 yeast
1 teaspoon (5 g) salt
4 teaspoons (20 ml) olive oil

Toppings
2 ¼ lb. (1 kg) fresh white onions
3 ½ tablespoons (50 ml) olive oil
2 ½ teaspoons (10 g) sugar
1 generous tablespoon (2 g)
 herbes de Provence
Freshly ground pepper
3 ½ tablespoons (50 ml) water
12 salt-packed anchovies
1 pinch dried thyme and/or
 herbes de Provence
12 small black Niçoise olives

CHEF'S NOTES

– When you place the
pissaladière in the oven, you can
spray a little water inside to
create steam, which helps the
dough rise in the oven and
ensures a thin, crispy crust.
– The anchovies add plenty of
salt to the onions, so there is no
need to add more. Sugar is
recommended to balance the
onions' acidity.

Prepare the bread dough with olive oil.
Place the flour, water, and yeast in the bowl of a stand mixer
fitted with the dough hook. Knead for 2 minutes on speed 1,
then let rest for 45 minutes (autolyze). Knead for 10 minutes on
speed 2 until the dough is smooth and elastic. Add a little
lukewarm water if needed, but take care not to add too much:
the dough should be firm, not sticky. Two minutes before the
end of the kneading time, add the salt and olive oil. Transfer to
a large bowl and cover with a clean tea towel. Let rise for 35–40
minutes, or until nearly doubled in size, depending on the room
temperature (bulk fermentation). Brush a baking sheet with
olive oil and line it with parchment paper. Roll out the dough to
fit the baking sheet and let it rise (proof) for about 40 minutes.

Prepare the toppings.
Peel the onions and cut them crosswise into rounds, ⅛–¼ inches
(3–5 mm) thick. Warm the olive oil over low heat in a large
skillet or Dutch oven. Add the onions, sugar, and *herbes de
Provence* and season with pepper. Add the 3 ½ tbsp (50 ml)
water to encourage the onions to soften. Cover and cook,
stirring regularly, until the onions are fall-apart tender and
lightly golden, but not caramelized (about 30 minutes). Let
cook uncovered for the final 10 minutes to allow excess liquid to
evaporate. Cooking the onions just right is the key to a
successful pissaladière. Remove from the heat, stir in half the
anchovies, and let sit for about 15 minutes to allow them to
dissolve. Let cool completely.

Preheat the oven to 430°F (220°C).

Spread the onion mixture across the dough and smooth over to
make an even layer. Sprinkle with the thyme and/or *herbes de
Provence*. Cut the remaining anchovies in half lengthwise and
arrange them over the onions in a crosshatch pattern. Scatter
the olives harmoniously over the onions and drizzle with olive
oil. Bake for 25–30 minutes, until the crust is golden all over.
Serve with a frisée salad, if you wish.

DID YOU KNOW?

Pissaladière is a specialty of the Nice region. It can be eaten warm or at
room temperature.

Olive fougasse ✳ ✳

SERVES 8

Preparation: **25 minutes**
Resting: **1 hour 35 minutes**
Cooking: **20 minutes**

INGREDIENTS

Dough
3 ¼ cups (400 g) all-purpose
flour
½ oz. (14 g) fresh (compressed)
yeast
1 cup (250 ml) lukewarm water
2 ¼ teaspoons (12 g) salt
3 ½ tablespoons (50 ml) olive oil
5 ¼ oz. (150 g) pitted green
olives
5 ¼ oz. (150 g) pitted black
olives

Toppings
2 ½ tablespoons (40 ml) olive oil
2 teaspoons (2 g) oregano
1 teaspoon (5 g) *fleur de sel*

TECHNIQUES

Cutting into fine dice
(*brunoise*) **64**

CHEF'S NOTE

– Fougasses come in many
different varieties today. Popular
flavorings include onions,
bacon, honey, and sesame
seeds.

Prepare the dough.

Place the flour, water, and yeast in the bowl of a stand mixer
fitted with the dough hook. Knead for 2 minutes on speed 1,
then let the dough rest for 45 minutes (autolyze). Knead for 10
minutes on speed 2 until the dough is smooth and elastic. Add a
little lukewarm water if needed, but take care not to add too
much: the dough should be firm, not sticky. Two minutes before
the end of the kneading time, add the salt and olive oil. Transfer
the dough to a large bowl and cover with a clean tea towel. Let
rise for 1 hour, or until doubled in size, depending on the room
temperature (bulk fermentation).

Finely dice (*brunoise*) the green and black olives and gently
knead them into the dough. Divide the dough into four equal
pieces. On a floured surface, shape each piece into an oval,
4 ¾ inches (12 cm) in diameter and ¾–1 ¼ inches (2–3 cm) thick.
Using scissors or a new box cutter blade, cut slits in the dough
to form a wheat-stalk shape.

Place the fougasses on a baking sheet greased with oil, dust the
surface with a little flour, and cover with a clean tea towel. Let
rise (proof) for 40–50 minutes in a warm place.

Meanwhile, preheat the oven to 410°F (210°C).

Brush the fougasses with the olive oil and sprinkle with the
oregano and *fleur de sel*. Bake for 20–25 minutes, until golden
all over. Let cool on a rack.

DID YOU KNOW?

The name "fougasse" comes from the old Occitan word "*fogatza*," which
meant "bread baked under the ashes." Traditional flavorings include
onions, olives, anchovies, and bacon. In the Southern Alps (Aigues-
Mortes), bakers make a sweet version.

Creamed lettuce soup (*velouté Choisy*) ✳

SERVES 8

Preparation: **35 minutes**
Cooking: **40 minutes**

INGREDIENTS

2 ½ lettuces
2 leek whites (200 g)
5 ½ tablespoons (80 g) butter,
  for the leeks
Generous ¾ cup (80 g) flour
9 cups (2 ¼ liters) clear white
  veal stock
⅔ cup (150 ml) heavy cream
2 egg yolks
2 tablespoons (30 g) butter
  for the lettuce chiffonade
8 slices sandwich loaf
Oil for frying
A few sprigs chervil, for garnish
Salt, freshly ground pepper

TECHNIQUE

Shredding (chiffonade) **58**

CHEF'S NOTE

– Use this recipe with other
vegetables, such as broccoli,
cauliflower, and zucchini
(courgette).

Remove and discard the hearts of two of the lettuces and blanch the leaves whole. Peel, wash, and cut the leek whites. Sweat the leek white in the butter. Add the flour and stir with a spatula. Pour in the veal stock and bring the liquid to a boil, stirring constantly. Add the blanched lettuce leaves. Cook for 30–45 minutes, until the lettuce is cooked. Process or blend and strain through a chinois.

Combine the cream and egg yolks and mix into the strained soup in a mixing bowl to thicken it. Season with salt and pepper.

Cut the half lettuce into a chiffonade. Sweat the chiffonade briefly in the butter. Add it to the velouté.

Cut the bread into small cubes (less than ½ in./1 cm). Fry them in a pan and drain on paper towel.

Pour the soup into a soup plate or tureen. Garnish with a nice sprig of chervil and a few croutons.

DID YOU KNOW?

Any dish that bears the name "Choisy" contains lettuce as its predominant ingredient. A Choisy omelet is filled with creamed shredded lettuce, while a Sole Choisy is garnished with julienned lettuce.

Fish and Shellfish

Gérald Passédat

presents his recipe

With the sea lapping three of France's long coasts, it is only natural that fish plays a primordial role in our culinary heritage, and our deep-rooted traditions of cooking fish—fish soups, in particular—certainly owe a great deal to geography. Each port, no matter its size, has a worthy variation on the theme, so we can sample a bouillabaisse at one, a *cotriade* at another, and a *matelote* elsewhere.

I have adopted the Mediterranean as my own. It is vital to me, providing me with not only peace and tranquility, but the fish of its coastlines and its depths. I share much with the fishermen who work it and respect it, and with them, I endeavor to protect it, supporting those who practice long-line fishing. I marvel when I discover humble, often long-forgotten fish such as the dentex, the prosaically named axillary sea bream, whose French name literally means "lovely eyes," and ocean catfish or sea bass, whose flavors are heightened by a light cuisine. Their rich textures and their wide range of flavors mean that I can give free rein to my imagination. Nature offers itself up to us on condition that we respect it, and I pick from my marine garden to serve dishes every day with the conviction that I am a mere link in a chain whose origin starts in the depths.

SERVES 4

Preparation: **2 hours**
Cooking: **40 minutes**

INGREDIENTS

1 sea bass weighing
   3 lb. 5 oz. (1.5 kg)
3 lemons
4 ripe vine tomatoes
2 stalks (20 g) basil
2 stalks (20 g) cilantro
   (coriander)
1 truffle weighing ²⁄₃ oz.
   (20 g)
1 cucumber
2 zucchini
3 tablespoons (50 ml)
   clarified butter
1 green tomato
2 pinches (2 g) wild
   fennel seeds
Olive oil
Mignonette pepper
Fleur de sel (preferably
   from Camargue)
Scant ½ cup (100 ml)
   truffle jus

Fish fumet
Bones of the sea bass
1 cup (250 ml) olive oil
6 cups (1.5 liters) water
1 shallot
1 carrot
½ leek
1 bouquet garni

Lucie's base
14 oz. (400 g) tomatoes
   (fresh off the stalk or
   beefsteak tomato,
   "coeur de boeuf"
   if possible)
1 teaspoon (5 ml)
   tomato paste
½ teaspoon (2.5 g)
   sugar
1 teaspoon (8 g)
   coriander seeds

Sea bass,
the way Lucie Passédat liked it

To prepare the fish
Remove the scales of the fish, gut it, and wash it. Prepare the fillets, removing the bones. Set them aside to use for the fish fumet. Slice the two fillets to make four equal servings of 5 ½ oz. (160 g). Make shallow, regular incisions in the skin.

Fish fumet
Prepare the aromatic garnish. Wash, peel, and chop the shallot, carrot, and leek half. Prepare the bouquet garni.

Crush the fish bones and sauté them with the olive oil. Add the garnish and pour in the water. Cook for 20 minutes, strain through a chinois, and set aside. You should have 4 ¾ cups (1.2 liters) clear fumet; keep 4 cups (1 liter) for Lucie's base and the remainder to cook the fish.

Lucie's base
Place 4 cups fish fumet in a pot with the chopped tomatoes, tomato paste, sugar, and coriander seeds and reduce by half. Strain through a chinois and set aside. This is the base.

While it is reducing, prepare the lemon zest of one lemon: dice it into a fine *brunoise*, blanch it 3 times, and refresh. Set the diced zest aside.

Peel four vine tomatoes and dice them to make a *brunoise*. Prepare the leaves of the basil and cilantro (fresh coriander). Wash and chop the leaves. Squeeze the other two lemons.

Prepare the four truffle shavings and cut them into round disks with a small pastry cutter. Dice the trimmings into a *brunoise*. Set aside.

Peel the cucumber and use a mandoline or peeler to cut the tagliatelle-shaped strips from the flesh. Do the same with the zucchini skin. Work carefully so that they are all nicely shaped and the same size.

Blanch them and refresh. Line a pan with parchment paper and arrange the vegetable tagliatelle on it, alternating seven zucchini skins with six cucumber strips.

Brush a stainless steel ovenproof dish with clarified butter and season it with salt and pepper.

Arrange the slices of green tomato and sea bass fillets in the dish, and season with the wild fennel seeds, olive oil, Camargue salt and mignonette pepper. Pour the reserved fish fumet over and cook for 12 minutes in a steam oven at 140°F (60°C), or use a steam cooker. When done, allow it to rest.

To assemble and serve
Take Lucie's base and add the chopped cilantro (coriander) and basil, diced lemon zest, tomato cubes, truffle *brunoise*, olive oil, juice of two lemons, and the truffle jus. Adjust the seasoning with salt and pepper. Re-heat slightly but do not allow to boil.

Place the vegetable tagliatelle on the cooked fish. Reheat slightly over steam. Take four truffle shavings, brush them with olive oil, and season them with salt and pepper. Reheat them in the oven at 300°F (150°C) and then place them carefully on the fish pieces just before serving.

Pour the base into soup plates, place the fish in this, drizzle the vegetable tagliatelle and base with a little olive oil. Sprinkle with a little Camargue salt or *fleur de sel*.

Dogfish stew in red wine with Brussels sprouts ✳✳

SERVES 8

Preparation: **1 hour 10 minutes**
Marinating: **3 hours minimum**
Cooking: **50 minutes**

INGREDIENTS

3 ½ lb. (1.6 kg) dogfish
4 oz. (120 g) bacon bits
Scant ²/₃ cup (60 g) flour
  (optional)
10 oz. (300 g) button mushrooms
3 tablespoons (40 ml) cognac
1 bouquet garni
1 oz. (30 g) beurre manié (see
  p. 155)
8 slices sandwich loaf
4 garlic cloves
2 lb. 4 oz. (1 kg) Brussels sprouts
1 tablespoon (15 g) butter
Fine salt, freshly ground pepper

Marinade
1 shallot
2 oz. (60 g) garlic chives or
  1 large white onion
4 garlic cloves
1 small carrot (2 oz./60 g)
1 bouquet garni
1 bunch of assorted fresh herbs,
  such as flat-leaf parsley, chives,
  thyme, and summer savory
½ teaspoon (2 g) peppercorns
4 cups (1 liter) red wine
Scant ½ cup (100 ml) cognac

Fumet
1 shallot
4 tablespoons (60 g) butter
1 lb. 5 oz. (600 g) fish bones
1 bouquet garni

TECHNIQUES

Raw marinade **144**
Fumet **141**
Quartering button mushrooms **60**
Beurre manié **155**

A day ahead (ideally), prepare the fish and marinade (see p. 144). Slice the dogfish into eight equal portions. Make a few incisions on the back so that the pieces do not curl up during cooking.

Peel and wash the vegetables for the marinade and slice them finely. Place half the vegetables at the bottom of a baking dish and arrange the pieces of fish over them. Then put in the other half of the vegetables with the dried and fresh herbs and peppercorns. Cover with the wine and cognac. Cover the dish with plastic wrap and chill for at least 3 hours. Drain the fish pieces over a bowl, and strain the marinade through a chinois. Use it to make a fumet (see p. 141). Rinse the fish bones well and sweat them together with the chopped shallot in butter. Pour in the wine and the marinade and add the bouquet garni. Cook over high heat for 30 minutes, skimming when necessary.

Preheat the oven to 325°F–350°F (160°C–170°C). In another pan, sauté the bacon bits without adding any fat. (At this point, if you have not marinated the fish, coat it in flour to add taste to the dish and thicken the sauce.) Quarter the mushrooms (see p. 60) and add them to sweat briefly. Flambé the ingredients with the cognac and then pour in the fumet. Add the fish pieces and bouquet garni, cover with a lid, and cook in the oven for 20–25 minutes. Remove the fish pieces and the bouquet garni. Reduce the cooking liquid by half over medium heat. Thicken the liquid with beurre manié (see p. 155) and adjust the seasoning.

Make the croutons: rub slices of toasted sandwich loaf with garlic.

Remove the outer leaves of the Brussels sprouts, wash, and boil them. Refresh immediately under cold water. Coat the Brussels sprouts with a knob of butter and season them.

Arrange the slices of dogfish in soup plates and pour the sauce over. Scatter the croutons in the plates.

DID YOU KNOW?

This dish is a specialty of the Bordeaux region, which enjoys a rich variety of fish, both sea and fresh water, as well as fish that migrate up river, such as the somewhat unappealingly named dogfish (also known as rock salmon). Its flesh withstands relatively longer cooking times and goes well with a robust wine—Bordeaux red is, of course, ideal. Eel and lamprey are equally good in this recipe.

Trout with almonds ✳

SERVES 6

Preparation: **25 minutes**
Cooking: **20 minutes**

INGREDIENTS

6 trout weighing about ½ lb.
  (250 g) each
1 cup (100 g) flour
$^1/_3$ cup (80 g) clarified butter
4 tablespoons (60 g) salted butter
1 cup (4 oz./100 g) sliced
  almonds
Juice of 1 lemon
½ bunch parsley, chopped
Fine salt, freshly ground pepper

Special equipment: oval frying
  pan

TECHNIQUE

Sauté meunière **123**

Dress the trout and dry them well, dabbing up all excess moisture with paper towel.

Spread out the flour in a conveniently sized flat dish and season it. Dip the trout in to coat. Shake lightly to remove any excess flour.

Heat an oval non-stick pan with the clarified butter over low to medium heat. Place the trout in the pan and gently brown them. Turn over and brown lightly on the other side. Check for doneness (the flesh should come away easily from the bone) and, if necessary place them in the oven at 325°F–350°F (160°C–170°C) for a few minutes to complete cooking.

Remove the skin.

Melt some butter in a small pan until it is brown (beurre noisette). Gently sauté the sliced almonds in the butter and deglaze with the lemon juice.

Arrange the trout on a large, flat serving platter, heads to the left.

Drizzle with the butter-almond mixture and scatter with chopped parsley.

Aniseed-flambéed sea bream ✳

SERVES 4

Preparation: **20 minutes**
Cooking: **25 minutes**

INGREDIENTS

2 gilthead sea bream (*Sparus
    aurata*) weighing about 1 ½ lb.
    (700 g) each
6 sprigs dill
4 star anise
A little olive oil
Scant ½ cup pastis (the French
    aniseed-flavored aperitif, similar
    to raki and ouzo)
Fine salt, freshly ground pepper

TECHNIQUE

Roasting **120**

CHEF'S NOTE

– Rice flavored with turmeric or
sautéed potatoes make good
sides for this fish dish.

Prepare the sea bream: remove the fins and scales, and gut them.

Preheat the oven to 325°F (160°C). Grease a baking tray.

Chop the dill and crush the star anise. Combine with salt and pepper. Fill the sea bream with this mixture. Arrange the sea bream on the baking tray. Use a brush to coat them with oil and season them with salt and pepper. Cook for 20–25 minutes.

Just before serving, flambé them with a generous dose of pastis.

Cut the sea bream, making sure you remove all the bones.

Serve nice and hot with a beurre blanc sauce (see p. 134) or a hollandaise sauce (see p. 150).

Fish papillotes with vegetable scoops ✶✶

Filleting a fish (two round, flat fillets) 72
Scooping 62
Gentle stewing 100
Cooking en papillote 107

SERVES 4

Preparation: **45 minutes**
Cooking: **25 minutes**

INGREDIENTS

2 whole whiting
14 oz. (400 g) fresh cod
1 turnip (5 oz./140 g)
2 carrots (5 oz./140 g)
2 small zucchini (5 oz./140 g)
3 tablespoons (40 ml) olive oil
1 egg white
6 sprigs dill
3 ½ tablespoons (45 ml) fish glaze (reduced fish fumet)
¼ cup (50 ml) Noilly Prat (white vermouth)
Fleur de sel
Fine salt, freshly ground pepper

TECHNIQUES

Filleting a fish (two round, flat fillets) **72**
Scooping **62**
Gentle stewing **100**
Cooking en papillote **107**

CHEF'S NOTES

– Most fish fillets can be prepared in papillotes.
– The vegetables can also be cut into julienne strips, diced, or finely sliced.

Trim and fillet the whiting and the cod (see p. 72). Remove the bones and cut portions weighing about 3 oz. (80 g) each.

Wash the vegetables. Peel the turnips and carrots. Leave the zucchini unpeeled. Using a small scoop, prepare the vegetable balls (see p. 62), keeping the three vegetables separate. Rinse to remove any residue. Braise the vegetables (separately) in a little olive oil and just enough water to half cover them. Season with salt and pepper.

Preheat the oven to 325°F (160°C).

Lightly whisk the egg whites with a pinch of salt using a fork.

Cut out parchment paper rectangles measuring 14 × 10 inches (35 × 25 cm). Fold in half lengthwise. Place two fish fillets, one of each kind, in the center of the bottom half of parchment paper and season with salt and pepper. Arrange a few sprigs of dill over the fillets and drizzle with the fish glaze and Noilly Prat. Now arrange a few of the vegetables scoops over the fillets, setting aside the rest to serve separately. Using a pastry brush, wet the edge of the parchment paper with the egg white. Fold the paper over and make a small fold at the edges. Keep in place with paper clips.

Place the papillotes on a baking tray and cook for 8–10 minutes.

Place each papillote on a plate and serve with a dish of the remaining vegetable scoops. Pass around some *fleur de sel* for each guest to sprinkle.

Salt cod purée (brandade) and mashed potatoes ✳

SERVES 6

Preparation: **35 minutes**
Soaking: **48 hours**
Cooking: **40 minutes**

INGREDIENTS

2 lb. (900 g) salted cod
1 bouquet garni
¼ cup (60 ml) olive oil
2 tablespoons (30 ml) whipping
   cream
Freshly ground pepper

Mashed potatoes
1 ½ lb. (800 g) potatoes
2 garlic cloves, peeled, shoots
   removed
Scant ⅔ cup (150 ml) milk
3 tablespoons (40 g) unsalted
   butter
A little grated nutmeg
1 pinch ground coriander
Freshly ground pepper

CHEF'S NOTE

– If you wish, serve this as a
gratin. Either prepare individual
portions in ramekins or serve in
a large dish, accompanied by a
salad or vegetables.

Soak the cod in cold water or milk for 48 hours to remove some of the salt. Drain the pieces of fish and poach them with the bouquet garni in boiling water for 1–2 minutes. Repeat as many times as you need to remove the excess salt, so taste as you proceed. When the cod is ready, remove the skin and bones and flake it.

Brush the potatoes with a vegetable brush and place them in a pot of cold water to bring to a boil. Cook for about 35 minutes. Peel them and press them through a vegetable mill.

Chop the garlic cloves. Add to the mashed potatoes with the remaining ingredients (milk, butter, grated nutmeg, ground coriander, and freshly ground pepper).

Using a spatula, vigorously stir the cod with the olive oil until it reaches a light texture. Thin with the cream and incorporate the mashed potatoes. Adjust the seasoning.

DID YOU KNOW?

The brandade—puréed salt cod, cream or milk, and olive oil—is a typical dish of the southern French regions of Languedoc and Provence, with regional variations that may or may not include garlic. Antoine Augustin Parmentier (1737–1813) was the man responsible for promoting the potato in France; it was intended to complement cereal production, which was more likely to suffer in difficult climatic conditions. He had soup kitchens opened in Paris where potato soup was served, and had an all-potato meal prepared for Benjamin Franklin. A number of dishes in which potatoes play a key role bear his name.

Roasted pike perch with meat jus ✳

SERVES 6

Preparation: **15 minutes**
Cooking: **20 minutes**

INGREDIENTS

2 lb. (1 kg) pike perch fillets
2 ½–3 tablespoons (40 g)
  clarified butter
1 lb. (500 g) assorted grains,
  such as barley, quinoa, wheat,
  and oats
2 ½ tablespoons (40 g) butter
2 cups (500 ml) meat stock,
  broth, or juice
Fine salt, freshly ground pepper

TECHNIQUE

Poaching (cold start): Shallow
  poaching **110**

Preheat the oven to 325°F (160°C).

Prepare fillets weighing about 5 oz. (140–160 g) each.

Butter a roasting tray. Place the fillets on the tray and drizzle the clarified butter over. Season with salt and pepper.

Poach the assortment of grains using the shallow poaching (cold start) technique as indicated on page 110. Add a knob of butter when they are done and season.

Reduce the meat jus until it coats the back of a spoon.

Spoon a layer of grains on each plate and place the pike perch fillets on the top.

Serve the sauce from a bowl.

Langoustine and pineapple skewers ✳

SERVES 6

Preparation: **40 minutes**
Cooking: **35 minutes**

INGREDIENTS

12 langoustines
1 pineapple
18 scallops
Scant ½ cup (100 g) clarified
    butter
5 ½ tablespoons (80 g) butter,
    softened
4 sprigs of tarragon
Five-pepper mix
10 oz. (300 g) quinoa
1 onion, chopped
Fleur de sel, freshly ground
    pepper

TECHNIQUES

Shelling crustaceans **69**
Poaching (cold start): Shallow
    poaching **110**

Shell the langoustines, leaving the heads on.

Peel the pineapple and cut it into large cubes.

Skewer two langoustines and three scallops, alternating them with pineapple cubes onto each of your six skewers. Set aside some pineapple cubes for garnish. Season with salt and pepper. Sauté them in clarified butter over high heat.

Combine the softened butter with the tarragon, setting aside a few leaves for garnish. Season with *fleur de sel* and the five-pepper mixture.

Prepare the quinoa with the chopped onion using the shallow poaching (cold start) technique on p. 110. When it is ready, mix in the tarragon-flavored butter.

Prepare small domes of quinoa and arrange a skewer with a few pineapple cubes attractively scattered on each plate.

Garnish with tarragon leaves.

Sea bass in a salt crust ✳

SERVES 8

Preparation: **25 minutes**
Resting: **15 minutes**
Cooking: **20 minutes**

INGREDIENTS

1 sea bass weighing about 1 ¾ lb.
 (800 g)
Aromatic ingredients, such as dill,
 thyme, or olive oil
½ lb. (250 g) kosher salt
1 cup (3 oz./100 g) flour
1 egg, beaten, plus 3 egg whites
Freshly ground pepper

TECHNIQUE

Cooking in a crust **101**

CHEF'S NOTES

— Use one of any number of
sauces to accompany this dish.
Even a simple squeeze of lemon
juice enhances it wonderfully.
— Do not leave the fish for more
than 15 minutes in the crust
before you cook it, because it
will absorb some of the salt.
— Try to find line-caught sea
bass as it is not damaged when
it is fished and you will be
supporting sustainable fishing
methods.

Remove the scales and fins of the fish and gut it. If you wish, remove the head. Season the cavity with pepper and add other aromatic ingredients if you wish.

Combine the kosher salt with the flour. Make a well in the center. Lightly beat the three egg whites with a fork. Incorporate them into the flour-salt mixture to make a smooth paste. Leave to rest for 15 minutes.

Preheat the oven to 350°F (180°C).

Using a rolling pin, roll the paste out to a thickness of about $\frac{1}{5}$ in. (4 mm). Make sure the paste is long and wide enough to roll around the fish, and seal the edges with a little water or egg white. When you have wrapped the fish, baste the paste with the whole egg.

Cook for 17–20 minutes until the crust turns a light golden color.

Serve immediately. Break the crust at the table and carefully take out the flesh of the fish.

DID YOU KNOW?

Cooking in salt is a technique that originated in ancient China. This method retains the moisture of fish, poultry, and even meat as it cooks. Because the crust is hermetic, all seasoning permeates the food; the crust (pure coarse or kosher salt, or a paste as in this recipe) creates a kiln effect, speeding up the cooking process. Cracking open a salt crust at a dinner table makes for a dramatic effect.

Pollack fillets bonne femme ✳ ✳

SERVES 6

Preparation: **45 minutes**
Cooking: **50 minutes**

INGREDIENTS

1 whole pollack weighing about
  3 ½ lb. (1.5 kg)
1 shallot
4 oz. (120 g) button mushrooms
5–6 sprigs parsley
1 tablespoon (15 g) plus
  3 tablespoons (40 g) butter
1 bouquet garni
²/₃ cup (150 ml) heavy cream

Fumet
About 14 oz. (400 g) fish bones
½ small leek (40 g), white only
1 shallot
½ onion
²/₃ cup (150 ml) white wine
1 bouquet garni
½ teaspoon (2 g) peppercorns

TECHNIQUES

Filleting fish (two round,
  flat fillets) **72**
Fumet **141**
Simple slicing (*émincer
  à la paysanne*) **57**
Poaching (cold start): Shallow
  poaching **110**

CHEF'S NOTES

– To gain time, use a good-
quality dried fumet mix instead
of making it yourself from
scratch.
– This dish is traditionally served
with rice pilaf (see p. 338).

Fillet the pollack and remove the skin. Keep the central bone to use for the fumet. Cut six portions weighing about 5–6 oz. (160 g) each. Prepare the aromatic base: chop the shallot, slice the button mushrooms, and chop the parsley.

Prepare the fumet (see p. 141).
Crush the central bone as well as the other bones, and soak them in cold water to remove any traces of blood. Peel, wash, and finely slice the vegetables (leek, shallot, and onion). Place all the ingredients in a large pot with 1 cup (250 ml) water and bring to a boil, skimming when necessary. Simmer lightly for 25–30 minutes, but do not stir as this would make the fumet cloudy. Strain through a chinois and chill over an ice bath.

Preheat the oven to 250°F (120°C).

Butter the bottom of a flameproof cooking dish or tray with 1 tablespoon (15 g) butter. Arrange the aromatic base in the dish (shallot, button mushrooms, and parsley). Place the fish fillets over the aromatic base and pour in just enough fumet and white wine to half cover the ingredients. Add the bouquet garni. Bring to a simmer over heat and cover with parchment paper. Cook in the oven for a few minutes. Remove the fish and keep it warm. Turn the oven to broil.

To make the sauce, reduce the cooking liquid by 90%. Incorporate the cream and reduce again until thick enough to coat the back of a spoon. Whip in the remaining butter.

Arrange the pollack fillets in a buttered serving dish and pour over the sauce. Reheat the dish in the oven briefly.

DID YOU KNOW?

Bonne femme literally means "good wife," and refers to dishes that are cooked simply, as one would eat them at an everyday family meal.

Steamed pout fillets in lettuce leaves ✳

SERVES 4

Preparation: **35 minutes**
Cooking: **30 minutes**

INGREDIENTS

1 lettuce
1 lb. (500 g) pout (bib) fillets
7 oz. (200 g) Basmati rice
3 tablespoons (45 g) butter, plus
  a little for the rice
½ red cabbage
2 tablespoons (30 ml) red wine
  vinegar
Scant ½ cup (100 ml) water
2 tablespoons (30 g) clarified
  butter
Fleur de sel
Fine salt, freshly ground pepper

TECHNIQUES

Steaming **125**
Cooking in a crust **101**
Poaching (hot start): Deep
  poaching **108**
Gentle stewing **100**

CHEF'S NOTE

– This recipe will work for most
types of fish fillets.

Wash the lettuce leaves. Blanch the larger leaves very briefly—no more than a few seconds—in boiling water. Refresh immediately under very cold water and dry carefully and thoroughly.

Remove the bones from the fish fillets. Season them and wrap them in the lettuce leaves. Steam them (use a steam cooker or steam oven if you have one) for 8–12 minutes.

Cook the basmati rice in boiling water according to instructions. Refresh briefly under cold water, add a knob of butter, and season with salt.

Cut the red cabbage into quarters. Remove the heart and shred the leaves finely.

Melt the 3 tablespoons (40 g) butter in a sauté pan. Add the red cabbage. Deglaze with the red wine vinegar. Add the water, cover with the lid, and leave to braise for about 20 minutes. Season.

Brush the fish fillets in their wrapping with the clarified butter to give them a nice gloss.

Arrange the braised red cabbage in a serving dish or in the plates. Center the fish fillets and sprinkle them with *fleur de sel*.

Bouillabaisse ✳ ✳ ✳

SERVES 8

Preparation: **1 hour**
Cooking: **1 hour 10 minutes**

INGREDIENTS

1 lb. (500 g) conger (sea eel)
2 red gurnards
1 ½ lb. (800 g) John Dory
7 oz. (200 g) crustaceans of your
  choice

Stock
½ large onion
½ leek (50 g), white only
10 oz. (300 g) tomatoes
4 garlic cloves
3 green crabs
Scant ¼ cup (50 ml) olive oil
1 bouquet garni
2 pinches (2 g) ground saffron, or
  8 filaments
Zest of ½ dried orange
Fine salt, freshly ground pepper

Rouille
5 oz. (150 g) mealy potatoes
4 garlic cloves, peeled, shoots
  removed
2 egg yolks
²/₃ cup (150 ml) olive oil
Scant ½ cup (100 ml) sunflower
  seed oil
1 pinch (1 g) ground saffron or
  4 filaments
Fine salt, freshly ground pepper

½ long loaf of country or
  sourdough bread

TECHNIQUES

Filleting a fish (two round,
  flat fillets) **72**
Peeling using hot water **63**
Rouille **147**

CHEF'S NOTE

– Boil potatoes in the stock as a
tasty side dish.

Prepare and trim the fish.
Fillet the fish and remove all the bones, setting them aside with the heads for the stock. Reserve the fillets in the refrigerator. You may either shell the crustaceans or leave them whole.

Prepare the stock.
Peel, wash, and dice the onion to make a mirepoix. Slit the leek white lengthwise in two, wash it thoroughly, and slice it finely. Peel the tomatoes and remove the seeds, and remove the shoots from the garlic cloves.

Cut the small crabs into halves. Heat a little olive oil in a low-sided pot and put in all the ingredients. Leave them to sweat briefly, then pour in 8 cups (2 liters) cold water. Bring to a boil and simmer for 45 minutes over medium heat. Filter and season with salt and pepper. Place in the refrigerator until needed.

Prepare the rouille (see p. 147).
Boil the potatoes in their jackets, then peel and press through a vegetable mill. Crush the garlic cloves. Mix in the egg yolks, one by one, and whisk in the oils. It is best to use a combination of a neutral oil with olive oil added for the taste. Add the saffron and adjust the seasoning.

Place the fish fillets and shellfish in the cold stock. Bring rapidly to a boil and lower the temperature after a few moments.

Prepare the croutons by slicing slice the bread and toasting it.

Serve the bouillabaisse in a soup tureen or in individual soup plates, with the rouille and croutons in separate dishes.

DID YOU KNOW?

Along the coast from Marseille to Toulon, restaurants and fishermen are proud of their beautifully colored soup, which they vary with the catch of the day.

Grilled salmon steaks with braised fennel ✴✴

SERVES 6

Preparation: **35 minutes**
Marinating: **2 hours**
Cooking: **1 hour 40 minutes**

INGREDIENTS

1 whole salmon weighing about
  2 lb. 10 oz. (1.2 kg)
3 fennel bulbs
½ carrot (50 g)
½ large onion
3 tablespoons (40 g) butter
4 cups (1 liter) white veal stock
  (ready-to-use mix or see recipe
  p. 138)
1 bouquet garni
¼ cup (60 ml) oil
Fine salt, freshly ground pepper

Instant marinade
1 lemon
¾ cup (200 ml) olive oil
A few sprigs of thyme
6 bay leaves
Five-pepper mix

TECHNIQUES

Instant marinade **143**
Braising vegetables **98**
Grilling **104**

CHEF'S NOTE

– Use tuna, sardines, or other
fatty fish for this recipe.

Remove the fins and scales from the salmon and gut it. Cut six steaks weighing about 7 oz. (200 g) each.

Prepare the instant marinade (see p. 143). Peel the lemon, removing all the white pith, and slice it.

Place the olive oil, aromatic ingredients, and lemon slices in a tray. Place the salmon steaks in the tray and marinate in the refrigerator for 2 hours, turning them every 30 minutes.

Preheat the oven to 300°F (150°C).

Cut the fennel bulbs in halves and remove the hearts. Blanch in boiling water for a few minutes and refresh.

Dice the carrot and onion to make a mirepoix. Sweat the mirepoix in the butter in a roasting pan over low heat. Place the fennel halves in the pan. Pour over the white veal stock and add the bouquet garni.

Cover with parchment paper. Cook in the oven for 1 hour 15 minutes, turning the fennel halves over after about 35–40 minutes. You will need to have the oven at the same temperature to finish cooking the salmon steaks, so don't turn it off.

Remove the fennel from its braising liquid.

Strain the liquid through a chinois and reduce over low heat until the consistency is thick. Return the fennel halves to the roasting pan to keep them warm.

Heat the grill pan and oil it. Place the salmon steaks at an angle so that the final pattern will be diamond shaped. Sear to make a diamond pattern on both sides. Place the salmon steaks on a baking tray and finish cooking them for 10–15 minutes in the oven.

Serve individually or in a large dish.

Langoustines with tarragon ✳

SERVES 4

Preparation: **40 minutes**
Cooking: **35 minutes**

INGREDIENTS

12 large langoustines
4 tablespoons (60 g) clarified
   butter
1 celery branch (10 oz./300 g),
   for the batons
3 tablespoons (40 g) butter
A few sprigs of tarragon, for
   garnish
Fine salt, freshly ground pepper

Sauce
1 shallot, minced
1 small piece (1 ½ oz./40 g)
   celery stalk, diced
A few sprigs of tarragon, leaves
   chopped
2 tablespoons (30 ml) cognac
²/₃ cup (150 ml) heavy cream
Fine sea salt, freshly ground
   pepper

TECHNIQUES

Cutting into batons
   (*jardinière*) **64**
Cutting fish and shellfish
   into chunks **71**

CHEF'S NOTE

– You can also make this recipe
with lobster.

Slice the langoustine into pieces comprising two segments. Break the claws in half and reserve the heads for the sauce.

Heat a pan with the clarified butter and sauté the segments and claws. Season with salt and pepper.

Prepare the sauce.
Remove the segments and claws from the pan and replace them with the heads. Sauté them for a few minutes and add the chopped shallot and diced celery. Flambé with cognac. Pour in the cream and add the chopped tarragon. Reduce by half and strain through a fine-meshed conical sieve. Season.

Remove the tough outer fibers from the celery branch and cut it into batons about $1/5$ in. (5 mm wide) and 2 in. (5–6 cm) long. Stew them for a few minutes in the butter and ¼ cup (50 ml) water. They should retain some of their crunch.

Arrange the langoustine pieces in soup plates and pour the sauce over them. Arrange the celery sticks attractively in rows at the side. Garnish with tarragon leaves.

Braised bacon-wrapped monkfish ✳✳

SERVES 6

Preparation: **35 minutes**
Cooking: **45 minutes**

INGREDIENTS

3 ½ lb. (1.5 kg) monkfish
12 slices bacon
½ carrot (1 ½ oz./40 g)
¼–⅓ leek (1 ½ oz./40 g), white
  part only
⅓–½ celery stalk (1 ½ oz./40 g)
3 cups (750 ml) fumet (see
  p. 141)
1 bouquet garni

Sauce
⅔ cup (150 ml) heavy cream
3 ½ tablespoons (50 g) butter
Fine salt, freshly ground pepper

Special equipment: ovenproof
  sauté pan with lid

TECHNIQUES

Preparing monkfish **69**
Tying up a roast **83**

CHEF'S NOTE

– It's important to have equal
weights of the vegetables for
the mirepoix.

Prepare the monkfish: remove the skin, membranes, and violet-colored parts of the tail (see p. 69).

Preheat the oven to 275°F (140°C).

Bard the fish with the bacon slices and tie with twine.

Peel, wash, and finely dice the vegetables to make a mirepoix.

Lightly color the monkfish in a sauté pan. Add the diced vegetables and pour in the fumet. Add the bouquet garni.

Cover with the lid and cook in the oven for 20–30 minutes, depending on the size of the monkfish. Remove the fish and keep it warm.

To make the sauce, reduce the cooking liquid, add the cream, and reduce until thick. Whip in the butter. Adjust the seasoning.

Remove the twine from the fish. Serve either whole or cut in individual portions. Pour over the sauce.

Sautéed John Dory fillets with seaweed ✳✳

SERVES 6

Preparation: **40 minutes**
Cooking: **45 minutes**

INGREDIENTS

6 fillets of John Dory
4 tablespoons (60 g) clarified
  butter
3 lb. 5 oz. (1.5 kg) potatoes
2 tablespoons (30 g) kosher salt
A little dried seaweed, soaked,
  for garnish
1 lemon, for garnish
Fine salt, freshly ground pepper

Sauce
2 shallots
A little dried seaweed, soaked
Juice of 2 lemons
¼ cup (60 ml) heavy cream
1 stick (120 g) butter, cubed
Piment d'Espelette
Fine salt
1 pinch sugar (optional)

TECHNIQUE

Sautéing **123**

CHEF'S NOTE

– If your seaweed is preserved in
salt, blanch it briefly in boiling
water and refresh immediately
in ice water.

Preheat the oven to 325°F (160°C).

Season the fish fillets. Heat a pan with the clarified butter and sauté them until lightly browned. It will probably be necessary to finish cooking them in the oven for just a few minutes.

Prepare the sauce.
Finely chop the shallots. Chop the seaweed. Place the shallots, the seaweed, and the lemon juice in a small pan. Reduce to a quarter of the original quantity. Stir in the cream and whisk in the butter. Season with salt and *piment d'Espelette*. If the sauce is too bitter because of the seaweed, add a pinch of sugar.

Cut the potatoes into small oval shapes and put them in a pot. Cover them with cold water and add the kosher salt. Bring to a boil and simmer for about 20 minutes. Check for doneness with the blade of a small sharp knife. The potato should fall apart immediately.

Arrange the fish fillets, potatoes, and sauce on a serving dish or on individual plates. Garnish with seaweed and/or sliced lemon.

Plaice *goujonnettes* with tartare sauce ✳ ✳

SERVES 6

Preparation: **45 minutes**
Cooking: **5 minutes**

INGREDIENTS

3 plaice, weighing 1 ¼ lb.
  (600 g) each
3 eggs
Scant ½ cup (100 ml) oil plus oil
  for frying
¾ cup (80 g) flour
1 cup (120 g) breadcrumbs
1 lemon, for garnish
Fine salt, freshly ground pepper

Tartare sauce
Yolks of 2 hard-boiled eggs
1 tablespoon (15 ml) French
  mustard
1 teaspoon (5 ml) wine vinegar
¾ cup (200 ml) sunflower seed
  oil
A few sprigs of chives
1 onion (3 oz./80 g)
1 pinch Cayenne pepper
Salt

TECHNIQUES

Filleting a fish (four flat fillets)
  73
Cutting strips (*goujonnettes*) **72**
Tartare sauce **151**
Crumbed sauté **124**

CHEF'S NOTE

– You can also use this recipe to prepare sole *goujonnettes*.

Remove the fins from the plaice and prepare the fillets (see p. 73). Remove the skin. Wash and dab carefully to dry. Cut the fillets into strips (see p. 72). Season with salt and pepper.

Beat the eggs with the oil. Prepare the fish strips for frying: dip first in the flour, then in the egg-oil mixture, and lastly in the breadcrumbs.

Prepare the tartare sauce (see p. 151).
Make a mayonnaise, using hard-boiled egg yolks instead of raw egg yolks. Add the snipped chives and finely chopped onions. Season with salt and Cayenne pepper.

Pour just under ½ in. (1 cm) oil into a frying pan and heat. When it is hot, begin frying the first batch of strips (*goujonnettes*) for 1–2 minutes. Drain on paper towel. Filter the oil and repeat for the next batch.

Arrange the fried plaice on a serving dish or flat plates with a few lemon wedges. Serve the tartare sauce on the side.

Mackerel in *escabèche* ✴

SERVES 6

Preparation: **40 minutes**
Cooking: **15 minutes**

INGREDIENTS

6 mackerel
1 cup (250 ml) dry white wine
2 cups (500 ml) water
2 oz. (60 g) button mushrooms
1 unsprayed or organic lemon
2 oz. (60 g) peas
2 oz. (60g) French green beans
12 baby carrots
2 oz. (60 g) baby onions
2 bay leaves
¾ teaspoon (2 g) peppercorns
Fine sea salt

TECHNIQUES

Filleting a fish (two round, flat
  fillets) **72**
Vegetable court bouillon **137**

CHEF'S NOTES

– It's essential to have a court
bouillon with a fine taste. There
are many variations possible,
depending on the herbs and
vegetables available. You may
also add a little seaweed to your
court bouillon.

Fillet the mackerel and remove the bones. Roll them up and
secure them with toothpicks or small wooden skewers. Arrange
them side-by-side in a deep pan.

Prepare the vegetable court bouillon (see p. 137).
Bring the 2 cups (500 ml) of water and the wine to a boil. Finely
dice the mushrooms (*brunoise* size) and slice the lemon. Add the
peas, beans, baby carrots, and baby onions to the liquid.
Simmer for 3–4 minutes. Add the lemon slices, finely diced
mushroom, bay leaves, peppercorns, and salt.

Bring to a boil again. As soon as it begins boiling, pour the
liquid over the mackerel fillets. Allow to cool gradually.

Place the mackerel fillets in soup plates and pour over the cold
court bouillon. Arrange the vegetables attractively around the
fillets.

Turbot poached in cardamom-infused milk, with hollandaise sauce ✳✳

SERVES 6

Preparation: **25 minutes**
Cooking: **35 minutes**

INGREDIENTS

3 ½ lb. (1.5 kg) turbot
1 unsprayed or organic lemon
6 cups (1.5 liters) full cream milk
2 cups (500 ml) water
30 green cardamom seeds
2 tablespoon (30 g) kosher salt
¾ teaspoon (2 g) peppercorns
1 lemon, for garnish
A few sprigs of dill, for garnish

Hollandaise sauce
½ cup (5 oz./140 g) clarified
  butter
4 egg yolks
1 ¹/₃ tablespoons (20 ml) water
Juice of 1 lemon
1 small pinch Cayenne pepper
Fine salt

TECHNIQUES

Cutting fish and shellfish
  into chunks **71**
Hollandaise sauce **150**
Cutting citrus segments **62**

CHEF'S NOTES

– Other flat fish are suitable for
this type of cooking, but they
must be thick. Examples are
halibut, flounder, and brill.
– Substitute other aromatic
ingredients, such as green tea,
rosemary, and spices in the
court bouillon.

Cut the turbot into chunks (see p. 71). Slice the lemon. Prepare a court bouillon: bring the milk and water to a boil in a pot with the lemon slices, cardamom seeds, kosher salt, and peppercorns. Simmer for 2–3 minutes. Strain through a fine-mesh sieve and refresh over ice.

Place the pieces of turbot in a sauté pan. Cover with the court bouillon and, over low heat, bring slowly to a temperature of 160°F (70°C). If you don't have a thermometer, turn off the heat as soon as the liquid begins to simmer. Leave for a few minutes and bring to a simmer again. Maintain the liquid at this temperature for 12–15 minutes and turn off the heat.

Prepare the hollandaise sauce (see p. 150).
Heat the clarified butter. Whisk the egg yolks with the water. Then put them in a bain-marie or over very low heat and whisk until the consistency is that of a thick sabayon. Whisk in the hot clarified butter. Season and stir in the lemon juice.

Remove the dark and white skin from the turbot pieces, as well as the central bone. Arrange the pieces in plates. Drizzle the hollandaise sauce over some of the fish.

Garnish with the lemon segments (see p. 62), sprigs of dill, and the remaining cardamom seeds.

Sole meunière and potatoes cocotte ✳ ✳

SERVES 4

Preparation: **40 minutes**
Cooking: **30 minutes**

INGREDIENTS

4 soles
2 lb. (900 g) potatoes
2 ¾ tablespoons (40 g) plus
   2 ¾ tablespoons (40 g)
   salted butter
½ cup (50 g) flour
4 tablespoons (60 g) clarified
   butter
Juice of 1 lemon
1 lemon, in segments, for garnish
   (see p. 62)
A few sprigs of parsley, for
   garnish
Fine salt

TECHNIQUES

Cutting citrus segments **62**
Sauté meunière **123**

CHEF'S NOTE

– Purists do not remove any skin
at all before cooking. They take
it off afterwards so that the flesh
of the sole is not soaked in
butter.

Begin by preparing the garnish: chop the parsley and cut the lemon segments. Remove the fins and scales from the soles. Make an incision at the head and pull off the dark skin from the top side. (The other side does not need to have its skin removed.)

Wash, peel, and rinse the potatoes. Cut them into oval shapes about 2 inches (5 cm) long. Place them in a pan and cover with cold water. Bring to a boil and leave to simmer for 2 minutes. Drain them, but do not refresh. Melt half the salted butter in a pan big enough to hold the potatoes in one layer and sauté them.

Dab the soles with paper towel to dry them. Season them with salt and dip them in the flour. Shake gently to remove any excess. Pour the clarified butter into an oval (or large) frying pan and heat over medium heat. Place the soles in the pan, white skin side downward. Leave them to brown gently. Turn over and cook the other side in the same way. While they cook, brown the other half of the salted butter in a small pan. Remove the fish from pan and spoon over the lemon juice and browned butter.

Place the soles on large flat plates. Sprinkle with chopped parsley and garnish with the lemon segments. Arrange the potatoes cocotte around.

Monkfish medallions
à l'américaine and rice pilaf ✳ ✳

SERVES 6

Preparation: **45 minutes**
Cooking: **50 minutes**

INGREDIENTS

1 monkfish tail weighing about
  2 ½ lb. (1.2 kg)
1 onion
5 ½ tablespoons (80 g) butter
10 oz. (300 g) long-grained rice
Bouquet garni
Scant ¼ cup (50 ml) olive oil
Zest of 1 unsprayed or organic
  lemon, for garnish
A few sprigs of tarragon, for
  garnish
Fine salt, freshly ground pepper

Sauce américaine
6 small crabs
3 tablespoons (40 ml) olive oil
½ onion
½ shallot
½ carrot (1 ½ oz./40 g)
½ tomato (⅔ oz./20 g)
1 ½ tablespoons (20 g) tomato
  paste
1 ⅓ tablespoons (20 ml) cognac
Scant ¼ cup (100 ml) white wine
1 ¼ cup (300 ml) fish fumet
2 garlic cloves, peeled, shoots
  removed
1 bouquet garni
A few sprigs of tarragon

For the roux
1 ¾ tablespoons (1 oz./25 g) butter
¼ cup (25 g) flour

TECHNIQUES

Preparing monkfish **69**
Cutting medallions **70**
Sauce américaine **148**
Velouté **152**
Poaching (cold start): Shallow
  poaching **110**

Prepare the monkfish tail for cooking (see p. 69). Cut the fillets along the central bone. Cut out six medallions (see p. 70) and flatten them slightly. Cover them in plastic wrap and chill.

Prepare the *sauce américaine* (see p. 148).
Finely dice the onion, shallot, and carrot to make a mirepoix. Cut the small crabs in halves. Sauté them over high heat in hot olive oil. Turn down the heat. Add the mirepoix and sweat. Pour in the chopped tomato and add the tomato paste. Flambé with cognac, then add the white wine. Reduce by half and pour in the fish fumet. Add the garlic cloves, the bouquet garni, and the whole tarragon leaves. Simmer for 30 minutes, skimming when necessary. Blend, with the shells, and strain through a very fine mesh sieve.

Prepare a cold blond roux (see p. 152) with the butter and flour. Pour the strained liquid over this and bring it all to a boil to thicken it. Adjust the seasoning and set aside over a hot bain-marie.

Preheat the oven to 250°F (120°C).

Peel, wash, and chop the onion. Sweat it in the 5 ½ tablespoons (80 g) butter in an ovenproof pot. Add the rice and cook until it is translucent. Pour in 1 ½ times the volume of cold water or fumet. Add the bouquet garni and season. Bring to a simmer and cover with a lid of parchment paper. Place in the preheated oven to cook for 15–20 minutes. Test for doneness: all the liquid will have been absorbed and the rice should be the right texture. Fluff the rice with a fork before serving.

Heat the olive oil in a sauté pan over medium heat. Season the monkfish medallions and cook without browning them. Be careful to cook them very briefly as monkfish dries out quickly and becomes rubbery.

Arrange them on individual plates or in a serving dish. Pour the sauce over. Garnish with grated lemon zest and chopped tarragon.

DID YOU KNOW?

If you use other crustaceans to prepare a *sauce américaine*, it is given the name "crustacean sauce."

Tagliatelle with fresh and smoked salmon ✳

SERVES 6

Preparation: **25 minutes**
Cooking: **15 minutes**

INGREDIENTS

¾ lb. (360 g) tagliatelle
1 tablespoon (20 g) kosher salt
¼ cup (65 ml) olive oil
½ lb. (250 g) fresh salmon
7 oz. (200 g) piece smoked
  salmon
1 cup (250 ml) tomato sauce with
  basil (see recipe p. 151)
A few sprigs of basil for garnish
Fine sea salt, freshly ground
  pepper

TECHNIQUES

Poaching (hot start): Deep
  poaching **108**
Tomato sauce **151**

Cook the tagliatelle in a large pot of boiling salted water and refresh under cold water immediately. Drizzle in a litle of the olive oil and mix through so that the tagliatelle do not stick.

Dice both the fresh and smoked salmon, keeping them separate. Sauté the cubes of fresh salmon in the remaining olive oil. Season and drain on paper towel.

Heat the tomato sauce.

Carefully combine all the ingredients.

Serve in a large dish or individual soup plates, topped with a leaf of basil.

Trout *au bleu* ✳

SERVES 4

Preparation: **35 minutes**
Cooking: **25 minutes**

INGREDIENTS

2 ¾ oz. (80 g) carrot
1 large onion
3 ½ cups (800 ml) water
¾ cup (200 ml) white wine
½ oz. (15 g) coarse sea salt
1 bouquet garni
1 teaspoon (5 g) peppercorns
4 very fresh (or live) trout
¾ cup (200 ml) white vinegar,
 lukewarm

TECHNIQUES

Vegetable court bouillon **137**

CHEF'S NOTE

— You can serve this trout with a
sauce of reduced court bouillon.

To prepare a court bouillon, peel, rinse, and thinly slice the carrot and onion. Combine the water, wine, and salt in a large saucepan and bring to a boil. Add the onion, followed by the carrot. Let simmer for 15 minutes over low heat, then add the bouquet garni and peppercorns. Continue to cook for 1 minute, then remove from the heat and let cool.

Preheat the oven to 250°F (120°C).

Dress the trout and drizzle with the lukewarm vinegar (the fish will turn light blue). Place the trout in a 10 × 6 × 2-inch (25 × 15 × 5-cm) baking dish and pour the cooled court bouillon over them. Bake for 15 minutes.

Shredded skate wing
with olives and anchovies ✳

SERVES 4

Preparation: **35 minutes**
Cooking: **20 minutes**

INGREDIENTS

4 skate wings, skinned
⅓ cup (80 ml) olive oil
16 anchovy fillets in oil
16 pitted black olives
Juice of 1 lemon
1 lemon, sliced, for garnish
A handful of chopped parsley,
   for garnish
Fine sea salt, freshly ground
   pepper

CHEF'S NOTE

– Skate is a fragile, cartilaginous
fish that does not keep well.
When buying skate, make sure
that it is extremely fresh. If it still
has its skin, it should be covered
in a viscous substance. If the
skin has been removed, smell it:
there should be no odor at all.

To prepare the garnish, chop the parsley and slice one lemon.

Heat the olive oil in the sauté pan. Season the skate wings.
When the oil is hot, cook each side of the wings, being careful
not to burn them, and baste them regularly with the oil.

To check for doneness, lift up the flesh next to the central bone.
If it is quite white, then the fish is ready to eat. Remove it and
keep warm.

Thread the anchovy fillets through the pitted olives and sauté
them lightly. Deglaze with the lemon juice.

Remove the fish from the wings and arrange it on plates. Pour
the sauce from the pan over the shredded skate wings. Scatter
with chopped parsley and garnish with slices of lemon.

Seafood and vegetables en cassolette ✷✷

SERVES 6

Preparation: **45 minutes**
Cooking: **45 minutes**

INGREDIENTS

Mussels marinière
2 lb. (1 kg) mussels
1 shallot
¼ bunch parsley
2 tablespoons (30 g) unsalted
  butter
⅓ cup (80 ml) dry white wine

Cassolettes
2 tablespoons (25 g) butter
2 ½ tablespoons (25 g) flour
1 ⅔ cups (400 ml) fish fumet
⅓ cup (80 ml) cream
5 ¼ oz. (150 g) celeriac
5 ¼ oz. (150 g) zucchini
10 ½ oz. (300 g) scallops
7 oz. (200 g) peeled shrimp
½ cup (50 g) dried breadcrumbs
Salt, freshly ground pepper

TECHNIQUES

Marinière **106**
Cutting into fine dice
  (*brunoise*) **64**
Gentle stewing **100**

Prepare the mussels marinière (see p. 106) using the ingredients listed. Remove the mussels from their shells and reserve the filtered cooking liquid.

To prepare the cassolettes, preheat the oven to 430°F (220°C). Make a seafood velouté using a roux: melt the 2 tablespoons (25 g) butter in a saucepan over low heat. Remove from the heat and whisk in the flour until smooth, then whisk in the fumet and the reserved mussel-cooking liquid. Stir in the cream and season with salt and pepper.

Cut the celeriac and zucchini into small dice (*brunoise*). Gently stew the celeriac and zucchini separately (see p. 100) for 5–6 minutes each.

Sear the scallops in a skillet over high heat, without cooking them all the way through.

Divide the vegetables between six 3-inch (8-cm) cassolettes, ¾–1 ¼ inches (2–3 cm) deep. Arrange the shrimp, mussels, and scallops over the vegetables. Cover with the seafood velouté, sprinkle with breadcrumbs, and bake for a few minutes, until warmed through and lightly golden.

Stuffed shellfish platter ✳ ✳

SERVES 6

Preparation: **35 minutes**
Soaking: **1 hour**
Cooking: **10 minutes**
Chilling: **1 hour**

INGREDIENTS

Coarse sea salt
12 venus clams (*praires*)
12 mussels
12 razor clams
12 cockles (*amandes de mer*)
24 clams (*palourdes*)
12 oysters
Scant ½ cup (100 ml) dry white
  wine
3 ½ tablespoons (50 ml) olive oil
½ bunch flat-leaf parsley
¼ bunch chervil
4 cloves garlic
1 shallot
1 stick plus 2 tablespoons (150 g)
  unsalted butter, at room
  temperature
¾ teaspoon (2 g) *piment
  d'Espelette*
Scant 2 tablespoons (25 ml)
  pastis
½ cup (50 g) grated Parmesan
Fleur de sel
Salt, freshly ground pepper

TECHNIQUE

Opening oysters and other
  shellfish **74**

CHEF'S NOTE

– You can also add lemon juice
to the compound butter.

Fill a large bowl with cool water and add a handful of coarse sea salt; stir or swish to dissolve. Add all the shellfish and let them soak for about 1 hour to purge any grit.

Drain the shellfish and place in a large saucepan with the white wine and olive oil. Set over high heat, cover, and cook just until the shells open. Drain, reserving the cooking liquid. Separate the shells at the hinge and remove and discard the empty half-shells; set aside the half-shells containing the meat.

Strain the cooking liquid and reduce by three-quarters over high heat. To prepare the stuffing, wash and de-stem the herbs and peel and chop the garlic and shallot. Place the herbs, garlic, and shallot in a food processor with the butter, *piment d'Espelette*, pastis, and reduced cooking liquid; process until well blended. Season with salt and pepper.

Cover the reserved shellfish with the stuffing, place on a baking sheet, and chill for 1 hour.

Preheat the broiler and line a serving platter with coarse sea salt. Sprinkle the grated Parmesan over the shellfish and place under the broiler until just lightly browned. Set over the bed of coarse salt to stabilize the shells and sprinkle with a pinch of *fleur de sel*. Serve immediately.

Poultry

Jean-François Piège

presents his recipe

Lebanon is a country I know a little, and one I like to recreate in my cooking, suggesting its colors, the hustle and bustle of its markets, lingering moments over meze, and early evening drinks that extend into the small hours. When I think of Lebanon, the bright red of its plump, juicy tomatoes, the thin round breads hot out of the bakers' ovens, the generosity of its herbs, the abundant bunches of parsley, and all the flavors of the Mediterranean, lemons, olives, toasted sesame seeds … and garlic—the essence of Lebanese cuisine—all come to mind.
The recipe I give here is an interpretation of *shish taouk*, a bouquet of flavor and freshness. It must be prepared ahead of time, but the simple generosity it conveys makes it well worth the effort. Serve it with arak, an aniseed-flavored liqueur, or a red Lebanese wine.

SERVES 4

Preparation:
45 minutes
Marinating:
12 hours or overnight
Cooking:
1 hour 20 minutes

INGREDIENTS

4 free-range chicken
  fillets
1 red onion
2 tomatoes, fresh off the
  stalk
½ bunch flat-leaf
  parsley
Juice of 1 lemon
4 tablespoons (60 ml)
  olive oil
4 pita breads
4 tablespoons (50 g)
  tomato paste
1 clove garlic, chopped
Salt, freshly ground
  pepper

Lebanese spice mix
1 tablespoon (10 g)
  cumin seeds, crushed
1 tablespoon (10 g)
  fennel seeds, crushed,
1 tablespoon (10 g)
  ground star anise
2 tablespoons (20 g)
  sumac
2 tablespoons (20 g)
  ground *piment
  d'Espelette*
1 tablespoon (10 g)
  thyme flowers, crushed
⅓ cup or 1 oz. (30 g)
  freshly shredded
  coconut
2 tablespoons (20 g)
  white sesame seeds,
  toasted

**Chickpea purée
(hummus)**
14 oz. (400 g) dry
  chickpeas
1 long shallot
4 tablespoons (60 ml)
  olive oil
2 garlic cloves, unpeeled
1 bunch flat-leaf parsley,
  stalks only
Juice of 1 lemon
A little sherry vinegar
Salt, freshly ground
  pepper

**Tomato salad with
  sumac vinaigrette**
2 tomatoes, fresh off the
  stalk, or other tasty
  tomatoes
½ bunch flat-leaf parsley
1 generous pinch (2 g)
  sumac
Juice of 1 lemon
3 tablespoons (45 ml)
  olive oil
1 bunch young spring
  onions
Salt, freshly ground
  pepper

Lebanese-style marinated chicken in pita

A day (or 12 hours) ahead
Marinate the chicken fillets. Mix together all the ingredients for the spice mix. Chop the flat-leaf parsley and slice the red onion finely.

Cut the tomatoes into quarters, remove the seeds, and cut them into strips.

Cut the chicken fillets into fine strips, ¼ in. (5 mm) wide.

Sprinkle the bottom of a dish with a third of the spice mix, place the chicken pieces on it, ensuring they are flat, scatter over half the onions, tomatoes, parsley, and another third of the spice mix. Repeat the procedure with the rest of the ingredients. Pour over the lemon juice and 4 tablespoons (60 ml) olive oil. Cover with plastic wrap and chill for at least 12 hours.

A day (or 12 hours) ahead
Chickpea purée (hummus)
Soak the chickpeas in water overnight or for 12 hours. Slice the shallot and drain the chickpeas. In a large pot with a little olive oil, sweat the sliced shallot. Add the chickpeas to the pot. Pour in water to just under double the volume of the chickpeas. Add the unpeeled garlic cloves and the parsley stalks, and simmer for about 1 hour.

Drain the chickpeas, reserving some of the liquid, and remove the parsley stalks and garlic cloves.

Place the chickpeas into the bowl of a food processor with a little of the cooking liquid. Add the juice of 1 lemon, a little sherry vinegar, and 3 tablespoons (45 ml) olive oil. Process for 5 minutes, adding more cooking liquid if necessary to obtain a soft texture. Transfer to a bowl and cover with plastic wrap flush with the surface of the purée.

To serve (or 12 hours later)
Prepare the pita bread
Remove the chicken fillets from the marinade, scraping off all the onions, tomatoes, and other ingredients. Season them with salt and grill rapidly on both sides, on a grill or in a very hot skillet without any fat. Drain the garnish ingredients and season with salt and freshly ground pepper. Set aside.

Preheat the oven to 400°F (200°C). Open the pitas. Combine the tomato paste and chopped garlic and spread the mixture inside the pitas. Spoon the chicken pieces, together with the marinade ingredients, into the pitas. Roll them up and place them on a baking dish. Cook for 4–5 minutes.

Tomato salad with sumac vinaigrette
Cut the two tomatoes into quarters. Set aside twenty large leaves of parsley and chop the rest. Make a vinaigrette with the sumac, lemon juice, and olive oil. Season the tomato quarters with salt and freshly ground pepper, and leave them to marinate. Scatter with chopped parsley and snipped young spring onions.

To assemble
On a flat plate, arrange an oval scoop of chickpea purée and some tomato quarters. Top the chickpea purée with a parsley leaf. Drizzle some marinade attractively round the plate. When the pitas are nice and crisp, cut them in two at an angle and arrange them on the plate.

Jean-François Piège presents his recipe

Bay leaf-infused young guinea hen with canapés ✳✳

SERVES 4

Preparation: **40 minutes**
Cooking: **50 minutes**

INGREDIENTS

1 young guinea hen
6 bay leaves
4 tablespoons (60 g) butter,
    divided
1 whole sandwich loaf (150 g)
A little oil for frying
1 lb. (500 g) green beans,
    prepared for boiling
8 thin rashers of bacon
Fine sea salt, freshly ground
    pepper

Gratin stuffing
3 oz. (80 g) cured bacon slab
4 ½ oz. (120 g) chicken livers
1 shallot
2 teaspoons (10 ml) cognac
Fine sea salt, freshly ground
    pepper

TECHNIQUES

Encrusting poultry **78**
Gratin stuffing (*farce à gratin*)
    161
Roasting **120**

Dress the young guinea hen and slip the bay leaves under its skin (see p. 78). Season the cavity with salt and pepper.

Preheat the oven to 350°F (180°C).

Lightly grease a roasting pan with a little butter and place the guinea hen on it. Melt 1 ⅓ tablespoons (20 g) butter and pour it over. Season the outside of the bird. Cook it for 15 minutes, then lower the temperature to 325°F (160°C) and cook for a further 20 minutes. Hollow out the center of the sandwich loaf, leaving a border of ¾ in. (1.5 cm) all round. Fry the hollowed-out loaf in oil until it is light brown and drain on paper towel.

Prepare the stuffing (see p. 161).
Dice the bacon and remove the veins of the livers. Chop the shallot. Sauté the bacon and liver on high heat, ensuring that the livers remain pink inside. Add the chopped shallots and flambé with cognac. Process the mixture, push through a fine-mesh sieve, and season with salt and pepper.

Boil the green beans in salted water. Lower the oven temperature to 300°F (150°C). Melt the remaining butter. Make eight bundles with the beans, wrap a slice of bacon round each one, and pour the butter over them. Season with salt and pepper. Place the bundles on a roasting pan and cover them with aluminum foil. Heat the beans for 10–12 minutes.

Fill the hollowed-out sandwich loaf with the stuffing and cut into thick slices to make the canapes. Place the guinea hen over the canapés, and arrange the bundles of green beans around it.

DID YOU KNOW?

Guinea fowl originated on the African continent; references to the bird on the tables of France are found from the Renaissance onward. Rabelais mentions them in *Pantagruel*. The meat is more delicate and has less fat than that of chicken.

Duckling à l'orange with sautéed potatoes and artichokes ✳ ✳

SERVES 4

Preparation: **1 hour 45 minutes**
Cooking: **1 hour 15 minutes**

INGREDIENTS

1 duckling
3 ½ oz. (100 g) bard
3 tablespoons (40 ml) oil
1 ½ lb. (600 g) potatoes
2 tablespoons (30 g) plus
  2 tablespoons (30 g) clarified
  butter
3 artichokes
Juice of 1 lemon
½ cup (50 g) flour
A few sprigs of flat-leaf parsley
1 orange, for garnish
Fine sea salt, freshly ground
  pepper

Sauce
2 unsprayed or organic oranges
Scant ½ cup (100 ml) wine
  vinegar
⅓ cup (70 g) sugar
2 teaspoons (10 ml) Cointreau or
  other orange liqueur
1 ¼ cups (300 ml) thickened
  brown veal stock (use an instant
  mix or see p. 140)
Fine sea salt, freshly ground
  pepper

TECHNIQUES

Dressing and trussing
  poultry **85**
Boiled vinegar and sugar
  (*gastrique*) **142**
Turning vegetables **66**
Poaching (hot start): Deep
  poaching (in a *blanc*) **108**
Cutting citrus segments **62**

Preheat the oven to 325°F (160°C).

Dress the duckling and season the cavity with salt and pepper. Truss it (see p. 85). Drizzle a little oil into an ovenproof pot and color the duckling all round. Season the outside of the duckling with salt and bard it. Tie with twine to keep the bard in place. Put a tight-fitting lid on the pot and cook for about 1 hour 15 minutes in the oven.

To prepare the sauce, cut fine julienne strips in the orange zest (see p. 61) and blanch them three times. Prepare a *gastrique* (see p. 142). Place the vinegar and the sugar in a saucepan. Slowly bring to a boil and reduce until it reaches a syrupy consistency. (This is the stage before it caramelizes.) Deglaze with the Cointreau and then add the juice of the oranges. Reduce again, and add the thickened brown veal stock and julienned orange zest. Season with salt and pepper.

Wash, peel, and rinse the potatoes. Cut them into cubes, sauté them in clarified butter, and season with salt.

Turn the artichokes (see p. 66). Squeeze lemon juice over them and cook them in a *blanc* (see the deep poaching [hot start] technique, p. 108). Cut them into cubes, sauté them in clarified butter, and season with salt. Combine the two vegetables and scatter chopped parsley over them.

Cut the duck fillets into two or three thin strips, and cut the thighs into two pieces.

Arrange two or three thin strips and a piece of thigh on each plate and pour over the sauce. Add the sautéed vegetables and garnish with orange slices and segments (see p. 62).

CHEF'S NOTE

– Duck pairs well with sweet-and-sour sauces, particularly those with a fruit base, such as peach, pineapple, and cherry.

Quail stew and potatoes
à la boulangère ✴ ✴

SERVES 6

Preparation: **50 minutes**
Cooking: **1 hour**

INGREDIENTS

6 quails
2 tablespoons oil
A few drops of cognac
2 lb. (900 g) potatoes
3 large onions
7 tablespoons (100 g) butter,
  clarified, divided
1 ¼ cups (300 ml) thickened
  white poultry stock
Fine sea salt, freshly ground
  pepper

Sauce
2 shallots
1 ¼ cups (300 ml) red wine
1 bouquet garni
6–8 peppercorns
1 scant cup (200 ml) thickened
  veal stock (use a mix or see
  recipe p. 138)
3 tablespoons (40 g) butter,
  cubed
Fine sea salt, freshly ground
  pepper

TECHNIQUES

Dressing and trussing poultry **85**
Game stew (salmis) **121**

CHEF'S NOTE

– Cooking in two stages—
roasting and then stewing—is a
method typically used for small
game birds. They contain little
fat, and it is a method that
prevents them from drying out.

Preheat the oven to 375°F (190°C).

Dress the quails and season the insides with salt and pepper. Truss them (see p. 85). Drizzle a little oil over them, and a little more into an ovenproof sauté pan. Cook the quails for 8–10 minutes until they are lightly browned. At this stage, though, they should be barely cooked—carefully check the color of the juice, which should still be red, with the tip of a very fine knife.

Cut each quail in two along the backbone—each piece will have a leg, a wing, and a breast. Reserve the carcass for the sauce. Drizzle a few drops of cognac over the quails and keep them warm.

To prepare the sauce, finely chop the shallots. Crush the quail carcasses and return them to the same sauté pan in which you browned them briefly. Add the chopped shallots and sweat them. Deglaze with the red wine, add the bouquet garni and peppercorns, and reduce by three-quarters. Heat the stock, pour it in, and bring back to a boil for a few minutes. Strain through a chinois and whisk in the butter. Adjust the seasoning.

Wash, peel, and rinse the potatoes. Slice them into very thin disks (¹/₁₀ in./2 mm), and rinse once more to remove some of the starch. Peel and wash the onions. Slice them thinly and sauté them in clarified butter until they are golden. Sauté the thin potato slices in clarified butter in another sauté pan.

Preheat the oven to 325°F (160°C). Butter an ovenproof gratin dish and arrange the sliced potatoes and onions in alternate layers, seasoning as you go. Begin and end with a layer of potatoes. Pour in the white stock and cook for about 30 minutes.

Pour the sauce over the quail pieces in a sauté pan and finish cooking them over low heat (as you would a stew). Allow about 15 minutes for the thighs, and about 10 minutes for the wings, so put the wings in 5 minutes after the thighs.

Arrange a bed of potatoes *à la boulangère* on each plate, place two quail halves on it, and drizzle the sauce over.

DID YOU KNOW?

A dish called *à la boulangère* (in the style of the baker's wife) was traditionally cooked in the baker's oven, after the bread baking was finished for the day and the oven had begun cooling.

Crumbed turkey escalopes with sautéed potatoes ✳

SERVES 6

Preparation: **35 minutes**
Cooking: **20 minutes**

INGREDIENTS

6 turkey escalopes
½ cup (50 g) flour
2 eggs
3 tablespoons (40 ml) oil, plus a
   little for frying
1 scant cup (100 g) ready-made
   breadcrumbs
2 tablespoons (30 g) butter
1 cup (250 ml) thickened brown
   veal stock (an instant mix or see
   p. 140)
A few sprigs of parsley, chopped,
   for garnish
1 lemon, for garnish
Fine sea salt, freshly ground
   pepper

Sautéed potatoes (without
   parboiling)
2 lb. 7 oz. (1.2 kg) potatoes
3 tablespoons (40 ml) oil
3 tablespoons (40 g) butter
Fine sea salt, freshly ground
   pepper

TECHNIQUES

Preparing escalopes **88**
Crumbed sauté **124**

CHEF'S NOTE

– It's best to cook the escalopes
as soon as you have breaded
them, otherwise the crumbs
become sticky.

Flatten the escalopes evenly and trim them (see p. 88). Season them with salt and pepper. Dust them with flour and then tap them lightly to remove any excess. Beat the two eggs with the oil. Dip the escalopes in the egg-oil mixture and then coat them in breadcrumbs. It is important not to leave them like this for more than 30 minutes before cooking.

Wash, peel, and rinse the potatoes. Using a mandoline, slice them into very thin disks (1/10 in./2 mm). Rinse them under water and dry well with paper towel to remove any moisture.

Heat a non-stick pan with the oil and butter. Place a single layer of potato slices in the pan and cook them until they turn a hazelnut color. Turn them over and leave until they are the same color on the other side. Remove them from the pan, place on paper towel, and season. Repeat the procedure with successive layers of sliced potatoes until they are all done. Keep them warm.

Heat a nonstick pan with oil and butter over medium heat. Place the breaded escalopes in the pan and cook until they are browned. Turn them over and cook until the same color. If they are not cooked through (test with the tip of a knife), finish them in the oven at 325°F (160°C) for a few minutes. Deglaze the pan with the veal stock.

Arrange the escalopes in a serving dish or individual plates. Arrange the sautéed potato slices in concentric circles and sprinkle them with chopped parsley. Serve lemon wedges with the escalopes, and pass round the sauce separately.

Duck confit and potatoes sarladaises ✴

SERVES 6

Preparation: **25 minutes**
Marinating: **12 hours minimum**
Cooking: **1 hour 45 minutes**

INGREDIENTS

6 duck thighs
Brine (sufficient to cover the
  duck thighs)
3 lb. (1.5 kg) duck or goose fat
  (buy at specialty stores or
  online)
6 cloves pink garlic, unpeeled
2 bay leaves
8 peppercorns

Potatoes sarladaises
2 lb. 7 oz. (1.2 kg) potatoes
3 ½ oz. (100 g) duck fat
½ bunch flat-leaf parsley
$\frac{1}{6}$ oz. (3 g) truffle bits
1 clove garlic
Fine sea salt, freshly ground
  pepper

TECHNIQUE

Slow cooking in oil or fat **98**

CHEF'S NOTES

– Filter the duck fat and reuse it
next time you make a confit.
Alternatively, use it to cook
vegetables such as potatoes or
Jerusalem artichokes.
– Make brine by combining
water with coarse sea salt (1 oz.
salt per 4 cups water, 30 g per
liter).

A day ahead, brine the duck thighs.
Remove the pin-feathers from the duck thighs (cylindrical,
tough feather case) and any remaining feathers. Make
superficial incisions in the skin. Trim the tips of the bones so
that the meat can retract more easily during cooking. Leave in
the brine for 24 hours, or at least overnight, in the refrigerator.

Rinse the duck thighs. Place a grilling rack at the bottom of a
large pot and place the duck thighs on it. Cover the thighs with
the fat and aromatic ingredients. Leave the garlic cloves
unpeeled. Bring slowly to a simmer, and leave to cook for
between 1 hour 30 minutes and 1 hour 45 minutes.

Prepare the potatoes sarladaises.
Wash, peel, and rinse the potatoes. Use a mandoline to cut
$\frac{1}{10}$-in. (2-mm) thick slices. Sauté them directly, without
parboiling, in the duck fat until golden.

Preheat the oven to 325°F (160°C).

Combine the potatoes and the chopped parsley and garlic
mixture. Add the truffle bits and season with salt and pepper.
Place the potatoes in a deep ovenproof dish, cover, and cook for
about 30 minutes.

Serve the duck confit and sarladaises potatoes in separate
dishes.

DID YOU KNOW?

Duck and duck fat are typical ingredients in the cooking of the Périgord
region. A dish cooked *à la sarladaise* is prepared with duck or goose fat,
and the name comes from the town of Sarlat, the capital of the Black
Périgord region.

Sliced chicken curry ✳

SERVES 4

Preparation: **25 minutes**
Cooking: **30 minutes**

INGREDIENTS

4 chicken escalopes
1 scant teaspoon (2 g) curry
   powder
2 tablespoons (30 g) butter
1 large onion
Scant ½ cup (100 ml) soy cream
Fine sea salt, freshly ground
   pepper

Sautéed zucchini
2 zucchini (courgettes)
2 tablespoons (30 ml) olive oil
A few thyme flowers
Fine sea salt, freshly ground
   pepper

TECHNIQUE

Canelling **56**

Cut the flattened chicken into thin strips. Season them with salt and pepper and sprinkle with curry powder.

Sauté the strips in half the butter in a sauté pan. Remove the chicken and keep it warm.

Chop the large onion and sweat it in the remaining butter, then deglaze with soy cream. Reduce the liquid until thick. Adjust the seasoning and return the chicken to the pan.

Wash and canelle the zucchini (see p. 56). Cut them into slices about $^1/_{10}$–$^1/_8$ in. (2–3 mm) thick. Heat the olive oil in a nonstick pan and sauté the slices, until just lightly browned. Season and scatter with thyme flowers.

Arrange in individual plates or serving dishes.

Rabbit stew with puréed Golden Hubbard squash ✳✳

SERVES 6

Preparation: **45 minutes**
Cooking: **1 hour 10 minutes**

INGREDIENTS

1 rabbit
3 tablespoons (40 g) butter
5 oz. (150 g) button mushrooms
1 shallot
A few sprigs of chives
1 ½ tablespoons (20 ml) cognac
⅔ cup (150 ml) white wine
Scant ½ cup (100 ml) heavy
  cream
2 cups (500 ml) thickened white
  chicken stock (use an instant
  mix or see p. 138)
1 bouquet garni
2 small leeks (150 g), white part
  only, for garnish
A little oil for frying
3 ½ oz. (100 g) All Blue
  potatoes, for garnish
Fine sea salt, freshly ground
  pepper

Puréed Golden Hubbard squash
1 ¾ lb. (800 g) Golden Hubbard
  squash or Hokkaido Orange
3 carrots (7 oz./200 g)
10 oz. (300 g) potatoes
4 cups (1 liter) milk
A little grated nutmeg
4 tablespoons (60 g) butter
Fine sea salt, freshly ground
  pepper

TECHNIQUES

Jointing rabbit **80**
Cutting into julienne strips **61**

Cut the raw rabbit into pieces (see p. 80). Season them with salt and pepper. Melt the butter in an ovenproof pot or dish and lightly brown the rabbit pieces over low heat. Place them on a rack.

Preheat the oven to 350°F (170°C).

Thinly slice the mushrooms, chop the shallot, and snip the chives. Sauté the mushrooms in the same pan in which you cooked the rabbit. Add the chopped shallot and chives. Flambé with cognac and deglaze with the white wine. Add the cream, the white stock, and the bouquet garni.

Return the rabbit pieces to the pot and cook for 1 hour with the lid on. Remove the pieces from the pot. Strain the cooking liquid through a chinois and reduce over low heat until thick enough to coat the back of a spoon. Season the sauce and return the rabbit pieces to the pan.

Peel and rinse the vegetables for the squash puree. Cut them into large cubes. Place them in a pot, add the cold milk and a little grated nutmeg and bring to a simmer. When the vegetables are tender, drain them and process. Dry the purée out over low heat, stirring constantly so that it does not burn. Stir in the butter and season with salt and pepper.

Cut the leek into julienne strips (see p. 61). Fry them in the oil and season with salt. Cook the All Blue potatoes in water, peel them, and slice finely.

Arrange the puréed squash in a circle on each plate and place a piece of rabbit in the center. Drizzle with sauce. Place a small bunch of fried leek white on top and garnish with a few slices of All Blue potatoes.

CHEF'S NOTE

– Try other vegetables, alone or in combination, to vary your purées. Broccoli, carrots, and mushrooms are some ideas to start with.

Lime and honey duck fillets on a bed of zucchini ✳

SERVES 4

Preparation: **35 minutes**
Cooking: **30 minutes**

INGREDIENTS

4 duck fillets
2 unsprayed or organic limes, sliced
2 ½ tablespoons (50 g) runny honey
1 ½ lb. (600 g) zucchini (courgettes)
Scant ¼ cup (50 ml) oil
A few sprigs of thyme
Fine sea salt, freshly ground pepper

Sauce
2 tablespoons (40 g) honey
Juice of 1 lime
Scant ¼ cup (50 ml) soy sauce
Freshly ground pepper

TECHNIQUE

Canelling **56**

CHEF'S NOTES

– Duck breast is best when pink, rare even.
– Although a wide range of honeys are available, with correspondingly varied tastes, a multi-floral honey is best for cooking.

Preheat the oven to 375°F (190°C).

Remove all visible nerves as well as the pin-feathers (cylindrical, tough feather case) from the duck fillets. Grill briefly skin-side down, making a diamond pattern, and season with salt and pepper. On the other side, make small incisions $^1/_5$ in. (5 mm) deep in which to slip the half-slices of lime. Drizzle the honey and grind some pepper over each piece of duck.

Wash the zucchini and canelle them (see p. 56). Slice them thinly (about $^1/_8$ in. or 3 mm). Sauté them in oil and season with salt and pepper. Keep warm.

Heat another sauté pan without any fat. When it is really hot, place the duck fillets in it, skin side down. Leave to brown over medium heat. When the skin is browned, transfer the fillets to the oven. Cook for 7–10 minutes, until the desired doneness.

To prepare the sauce, place the honey and lime juice in a small saucepan and reduce until it reaches a thick consistency. Deglaze with the soy sauce and season with pepper.

Arrange the zucchini slices in a circle and scatter with thyme. Place the duck fillet in the middle and drizzle with sauce.

DID YOU KNOW?

The description "*magret*" is used only for the breast of a duck fattened for its foie gras.

Stuffed chicken legs with chestnuts ✳ ✳

SERVES 8

Preparation: **1 hour 10 minutes**
Cooking: **45 minutes**

INGREDIENTS

2 free-range or organically raised
  chickens, around 2 ½ lb. (1 kg)
  each
10 oz. (300 g) caul
3 tablespoons (50 g) butter,
  to sauté the chicken
2 shallots
2 celery stalks (100 g)
5 sage leaves
3 ½ lb. (1.6 kg) chestnuts
4 tablespoons (60 g) butter,
  for the chestnuts
8 marigolds, fresh or dried
Fine sea salt, freshly ground
  pepper

Mousseline stuffing
1 egg white
1 scant cup (200 ml)
  whipping cream
Fine sea salt, freshly ground
  pepper

TECHNIQUES

Cutting up raw, dressed
  poultry **79**
Boning and stuffing a chicken
  leg **90**
Mousseline stuffing (cream-
  based) **159**

CHEF'S NOTE

– Try roasting the chestnuts on a
wood fire—this will give them a
lovely color and impart a slight
grilled taste to them.

Cut each chicken into four pieces (two wings and two thighs). Remove the small fillet from the wings and cut off the tips of the wing bones. Remove the thigh bone and the drumstick bone, being careful not to cut the meat (see p. 79). Set aside ½ lb. (250 g) of the chicken meat to use for the stuffing. Season this meat with salt and pepper.

Prepare the mousseline stuffing (see p. 159). Place the seasoned meat in the bowl of a food processor and with the blade attachment grind it finely. Add the egg white and process for a few more seconds. Push the stuffing through a sieve. Transfer it to a stainless steel bowl over a bowl of ice water. Gradually stir in the cream.

Fill the wings and thighs with the stuffing. Fold over the meat to form nice plump thighs, and roll them in caul. If necessary, tie with kitchen twine.

Preheat the oven to 350°F (170°C).

Finely dice the shallots and celery to make a mirepoix. Melt 3 tablespoons (50 g) butter in a pot or sauté pan and brown the chicken pieces. Remove from the heat and add the diced shallots and celery. Add a few sage leaves. Put the chicken pieces back into the pot. Cover the pot or pan and cook for about 35 minutes in the oven until the chicken is cooked through.

Transfer the chicken pieces to another dish. Reduce the cooking liquid and strain it through a chinois. Season it and return the chicken pieces to the pot.

Prepare a pot of boiling water. Make one incision on the rounded side of each chestnut. When the water is boiling, add the chestnuts and boil them for 3 minutes. Remove the skin while they are still hot, taking care not to burn yourself.

Melt the 4 tablespoons (60 g) of butter over the chestnuts and coat them. Season just before serving. Place in a serving dish or on individual plates. Drizzle the sauce over the chicken pieces and surround them with chestnuts. Garnish with edible marigolds and sage leaves, or other seasonal flowers.

Squab fricassee and garden peas *à la française* ✳ ✳

SERVES 6

Preparation: **50 minutes**
Cooking: **45 minutes**

INGREDIENTS

3 squab (pigeons)
1 large onion
1 large leek (100 g), white part only
7 tablespoons (100 g) butter, divided (to sear the squab, glaze the onions, and stew the lettuce)
3 cups (750 ml) thickened white chicken stock (use an instant mix or see p. 138)
Scant ½ cup (100 ml) heavy cream
2 lb. (1 kg) garden peas
3–4 new onions (4 ½ oz./120 g)
1 ½ tablespoons (20 g) sugar
1 lettuce
Fine sea salt, freshly ground pepper

TECHNIQUES

Simple slicing (*émincer à la paysanne*) **57**
Brown braising (meat, poultry, offal) **97**
Glazing vegetables **102**
Shredding (chiffonade) **58**

CHEF'S NOTE

– This recipe may be used with most types of poultry.

Cut the squab in half. Bone each half partially, removing most of the superficial bones, and season with salt and pepper.

Peel, wash, and finely chop the large onion. Slit the leek white in two lengthwise and cut into fine slices (*à la paysanne*).

Preheat the oven to 350°F (170°C).

Sear the squab halves in a pot with half of the butter, ensuring that they do not brown. Add the chopped onion and sliced leek white, and sweat with the lid on. Cover the contents of the pot with the chicken stock, and place in the oven, still with the lid on, for 30–35 minutes.

Remove the squab pieces. Reduce the cooking liquid until it is thick. Add the cream (spoon a little hot liquid into the cold cream, mix, and then put it all into the pot) and reduce again until the sauce coats the back of a spoon. Strain through a chinois, season with salt and pepper, and return to the pot. Return the squab pieces to the pot to keep them warm.

Prepare a pot of salted boiling water and boil the peas. Glaze the new onions with 1 ⅓ tablespoons (20 g) butter and the sugar (see p. 102). Shred the lettuce (make a chiffonade—see p. 58) and braise it in 2 tablespoons (30 g) butter and a scant ¼ cup (50 ml) water. Combine the garden peas, onions, and shredded lettuce in a sauté pan. Season with salt and pepper.

Serve the fricassee in a casserole dish, surrounded by the vegetables.

DID YOU KNOW ?

Until the French Revolution, only the nobility enjoyed squabs. Today, they are still considered to be a refined dish for special occasions. La Varenne (1618–1678) wrote a recipe for squab with peas (it included lettuce and bacon bits) that is still found on French tables.

Grilled cockerel and *diable* sauce ✳✳

SERVES 4

Preparation: **1 hour**
Cooking: **50 minutes**

INGREDIENTS

2 cockerel (young cock of
  about 1 lb./500 g)
Scant ⅓ cup (70 ml) oil
2 ½ tablespoons (40 g)
  French mustard
½ cup (60 g) packaged
  breadcrumbs
3 tablespoons (40 ml) oil
1 ½ lb. (600 g) potatoes
4 cloves garlic
2 tomatoes
A little *herbes de Provence*
4 bay leaves
4 button mushrooms
Fine sea salt, freshly ground
  pepper

Diable sauce
2 shallots
1 teaspoon (2 g) mignonette
  pepper
3 ½ tablespoons (50 ml)
  red wine vinegar
3 ½ tablespoons (50 ml)
  dry white wine
1 cup (250 ml) thickened brown
  veal stock (use an instant mix
  or see p. 140).
A few sprigs of tarragon,
  leaves chopped

TECHNIQUES

Cutting wafers **65**
Grilling **104**

CHEF'S NOTE

– Use this recipe for other types
of poultry, whole or in pieces.

Preheat the oven to 350°F (170°C).

Cut the cockerels in two, lengthwise, along the backbone. Remove the bones from the ribcage, the wishbone, and the cartilage attached to it. Heat a ridged grill pan. Brush the skin of the cockerel with oil, and grill the pieces on the pan, making a diamond pattern with the ridges, skin side first, and then flesh side. Place them on a baking tray. Baste the skin with mustard using a pastry brush, and sprinkle with breadcrumbs. Cook the cockerels for 25–30 minutes. (You will need to have the oven at the same temperature to broil the vegetables afterward.)

Wash, peel, and rinse the potatoes. Cut them into wafers (see p. 65) using a mandoline. Rinse twice and dry thoroughly, dabbing with paper towel to remove any excess moisture.

Peel the garlic, remove the shoots, and chop. Wash the tomatoes, remove the stems, and cut them in half. Season them with salt and pepper, and then with the *herbes de Provence* and chopped garlic. Drizzle a little oil and place 1 bay leaf on each piece. Arrange them on a roasting pan. Rinse the mushrooms and dry them well. Baste them with oil and grill them, cap side down. Remove the stems and place the caps in the roasting pan with the tomatoes. Season the vegetables with salt and pepper.

Prepare the *diable* sauce. Peel and wash the shallots and chop them. In a small saucepan, place the shallot, mignonette pepper, vinegar, and dry white wine. Reduce slowly, over low heat, until almost dry. Pour in the veal stock and add the chopped tarragon leaves.

Place the vegetables in the oven and cook for 10–15 minutes, until softened. Fry the potato wafers and drain well.

Cut the cockerel pieces in two and serve one wing and one thigh to each person. Serve the vegetables and the sauce separately.

Chicken breasts with baby vegetables ✳

SERVES 6

Preparation: **30 minutes**
Cooking: **35 minutes**

INGREDIENTS

6 chicken breasts
3 tablespoons (40 g) butter,
  to sauté the chicken
2 cups (500 ml) vegetable broth
2 tablespoons (20 g) cornstarch
  or 1 ½ tablespoons (20 g)
  butter, to thicken the sauce
  (optional)
2 bunches of baby vegetables,
  such as carrots, zucchini
  (courgettes), fennel, onions
2 tablespoons (30 g) butter,
  clarified, for the vegetables
Fine sea salt, freshly ground
  pepper

CHEF'S NOTE

– Baby vegetables are best left
slightly crunchy, so don't
over-boil them. If you use this
boiling method, you can also
marinate them afterward.

Preheat the oven to 350°F (170°C).

Trim the skins of the breasts and make incisions in the skin.
Season with salt and pepper. Sauté them, skin side down, in the
butter, using an ovenproof pan or skillet. Pour the vegetable
broth over the chicken pieces. Finish the cooking in the oven.
This will take 25–30 minutes.

Remove the chicken breasts from the pan and reduce the
cooking liquid to one quarter of its volume. Use a little butter or
starch to thicken it. Whisk in 1 ½ tablespoons (20 g) butter, or
dilute 2 tablespoons (20 g) cornstarch in a little liquid before
pouring it into the liquid. Bring to a boil and remove from the
heat. Adjust the seasoning.

Cook the vegetables separately in a pot of salted boiling water.
To remove the thin skin of the carrots when they are cooked,
simply press them downward with your fingers. Give the
vegetables a nice gloss by brushing them with the clarified
butter.

Cut the breasts into thin strips. Arrange the chicken pieces in
the plates with the baby vegetables in attractive rows.

Meats

Régis Marcon

presents his recipe

In Auvergne, my region, meat used to be cooked in a broth with hay. Mountain hay in particular is very flavorful—it is packed with sweet-smelling grasses and flowers, especially spignel, an aromatic plant that grows wild in pastures. And naturally, it is organic. A method my mother used to cook rabbit by coating it in wild thyme gave me the idea of preparing lamb in a hay crust. I serve the lamb in a juice infused with a little hay, and use what is known as *épice au loup* (literally, the wolf's spice), a ground mixture of garlic, dried orange peel, ginger, juniper, and black pepper, in homage to the wonderful Suzanne Robaglia who, in 1935, published *Margaridou*, far more than just a cookery book, on the traditional recipes of Auvergne.

SERVES 4

Preparation:
35 minutes
Cooking:
1 hour

INGREDIENTS

1 leg of milk-fed lamb
1 ½ lb. (650 g) of your
  choice of seasonal
  vegetables
4 ¼ pints (2 liters)
  white chicken stock
1 ⅔ cups (400 ml)
  prepared lamb jus
  (make ahead or buy at
  specialty stores)
1 handful of spignel-
  infused hay
2 lb. 4 oz. (1 kg) herbed
  bread dough
3 tablespoons (40 g)
  butter
4 slices of rolled pork
  belly
Épice au loup (ground
  juniper, ginger, dried
  garlic, dried orange
  peel, black pepper)
Salt, pepper

Lamb cooked in a spignel-infused hay crust, *épice au loup*, and seasonal vegetables

To prepare the lamb and vegetables
Trim and season the leg of lamb. Brown it all round over high heat and set it aside. Prepare your seasonal vegetables. Boil them separately in the white chicken stock.

To make the jus
Heat the lamb jus with a little hay. Leave to infuse, then strain through a chinois and season.

To assemble and cook
Roll out the bread dough and cover it with the remaining hay. Place the leg of lamb in the center and wrap the dough around it. Cook at 400°F (200°C) for about 45 minutes.

To finish
Melt the butter with the pork belly and glaze the cooked vegetables in the mixture.

To serve
Cut open the hay crust and remove the leg of lamb to slice it. Place a slice on each plate and arrange the vegetables attractively around it. Drizzle with sauce.

Serve the spice mixture separately.

Grilled rib roast and béarnaise sauce ✳✳

SERVES 8

Preparation: **30 minutes**
Cooking: **25 minutes**

INGREDIENTS

2 double-cut rib steaks (prime
  beef) about 2 lb. (1 kg) each
3 tablespoons (40 ml) oil, for
  cooking
1 teaspoon (4 g) *fleur de sel*
1 teaspoon (2 g) mignonette
  pepper

Béarnaise sauce
2 shallots
Scant ½ cup (100 ml) dry white
  wine
Scant ¼ cup (50 ml) wine vinegar
A few sprigs of tarragon
2 sticks (220 g) unsalted butter,
  clarified
5 egg yolks
1 teaspoon (2 g) mignonette
  pepper
Fine salt

TECHNIQUES
Grilling **104**
Béarnaise sauce **149**

CHEF'S NOTES

– Potatoes or green vegetables
are the classic, and still much
appreciated, side dishes for this
cut of beef.
– Bear in mind that the resting
time for the beef is the same as
the time you will need to make
the sauce; get all your
ingredients and equipment
ready beforehand.

Trim the ribs and tie them with twine so that they maintain their shape. Make sure the rack of your barbecue is clean and begin heating it, or heat a ridged grill pan. Lightly oil the beef and sear each side, making a diamond pattern. Leave it to cook until it reaches the desired degree of doneness. If you prefer your meat well done, finish cooking it in a hot oven, heated to 350°F (180°C), for a few minutes. When it is done, sprinkle with *fleur de sel* and mignonette pepper. Wrap it well in aluminum foil and leave to rest in a warm place.

Prepare the béarnaise sauce (see p. 149).
Peel, wash, and finely chop the shallots. Pour the white wine, vinegar, shallots, and a little tarragon into a saucepan and prepare the reduction over low heat. While the sauce reduces, melt the clarified butter and keep it warm. Do not reduce until dry; there should be a few tablespoons of liquid left and the shallots will be moist. Most of the acidity will have disappeared. Add the egg yolks to the reduction with 5 tablespoons (75 ml) water. Place the pot over hot water (bain-marie) or very low heat and whisk until the consistency is nice and thick—it should resemble a sabayon (see p. 52). Pour in the warm melted butter gradually, continuing to whisk. Add the salt. Strain through a fine-mesh sieve and serve immediately.

Cut the beef, parallel to the bone, into strips. Place them in a serving dish so that the guests can immediately see which portion is done to their taste. Serve the sauce separately, in a sauce dish.

Provençal shoulder of lamb and vegetable *tian* ✳✳

SERVES 5

Preparation: **50 minutes**
Cooking: **55 minutes**

INGREDIENTS

1 shoulder of lamb
3 cloves garlic, unpeeled
3 ½ tablespoons (50 ml) olive oil
Salt, freshly ground pepper

Vegetable tian

2 large onions
2 tomatoes
1 zucchini (courgette)
1 eggplant (aubergine)
3 ½ tablespoons (50 ml) olive oil
A scattering of *herbes de Provence*
A few sprigs of basil
Salt, freshly ground pepper

Pistou

4 garlic cloves, peeled, shoots
   removed
½ bunch basil
3 ½ tablespoons (50 ml) olive oil
Juice of 1 lemon

TECHNIQUES

Boning a shoulder of lamb **80**
Cutting round slices **58**

CHEF'S NOTE

– Try to select vegetables that are the same diameter. This will make it easier to put your *tian* together and your presentation will be just that much more attractive.

Preheat the oven to 425°F (220°C).

Bone the shoulder (see p. 80).

Prepare the *pistou*. Crush the garlic cloves with the basil leaves using a pestle and mortar. Drizzle the olive oil in as you crush and then thin with the lemon juice.

Brush the cavity with the *pistou* (see p. 146) and season with salt and pepper. Roll the shoulder up and tie with twine (see p. 83). Baste it with oil and season with salt and pepper. Cook for 10 minutes, then lower the temperature to 350°F (170°C). Add the garlic cloves and cook for an additional 45 minutes. Remove the lamb from the baking dish, wrap it in aluminum foil, and keep warm. You will need to have the oven at the same temperature for the vegetable *tian*.

Peel and wash the onions and wash all other the vegetables. Cut them into disks ⅛ in. (2–3 mm) thick (see p. 58). Oil a baking dish. Arrange the vegetable slices—tomatoes, zucchini, onions, and eggplant—vertically in rows. It's best to alternate all the vegetables in each row, rather than placing one vegetable in each row. Scatter with *herbes de Provence*, tuck in a few sprigs of basil, drizzle over a little olive oil, and season with salt and pepper. Cook the vegetables for 30 minutes until soft, allowing them to stew a little in their own liquid.

Heat the plates before serving and cut up the meat as it is required.

DID YOU KNOW?

A *tian* is a Provençal earthenware baking dish used to make gratins. It has given its name to this assortment of typically southern vegetables, cooked to a confit texture, that accompany the lamb flavored with olive oil and basil, other typical ingredients of the region.

Veal medallions, green lentils, and horn of plenty mushrooms ✳ ✳

SERVES 6

Preparation: **35 minutes**
Cooking: **40 minutes**

INGREDIENTS

2 lb. (900 g) veal fillet (filets
  mignons or chops)
¼ carrot
1 large onion
2 garlic cloves
14 oz. (400 g) green lentils,
  if possible *lentilles vertes
  du Puy AOC*
2 bay leaves
2 cloves
1 ½ oz. (40 g) slab smoked bacon
2 oz. (60 g) horn of plenty
  or black trumpet mushrooms
5 tablespoons (70 g) butter
Salt, freshly ground pepper

Sauce
2 shallots
1 ⅓ tablespoons (20 ml) cognac
1 cup (250 ml) brown veal stock
3 tablespoons (40 g) butter,
  cubed
Salt, freshly ground pepper

TECHNIQUES

Cutting medallions
  and noisettes **93**
Poaching (cold start): Shallow
  poaching **110**

CHEF'S NOTE

– You can replace veal
medallions with loin chops.

Cut twelve thin round medallions of veal, about ⅓ in. (1 cm) thick. Season them with salt and pepper.

Peel and wash the carrot and the onion, and remove the shoots from the garlic cloves. Chop the vegetables into thick sticks so that you can remove them from the lentils before serving if you wish; if you intend to serve them with the lentils, chop them finely. Place the lentils in a pot and pour in twice their volume of cold water (see the shallow poaching [cold start] technique p. 110). Add the aromatic garnish (carrot, onion, garlic, bay leaves, cloves, and smoked bacon) and bring to a boil. Leave to simmer gently until cooked, about 15 minutes.

Brush the horn of plenty mushrooms, wash them if necessary, and cut them in half lengthwise. Sauté them half of the butter and then add them to the lentils. Remove the piece of bacon and season the lentils.

Heat a sauté pan. Melt the remaining butter and place the veal medallions in to brown on both sides. Check for doneness and transfer to a rack, keeping them warm.

Make the sauce: chop the shallots and sweat them in the same sauté pan. Flambé them with the cognac. Add the veal stock, and whip in the butter. Season with salt and pepper.

Spoon servings of lentils in soup plates and arrange the veal medallions on top. Pour the sauce over.

Boeuf bourguignon with fresh pasta ✳ ✳ ✳

SERVES 8

Preparation: **40 minutes**
Resting and drying: **12 hours**
(for pasta dough)
Cooking: **2 hours 45 minutes**

INGREDIENTS

3 ½ lb. (1.6 kg) stewing beef
4 cups (1 liter) red Burgundy
  wine
½ carrot
1 large onion
¼ cup (60 ml) oil
6 cups (1.5 liters) thickened
  brown veal stock (use an instant
  mix or see p. 140)
1 bouquet garni
3 garlic cloves, peeled, shoots
  removed
5 oz. (150 g) slab bacon
3 ⅓ tablespoons (50 g) butter
7 oz. (200 g) button mushrooms
5 oz. (150 g) new onions
1 ½ tablespoons (20 g) sugar
Salt, freshly ground pepper

Fresh pasta

2 ½ cups (220 g) cake flour
2 eggs, beaten
1 ½ tablespoons (20 ml) oil
1 teaspoon (5 g) salt

TECHNIQUES

Pasta and noodle dough **17**
Quartering button mushrooms
  60
Glazing vegetables **102**

CHEF'S NOTES

— Cooking this dish in the oven is
preferable to cooking it over the
stove top as the heat will be
more evenly distributed.
— Boeuf bourguignon is excellent
when reheated a day later.

A day ahead, prepare the fresh pasta (see p. 17).
Sift the flour. Beat the eggs and combine with the oil and salt. Make a well in the center and pour in the liquid ingredients. Rapidly knead the ingredients so that they form a ball. Do not overwork or else the dough will become too elastic. Chill for 30 to 45 minutes. Roughly spread the dough out using a pastry roller, then process it through a pasta maker. Use the pasta maker to cut out tagliatelle (p. 17: images 5, 6). Allow the pasta to dry for several hours before using it.

To prepare the main dish, pour the wine into a pot and reduce it by half over high heat. While it is simmering, peel and wash the carrot piece and the onion. Dice them to make a mirepoix. Oil a sauté pan and, over high heat, brown the meat. Add the diced carrot and onion. Lower the heat and sweat the vegetables. When they have softened, pour in the reduced red wine and veal stock. Add the bouquet garni and garlic cloves. Bring to a simmer and cover with the lid. Now you may either leave it on low heat, or cook in the oven at 325°F (160°C), for 2 ½ hours.

Cut the bacon into lardons, making sure you leave no rind or cartilage. Place them in a pot of cold water to blanch them. When they are done, lightly butter a pan to sauté them.

Wash the mushrooms, pat them dry immediately, and quarter them (see p. 60). Place a knob of butter in a pan and sauté the mushrooms over high heat until all their liquid evaporates. When they are done, season them with salt and freshly ground pepper.

Glaze the baby onions with the sugar until brown (see p. 102). Cook the pasta in a large pot of boiling salted water.

Remove the pieces of beef from the pot. Strain the sauce through a chinois and reduce it if there is too much or if it is thin. Season the sauce and return the meat to the pot with the mushrooms, onions, and lardons.

Serve in a large serving dish or individual soup plates.

Roast veal with balsamic reduction ✳ ✳

SERVES 8

Preparation: **35 minutes**
Cooking: **1 hour 55 minutes**

INGREDIENTS

3 ½ lb. (1.6 kg) boneless veal
  roast
3 tablespoons (40 g) butter,
  clarified
²/₃ cup (150 ml) balsamic vinegar
4 lb. (1.8 kg) carrots
¼ cup (2 ¼ oz./60 g) plus ¼ cup
  (2 ¼ oz./60 g) butter
3 ½ tablespoons (40 g) sugar
7 oz. (200 g) dried plums
  (prunes)
Scant ½ cup (100 ml) red wine
Salt, freshly ground pepper

Special equipment: a large
  ovenproof pot or Dutch oven

TECHNIQUES

Turning vegetables **66**
Glazing vegetables **102**

Preheat the oven to 350°F (180°C).

Trim the veal roast and tie it with twine. Place it in a large pot or Dutch oven and pour over the clarified butter. Season with salt and pepper. Place over low heat and brown lightly. Deglaze with balsamic vinegar. Place the pot in the oven and cook for 1 hour 45 minutes, turning the roast over every 20 minutes.

Wash, peel, and rinse the carrots. Turn them (see p. 66) to make oblong shapes 2 in. (5 cm) long. Place the carrots in a pot and cover with water. Add 4 tablespoons (60 g) butter, a little salt, and the sugar. Cover with a parchment paper lid and bring to a boil. When all the water has evaporated (by now, the carrots should be easy to cut), coat them in the butter and sugar mixture by whirling them in the pot.

Place the dried plums and red wine in a saucepan. Slowly bring to a simmer and remove from the heat.

When the veal roast is done, remove it from the pot and cover it with aluminum foil to keep it warm. Remove the fat from the cooking liquid and whip in the remaining 4 tablespoons (60 g) butter.

Adjust the seasoning. Slice the meat, arrange it in a dish, and pour the sauce over. Surround the sliced veal with carrots and dried plums.

Lamb stew (navarin) with turnips ✳✳

SERVES 8

Preparation: **35 minutes**
Cooking: **1 hour 25 minutes**

INGREDIENTS

4 lb. (2 kg) boned shoulder
   of lamb
1 large onion
3 garlic cloves
3 ⅓ tablespoons (50 ml) oil
Scant ⅔ cup (60 g) flour
Scant ½ cup (100 ml) white wine
3 tablespoons (40 g) tomato
   paste
1 bouquet garni
Salt, freshly ground pepper

Sautéed turnips
3 lb. (1.5 kg) turnips
4 tablespoons (60 g) butter
3 ½ tablespoons (40 g) sugar
Salt

TECHNIQUE

Gentle stewing **100**

CHEF'S NOTE

– The turnip quarters will be
considerably tastier if you use
the cooking liquid from the meat
instead of water.

Preheat the oven to 350°F (180°C).

Trim the lamb and cut it into 2–2 ½ oz. (60–70 g) pieces.

Dice the large onion to mirepoix size. Peel, wash, and crush the garlic cloves. Heat a low-sided pan over high heat and pour in the oil. Brown the pieces of lamb evenly all over.

Tip the pan to the side to remove the fat, holding the lid to retain the lamb. (Cool the fat before discarding it.) Add the diced onion and leave it to sweat with the lid on. When it is translucent, sprinkle the flour over. Place the pot in the oven for 5 minutes (this will cook the starch). Pour in the white wine, and add enough water to just cover the meat. Then add the tomato paste, bouquet garni, and garlic, and season with salt and pepper. Cover with the lid and cook for 1 hour 15 minutes.

Peel and wash the turnips, and cut them into quarters. Gently stew them with butter, sugar, salt, and a little water for 7–8 minutes. Check for doneness with the tip of a knife, which should slide in easily.

Skim the surface of the lamb stew and remove the fat when you take the pot out of the oven. Remove the bouquet garni.

Serve the meat and turnips separately.

Kidneys in mustard sauce ✳

SERVES 5

Preparation: **35 minutes**
Cooking: **15 minutes**

INGREDIENTS

2 veal kidneys
2 tablespoons (30 g) butter, clarified
1 tablespoon (20 ml) red port
Scant ¼ cup (50 ml) heavy cream
Scant ½ cup (100 ml) thickened brown veal stock (use an instant mix or see p. 140)
1 scant tablespoon (20 g) *moutarde à l'ancienne*, French mustard with crushed brown mustard seeds
Salt, freshly ground pepper

TECHNIQUE

Preparing kidneys **90**

CHEF'S NOTES

– Rice, sautéed potatoes, or vegetable flans make excellent side dishes to eat with kidneys.
– Veal kidneys are considered to have the finest taste of all types of kidney.
– They should always be served pink, with a little drop of clear juice appearing in the center, or else they become rubbery.

Remove the fine membrane from the kidneys (see p. 90). Cut them in half and remove the nerves. Separate the lobes, cutting them into pieces of about 1 oz. (25–30 g) each.

Pour the clarified butter into a sauté pan and heat over high heat. Brown the kidney lobes, making sure that they do not dry out—they should remain pink inside. Transfer them to a rack to let their juices drip out. Season with salt and pepper. Discard the fat from the pan.

Deglaze with port and reduce by half. Add the cream, followed by the thickened veal stock. Stir in the mustard but do not allow the sauce to boil, or else it will separate. Adjust the seasoning.

Arrange the kidneys in a serving dish and pour the sauce over them.

Roasted rack of lamb with garden vegetables ✳ ✳

SERVES 8

Preparation: **50 minutes**
Cooking: **30 minutes**

INGREDIENTS

2 racks of lamb with 8 chops in
   each
3 tablespoons (40 ml) oil for
   cooking
½ carrot
½ large onion
Scant ½ cup (100 ml) white wine
1 bouquet garni
1 scant cup (200 ml) water or
   clear stock
Salt, freshly ground pepper

Garden vegetables
4 carrots (14 oz./400g)
4 turnips (14 oz./400 g)
10 oz. (300 g) shelled peas
10 oz. (300 g) green beans
4 tablespoons (60 g) butter
Salt, freshly ground pepper

TECHNIQUES

Preparing a rack (pork, veal,
   lamb) **86**
Cutting into batons
   (*jardinière*) **64**

CHEF'S NOTE

– Your butcher will be able
to dress the racks of lamb
for you if you prefer.

Preheat the oven to 425°F (220°C).

Trim the racks and remove the backbones (see p. 86). Make small, shallow incisions in the fine membrane that covers the racks. Tie them with kitchen twine. Oil a roasting pan and place the racks on it. Baste them with oil and season with salt and pepper. Cook for 10 minutes at 425°F (220°C), and then turn the temperature down to 350°F (170°C) to cook for a further 10 minutes.

Remove the racks from the pan and tent them under aluminum foil. Keep them warm, and set aside the pan. Discard the fat.

Peel and wash the carrot and the large onion. Dice them finely to make a *brunoise*. Place the roasting pan over medium heat to caramelize the juices from the lamb. Add the finely diced vegetables, and sweat over low heat. Deglaze with the white wine and reduce by half. Add the bouquet garni and pour in the scant cup water or clear stock. Reduce by half again. Strain through a chinois and season.

To prepare the garden vegetables, peel and wash the carrots and turnips. Cut them into little sticks ¹/₅ in. × 1 ¼ in. (5 mm × 30 mm). Cook the carrots, turnips, peas, and beans separately in boiling salted water. As soon as they are done, cool them briefly under cold running water and dry on paper towel. Cut the beans so that they are they same length as the carrot and turnip sticks. Gently heat all the vegetables together with butter.

Cut the racks, allowing two chops per person. Serve on flat plates with the garden vegetables, and pour over the hot sauce.

389

Duck *magret* with honey, black currant, and Timut pepper ✳

SERVES 4

Preparation: **15 minutes**
Cooking: **25 minutes**

INGREDIENTS

4 large duck *magrets* (or breasts)
1 tablespoon (25 g) lavender honey
1 tablespoon (15 ml) raspberry vinegar
Scant ½ cup (100 ml) Banyuls sweet wine
10 ½ oz. (300 g) fresh black currants (or use frozen)
Generous ¾ cup (200 ml) thickened brown veal stock (use an instant mix or see p. 140)
1 teaspoon (2 g) ground Timut pepper
Salt, freshly ground black pepper

Preheat the oven to 350°F (180°C).

Using a knife, score the skin side of the duck *magrets* in a crosshatch pattern. Sear the *magrets* skin-side down in an oven-safe nonstick skillet over high heat to render the fat. Turn them over and cook until browned but still pink in the center. Remove from the skillet (set the skillet aside, unwashed, for the sauce) and let sit on a rack for about 10 minutes to let the excess fat drip off.

Place the *magrets* skin-side down in a baking dish and finish cooking them in the oven for 10–15 minutes, depending on the thickness and desired doneness (pink or well done).

To prepare the sauce, warm the skillet used to sear the *magrets* in order to melt the fat, then pour in the honey and raspberry vinegar. Deglaze over high heat for 1–2 minutes, stirring with a spatula to release any brown bits stuck to the pan.

Reduce by half, then deglaze with the Banyuls sweet wine and stir in the black currants. Let simmer for 1–2 minutes over medium heat, then pour in the veal stock. Add the Timut pepper and season with salt and black pepper to taste.

Check that the *magrets* are cooked to the desired doneness, then slice them crosswise. Arrange on individual plates (or a platter). Immediately pour the sauce over them and serve.

Flank steak with shallots ✳

SERVES 6

Preparation: **20 minutes**
Cooking: **20 minutes**

INGREDIENTS

6 flank steaks
5 ¼ oz. (150 g) shallots
3 ½ tablespoons (50 ml) oil
Scant ½ cup (100 ml) white wine
Generous ¾ cup (200 ml)
   thickened brown veal stock (use
   an instant mix or see p. 140)
1 tablespoon (20 g) butter
Salt, freshly ground pepper

CHEF'S NOTE

– You can add a pinch of sugar
to the shallots to temper any
bitterness.

Score the flank steaks, then flatten them using a meat mallet or rolling pin.

Peel, rinse, and thinly slice the shallots.

Sear the steaks in a very hot skillet with the oil over high heat. Cook them a little less than desired—they will finish cooking when you reheat them in the sauce before serving. Transfer to a rack and cover with aluminum foil.

Return the skillet to high heat to melt the fat and make the brown bits (*sucs*) stick to the bottom, in order to intensify the flavor. Reduce the heat to low, add the shallots, and cook until softened. Deglaze with the white wine. Reduce until nearly all the liquid has evaporated, then pour in the stock. Stir in the butter to thicken.

Place the flank steaks in the sauce until warmed through and cooked to the desired doneness. Serve immediately.

Normandy-style veal chops ✳

SERVES 6

Preparation: **30 minutes**
Cooking: **35 minutes**

INGREDIENTS

6 veal chops
1 ¼ sticks (5 oz./140 g) unsalted
   butter
1 ¾ lb. (800 g) green beans
12 rashers bacon
Salt, freshly ground pepper

Sauce
5 oz. (150 g) button mushrooms
2 shallots
1 tablespoon (15 ml) calvados or
   other apple brandy
Scant ½ cup (100 ml) hard cider
½ cup (120 ml) crème fraîche
Scant cup (200 ml) thickened
   brown veal stock (use an instant
   mix or see recipe p. 140)
Salt, freshly ground pepper

TECHNIQUE

Preparing chops **88**

CHEF'S NOTE

– The secret to getting the veal
chops just right is to cook them
in hot butter without allowing
them to burn.

Trim the chops and cut off the tips of the bones. Make a small incision on the nerve on the outside (curved side) so that the meat does not shrink during cooking. Season the chops with salt and pepper. If you like your veal chops well done, you will need to finish cooking them in the oven. In this case, preheat it to 350°F (180°C). Begin heating 7 tablespoons (100 g) unsalted butter in a sauté pan. When it is sizzling, place the chops in the pan over low heat and brown gently on both sides, spooning the butter frequently over the meat as it cooks. Check for doneness and, if necessary, place the chops in the oven for a few minutes. Remove from the oven as soon as they are done to your liking, cover with aluminum foil, and keep warm.

Discard some of the fat from the sauté pan. Finely slice the mushrooms and chop the shallots. Sauté the mushrooms until brown. Add the shallots and cook until translucent. Flambé the contents of the pan with calvados (apple jack brandy) and deglaze with the hard cider. Reduce to a quarter of the original quantity. Stir in the crème fraîche. Pour in the veal stock and reduce again until the sauce is thick. Whip it well and season with salt and pepper. Ensure that your oven is at 300°F (150°C) so that you can heat your beans at the last moment.

Prepare a pot of salted boiling water and cook the green beans. Refresh them briefly under cold running water and pat dry to remove all moisture. Arrange the green beans in bundles and wrap each one with a thin rasher of bacon.

Butter a roasting pan and arrange the bundles of beans on it. Brush them with a little butter to give them a nice gloss and season them. Ten minutes before you are ready to serve, place the beans in the oven to re-heat them. Arrange the chops and bundles of beans on the plates and drizzle with mushroom sauce.

DID YOU KNOW?

Normandy is a fertile region in northwestern France, famous for its dairy products, including cream and butter, and apples, from which wonderful hard cider and calvados are made. This dish showcases the best of the produce.

Fillet of beef in a brioche crust ✳ ✳

SERVES 6

Preparation: **45 minutes**
Resting: **1 hour 55 minutes**
Cooking: **30 minutes**

INGREDIENTS

2 lb. (900 g) tenderloin or fillet of
 beef
3 tablespoons (40 ml) oil for
 cooking
Generous ²/₃ cup (100 g)
 packaged breadcrumbs
5 sprigs flat-leaf parsley
6 sprigs chervil
3 ½ tablespoons (50 ml) olive oil
1 egg
2 tablespoons (30 g) butter,
 clarified
Salt, freshly ground pepper

Brioche dough
¹/₆ oz. (5 g) fresh (compressed)
 yeast
2 ¼ cups (220 g) flour
1 generous tablespoon (15 g)
 sugar
2 eggs
7 ½ tablespoons (110 g) unsalted
 butter, room temperature
Salt

TECHNIQUES

Brioche dough **27**
Cooking in a crust **101**

CHEF'S NOTES

– Instead of the herbed crust, try
a basic mushroom duxelles (see
p. 158).
– Sugar is included in the
brioche recipe to ensure the
dough begins rising; it will not
impart a sweet taste to your
dish.

Prepare the brioche dough (see p. 27).
Dilute the yeast in 2 tablespoons (30 ml) of water at room
temperature. Sift the flour onto a flat surface and make a well in
the center. Sprinkle the salt and sugar outside the well so that
they do not come into direct contact with the yeast. Beat the
eggs and incorporate them into the mixture using a rubber
scraper. Knead the dough energetically to give it elasticity. You
may use a stand mixer fitted with the dough hook to do this. If
you opt for the stand mixer, use medium speed for about 10
minutes. Then knead in the butter at room temperature until it
is completely incorporated and the dough is smooth, and place
the dough in a mixing bowl. Cover with plastic wrap (otherwise
an unwanted crust will form) and leave to rise for 30 to 40
minutes at a temperature of 77°F–82°F (25°C–28°C) with a bowl
of water. When the dough has doubled in volume, remove from
the bowl and turn out onto a lightly floured surface. Flatten it
and fold into three. Shape into a ball and chill until it hardens,
about 45 minutes.

Trim and season the beef. Brown it lightly over high heat in the
oil. Place it on a rack to allow it to drain. Combine all the
ingredients for the herbed crust (breadcrumbs, parsley, chervil,
and olive oil) and season them with salt and pepper.

Take the brioche pastry out of the refrigerator and roll it out
into a rectangle about ¹/₁₀–⅛ in. (3–4 mm) thick. Spread the
herbed crust over the brioche pastry, place the piece of beef in
the middle, and roll it up. If you have any leftover pieces of
pastry, use them to make decorative pieces. Leave to rise for
30 minutes at 82.5°F–86°F (28°C–30°C). The brioche dough
should almost double in volume.

Preheat the oven to 375°F (190°C), ensuring there is no residual
steam in the oven.

Beat the egg and baste the
pastry with it. Cook for about
30 minutes, depending on how
well done you like your beef.
When you remove it from the
oven, brush the brioche pastry
with a little clarified butter and
serve whole.

Slow-cooked caramelized pork ✳

SERVES 6

Preparation: **15 minutes**
Cooking: **1 hour 15 minutes**

INGREDIENTS

2 ½ lb. (1.2 kg) top of pork
  shoulder butt (US) or top of
  spare rib (UK)
3 tablespoons (40 g) butter,
  clarified
3 ½ tablespoons (40 g) sugar
Salt, freshly ground pepper

Preheat the oven to 350°F (170°C).

Brown the pork in a pot with the clarified butter and sugar.
Season it with salt and freshly ground pepper. Cover with the
lid and cook for 1 hour 15 minutes.

Slice the meat and pour over the sauce from the pot.
Serve this dish with tagliatelle or potatoes in their jackets.

DID YOU KNOW?

Since the time of the Gallic tribes, pork has been widely eaten in France
in many forms, with new recipes constantly being created. Spiced
vegetables, such as cumin-flavored carrots, make an excellent side
dish here.

Roast beef with onions ✳

SERVES 6

Preparation: **15 minutes**
Cooking: **30 minutes**
Resting: **20 minutes**

INGREDIENTS

4 large onions
2 ¼ lb. (1 kg) boneless beef roast
  (rump steak, sirloin, round, etc.)
2 ½ tablespoons (40 ml)
  sunflower oil
Salt, freshly ground pepper

TECHNIQUE

Roasting 120

Preheat the oven to 375°F (190°C).

Peel, rinse, and roughly chop the onions.

Brown the beef roast all over in a Dutch oven with the
sunflower oil over high heat. Season with salt and pepper and
add the onions, placing them around the meat.

Roast in the oven, uncovered, for 30 minutes. To ensure your
roast is perfectly cooked to your liking, test it with a meat
thermometer: the center should reach 133°F (56°C) for rare and
136°F (58°C) for medium-rare.

Remove the roast from the oven and immediately wrap it in
aluminum foil. Place on a rack just inside the oven and leave the
door open. Let rest for about 20 minutes.

Slice the roast and drizzle with the pan juices. Place the onions
in a separate serving dish. Serve with baby potatoes, mixed
garden vegetables (see p. 416), and/or Provençal-style tomatoes
(see p. 427).

Veal stew (blanquette) ✳

SERVES 8

Preparation: **25 minutes**
Cooking: **1 hour 30 minutes**

INGREDIENTS

4 lb. (1.8 kg) veal shoulder
1 tablespoon (20 g) kosher salt
1 large onion
3 cloves
1 large green leek leaf
1 stalk celery
1 bouquet garni
5 peppercorns
½ cup (125 ml) heavy cream

For the roux
4 tablespoons (60 g) butter
Scant ⅔ cup (60 g) flour
  (You may need slightly more or
  less, depending on the final
  volume of your cooking liquid.)

TECHNIQUE

Poaching (cold start): Deep
  poaching 113

Trim the veal and cut it into pieces weighing about 2–2 ½ oz. (60–70 g). Place them in cold water in a pot and bring to a boil to blanch. Remove as soon as the water begins to boil. Discard the cooking liquid. Place the pieces of veal in a clean pot, cover with water, and add the kosher salt.

Peel and wash the onion. Cut it in half and stud it with the cloves. Add the aromatic ingredients (onion, leek, celery stalk, bouquet garni, and peppercorns) to the meat. Slowly bring to a simmer. Leave to cook for 2–2 ½ hours, skimming when necessary.

Remove the meat from the cooking liquid and strain the liquid through a fine-mesh sieve, if possible into a large measuring jug so that you can calculate how much roux you will need (see below). Discard the aromatic ingredients.

Prepare a white roux with the butter and flour. For every 4 cups (1 liter) of cooking liquid, you should have 2 oz. (55 g) of roux, i.e. 1 oz. butter for 1 oz. or ¼ cup (27.5 g) flour. Combine the butter and flour without heating. Pour half of the cooking liquid over the roux, whisking as you pour. Add the remaining cooking liquid, still whisking. Stir in the cream. When the cream and the liquid are thoroughly combined, pour this mixture back into the cooking liquid with the roux and stir in until heated, without bringing it to a boil.

Transfer the veal stew to a large serving dish and serve with vegetables and rice.

DID YOU KNOW?

Another classic of French cuisine, the recipe for *blanquette de veau* has remained practically unchanged since the eighteenth century. The secret lies in mastering the liaison (thickening) of its sauce.

Breton-style braised leg of lamb ✳

SERVES 10

Preparation: **40 minutes**
Soaking: **12 hours**
Cooking: **1 hour 20 minutes**

INGREDIENTS

1 ½ lb. (700 g) *cocos de Paimpol AOC*, white haricot beans
1 leg of lamb, about 4 ½ lb. (2 kg), allow 7–9 oz. (200–250 g) per person, with shrinkage
3 ½ tablespoons (50 g) butter
¾ cup (200 ml) hard cider
1 onion
½ carrot (2 oz./60 g)
2 cloves
½ leek greens
3 tomatoes
1 bouquet garni
15 peppercorns
Salt, freshly ground pepper

Special equipment: a Dutch oven or flameproof dish with a tight-fitting lid.

TECHNIQUES

Preparing a leg of lamb **87**
Brown braising (meat, poultry, offal) **97**
Peeling using hot water **63**

CHEF'S NOTE

– A light, green salad is a welcome accompaniment to this dish.

A day ahead, shell the beans and leave them to soak overnight in cold water.

Preheat the oven to 350°F (170°C).

Prepare the lamb for cooking. Trim it and remove the pelvic bone (see p. 87). Remove the fine membrane, tie it with twine, and season with salt and pepper. Melt the butter in a pot and brown the lamb all over. Pour over the hard cider, cover with the lid, and transfer the pot to the oven. Cook for 30 minutes, or longer, depending on how pink you like it. Peel and wash the onion and half-carrot, and cut in half lengthwise. Push the cloves into the base of each onion half.

Wash the leek greens and tie them together. Peel the tomatoes, remove the seeds, and dice the flesh. Place the dry beans in a large pot and cover them with cold water. Add the aromatic vegetables, the bouquet garni, and the peppercorns. Bring to a boil and simmer over low heat for at least 1 hour, adding extra boiling water if necessary. They should be completely softened, almost stewed. Drain the beans, remove the bouquet garni, and season with salt and pepper.

Slice the leg of lamb when you serve it. Pour the cooking liquid over the sliced meat and accompany with the coco beans, served separately in a vegetable dish.

DID YOU KNOW?

Inland Brittany, like Normandy, is an apple-producing region, and excellent hard cider is made there. This recipe brings together two of its many star products, its manually harvested semi-dry *coco de Paimpol* bean, and its popular cider.

Pot-au-feu ✳

SERVES 8

Preparation: **35 minutes**
Cooking: **2 hours 30 hours**

INGREDIENTS

1 lb. (500 g) beef ribs (US) or
   fore/thin ribs (UK)
2 lb. (1 kg) beef chuck (US) or
   chuck and blade (UK)
1 tablespoon (20 g) kosher salt
1 ¼ lb. (600 g) marrow bones
1 ¼ lb. (600 g) potatoes
1 ¼ lb. (600 g) carrots
1 lb (400 g) zucchini (courgettes)
Fleur de sel
French mustard

Aromatic ingredients
1 large onion
1 carrot
Green leaf of 1 leek
2 cloves
1 bouquet garni
6–8 peppercorns

TECHNIQUE

Poaching (cold start): Deep
   poaching **113**

CHEF'S NOTES

– Use other types of meat
besides beef, like pork and veal.
You may even try fresh, cured,
or smoked meats. If you opt for
this kind of variation, don't cook
the meats together. Choose your
vegetables according to the
seasons.
– Every European country has its
own version of this boiled dish.
The pot-au-feu, the hearty
winter meal par excellence, is a
one-pot dish comprising of
broth, meat, and vegetables;
and leftover meat may be eaten
cold, reheated, or minced to
make a pie.

Trim the meat, leaving each piece whole.

Prepare the aromatic ingredients. Peel and wash the onion and carrot. Wash the leek green. Cut the vegetables in two and push the cloves into the onions near the base.

Place the pieces of meat in a large pot, cover with cold water, and bring to a boil. Remove the meat immediately and transfer the pieces to another pot. Cover them with cold water. Add all the aromatic ingredients and put in the kosher salt. Bring to a boil, turn down the heat, and simmer for 2 ½ hours. Thirty minutes before the time is up, add the marrow bones. Remove the aromatic ingredients and adjust the seasoning.

Wash, peel, and rinse the potatoes and carrots. Wash the zucchini. Shape the vegetables into regular oval "egg" shapes weighing about 2–2 ½ oz. (50–60 g) per piece. Take 4 cups (1 liter) of the cooking liquid and cook the vegetables in it separately for just the time required for each.

Serve the vegetables with the meat, and the broth in a tureen or vegetable dish. Accompany with *fleur de sel* and French mustard in small dishes.

Hachis Parmentier ✳

SERVES 6

Preparation: **40 minutes**
Cooking: **50 minutes**

INGREDIENTS

Mashed potatoes
2 ¼ lb. (1 kg) medium-starch
  potatoes (such as Bintje)
²/₃ cup (150 ml) milk
Scant ½ cup (100 ml) heavy
  cream, min. 35% fat
Freshly grated nutmeg
3 tablespoons (50 g) unsalted
  butter, at room temperature and
  diced
Salt, freshly ground pepper

Filling
1 carrot
2 onions
2 cloves garlic
4 teaspoons (20 ml) olive oil
1 tablespoon (15 g) unsalted
  butter
1 lb. (500 g) ground beef
½ bunch parsley, chopped
Salt, freshly ground pepper

TECHNIQUE

Cutting into fine dice
  (*brunoise*) **64**

CHEF'S NOTES

– Milk can be used instead of
water to cook the potatoes, if
wished.
– You can top the potatoes with
a sprinkling of grated cheese or
breadcrumbs before baking.
– You can also brown your
hachis Parmentier by placing it
under the broiler for a few
minutes.

To prepare the mashed potatoes, peel, rinse, and quarter the
potatoes. Cook in simmering salted water for about 30 minutes,
until easy to pierce with a knife. Pass the potatoes through a
ricer or food mill or mash them well with a fork. Warm the
milk, cream, and a little freshly grated nutmeg in a saucepan;
let infuse for 5 minutes, or just until the mixture comes to a boil.
Remove from the heat. Stir the butter into the mashed potatoes,
followed by the hot milk mixture. Stir until smooth. Season
with salt and pepper and keep warm.

To prepare the filling, peel and finely dice the carrot (*brunoise*),
then peel and finely chop the onions. Peel the garlic, remove the
green shoots, and chop finely. Sweat the carrot in a sauté pan
with the olive oil and butter for about 1 minute, then add the
onion and garlic. Cook for a few more minutes, until softened,
then add the ground beef. Season with salt and pepper and
cook, stirring, for 5-6 minutes, until no longer pink. Stir in the
parsley and remove from the heat.

Preheat the oven to 400°F (200°C).

Grease a 10 × 6 × 2-inch (25 × 15 × 5-cm) baking dish and rub
with a garlic clove. Spread half the mashed potatoes across the
base of the dish and cover with the meat filling. Add the
remaining potatoes and spread them into a smooth, even layer.
Bake for about 10 minutes, until the surface is golden.

Serve the hachis Parmentier as soon as you take it out of the
oven, with a green salad on the side.

DID YOU KNOW?

Born in 1737 in Montdidier, in the Picardy region, Antoine Augustin
Parmentier served as a pharmacist in the French army and later at the
Hôtel des Invalides in Paris, after being wounded. He loved chemistry
and agronomy and put all his knowledge and energy into finding foods
and/or substances that could alleviate shortages due to poor harvests.
His research on extracting starch from various plants (including chestnuts
and corn) and sugar from grapes earned him widespread recognition, and
he is especially remembered for his role in popularizing the potato.

Frogs' legs ✳

SERVES 8

Preparation: **30 minutes**
Cooking: **20 minutes**

INGREDIENTS

½ bunch parsley
¼ bunch tarragon
¼ bunch chervil
6 cloves garlic
96 large frogs' legs
Scant 1 cup (100 g) flour
Scant ½ cup (100 ml) olive oil
3 tablespoons (40 g) unsalted
  butter
Salt, freshly ground pepper

Wash and finely chop the herbs (parsley, tarragon, and chervil). Peel the garlic, remove the green shoots, and chop finely.

Season the frogs' legs with salt and pepper. Dredge them in the flour and shake them in your hands to remove any excess.

Brown the legs in a skillet with the olive oil over high heat, taking care not to damage them. Work in batches to avoid crowding the pan.

Add the butter, return all the legs to the pan, and cook until uniformly golden. Remove from the heat and gently stir in the chopped garlic and herbs. Cover and let sit for 2 minutes, then serve immediately.

Turkey paupiettes ✳

SERVES 6

Preparation: **25 minutes**
Cooking: **20 minutes**

INGREDIENTS

6 turkey cutlets
7 oz. (200 g) turkey breast
1 egg white
⅔ cup (150 ml) heavy cream
1 teaspoon (5 g) salt
1 teaspoon (2 g) freshly ground
  pepper
3 tablespoons (50 g) butter

Sauce
3 ½ tablespoons (50 ml) port wine
Scant ½ cup (100 ml) heavy
  cream, well chilled
Generous ¾ cup (200 ml)
  thickened brown veal stock (use
  an instant mix or see p. 140)

Preheat the oven to 350°F (180°C).

Place the turkey cutlets between two layers of plastic wrap, ensuring they lie flat. Using a rolling pin or meat mallet, flatten them until evenly thin. Trim and remove any veins, if necessary.

To prepare the stuffing, dice the turkey breast and place in the bowl of a food processor with the egg white. Process until smooth, then press through a fine-mesh sieve. Transfer to a large stainless steel bowl, place over ice, and gradually stir in the cream. Season with salt and pepper. Place about 1 tablespoon of stuffing in the center of each cutlet. Roll the cutlets up around the filling and tie into the desired shape using kitchen twine.

Brown the paupiettes all over in a skillet with the butter, then transfer them to a baking dish and finish cooking through in the oven (about 15 minutes).

To prepare the sauce, return the skillet to high heat to make the brown bits (*sucs*) stick to the bottom, to intensify the flavor. Pour off the excess grease. Deglaze the pan with the port wine and reduce by one-third, then add the cream, followed by the stock. Let reduce to the desired consistency and adjust the seasoning. Serve the paupiettes with the sauce.

Beef tournedos with foie gras ✳

SERVES 4

Preparation: **20 minutes**
Cooking: **25 minutes**

INGREDIENTS

½ lb (250 g) whole fresh foie
  gras
4 beef tournedos (medallions)
4 teaspoons (20 ml) grape-seed
  oil
Salt, freshly ground pepper

Sauce
Scant ½ cup (100 ml) sweet
  white wine
Scant ½ cup (100 ml) thickened
  brown veal stock (use an instant
  mix or see p. 140)
⅕ oz. (5 g) black truffle bits
1 ½ tablespoons (20 g) butter,
  cubed
Salt, freshly ground pepper

TECHNIQUES

Cutting medallions and
  noisettes **93**
Sautéing **123**

CHEF'S NOTES

– Any number of side dishes,
from the simplest to the most
elaborate, go well with this dish.
– This is a simple recipe for a
gastronomic treat with a
decidedly southwestern French
influence.

Cut the foie gras into slices less than ½ in. (1 cm) thick. Season them with salt and pepper.

Sauté the tournedos in oil until it is cooked to your liking, and season with salt and pepper.

Transfer to a rack and keep warm.

Heat a non-stick pan without adding any fat to it. When it is hot, sauté the slices of foie gras. When they have reached the desired degree of doneness, place them on paper towel to drain.

Prepare the sauce. Discard the fat from the sauté pan and deglaze with white wine. Reduce the liquid by half and pour in the veal stock.

Add the truffle bits and whisk in the butter. Adjust the seasoning. Place each tournedos on a plate and top with a slice of foie gras. Drizzle the sauce attractively around the meat.

DID YOU KNOW?

The story goes that Gioacchino Antonio Rossini (1792–1868), composer, fine musician, and true gourmet, who spent many years in Paris, had a variation on this dish created for him by the chef of one of his favorite restaurants. When it is served with a generous slice of truffle, it is known as Tournedos Rossini.

Lamb medallions with licorice-infused foamed milk and duchess potatoes ✳ ✳

SERVES 6

Preparation: **50 minutes**
Cooking: **1 hour 30 minutes**

INGREDIENTS

2 racks of lamb with 6 chops each
2 lb. (1 kg) potatoes
3 egg yolks
1 stick (4 ½ oz./120 g) butter, divided
Salt, freshly ground pepper

Sauce
2 leaves gelatin (4 g)
2 cups (½ liter) whole (full-cream) milk
2 licorice sticks
Salt, freshly ground pepper

TECHNIQUES

Preparing a rack (pork, veal, lamb) **86**
Cutting medallions and noisettes **93**
Duchess potatoes **163**

CHEF'S NOTE

– Licorice-infused milk may be used to braise a leg of lamb or to cook the vegetables served as a side dish. The method of infusing an aromatic ingredient in milk can be used with many varied aromatics.

Remove all the bones from the racks of lamb (see p. 86) to prepare the filets mignons, or ask your butcher to prepare them for you. Remove the outer membrane. Season them on both the flesh side and the fatty side, and roll the belly flap over the filets. Tie every 1 ¼ in. (3 cm) to keep the meat in place as it cooks. Cut between every round of string to create regular medallions that will cook evenly (see p. 93). Allow 3 medallions per person.

Prepare the sauce.
Soak the sheets of gelatin in cold water. Slowly bring the milk to a simmer with the licorice sticks. Leave to infuse for at least 1 hour at about 120°F–140°F (50°C–60°C). If you don't have a thermometer, leave it over a hot water bath that is below simmering point. Drain the gelatin, squeezing it between your fingers to eliminate the water, and mix it into the milk until no traces are visible. Strain the milk through a chinois.

Prepare the duchess potatoes (see p. 163).
Brush and wash the potatoes. Boil them in their jackets for about 30 minutes. Peel them and purée them through a food mill. Place the puréed potatoes in a sauté pan and, stirring with a spatula, dry them out over low heat for a few minutes. Remove from the heat and add the egg yolks and 5 ½ tablespoons (80 g) cubed butter. Season with salt and pepper. Spoon the potato mixture into a piping bag fitted with a star tip to create decorative mounds of potato mixture on parchment paper.

Heat a sauté pan. Add the remaining butter and, when it begins sizzling, place the lamb medallions in it to cook. Brown both sides until the meat reaches the desired degree of doneness. Transfer the medallions to a rack and keep them warm. Preheat the oven to 400°F (200°C) to reheat the duchess potatoes before serving. Deglaze the pan juices with the licorice-infused milk, and allow to reduce over low heat. Strain through a chinois and season with salt and pepper. Place the duchess potatoes in the oven for 5 minutes. Stand the medallions on the plates on their sides. Whisk the sauce until it is foamy, pour it over the meat, and serve with the duchess potatoes.

Vegetables

Alain Passard

presents his recipe

I want to make vegetables the equivalent of wines; they should have their own *grand cru* labels. The idea of talking about a carrot as one talks about a sauvignon grape variety is one I find particularly appealing. In culinary terms, the vegetable is first and foremost a product of the four seasons—marked differences in the range of flavors available are detectable with every change. The vegetable also constitutes a true source of inspiration, each one with its particular texture, skin, color, and design. Believe it or not, the curve of an eggplant can become an invaluable starting point when a recipe is created.

We have three vegetable gardens, each one with its own terroir: sandy earth in the Sarthe, a region southwest of Paris; clay in the Eure in Normandy; and alluvial deposits in the Bay of Mont Saint-Michel. These three quite different types of soil have led us to think about just what a vegetable needs for optimum growth, and we plant specific seeds according to what the soils can best support. The Eure is perfect territory for bulbs like new garlic, red and yellow onions, and gray shallots. In the Sarthe, we have our carrots, asparagus, and leeks, and in the microclimate of the Bay of Mont Saint-Michel, we cultivate our aromatic plants. After a tasting session, we choose the best produce.

SERVES 4

Preparation:
40 minutes
Cooking:
50 minutes

INGREDIENTS

4 yellow carrots
4 orange carrots
2 round turnips
2 golden turnips
4 green cabbage leaves
A few broccoli florets
2 black radishes
4 green radishes
4 red radishes
½ lb. (220 g) salted
  butter
36 currants
Juice of 1 lemon

Semolina
7 oz. (200 g) extra-fine
  semolina
4 drizzles of olive oil
2 teaspoons argan oil
4 pinches *fleur de sel*

Onion sauce
4 sweet Cévennes
  onions, or other sweet
  onions
1 stick (120 g) salted
  butter
1 ⅔ cups (400 ml)
  whipping cream
Fleur de sel

Eggplant caviar
4 eggplants, weighing
  3 ½ oz. (100 g) each
4 teaspoons hazelnut oil
2 teaspoons fresh
  chopped ginger
4 pinches four-spice
  mixture
4 pinches *fleur de sel*

Harlequin vegetable platter

Vegetables
Wash and peel the vegetables. Cook in boiling water in separate pots: the yellow and orange carrots ; the round and golden turnips ; the broccoli; and the green cabbage—each with 2–3 tablespoons of butter. Cook the three types of radishes with 4 tablespoons of butter. Set aside a total of 1 ⅔ cups (400 ml) of the cooking liquid, taken from each of the pots.

Semolina
Place the semolina and olive oil in a saucepan. Heat together, whisking as you incorporate 20 fl. oz. (2 ½ cups or 600 ml) hot water. Set aside.

Onion sauce
Peel the onions, slice them finely, and sauté them in a pan with the salted butter and 1 ⅔ cups (400 ml) water. Be careful not to brown them, but cook until they reach a confit texture (see p. 98). When they are done, process them with the whipping cream, strain through a chinois, and adjust the seasoning with *fleur de sel*.

Eggplant caviar
Place the eggplants on a baking tray and broil at 425°F (220°C) for 20 minutes, turning regularly, to scorch the skin. When they are done, peel them, and chop the flesh, incorporating the hazelnut oil, chopped ginger, four-spice mixture, and *fleur de sel*. Transfer to a bowl.

To assemble
Cut each vegetable into pieces. Place them together in a sauté pan with the currants, the vegetable cooking liquid, 4 tablespoons (60 g) salted butter, and a few drops of lemon juice.

Heat it all together, swirling the pan so that all the vegetables are glazed. Arrange them on four plates. Flavor the semolina with the argan oil and *fleur de sel*. Place two oval scoops of eggplant caviar on each plate and sprinkle some of the semolina over the vegetables, dotting the onion sauce attractively around.

Florentine-style gnocchi ✳ ✳

SERVES 8

Preparation: **55 minutes**
Cooking: **40 minutes**

INGREDIENTS

1 ½ lb. (650 g) fresh spinach
3 garlic cloves, peeled, shoots
  removed
3 ½ tablespoons (50 g) salted
  butter
1 ¼ cups (120 g) grated Gruyère
  cheese
Freshly ground pepper

Choux pastry
6 tablespoons (90 g) butter,
  cubed
1 ²/₃ cups (150 g) flour
3 eggs
Salt, ground white pepper

Béchamel sauce
4 tablespoons (60 g) butter
Scant ²/₃ cup (60 g) flour
4 cups (1 liter) milk
A little grated nutmeg
Salt, freshly ground pepper

TECHNIQUES

Choux pastry **22**
Béchamel or white sauce **133**

CHEF'S NOTE

– If you can, use fresh spinach
rather than frozen for a far
better taste.

Remove the stems of the spinach leaves and wash them well.
Chop the garlic cloves. Prepare a beurre noisette (butter that is
melted until brown) with garlic and sauté the spinach in it.
Leave to cook over low heat for 5 minutes and then season.

To make the gnocchi, prepare a choux pastry (see p. 22). Sift the
flour. Bring to a boil 1 cup (250 ml) water, the cubed butter, salt,
and ground white pepper. Remove from the heat and add all the
sifted flour at once. Return the saucepan to the heat and dry the
batter by stirring energetically with a spatula until the moisture
has evaporated. Transfer the choux batter to a bowl and leave to
cool. Mix in the eggs one by one, using a spatula to stir them in
until completely incorporated. Bring about 4 ½ pints (2 liters)
salted water to a boil. Spoon the choux pastry into a piping bag
with a plain, medium-sized tip. Pipe small cylinder shapes into
the boiling water, cutting them off with a paring knife. Simmer
for 4–5 minutes. Remove from the water and strain.

Prepare the béchamel sauce (see p. 133). Make a white roux with
the butter and flour. Pour over half the cold milk and add the
grated nutmeg. Bring the mixture to a boil over high heat,
stirring constantly with your whisk. Pour in the remaining
milk, bring to a boil again, and season. Cover with plastic wrap
flush with the surface to prevent a skin from forming.

Preheat the oven to 425°F (220°C).

Spread a little béchamel sauce at the bottom of an ovenproof
dish. Arrange the spinach over it, and then the gnocchi. Cover
with béchamel sauce. Scatter with grated Gruyère cheese and
bake until brown and crisp on top, about 15–20 minutes.

Stuffed round zucchini ✳

SERVES 6

Preparation: **30 minutes**
Cooking: **30 minutes**

INGREDIENTS

6 round zucchini
1 large onion
2 tablespoons (30 ml) olive oil
6 ½ oz. (180 g) fresh goat cheese
Scant 1 cup (100 g) grated
  Gruyère
Salt, freshly ground pepper

Steam the zucchini for 3 minutes.

Cut the tops off the zucchini and set aside for serving. Scoop out the insides using a spoon, taking care not to pierce the skin. Roughly chop the scooped-out flesh.

Peel and finely chop the onion and sauté in a skillet with the olive oil over high heat, until softened and browned. Stir in the chopped zucchini and cook until tender.

Remove from the heat, stir in the goat cheese, and season with salt and pepper.

Stuff the hollowed out zucchini with the zucchini-goat cheese mixture. Sprinkle with the Gruyère and place in a 10 × 6 × 2-inch (25 × 15 × 5-cm) baking dish.

Place under the broiler for 10 minutes, until golden.

Replace the tops and serve.

Arlie potatoes ✳

SERVES 6

Preparation: **35 minutes**
Cooking: **45 minutes**

INGREDIENTS

2 ¾ lb. (1.2 kg) potatoes of the
  same size (about 7 oz./200 g
  each)
Generous ¾ cup (200 ml) heavy
  cream, warm
½ bunch chives, snipped
Generous 1 cup (120 g) grated
  Gruyère
Salt, freshly ground pepper

Preheat the oven to 340°F (170°C).

Scrub and wash the potatoes and place them whole in a baking dish or on a baking sheet. Bake for about 40 minutes, until completely tender—a paring knife inserted into the center should meet no resistance.

Cut the tops off the potatoes. Scoop out the insides using a small spoon, leaving an approximately ¼-inch (6-mm) shell with the skin intact. Set aside.

Pass the scooped-out potato through a ricer or food mill, then stir in the warm cream, followed by the chives. Divide between the potato shells.

Sprinkle with the Gruyère and place under the broiler for 5 minutes, until golden.

Asparagus with mousseline sauce ✳

SERVES 6

Preparation: **20 minutes**
Cooking: **20 minutes**

INGREDIENTS

Poached white asparagus
30 stalks white asparagus
Juice of 1 lemon
8 cups (2 liters) water
½ cup (50 g) flour
Scant ¼ cup (50 ml) neutral oil

Mousseline sauce
4 egg yolks
⅓ cup (80 ml) heavy cream
1 ½ sticks (180 g) butter, melted
Juice of 1 lemon
Cayenne pepper
Salt

TECHNIQUES

Peeling **59**
Poaching (hot start): Deep
    poaching (in a *blanc*) **108**

Peel the asparagus (see p. 59) and drizzle it with the lemon juice. Deep poach it for 12 minutes in a *blanc* prepared with the ingredients listed (see deep poaching [hot start] technique, p. 108).

Meanwhile, prepare the mousseline sauce. Whisk the egg yolks and cream together in a saucepan off the heat. Place over a hot water bath (bain-marie) or over very low heat and continue whisking until very thick. Remove from the heat and whisk in the melted butter. Stir in the lemon juice and season with Cayenne pepper and salt.

Place the hot asparagus on a clean tea towel to absorb excess moisture.

Serve with the mousseline sauce on the side, in a sauce dish.

Mixed garden vegetables ✳

SERVES 6

Preparation: **30 minutes**

INGREDIENTS

1 orange bell pepper (150 g)
1 large carrot (150 g)
6 violet asparagus spears
7 oz. (200 g) button mushrooms
10 pink radishes
2 lettuce hearts
A few sprigs of chervil, for
  garnish
A few sprigs of chives, for
  garnish

Vinaigrette
Scant ¼ cup (50 ml) vinegar
²/₃ cup (150 ml) oil
Salt, freshly ground pepper

TECHNIQUES

Cutting into julienne strips **61**
Peeling using oil **63**
Vinaigrette **152**

CHEF'S NOTE

– This garden salad will vary
with the seasons; what's
essential is to use the freshest
produce. Make it more
interesting by using different
types of oil and vinegar; the
juxtaposition of varied colors
will whet your appetite!

Wash the vegetables. Peel the bell pepper, either with a vegetable peeler or by roasting in a hot oven and removing the charred skin (see p. 63). Peel the carrot. Finely slice the asparagus, button mushrooms, and pink radishes lengthwise.

Remove the stem of the bell pepper. Cut it into quarters, remove the seeds and all the white ribs, and slice it finely. Cut the carrot into fine julienne strips. Remove the leaves of the lettuce hearts and wash them.

Dissolve a little salt in the vinegar and season with pepper. Whisk in the olive oil.

Arrange the vegetables attractively and garnish with chervil and chives. Drizzle the vinaigrette over at the last moment.

Cauliflower gratin ✳

SERVES 6

Preparation: **30 minutes**
Cooking: **45 minutes**

INGREDIENTS

Béchamel sauce
4 tablespoons (60 g) butter
⅔ cup (60 g) flour
3 cups (750 ml) milk, divided
Pinch grated nutmeg
Salt, freshly ground pepper

Gratin
3 ½ lb. (1.5 kg) cauliflower
1 ¼ cups (150 g) grated Gruyère
Salt, freshly ground pepper

TECHNIQUE

Béchamel or white sauce **133**

Prepare the béchamel sauce using the ingredients listed (see p. 133). Keep warm.

To prepare the gratin, preheat the oven to 430°F (220°C). Generously grease a 10 × 6 × 2-inch (25 × 15 × 5-cm) baking dish with butter.

Cut the cauliflower into florets and wash. Immerse in a pot of boiling salted water and let cook, uncovered, over high heat. Cook for several minutes, or until tender: a knife inserted into the stalks should meet no resistance. Drain well.

Transfer the florets to the baking dish, season with salt and pepper, and cover with the béchamel sauce. Sprinkle with the Gruyère.

Bake for about 20 minutes, until the top is golden.

Autumn skillet ✳

SERVES 6

Preparation: **40 minutes**
Cooking: **40 minutes**

INGREDIENTS

14 oz. (400 g) chestnuts
1 ¼ lb. (600 g) rutabagas
4 tablespoons (60 g) butter,
    divided
About ¼ cup (60 ml) water
2 cloves pink garlic
¼ bunch flat-leaf parsley
7 oz. (200 g) assorted
    mushrooms (porcini, girolles,
    black trumpets, etc.)
Salt, freshly ground pepper

TECHNIQUE

Scooping **62**

Cook the chestnuts in boiling water for 3 minutes. Refresh them in cold water, then peel them.

Peel the rutabagas and scoop out balls using a melon baller. Cook in a sauté pan with half the butter and the water over low heat until tender (about 12 minutes).

Meanwhile, peel the garlic, remove the shoots, and chop together with the parsley.

Quickly rinse the mushrooms in cold water, then dry them and cut them into ¾-inch (2-cm) dice. Sauté in a skillet with the remaining butter.

Combine the rutabaga, mushrooms, and peeled chestnuts in the same skillet and sprinkle with the garlic and parsley. Reheat for a few minutes, season, and serve.

Zucchini gratin ✳

SERVES 6

Preparation: **30 minutes**
Cooking: **45 minutes**

INGREDIENTS

Savory custard base
Generous ¾ cup (200 ml) milk
Scant ½ cup (100 ml) heavy cream
3 eggs
1 egg yolk

Gratin
2 tablespoons (30 g) butter
½ bunch chives
2 ¼ lb. (1 kg) zucchini
⅓ cup (80 ml) olive oil
½ teaspoon *herbes de Provence*
Generous 1 cup (120 g) grated
  Gruyère
Salt, freshly ground pepper

TECHNIQUES

Savory custard base for baking
  132
Cutting round slices **58**

Prepare the savory custard base using the ingredients listed (see p. 132).

Preheat the oven to 375°F (190°C) and grease a 10 × 6 × 2-inch (25 × 15 × 5-cm) baking dish with the butter.

Wash and snip the chives. Wash the zucchini and cut it, unpeeled, into thin rounds, about ⅛ inch (2–3 mm) thick. Sauté in a skillet with the olive oil until softened and lightly browned. Add the chives and *herbes de Provence* and season with salt and pepper.

Add the zucchini to the savory custard base. Using a spatula, gently stir to combine.

Pour into the baking dish, sprinkle over the Gruyère, and bake for about 30 minutes, until set and golden.

Spring skillet ✳

SERVES 6

Preparation: **40 minutes**
Cooking: **30 minutes**

INGREDIENTS

4 ¼ oz. (120 g) spring carrots
4 ¼ oz. (120 g) baby turnips
5 ¼ oz. (150 g) peas in their
  pods
7 oz. (200 g) fava beans in their
  pods
4 tablespoons (60 g) butter
Salt, freshly ground pepper

Wash and scrub the carrots and turnips, leaving them unpeeled. Shell the peas and fava beans.

Cook all the vegetables separately until just tender in an uncovered pot of boiling salted water. Check for doneness using the tip of a knife. As soon as the vegetables are done, refresh them in ice-cold water. Drain well. Cut the carrots and turnips into bite-size pieces.

Reheat all the vegetables together briefly in a skillet. Toss with the butter, season with salt and pepper, and serve.

Salade Niçoise ✳

Vegetables

SERVES 6

Preparation: **35 minutes**
Cooking: **12 minutes**

INGREDIENTS

6 tomatoes
2 celery stalks (180 g)
1 red bell pepper (180 g)
3 small violet artichokes
4 new onions
½ lb. (240 g) canned tuna in
  brine
5 pink radishes
2 eggs
18 black olives, for garnish
12 salted anchovy fillets, for
  garnish
A few sprigs of basil, for garnish

Vinaigrette
2 tablespoons (30 ml) wine
  vinegar
5 tablespoons (25 ml) olive oil
Salt, freshly ground pepper

TECHNIQUES

Hard-boiled eggs **41**
Vinaigrette **152**

CHEF'S NOTE

– You can rub the salad dish with
a garlic clove for extra taste.

Finely slice the vegetables, choosing the cut you prefer (for example slices, quarters, or sticks).

Drain and flake the tuna.

Finely slice the pink radishes.

Prepare the hard-boiled eggs (see p. 41). Remove the shells and cut them into quarters.

Prepare the vinaigrette. Dissolve a little salt in the vinegar, add pepper, and whisk in the olive oil.

Arrange the vegetables and tuna attractively in a large salad dish or serving platter. Add the garnish (olives, anchovy fillets, and basil). Drizzle with the vinaigrette just before serving.

DID YOU KNOW?

This refreshing yet satisfying salad contains the best of what the Mediterranean city of Nice and its surroundings have to offer, hence its name. The exact ingredients of this dish have been the subject of much debate, the use of lettuce and potatoes being the most controversial.

Ratatouille ✳

SERVES 4

Preparation: **40 minutes**
Cooking: **30 minutes**

INGREDIENTS

3 ½ oz. (100 g) eggplant
3 ½ oz. (100 g) zucchini
3 ½ oz. (100 g) red bell pepper
1 large onion
2 ½ tablespoons (40 ml) olive oil
2 cloves garlic
3 ½ oz. (100 g) tomatoes
Herbes de Provence
Piment d'Espelette
Salt

TECHNIQUES

Peeling using hot water **63**
Chopping tomatoes **57**

Wash the eggplant, zucchini, and bell pepper. Peel the onion. Cut the vegetables separately into ¼-inch (5-mm) dice; keep apart.

Sauté each vegetable separately in a skillet with olive oil, until softened and lightly browned.

Peel the garlic, remove the shoots, and chop finely. Peel the tomatoes (see p. 63), remove the seeds, and cut into ¼-inch (5-mm) dice (see p. 57). You can save the peel and fry it for decoration.

Combine all the vegetables in a Dutch oven and add a pinch or two of *herbes de Provence*. Cover and let cook over very low heat for about 30 minutes, stirring occasionally, until the vegetables are completely tender.

Season with salt and a little *piment d'Espelette*.

Provençal vegetable *tian* ✳

SERVES 6

Preparation: **30 minutes**
Cooking: **45 minutes**

INGREDIENTS

2 tomatoes
2 zucchini
1 eggplant
2 large onions
2 cloves garlic
¼ bunch basil
Scant ½ cup (100 ml) olive oil
½ teaspoon *herbes de Provence*
Salt, freshly ground pepper

TECHNIQUE

Cutting round slices **58**

Preheat the oven to 340°F (170°C).

Wash the tomatoes, zucchini, and eggplant. Peel the onion. Cut all the vegetables into thin rounds, about ⅛ inch (3–4-mm) thick.

Peel the garlic, remove the shoots, and chop finely. Finely chop the basil. Combine in a bowl and add half the olive oil and the *herbes de Provence*.

Brush the inside of a 10 × 6 × 2-inch (25 × 15 × 5-cm) earthenware baking dish with some of the olive oil, garlic, and herb mixture.

Arrange the vegetable slices in the baking dish, alternating them and packing them tightly together. Drizzle with the remaining olive oil.

Bake for about 45 minutes, until the vegetables are completely tender.

Basque-style vegetables ✳

SERVES 6

Preparation: **30 minutes**
Cooking: **35 minutes**

INGREDIENTS

1 slice cured ham (preferably
  Bayonne), ¼-inch (5-mm) thick
1 ¾ lb. (800 g) tomatoes
1 large onion
3 ½ oz. (100 g) mild green chili
  peppers
2 tablespoons duck fat
2 cloves garlic
Piment d'Espelette
Salt

TECHNIQUES

Peeling using hot water **63**
Chopping tomatoes **57**

Cut the ham into ¼-inch (5-mm) dice.

Peel the tomatoes (see p. 63), remove the seeds, and chop (see p. 57). Peel and thinly slice the onion, then thinly slice the chili peppers. Peel the garlic and remove the shoots.

Cook the ham and onion in a Dutch oven over low heat for 2–3 minutes, until softened. Add the tomatoes and the garlic crushed through a garlic press.

Cook over low heat for 30 minutes, stirring often, until the vegetables are completely tender. Season with salt and *piment d'Espelette*.

Soft-boiled eggs on a bed of artichokes with eggplant caviar ✳ ✳

SERVES 6

Preparation: **1 hour**
Cooking: **45 minutes**

INGREDIENTS

6 eggs
3 tablespoons (40 ml) vinegar
3 large green artichokes
2 lemons
2 ½ teaspoons (15 g) kosher salt
1 tablespoon (15 ml) oil
⅓ cup (1 oz./30 g) flour
6 sprigs rosemary, for garnish

Eggplant caviar
1 large eggplant (aubergine)
　(10 oz./300 g)
Herbes de Provence
Scant ¼ cup (50 ml) olive oil
Salt, freshly ground pepper

Red wine sauce
1 ¼ cups (300 ml) red wine
2 shallots
1 scant cup (200 ml) thickened
　brown veal stock (use an instant
　mix or see p. 140)
2 tablespoons (30 g) butter,
　cubed
Fine sea salt, freshly ground
　pepper

TECHNIQUES

Soft-boiled eggs
　(*oeufs mollets*) **42**
Turning vegetables **66**
Poaching (hot start): Deep
　poaching (in a *blanc*) **108**

Prepare a pot of boiling water. Pour in the vinegar and immediately place the eggs gently in the pot. Leave to simmer for 4 ½ to 5 minutes. Cool under running water immediately. Remove the shells.

Turn the artichokes (see p. 66). Break the stems and remove the leaves using a knife with a short, rigid blade (a boning knife). Trim the bottoms neatly so that there are no traces of green left, as these parts taste very bitter. Shave off the top a short distance (under 1 inch or a couple of centimeters) from the bottom at the level of the fuzzy choke. Squeeze lemon juice over the entire artichoke bottom so that it doesn't go black. You may also tie a slice of lemon to the bottom (stem end) during cooking. Keep the prepared artichokes in water with lemon juice until you are ready to cook them.

Prepare a *blanc* (see p. 108). Bring 6 cups (1.5 liters) water to boil with the juice of 1 lemon, kosher salt, and oil. Dilute the flour in cold water and pour into the boiling liquid. Simmer until it thickens—it will make a light velouté. Place the artichokes in the *blanc* and cook for 10 minutes. Refresh as soon as they are done.

Prepare the eggplant caviar. Preheat the oven to 340°F (170°C). Wash the eggplant and cut it in half lengthwise. Make fairly deep incisions in the flesh. Season with salt and pepper and scatter with *herbes de Provence*. Drizzle a little oil into a roasting pan. Place the eggplant halves in the pan, drizzle them with a little olive oil, and cook for 25–30 minutes. Scoop out the eggplant flesh. Chop it and adjust the seasoning.

To make the sauce, chop the shallots and place them in a small pot with the red wine. Reduce over medium heat until practically dry. Add the thickened brown veal stock. Whip in the butter and season.

Fill the artichoke bottoms with the eggplant caviar and top with a soft-boiled egg. Pour over the red wine sauce and garnish with a small sprig of rosemary on the side.

CHEF'S NOTE

– The success of this dish depends on how you cook the egg and the choice of your wine, which should be slightly tannic and not acidic. You can enjoy it cold or hot. If you are going to eat it hot, prepare the eggs last or reheat them by dipping them for a few moments in a pot of salted boiling water.

Potato and sweet potato purée ✳

SERVES 6

Preparation: **30 minutes**
Cooking: **30 minutes**

INGREDIENTS

1 ¼ lb. (600 g) potatoes
1 ¼ lb. (600 g) sweet potatoes
Generous ¾ cup (200 ml) milk,
   hot
4 tablespoons (60 g) butter, at
   room temperature and diced
½ teaspoon curry powder
Salt, freshly ground pepper

Wash and scrub the potatoes and sweet potatoes. Leave the skin on.

Either place the potatoes and sweet potatoes in a pot of cold salted water and bring to a simmer or steam them. In both cases, let them cook for 30 minutes, or until completely tender—a paring knife inserted into the center should meet no resistance.

Peel and pass through a ricer or food mill to make a purée.

Thin the purée with the hot milk, then stir in the butter until silky and smooth. Season with the curry powder, salt, and pepper.

Potato gratin ✳

SERVES 6

Preparation: **30 minutes**
Cooking: **45 minutes**

INGREDIENTS

2 ¾ lb. (1.2 kg) potatoes
2 cloves garlic
Generous ¾ cup (200 ml) heavy
   cream
1 cup (250 ml) milk
1 bay leaf
1 pinch ground nutmeg
1 ¼ cups (150 g) grated Gruyère
Salt, freshly ground pepper

TECHNIQUE

Cutting round slices **58**

Preheat the oven to 430°F (220°C). Generously grease a 10 × 6 × 2-inch (25 × 15 × 5-cm) baking dish with butter.

Wash, scrub, and peel the potatoes. Cut them crosswise into very thin slices, about 1/16 inch (2 mm) thick; do not rinse. Peel the garlic, remove the shoots, and chop finely.

Combine the cream, milk, garlic, bay leaf, and nutmeg in a large saucepan. Season with salt and pepper. Warm over medium heat.

Add the potato slices and cook over medium heat, stirring constantly, until the potatoes are halfway cooked (one out of every two potato slices should break easily).

Transfer the contents of the saucepan to the baking dish, arranging the potatoes attractively. Sprinkle with the Gruyère.

Bake for 30 minutes, until the potatoes are cooked through and the top is golden.

Provençal-style tomatoes ✳

SERVES 6

Preparation: **20 minutes**
Cooking: **20 minutes**

INGREDIENTS

6 large tomatoes
4 cloves (20 g) garlic
½ bunch flat-leaf parsley
Scant 1 cup (100 g) breadcrumbs
½ teaspoon *herbes de Provence*
5 cl olive oil
Salt, freshly ground pepper

Preheat the oven to 350°F (180°C).

Wash the tomatoes, remove the stems, and cut in half crosswise. Arrange cut-side up in a 10 × 6 × 2-inch (25 × 15 × 5-cm) baking dish.

Peel the garlic, remove the shoots, and chop together with the parsley. Combine in a bowl with the breadcrumbs and *herbes de Provence* and stir in the olive oil to bind everything together.

Spoon a little of this Provençal mixture over each tomato half.

Bake for about 20 minutes, until the tomatoes just start to collapse.

Potato galettes ✳

SERVES 6

Preparation: **30 minutes**
Cooking: **25 minutes**

INGREDIENTS

2 ¾ lb. (1.2 kg) potatoes
2 eggs, lightly beaten
4 tablespoons (60 g) butter
Salt, freshly ground pepper

Preheat the oven to 350°F (180°C).

Wash, scrub, and peel the potatoes. Grate them on the large holes of a box grater; do not rinse.

Place the grated potatoes in a large bowl, add the eggs, and season with salt and pepper. Combine the ingredients well using your hands.

Shape the potato mixture into 3-inch (8-cm) round galettes or pancakes, about ¾ inch (2 cm) thick.

Melt the butter in a nonstick skillet over medium-high heat. Working in batches, brown the galettes for about 2 minutes on each side.

Finish cooking the galettes in the oven, for about 10 minutes.

Rolled Picardy crêpes ✳✳

Preparation: **1 hour**
Cooking: **1 hours**

INGREDIENTS

3 ½ tablespoons (50 g) butter
  plus 1 ½ tablespoons (20 g) to
  butter crepes before filling
¾ lb. (350 g) button mushrooms
1 shallot (50 g)
1 onion (80 g)
1 ½ tablespoons (20 g) parsley,
  chopped
½ lb. (250 g) ham
4 oz. (120 g) grated Gruyère
  cheese
Salt, freshly ground pepper

Crêpe batter
2 ¾ cups (250 g) cake or
  all-purpose flour
3 eggs
2 cups (500 ml) low-fat (semi-
  skimmed) milk, room
  temperature
5 ½ tablespoons (80 g) butter
10 sprigs of chives, snipped
1 pinch of salt
Oil for the skillet

Béchamel sauce
4 tablespoons (60 g) butter
⅔ cup (60 g) flour
4 cups (1 liter) milk
A little grated nutmeg
Salt, freshly ground pepper

TECHNIQUES

Crêpe batter **20**
Basic duxelles (mushroom) **158**
Béchamel or white sauce **133**

CHEF'S NOTE

– The traditional filling for rolled
crêpes uses mushrooms and
ham, but feel free to add the
fillings of your choice.

Prepare the crêpe batter (see p. 20).
Sift the flour and salt into a mixing bowl. Crack the eggs one by
one into the mixture and whisk briskly with a little of the milk.
Incorporate the remaining milk, beating energetically until the
batter is smooth and fluid. Strain through a fine-mesh sieve.
Melt the butter until it browns to a hazelnut color. Mix it into
the batter with the snipped chives and chill for about
30 minutes. Heat a skillet over high heat. Drizzle a little oil in
and cook the crêpes one by one, turning them when they begin
to brown at the edges.

Prepare the mushroom duxelles (see p. 158).
Chop the button mushrooms, the shallots, and the onion. Melt
the 3 ½ tablespoons of butter and sweat the chopped shallot and
onion. Add the button mushrooms and cook, lid off, until all
the liquid has evaporated. Season with salt and pepper and add
the chopped parsley. Finely dice the ham. Prepare the béchamel
sauce (see p. 133) using the butter and flour to make a white
roux. Add 2 cups (500 ml) milk and the grated nutmeg. Bring
the mixture to boil over high heat, whisking constantly. Pour in
the remaining milk, bring to a boil again, and season. Transfer
to a bowl and cover with plastic wrap flush with the surface.
This will prevent a skin from forming.

Preheat the oven to 425°F (220°C).

Place the mushroom preparation, the diced ham, and a little of
the béchamel sauce in a mixing bowl and combine. Adjust the
seasoning. Spread the crêpes out and butter them with the
remaining butter. Fill them with the mushroom and ham
mixture and roll up. Arrange them in a shallow ovenproof dish.
Pour over the béchamel sauce and scatter the grated cheese on
top. Bake for 15–20 minutes.

Cheese

Xavier Thuret

presents his recipe

Cheese came into being when humankind felt the need to preserve milk, the divine drink that is also known as "white gold" because it is the first nourishment of life. The cheese maker's art is akin to that of the alchemist: he solidifies milk using the action of an acid, rennet in particular. This seemingly simple process has given rise to the diversity of cheeses we find on our cheese platters. The personality of a cheese stems first and foremost from its type of milk: cow, goat, sheep, or buffalo. What these animals feed on depends on what we call terroir, which varies from the plains to the mountains, from the pastures of Normandy, to the Alps, and the plateaus of the Larzac. France has an unrivaled range of this fine foodstuff. The specialist *affineurs*, ripeners, take the milk and transform it into a signature product, giving it creaminess, elasticity, suavity, and aromas that may be fruity, toasty, animal, or strong.

Tasting cheese is an experience to be shared, a moment of pure conviviality. But what will make it a truly sublime event is the wine— preferably a white wine. Don't ever forget: cheese doesn't like water! Cheese is part of France's gastronomic heritage and is an essential element in many dishes. It works wonders in binding ingredients, and its flavorful generosity constantly inspires new culinary creations.

SERVES 4

Preparation:
20 minutes
Chilling:
3–4 hours

INGREDIENTS

10 oz. (300 g) raw beets, cooked and peeled, or precooked beets if available
7 oz. (200 g) Roquefort Baragnaudes, or other good strong blue cheese
1 oz. (30 g) pine nuts
1 oz. (30 g) shelled pistachios
8 sheets gelatin (16 g)
Scant ½ cup (100 ml) hazelnut oil
Fine sea salt
Freshly ground pepper

Balsamic jelly
4 sheets gelatin (8 g)
½ cup (120 ml) balsamic vinegar

Beet nougat with Baragnaudes Roquefort chips

Balsamic vinegar jelly

Soften four sheets of gelatin in water at room temperature. Pour the vinegar into a small saucepan and warm it. When the gelatin sheets have softened, squeeze them out and incorporate them into the vinegar, allowing them to dissolve completely. Pour the mixture into a terrine and chill.

Beet purée

Cook the beets if using raw beets, and peel them. Peel the precooked beets if that is what you have. Place them in the blender and process until completely smooth. Finely dice the Roquefort. Mix the pine nuts, pistachios, and cubed Roquefort into the puréed beets. Season with salt and freshly ground pepper. Soften the eight remaining sheets of gelatin in a bowl of water. Slightly heat the scant ½ cup (100 ml) hazelnut oil. Dissolve the softened gelatin sheets in the warm oil, and then incorporate the mixture into the beet puree.

When the balsamic vinegar jelly has completely set in the terrine, pour the rest of the mixture over it. Chill for at least 3–4 hours.

To assemble

Dip a knife into warm water and cut nice, thick slices of terrine.

Serve with oak leaf salad seasoned with hazelnut oil and scattered with a few slightly crushed nuts and dried fruit.

Xavier Thuret presents his recipe

Brie fritters with spicy stewed black cherries ✳

SERVES 10

Preparation: **25 minutes**
Cooking: **35 minutes**

INGREDIENTS

Spicy stewed black cherries
7 oz. (200 g) black cherries
¾ cup (150 g) sugar
8 star anise
2 heaped tablespoons (10 g)
   cinnamon
1 vanilla bean, slit lengthways
1 teaspoon (5 g) ground ginger

Frying batter
2 cups (200 g) all-purpose flour
1 teaspoon (5 g) salt
2 whole eggs plus 3 egg whites
1 ⅓ tablespoons (20 ml)
   sunflower seed oil
¾ cup (200 ml) milk or beer

2 lb. 4 oz. (1 kg) Brie cheese
Oil for frying

TECHNIQUE

Frying batter **25**

Prepare the spicy stewed black cherries.
Remove the stems and pits of the black cherries. Place them in a pot with the sugar and spices and cover with water. Leave to stew gently until practically all the water has evaporated. Allow to cool.

Prepare the frying batter (see p. 25).
Sift the flour into a mixing bowl and add the salt. Break the whole eggs one by one, and whisk them in to the dry ingredients. Incorporate the oil. Pour in the liquid (milk or beer) and whisk until the mixture is smooth. Stiffly beat the egg whites. Gently fold in the beaten egg whites using a flexible rubber spatula.

Cut the Brie into fairly large cubes, just under 1 in. (2 cm). Heat an oil bath to 325°F (160°C). Dip the Brie cubes in the batter, ensuring that they are evenly coated, and place in the oil bath. When they are lightly golden to brown all over, remove them from the oil with a slotted spoon and place on paper towel to drain. Serve immediately with the spicy stewed black cherries.

Goat cheese, honey, rosemary, and toasted pink peppercorn parcels ✳

SERVES 8

Preparation: **25 minutes**
Baking: **15 minutes**

INGREDIENTS

3 teaspoons (10 g) pink
 peppercorns
4 sheets brick pastry (or 8 sheets
 filo)
8 baguette croutons
⅓ cup (80 ml) olive oil
1 log of fresh goat milk cheese,
 preferably coated with ash
Scant ⅓ cup (100 g) acacia
 honey
8 sprigs fresh rosemary
8 sprigs chives
Freshly ground pepper

Toast the pink peppercorns in the oven. Leave them to cool, then rub them between your hands to remove some of the skin. Crush roughly and set aside.

Preheat the oven to 325°F (160°C).

Cut the sheets of brick (or filo) pastry in half. (Note that brick pastry is sold in disks. Filo pastry is more fragile and should be doubled, though you will still need to cut them in half.) In the center of each piece of pastry, place a crouton of fresh baguette and drizzle it with a little olive oil.

Place a piece of goat milk cheese less than ½ in. (1 cm) thick on each crouton. Brush some acacia honey over it and top with a small sprig of rosemary. Season with freshly ground pepper and sprinkle over a little of the crushed pink peppercorns.

Fold the pastry upward to make small parcels, holding them together with a toothpick.

Bake for about 10 minutes, until the pastry is a nice, even golden color. When you remove them from the oven, take out the toothpick and make a knot with a chive sprig so that it looks like a little parcel.

Serve hot, accompanied by a salad.

Lyonnaise cream cheese with fines herbes (*cervelle de canut*) ✳

SERVES 8

Preparation: **40 minutes**
Draining: **overnight (optional)**

INGREDIENTS

3 lb. (1.5 kg) *faisselle* cheese
1 shallot
1 bunch (20 g) chives, plus a few
   extra sprigs for garnish
A few sprigs (10 g) chervil
Scant ¼ cup (50 ml) dry white
   wine (optional)
2 teaspoons (10 ml) white
   vinegar, flavored if you wish
   (tarragon, for example)
1 cup (250 ml) whipping cream,
   min. 35% fat, well chilled
Salt, pepper

Drain the *faisselle* cream cheese, overnight if possible.

Peel the shallot and chop it finely. Finely snip the chives and chop the chervil.

Combine the shallot and herbs with the drained cream cheese using a spatula. Add the white wine and/or vinegar, salt, and pepper and mix again.

Whip the chilled cream stiffly and carefully fold it into the cream cheese mixture.

Garnish the top with finely snipped chives. Chill until serving—it should be very cold. Accompany with breads with dried fruit or seeds, or crudités.

DID YOU KNOW?

This is a specialty of the region of Lyon, a city where silk weaving was a major industry. The dish takes its name from the *canuts*, silk workers who rose up against their working conditions in the nineteenth century. It literally means "silk workers' brains"! *Faisselle* actually means a cheese strainer, but it now refers to a type of fresh, unsalted cheese packed with its own strainer for the whey to drain out. It is popular in France served with fruit coulis as a dessert, and works equally well with savory ingredients. To make this recipe, you may use any light cream cheese, and even fresh goat milk cheese.

Cheese fondue (*fondue savoyarde*) ✳

SERVES 8

Preparation: **30 minutes**
Cooking: **25 minutes**

INGREDIENTS

1 large loaf of country bread
1 garlic clove, peeled, shoot
   removed
1 lb. (500 g) Beaufort cheese
14 oz. (400 g) Comté or
   Appenzell cheese
10 oz. (300 g) Tome de Savoie
   (hard cheese from the Savoy
   region) or Emmental
2 tablespoons (20 g) cornstarch
2 tablespoons (30 ml) kirsch
2 ¼ cups (600 ml) young white
   wine (Swiss Fendant, French
   Apremont, etc.)
A little grated nutmeg
Freshly ground pepper

Special equipment: fondue pot

CHEF'S NOTES

– Flambé the wine before
stirring in the cheese cubes.
– If these particular cheeses are
not available, substitute half
Gruyère, half Emmental.

Cut the bread into bite-size cubes and leave them out to dry.

Rub the inside of the fondue pot with a garlic clove.

Dice the cheese. If you want to save time, you may grate it in the food processor. Dilute the cornstarch in the kirsch.

Slowly heat the white wine. When it begins to simmer, gradually add the cheese cubes, stirring with a wooden spoon to mix them well. When all the cheese has melted, incorporate the cornstarch and kirsch mixture. First spoon a little hot cheese into the liquid, mix thoroughly, then pour this into the fondue mixture.

Season with pepper and grate in a little nutmeg.

Place the pot on the burner in the center of the table (if possible, use an electric burner or a spirit burner). Give the guests fondue forks so that they can swirl their bread cubes in the fondue mix.

Roquefort and caramelized pear *tartes fines* ✶✶

SERVES 8

Preparation: **50 minutes**
Resting: **1 hour 20 minutes**
Cooking: **15 minutes**

INGREDIENTS

4 Conference or other firm winter
  pears
Juice of 1 lemon
½ cup (125 ml) water
²/₃ cup (125 g) sugar
1 ½ lb. (640 g) Roquefort
8 walnuts

Puff pastry
2 ¾ cups (250 g) cake flour
1 teaspoon (5 g) salt
½ cup (125 ml) water
1 ½ sticks (185 g) unsalted
  butter

TECHNIQUES

Puff pastry **19**
Syrup **172**

Prepare the puff pastry (see p. 19).
Sift the flour and add the salt. Pour the water into the flour and stir with your fingers to combine. Blend the ingredients together rapidly until thoroughly mixed. You should have a smooth paste, known as the *détrempe*. Form it into a ball, and chill, covered, for about 20 minutes. Check that the butter has the identical consistency of the dough mixture. Beat it, if necessary, between two sheets of parchment paper, with your rolling pin. This enables it to be incorporated more easily into the dough, and gives it a longer rectangular shape. Now roll out the dough mixture to form a cross shape, leaving the center—where you will place the butter—thicker (about ⅓ in./8 mm) than the four other parts. The butter should fit over this part of the dough. Place the butter in the center of the dough (see p. 18: image 1) and fold over each of the four parts of the cross. The final result will look like the back of an envelope.

Lightly dust a cool working counter with flour (use as little as possible each time, so that the pastry does not become too hard). Roll out the dough (called a *paton*) to form a rectangle whose length is three times greater than its width (see p. 18: 2). Fold this into three, starting at each end (three layers) (see p. 18: 3). Rotate the folded dough a quarter turn and roll out again to form the same shape as previously, a rectangle three times its width. Repeat the folding operation. Cover with plastic wrap and chill again for about 20 minutes. Repeat this procedure—rolling out and folding—five more times (a total of six times), chilling for 20 minutes between each stage. Roll out the pastry very thinly and cut out eight 6-in. (15-cm) diameter circles.

Prepare a syrup with the water and the sugar. Allow the syrup to cool. (It will be poured over the pastry, so it should not soften or melt the butter it contains.)

Preheat the oven to 350°F (180°C).

Leave the pears unpeeled. Cut them in half, squeezing a little lemon juice over so that they don't go brown, then cut the halves into fans. Place the cut pears on the pastry disks. Baste the tops of the tarts with the cooled syrup. Crumble the Roquefort cheese over the tarts and bake for about 15 minutes, until the cheese has melted and the pastry is a nice golden brown. Garnish with the walnuts.

Comté and grape skewers ✳

SERVES 8

Preparation: **10 minutes**

INGREDIENTS

1 lb. (500 g) Comté cheese
(alternatively, Gruyère or
Emmental)
32 green grapes
32 red grapes

Take 16 wooden skewers and alternate the fruit and cheese in
the following order: 1 green grape, 1 cheese cube, 1 red grape,
1 cheese cube, and so on.

CHEF'S NOTES

– Use small skewers to serve this at buffet meals.
– Try various other types of cheese, and pair them with seasonal
fruits for a tasty mix. Berries also work well.
– A strong contrast in flavors, for example a mild cheese with a tangy
fruit, makes an interesting variation. Alternately, try a mild fruit with
a tangy cheese.

Cheese soufflés ✳ ✳

SERVES 8

Preparation: **35 minutes**
Cooking: **35 minutes**

INGREDIENTS

Béchamel sauce
3 tablespoons (45 g) butter
1/3 cup (45 g) flour
2 cups (500 ml) milk, divided
Salt, freshly ground pepper

Soufflés
2 teaspoons (10 g) butter
1 tablespoon (10 g) flour
5 egg whites
4 teaspoons (20 g) powdered
milk
3 egg yolks
1 ¼ cups (150 g) grated Gruyère

TECHNIQUES

Béchamel or white sauce **133**

Prepare the béchamel sauce using the ingredients listed (see
p. 133). Season, press plastic wrap over the surface, and let cool
to around 86°F (30°C).

Preheat the oven to 350°F (180°C).

Grease eight individual (8-cm) round soufflé dishes with
the 2 teaspoons (10 g) butter and dust with the 1 tablespoon
(10 g) flour.

Beat the egg whites until they begin to hold their shape, then
add the powdered milk and continue beating until they hold
firm peaks.

Whisk the egg yolks into the béchamel to thin it out, then stir in
the Gruyère. Gently fold in the egg whites.

Pour the batter into the soufflé dishes until two-thirds full. Bake
for 15–20 minutes, until a knife tip inserted into the center
comes out clean.

Cream cheese-filled mushroom caps ✳

SERVES 8

Preparation: **40 minutes,
+ 20 minutes marinating**
Cooking: **5 minutes**

INGREDIENTS

8 caps of large white button
   mushrooms
6 garlic cloves, peeled shoots
   removed
½ bunch chives
3 dill sprigs
1 lb. 5 oz. (600 g) *faisselle*
   (alternatively, unsalted ricotta,
   Philadelphia, or other fresh
   cheese with a high water
   content)
Fleur de sel, freshly ground
   pepper

Marinade
Scant ½ cup (125 ml) olive oil
2 sprigs thyme
2 bay leaves
¼ bunch parsley
1 lemon
1 tablespoon (20 g) mignonette
   pepper

TECHNIQUES

Instant marinade **143**
Grilling **104**

Prepare an instant marinade (see p. 143).
Pour half of the oil into a pan. Add the dried or fresh herbs, the thyme, and the bay leaves. Arrange the mushroom caps in the pan and pour over the rest of the olive oil.

Peel the lemon, removing all the white pith, and slice it. Place the lemon slices in the marinade and sprinkle with mignonette pepper. Cover with plastic wrap and chill for 10 minutes.

Turn the mushroom caps over and return to the refrigerator, covered, for another 10 minutes.

Snip the chives and finely chop the dill. Add the herbs and the garlic immediately to the cream cheese and chill.

Remove the mushroom caps from the marinade and grill the tops, making a diamond pattern when you sear them. Spoon the cream cheese-herb mixture into the hollow of the mushroom caps. Sprinkle with a few grains of *fleur de sel* and serve.

Baked Mont d'Or and *vin jaune* ✳

SERVES 8

Preparation: **15 minutes**
Cooking: **35 minutes**

INGREDIENTS

1 baguette
⅓ cup (80 ml) olive oil
10 garlic cloves, peeled, shoots removed
1 Mont d'Or cheese
2 ½ cups (600 ml) *vin jaune* (this wine is sold exclusively in 620 ml bottles)
Freshly ground pepper

Preheat the oven to 300°F–325°F (150°C–160°C).

Prepare some croutons: cut the bread, drizzle with olive oil, and grill in the oven until light brown.

Rub the croutons with the garlic and set aside.

Cut a hole into the center of the Mont d'Or, reserving the top, and pour in the amount of *vin jaune* you desire, no less than a scant ½ cup (100 ml). Press the pieces of garlic into the cheese.

Cover the central hole with the reserved piece of cheese. Place the cheese in its box, wrap the box in aluminum foil, and bake for about 35 minutes.

Remove as soon as it is melted to your liking. Give a few grinds of the pepper mill and serve immediately, to eat with spoons and croutons.

DID YOU KNOW?

The Mont d'Or cheese is a specialty of the Jura region in eastern France, and takes its name from the highest mountain there. It is sold in a box made of spruce. Highly prized *vin jaune*, or yellow wine, is produced in the same region from the Savagnin grape, and is aged for a requisite time of six years and three months, during which time it acquires its characteristic yellow color.

Desserts

Yves Thuriès

presents his recipe

Pastry tasting has literally become a voyage of discovery. In its modern-day form, it allows food lovers a three-in-one treat, for less time and at less cost. This is why, in pastry making and cuisine, tasting plates have come into being. Three recipes, three different products, and three different flavors, all in one plate and part of the same course. A seven-course menu gives the client the opportunity to taste twenty-one different recipes. This technique, when completely mastered, simplifies the preparation and the plating in both the kitchen and the restaurant.

Food stylists, all impassioned food lovers themselves, work in close collaboration with the great chefs. They too have the know-how to adapt their creations to all types of restaurant service. Pastry chefs, today more than ever before in history, work hand in hand with designers—invaluable allies—to create the elements of a tasting plate (here, in a trilogy). These tasting plates convey the essence of what a pastry chef can do. The aim is to seduce an epicurean public, sensitive to nuances even when pressed for time. What we have here is a new style of pastry and cuisine, service and menus *à la française* for all those who, today, aspire to create the gastronomy of tomorrow.

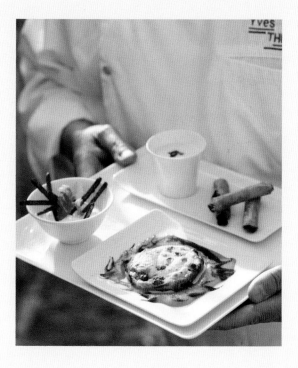

SERVES 10

Preparation:
45 minutes
Cooking:
45 minutes
Freezing:
3–4 hours

Sweet trilogy on a tasting plate

I. Spiced cream and crisp rolled wafers

INGREDIENTS

Spiced cream
¾ cup (200 g) milk
1 star anise
1 cinnamon stick
3 cloves
1 vanilla bean, slit
lengthwise and scraped
2 egg yolks (50 g)
¼ cup (50 g) sugar
1 ½ sheets gelatin (1.5 g),
soaked and drained
1 sprig of mint, for garnish

Crisp wafer tubes
2 ⅔ oz. (75 g) dark
couverture chocolate,
64% cacao
2 oz. (50 g) praline paste
(50% hazelnut, 50% sugar;
buy online or at specialty
stores)
2 oz. (60 g) *feuillantine*
(from professional
suppliers), or fine, crushed
wafers

Spiced cream
Bring the milk to a boil, add
the spices, and leave to infuse
for about 15 minutes. Strain
and prepare a custard (see
p. 177) with the egg yolks and
sugar using the spiced milk.
Remove from the heat and
incorporate the gelatin. Pour
the cream into small bowls
and chill to set.

Crisp wafer tubes
Melt the couverture chocolate
in a bain-marie. Add the
praline paste and then the
feuillantine. Roll out the
mixture very finely
(1/10 in./2 mm) between two
sheets of parchment paper.
Cut out rectangles and roll
them up to form cylinders.
Leave them to crystallize.

To assemble
Arrange the rolled wafer
tubes over the spiced cream
and garnish with a sprig of
fresh mint.

Yves Thuriès presents his recipe

II. Lemon and wild strawberry gratin with apricot coulis

INGREDIENTS

Soufflé cream
For the lemon cream
1 cup (250 ml) lemon juice
1 cup (250 ml) whipping
cream, min. 35% fat
12 egg yolks (240 g)
½ cup (100 g) sugar
7 tablespoons (1 ½ oz./40 g)
cake flour
4 sheets gelatin (8 g),
soaked and drained

For the Italian meringue
1 ½ cups (300 g) granulated
sugar
12 egg whites (360 g)
Wild strawberries as needed
for 10 soufflés
A little confectioners' sugar,
for dusting
Apricot coulis, to serve on
the side

Soufflé cream
Lemon pastry cream (first stage of soufflé cream)
Bring the lemon juice to boil with the whipping cream. Whisk the egg yolks with the sugar and flour together until the mixture is thick and pale. Pour the hot lemon cream over, whisking constantly. Return the mixture to the heat and bring to a fast boil for a few minutes, continuing to whisk. Remove from the heat and incorporate the gelatin.

Italian meringue (second stage of soufflé cream)
(see p. 51)
Cook the sugar with a scant ⅔ cup (150 ml) water and bring it to a temperature of 250°F (120°C). In the meanwhile, begin beating the egg whites. Pour the syrup over the beaten egg whites.

Immediately begin to incorporate the hot meringue into the boiling cream, pouring slowly and folding it in carefully.

As soon as the ingredients are combined, line the base and sides of the individual pastry rings with the hot soufflé cream. Scatter wild strawberries inside. Fill the rings with the cream and smooth over. Freeze for a few hours.

To bake
Preheat the oven to 400°F (200°C). Turn the frozen gratins out of the pastry rings and dust with confectioners' sugar. Bake for 10–12 minutes, until browned. Serve the hot apricot coulis separately.

III. Caramelized chocolate crisp rolls and coconut ivory sauce

INGREDIENTS

Ganache
Scant ½ cup (100 ml)
  whipping cream,
  min. 35% fat
3 tablespoons (40 ml) milk
3 ½ oz. (100 g) dark
  couverture chocolate,
  64% cacao
2 teaspoons (10 g) butter,
  softened
1 egg yolk (20 g)

Caramelized crisp
  chocolate rolls
Filo pastry as needed
A little clarified butter
A little granulated sugar

Coconut-flavored ivory
  sauce
3 ¼ oz. (90 g) coconut milk
4 ½ oz. (125 g) white
  couverture chocolate
1 ¾ oz. (50 g) clear glaze

Ganache
Bring the cream and the milk to a boil. Pour the hot liquid over the couverture chocolate to melt it. Whisk until smooth, add the softened butter and then the egg yolk. Set aside.

Caramelized crisp chocolate rolls
Cut strips of filo pastry measuring 2 ½ in. (6 cm). Baste them with clarified butter. Place the ganache on the strips and roll them up to form cigarette shapes. Sprinkle with granulated sugar and bake for about 5 minutes at 350°F (180°C). If they have not already caramelized, finish the process under a salamander or with a caramelizing iron.

Coconut-flavored ivory sauce
Bring the coconut milk to a boil. Add the couverture chocolate and mix until smooth. Heat the glaze to 140°F (60°C) and incorporate it into the chocolate-coconut mixture.

To assemble
Cut the rolled filo. Arrange three crisp chocolate rolls and a ramekin of coconut-flavored ivory sauce on an attractive plate.

Apricot tartlets ✳

SERVES 8

Preparation: **45 minutes**
Resting: **20 minutes**
Cooking: **25 minutes**

INGREDIENTS

4 large sweet, juicy apricots
4 ½ oz. (125 g) apricot glaze
  or preserves

Crumbled sweet short pastry
2 ¾ cups (250 g) cake flour
1 generous teaspoon (5 g) salt
1 stick (125 g) unsalted butter,
  softened
1 egg yolk
3 ½ tablespoons (40 g) sugar
4 ½ tablespoons (50 ml) water

Almond cream
7 tablespoons (100 g) unsalted
  butter, softened
½ cup (100 g) granulated sugar
1 generous cup (100 g) ground
  almonds or almond meal
2 eggs
A few drops of vanilla extract
1 tablespoon (15 ml) rum

TECHNIQUES

Crumbled sweet short pastry
  (*pâte sablée*) **15**
Almond cream **181**

Prepare the crumbled sweet short pastry (see p. 15).
Sift the flour with the salt. Rub the butter into the flour with your fingertips until you have the texture of coarse crumbs. Incorporate the egg yolk, sugar, and water. Be careful not to overwork the dough, which would make it too elastic, and form it into a ball. Flatten it out with the palm of your hand to ensure it is thoroughly mixed. Chill, covered in plastic wrap, for 20 minutes.

Preheat the oven to 350°F (180°C).

Roll the dough out with a pastry roller into a circle about ⅛ in. (3 mm) thick. Cut out circles big enough to line the tartlet molds and transfer them to the molds. Make a decorative pattern around the edges.

Prepare the almond cream (see p. 181).
Cream the softened butter well with the sugar. Add the ground almonds, and then the eggs, mixing them in one by one. Add the flavorings and whisk until smooth. Half fill the tart shells with the almond cream.

Wash the apricots, cut them in half, and remove the pits. Place an apricot half in the center of each tartlet, pressing it into the almond cream.

Bake for about 20–25 minutes. When they are almost done, remove the tartlets from the molds and return to the oven for a few minutes so that the edges of the pastry shells can brown lightly. Transfer to a cooling rack immediately and brush them with apricot glaze. If you are using apricot preserves, liquefy it a little over low heat first.

Mint-chocolate entremets ✳ ✳ ✳

SERVES 8

Preparation: **1 hour 50 minutes**
Cooking: **10 minutes**
Chilling: **3–4 hours**

INGREDIENTS

Joconde sponge
¾ cup (140 g) plus ¼ cup (50 g)
  granulated sugar
1 ²/₃ cups (5 oz./140 g) ground
  almonds
4 eggs plus 4 egg whites
8 tablespoons (45 g) flour, sifted
1 ¾ tablespoons (scant 1 oz./25 g)
  butter, melted

Mint Bavarian cream mousse
5 sheets (10 g) gelatin
2 cups (500 ml) milk
1 vanilla bean, slit lengthwise,
  seeds scraped
10 sprigs of fresh mint
5 egg yolks
²/₃ cup (125 g) granulated sugar
1 ²/₃ cups (400 ml) whipping
  cream, min. 35% fat
1 ¹/₃ tablespoons (20 ml) mint
  liqueur

Chocolate mousse
4 ½ oz. (125 g) dark chocolate,
  64% cacao
1 ¾ tablespoons (25 g) butter
¾ cup (150 g) sugar
²/₃ cup (150 ml) water
3 egg yolks
¾ cup (200 ml) whipping cream,
  min. 35% fat

²/₃ cup (150 g) neutral glaze
  (available at specialty stores)

TECHNIQUES

Joconde sponge **196**
French meringue **51**
Egg-based Bavarian cream **193**
Pâte à bombe **212**

Prepare the joconde sponge (see p. 196).
Preheat the oven to 350°F (180°C).

Sift together the ¾ cup (140 g) sugar and ground almonds. Beat in the whole eggs until the mixture reaches the ribbon stage. Fold in the sifted flour, followed by the melted butter. Beat the four egg whites until they form stiff peaks. Add the remaining sugar and beat until the mixture is firm and shiny. Carefully fold this French meringue into the egg and butter mixture. Spread the batter very thinly (¹/₅ in. /3–5 mm) on a baking sheet lined with parchment paper. Bake for 8–10 minutes. As soon as it is done, turn it over onto a rack to cool. Cut out eight disks the size of the base of your molds.

Prepare the mint Bavarian cream mousse (see p. 193).
Soak the gelatin sheets in very cold water until soft. Heat the milk in a saucepan with the vanilla bean and its seeds and the mint leaves. Leave to infuse for 15 minutes. Energetically whisk the egg yolks with the sugar. Pour half of the hot milk over the beaten egg yolks, beating constantly. Pour the rest of the milk in and then return to the pan. Heat gently, removing the pan from the heat from time to time, until the cream coats the back of a spoon or to 185°F (85°C). The cream must not be subjected to continuous heat, as the egg yolks might coagulate. Strain the custard through a chinois into a bowl. Squeeze the water out of the gelatin sheets and mix thoroughly into the custard. Cover the bowl with plastic wrap and leave to cool.

Whip the cream until it forms firm peaks, to a Chantilly consistency. When the custard has cooled to room temperature (about 68°F or 20°C), whisk in the mint liqueur. Gradually fold in the whipped cream using a rubber spatula, taking care not to deflate the mixture. Pour the mint Bavarian cream into eight individual molds and chill to set.

Prepare the chocolate mousse.
Melt the chocolate and butter together over a hot water bath. Do not let the mixture exceed 122°F (50°C). Bring the water and sugar to a boil. Pour the egg yolks into the bowl of a stand mixer and begin beating them. Gradually pour the hot syrup over the beaten yolks (see *pâte à bombe* p. 212). Continue beating until the mixture has completely cooled down. Beat the cream until soft peaks form. When the chocolate-butter mixture has cooled to 82°F–83°F (28°C), carefully fold it into the *pâte à bombe*, then carefully fold in the whipped cream.

Spoon a layer of chocolate mousse over the mint Bavarian cream. Top with a disk of joconde sponge. Chill until set, about 2–3 hours, before turning out of the molds. Coat with neutral glaze and garnish attractively before serving.

French fruit loaf ✳

SERVES 8

Preparation: **20 minutes**
Cooking: **40–50 minutes**

INGREDIENTS

1 ½ sticks (6 oz./175 g) unsalted
  butter, softened, and a little
  extra for the pan
²/₃ cup (125 g) granulated sugar
½ teaspoon (3 g) fine sea salt
3 eggs
3 ⅓ cups (330 g) flour, divided
1 slightly heaped teaspoon (5 g)
  baking powder
1 teaspoon (5 ml) vanilla extract
Zest of 1 unsprayed or organic
  orange
Zest of 1 unsprayed or organic
  lemon
½ teaspoon (3 g) freshly grated
  ginger
2 oz. (50 g) dried figs
2 oz. (50 g) candied cherries
2 oz. (50 g) candied pineapple
2 oz. (50 g) candied apricots
2 oz. (50 g) mixed candied fruit

TECHNIQUE

French fruit cake **34**

Prepare the loaf batter (see p. 34).
Preheat the oven to 300°F–325°F (150°C–160°C). Grease a loaf
pan.

Energetically cream the softened butter with the sugar and salt.
Add the eggs, one by one, mixing thoroughly each time. Sift
2 ½ cups (250 g) flour and the baking powder together and stir
into the batter. Stir in the vanilla extract. Add the orange and
lemon zests and the ginger.

Lightly coat all the pieces of fruit in the remaining flour so that
they don't fall to the bottom during baking.

Pour the batter into the greased pan, scattering the pieces of
dried fruit evenly throughout. Bake for 40–50 minutes. Test for
doneness: a tip of a knife should come out clean.

Turn the loaf out onto a cooling rack.

DID YOU KNOW?

What the French call a "cake" is more commonly known in the English-
speaking world as a fruit cake, originally from Scotland. A raised dough
with generous helpings of raisins and rum-soaked, candied fruits make up
the basic recipe, and it is usually topped with sliced almonds and bright
red glacéed cherries. This multicolored, multiflavored cake was invented
by a pastry chef by the name of Michel, who took his inspiration from the
Dundee Cake. He owned a tearoom, and Parisians thronged there to taste
this new wonder, whose slices displayed cheerily bright fruits. Not only
was it attractive, it was also mouthwatering. For added chic, the English
word "cake" was used to describe it, and Monsieur Michel's creation
became the new "must-have" treat.

Lemon meringue tartlets ✳

SERVES 8

Preparation: **45 minutes**
Resting: **20 minutes**
Cooking: **1 hour 10 minutes**

INGREDIENTS

Crumbled sweet short pastry
3 ²/₃ cups (250 g) cake flour
1 teaspoon (5 g) salt
1 stick (125 g) unsalted butter, softened
²/₃ cup (125 g) sugar
1 egg

Lemon cream
1 cup (200 g) sugar, divided
1 ¼ cup (300 ml) lemon juice
3 eggs plus 4 egg yolks
Scant ¼ cup (35 g) cornstarch
Zest of 1 unsprayed or organic lemon
4 tablespoons (60 g) unsalted butter, cubed
¾ cup (200 ml) whipping cream, min. 35% fat

Lemon garnish
2 unsprayed or organic lemons
1 cup (200 g) granulated sugar

Italian meringue
Generous 1 cup (210 g) granulated sugar
4 egg whites
1 pinch salt

Special equipment: sugar thermometer

TECHNIQUES

Crumbled sweet short pastry (*pâte sablée*) **15**
Candying (crystallizing) **99**
Italian meringue **51**

Prepare the crumbled sweet short pastry (see p. 15).
Sift the flour with the salt. Dice the butter and blend it in with your fingers until it forms coarse crumbs. Make a well and incorporate the sugar and the egg until just mixed. Shape the dough into a ball, cover with plastic wrap, and chill for 20 minutes.

Preheat the oven to 350°F (180°C). Roll out the dough to form a disk about ⅛ in. (3 mm) thick. Cut out disks big enough to line tartlet molds or rings and place one in each mold. Line them with parchment paper and fill with dry beans. Blind-bake for about 15 minutes, until the pastry is lightly golden all over.

Prepare the lemon cream.
Bring ½ cup (100 ml) water, half the sugar, and the lemon juice to a boil. Whisk the eggs, egg yolks, and the remaining sugar together until the mixture is thick and pale. Whisk in the cornstarch and blend thoroughly. Pour the lemon syrup over the egg mixture, beating constantly, and then return all the liquid to a low heat. Add the lemon zest and cook it using the same method as for a pastry cream, stirring constantly until it thickens and coats the back of a spoon, or until it reaches 185°F (85°C). Remove from the heat and whisk the butter in while still hot. Transfer to a bowl, cover with plastic wrap flush with the surface, and chill. When the lemon cream is at room temperature, or 68°F–77°F (20°C–25°C), whip the cream stiffly. Fold it carefully into the lemon cream and spoon the mixture into the pastry shells. Chill.

Prepare the lemon garnish.
Slice one lemon very finely and dry the slices in the oven at 200°F (100°C) for about 30 minutes. Using a vegetable peeler, peel off the skin of the remaining lemon. Cut it into fine julienne strips and blanch them three times, changing the water each time. Bring ¾ cup (200 ml) water and 1 cup (200 g) sugar to a boil. Add the julienne strips to candy them (see p. 99).

Prepare the Italian meringue (see p. 51).
Begin heating the sugar with a scant ½ cup (70 ml) water. When the syrup reaches 230°F (110°C), start beating the egg whites with a pinch of salt. When the syrup reaches 243°F–250°F (117°C–120°C), begin pouring it gradually into the egg whites. Continue beating until the meringue has cooled down completely. It will be dense and shiny, and will form many small peaks. Spoon into a piping bag and pipe out in decorative patterns on the tops of the tarts. Set the oven to broil. Lightly brown the meringue under the broiler, then allow to cool. Garnish with the dried lemon slices and candied julienne strips.

Canelés ✳

SERVES 8

Preparation: **35 minutes**
Resting: **overnight**
Cooking: **55 minutes**

INGREDIENTS

3 ½ tablespoons (50 g) butter,
  plus a little extra to grease the
  molds
½ vanilla bean
2 cups (500 ml) full cream milk
1 generous cup (110 g) all-
  purpose flour
2 teaspoons (10 g) fine salt
1 ¼ cups (250 g) sugar
2 eggs plus 2 yolks
Zest of ½ unsprayed or organic
  orange
1 ⅓ tablespoons (20 ml) rum

Special equipment: a *canelé* pan

A day ahead, prepare the batter.
Melt 3 ½ tablespoons (50 g) butter in a small saucepan until it browns.

Slit the vanilla bean lengthwise and scrape out the seeds. Bring the milk to a boil with the seeds and the vanilla bean.

Combine the flour, salt, and sugar. Pour in the whole eggs and egg yolks together and whisk vigorously to combine with the flour and sugar.

Pour the boiling milk into the batter and stir to combine. Pour in the melted brown butter and mix gently. Your batter should be liquid—the texture of a crêpe batter. Add the orange zest to the batter and stir in the rum. Chill overnight.

Place a flat baking tray on the center rack of the oven and preheat it to 525°F (270°C). If you cannot heat your oven to this temperature, the *canelés* will bake on a hot tray at 475°F (240°C). Butter the *canelé* molds. Half fill the molds with the batter and place the pan on the hot baking tray. Bake for 5 minutes, then lower the temperature to 300°F (150°C) and continue baking for about 40 minutes. The *canelés* should have a brown crust and a nice soft crumb.

DID YOU KNOW?

Canelés, sometimes spelled *cannelés*, are a specialty of Bordeaux.

Kouign amman ✳ ✳ ✳

SERVES 8

Preparation: **45 minutes**
Resting: **1 hour 45 minutes**
Cooking: **30–40 minutes**

INGREDIENTS

¾ oz. (20 g) fresh (compressed)
    yeast
5 cups (500 g) all-purpose flour
2 teaspoons (10 g) fine salt
1 ⅔ cups (375 g) salted butter
1 ¼ cups (250 g) granulated
    sugar
1 egg yolk
Scant cup (200 ml) warm water

TECHNIQUE

Puff pastry **19**

Heat the oven to a temperature of 77°F–82°F (25°C–28°C) and place a bowl of water at the bottom.

Dilute the yeast in ¼ cup (50 ml) warm water. Combine the flour with the salt. Add the yeast diluted in the water and work it in. Slowly pour in ¾ cup (200 ml) warm water and knead until the dough is smooth, just like a bread dough. If you are using the dough hook of your stand mixer, knead at medium speed.

Place the dough in the oven to rise until it doubles in volume.

Dust the work counter with a little flour and deflate the dough. Roll it out into a rectangle just under 1 in. (1.5–2 cm) thick.

Cut the butter into small cubes and arrange them on the entire surface of the rectangle. Sprinkle the sugar over evenly. Using the same method as required for puff pastry (see p. 19), fold and roll it out four times, chilling it 20 minutes between each operation.

Roll out the dough into a circle and baste it with beaten egg yolk. Leave to rest for 45 minutes in an unbuttered baking pan.

Preheat the oven to 450°F (230°C). Bake for 30–40 minutes, keeping a close eye on the color. It should turn a lovely golden color. When it comes out of the oven, the *kouign amman* is literally swimming in butter, but that will be absorbed as it cools.

DID YOU KNOW?

Kouign amman (pronounced "kween a-mun") is a specialty of Brittany. The name comes from the Breton words for "bread" and "butter."

Orange liqueur soufflé ✳ ✳

SERVES 8

Preparation: **40 minutes**
Cooking: **35 minutes**

INGREDIENTS

2 tablespoons (30 g) butter
2 generous tablespoons (30 g)
  sugar for the molds plus ⅓ cup
  (60 g) granulated sugar
¼ cup (60 ml) Cointreau or other
  orange liqueur
2 eggs, separated, plus 6 egg
  whites
1 small pinch of salt (2 g)

Pastry cream
2 cups (500 ml) milk
1 vanilla bean
4 egg yolks
⅔ cup (125 g) sugar
⅓ cup (2 oz./60 g) cornstarch

TECHNIQUE

Hot pastry cream soufflé **205**

Prepare a pastry cream (see p. 185).
Slit the vanilla bean lengthwise and scrape the seeds into the milk. Place the milk and vanilla bean in a saucepan to heat. In a mixing bowl, energetically whisk the egg yolks, sugar, and cornstarch until the mixture is pale and thick. When the milk is simmering, pour half of it over the egg yolk mixture, beating all the time. Pour in the remaining milk and return all the liquid to the heat. Bring to a simmer. Leave to simmer for no longer than 2–3 minutes, stirring constantly so that it does not burn. Pour it into a mixing bowl and cover with plastic wrap flush with the pastry cream to prevent a skin from forming. Chill rapidly.

Use a pastry brush to grease the molds or ramekins with butter. Then sprinkle the molds all over with 2 generous tablespoons (30 g) sugar. Turn them over and give them a rap to remove any excess sugar.

Stir the Cointreau into the pastry cream. Whisk the 8 egg whites stiffly with the pinch of salt. When they are firm, whisk in the remaining ⅓ cup (60 g) sugar until the mixture is shiny.

Place a baking tray in the oven and preheat the oven to 400°F (200°C).

Stir the 2 egg yolks into the pastry cream. Carefully fold in the stiffly beaten egg whites using a rubber spatula. Fill the soufflé molds to the top and smooth the surface.

Place the soufflé molds on the hot baking pan and bake for about 20 minutes, depending on the size. The soufflés should be well risen, have a nice brown crust, and be soft inside.

Passion fruit and orange mousse ✶✶

SERVES 8

Preparation: **45 minutes**
Cooking: **35 minutes**
Chilling: **3–4 hours**

INGREDIENTS

Genoese sponge
4 eggs
²/₃ cup (125 g) granulated sugar
1 ¹/₃ cups (125 g) cake flour, plus
    a little extra

Orange mousse
3 sheets gelatin (6 g)
4 oz. (125 g) puréed orange
3 egg whites
3 ½ tablespoons (40 g)
    granulated sugar
Scant ½ cup (110 ml) whipping
    cream, min. 35% fat
A few drops of Cointreau or other
    orange liqueur

Syrup
1 ½ cups (300 g) granulated
    sugar
1 ¹/₃ tablespoons (20 ml)
    Cointreau
Zest of ½ unsprayed or organic
    orange
¾ teaspoon (2 g) ground
    cinnamon

Passion fruit mousse
9 sheets gelatin (18 g)
17 ½ oz. (500 g) passion fruit pulp
10 egg whites
¾ cup (150 g) granulated sugar
2 cups (500 ml) whipping cream,
    min. 35% fat

2 ½ oz. (70 g) neutral glaze
    (available at specialty stores)
1 orange to garnish

TECHNIQUES

Genoese sponge **195**
Fruit mousse **199**
Italian meringue **51**

Prepare a Genoese sponge (see p. 195).
Preheat the oven to 350°F (180°C). Beat the eggs and sugar together in a round-bottomed bowl over a hot water bath until the mixture reaches the ribbon stage (140°F/60°C). Sift in the flour in two stages, folding it in gently with a rubber spatula. Work carefully so as not to deflate the batter. Pour onto a baking sheet lined with parchment paper to a thickness of about ⅛ in. (4 mm). Bake for 15–20 minutes. Test for doneness (the tip of a knife should come out dry) and turn out onto a cooling rack. Remove the parchment paper. When cooled, cut out an 8 inch (20 cm) disk for an 8 ½ inch (22 cm) cake or entremets ring.

Prepare the orange mousse (see p. 199).
Soak the gelatin sheets in cold water until softened. Bring the orange purée to a boil and simmer for 2 minutes. Squeeze the water from the gelatin sheets and incorporate into the orange purée. Leave to cool. Prepare an Italian meringue with the 3 egg whites, sugar, and 1 tablespoon (15 ml) water (see p. 51). Whip the cream until it forms stiff peaks. When the purée has reached room temperature, whisk in the orange liqueur. Gently fold the cooled Italian meringue into the purée. When it is completely incorporated, carefully fold in the whipped cream. Chill.

In a small saucepan, bring the sugar, Cointreau, orange zest, and ground cinnamon to a boil in 1 ¼ cups (300 ml) water to make a syrup. Place the disk of Genoese sponge at the center of your ring set on a baking sheet. Using a pastry brush, soak the disk with the syrup. Spoon in the orange mousse until it reaches quarter of the way up the ring. Freeze to set.

Prepare the passion fruit mousse (see p. 197).
Soak the gelatin sheets in cold water until softened. Bring the passion fruit pulp to a boil and simmer for 2 minutes. Squeeze the water from the gelatin sheets and incorporate into the pulp. Leave to cool. Prepare an Italian meringue with the 10 egg whites, sugar, and scant ¼ cup (50 ml) water (see p. 51). Whip the cream until it forms stiff peaks. When the passion fruit pulp has reached room temperature, whisk it to ensure it is smooth. Gently fold the cooled Italian meringue into the pulp. When it is completely incorporated, carefully fold in the whipped cream. Chill.

When well cooled, fill the ring to the top with the passion fruit mousse and smooth the surface. Place in the freezer until set, 30 minutes to 1 hour. When set, glaze with the neutral glaze, using a colorant for a marbled effect, if desired. Place on a serving dish and remove the ring with the help of a blowtorch or hot towel.

Assorted almond macarons ✳ ✳ ✳

SERVES 8

Preparation: **55 minutes**
Resting: **20 minutes**
Cooking: **45 minutes**

INGREDIENTS

1 ¾ cup (5 ¼ oz./150 g) ground
  almonds
1 generous cup (5 ¼ oz./150 g)
  confectioners' sugar
1 ¾ oz. (50 g) egg whites
¾ cup (5 ¼ oz./150 g) caster
  sugar
Scant 2 oz. (55 g) egg whites,
  whipped
1 small pinch ground red colorant

Raspberry preserves (with
  seeds)
1 lb. 2 oz. (500 g) raspberries
1 lb. 2 oz. (2 ⅔ cups or 500 g)
  granulated sugar
1 vanilla bean
1 ⅓ tablespoon (20 ml)
  raspberry brandy or liqueur

Salted butter caramel
⅔ cup (125 g) sugar
3 tablespoons (45 g) salted butter
Scant ½ cup (125 ml) whipping
  cream, min. 35% fat

TECHNIQUES

Almond macarons **197**
Italian meringue **51**

CHEF'S NOTE

– This recipe requires precisely
measured ingredients and just
the right baking temperature.

Prepare the macaron batter (see p. 197).
Prepare a silicone baking sheet or a baking tray lined with parchment paper. If you use parchment paper, drizzle a little cold water between the paper and the tray. Process the ground almonds and confectioners' sugar finely in a food processor. If the powder is not uniformly fine, you may need to sift it through a fine-mesh sieve. Finely ground almonds are essential to the quality of macarons. Add the 2 oz. (50 g) of egg whites and stir in until the mixture reaches a fairly firm texture.

Begin cooking the sugar and 3 ½ tablespoons (50 ml) water to form a syrup. When it reaches a temperature of 250°F (121°C) prepare an Italian meringue (see p. 51) using the beaten egg white. When it has cooled, carefully fold the Italian meringue into the almond mixture, taking care not to deflate the mixture. Stir until it reaches a consistency that is firm but still fluid.

Divide the macaron batter in two and incorporate the red colorant into half of it to make the raspberry macarons. Spoon the mixture into a piping bag and pipe out small rounds on to the baking sheet. If you are making mini macarons, pipe out circles just under 1 in. (2 cm), and for individual desserts, make them about 2 ½–3 in. (5–8 cm). Leave them out to dry for about 20 minutes. They will form a light crust—make sure it has formed before you bake them!

Ensure that the oven is completely dry (no residue of steam from previous use) and preheat it to 300°F (150°C). Cook for 8–10 minutes. When they are done, leave them to cool on the baking sheet. Transfer them to a rack only when they are cold.

Prepare the raspberry preserves.
Begin cooking the raspberries with the sugar. Slit the vanilla bean lengthwise and scrape the seeds into the mixture. Add the vanilla bean to the pan. Slowly bring the temperature to 225°F (107°C). Stir in the raspberry brandy or liqueur and crush the raspberries roughly using a fork. Leave to cool completely. Take pairs of raspberry macarons the same size and sandwich them together with the raspberry preserves.

Prepare the salted butter caramel.
Cook the sugar until it reaches a dark caramel color—350°F (180°C). Remove from the heat and stir in the salted butter. When it has melted, pour in the whipping cream. Return to the heat so that the caramel sauce liquefies. Allow it to cool. When it has cooled, sandwich together pairs of equally sized plain macarons with the caramel.

Kings' cake (*galette des rois*) ✳ ✳

SERVES 8

Preparation: **1 hour 30 minutes**
Resting: **1 hour 40 minutes**
Cooking: **50 minutes**

INGREDIENTS

Puff pastry
2 ¾ cups (250 g) cake flour
1 teaspoon (5 g) salt
½ cup (125 ml) water
¾ cup (185 g) unsalted butter

Frangipane cream:
Pastry cream
1 cup (250 ml) milk
½ vanilla bean
2 egg yolks
⅓ cup (65 g) granulated sugar
6 ⅓ tablespoons (generous
  ⅓ cup or 60 g) cornstarch
A few drops of bitter almond
  extract

Almond cream
1 generous cup (100 g) blanched
  ground almonds or almond meal
7 tablespoons (100 g) unsalted
  butter, softened
½ cup (100 g) granulated sugar
2 eggs

For basting
1 egg, lightly beaten
1 ½ cups (300 g) sugar
2 tablespoons (30 ml) water

TECHNIQUES

Puff pastry **19**
Frangipane cream **181**
Pastry cream **185**
Almond cream **181**

Prepare the puff pastry (see p. 19).
Make the puff pastry according to the technique on page 19, using the ingredients listed here.

Prepare the frangipane cream (see p. 181).
First, make a pastry cream (see p. 185) using the ingredients listed here and leave it to cool. While it cools, prepare the almond cream (see p. 181) using the ingredients listed here. Stir the bitter almond extract into the pastry cream. Incorporate the almond cream, and stir energetically.

Preheat the oven to 425°F (210°C).

Roll the puff pastry out: you will have to cut out two circles so make sure it is long enough. It should be about ⅛ in. (4–6 mm) thick. Cut out one disk (for the bottom of the cake) with a diameter of just under 10 in. (24 cm). The top disk must be just slightly bigger—just under 1 in. (2 cm)—as it has to cover the low mound of frangipane. Transfer the smaller circle to a baking tray (lined with parchment paper, if you wish). Baste the edge of the circumference, no more than ½ in. (1–1.5 cm) with the beaten egg. This will help seal the cake.

Spread the frangipane out evenly on the pastry, taking care not to put any on the egg-basted edge. One way to do this is to pipe it out from a piping bag, starting in the center. Cover the frangipane with the larger pastry circle. If you are including the traditional lucky charm or trinket, put it in now, pressing it in very lightly. To seal the two parts together, press lightly with your fingers all round the edges. Then take a small, sharp knife and make shallow, angled incisions in the two layers around the edge at fairly close intervals. This will help prevent the frangipane from seeping out as it bakes. You may make a small hole in the center to allow steam to escape during baking. Baste the top with the beaten egg yolk, but stop short of the edges. Then use the back of a knife (so that you don't cut into the top pastry) to make a decorative pattern, radiating arcs or criss-crossing lines. Chill for 20 minutes. Place in the oven and bake for 35–45 minutes altogether.

While the cake is baking, prepare a syrup with the 1 ½ cups (300 g) sugar and 2 tablespoons (30 ml) water. When the cake has puffed and started to turn golden, near the end of the baking time, brush the top with the syrup and return it to the oven for a few minutes. Repeat the procedure two more times during the last 5 minutes. The cake top should be golden brown and lightly caramelized. Do not let it get too dark. When it is the right color, transfer it to a rack and allow to cool. Serve the same day.

Mixed berry tart ✳

SERVES 8

Preparation: **45 minutes**
Resting: **20 minutes**
Cooking: **45 minutes**

INGREDIENTS

A total of 4 ¼ oz. (120 g) of
  mixed berries, including:
Raspberries
Black currants
Red currants
Strawberries
Wild strawberries
⅓ cup (80 g) smooth apricot
  preserves or glaze

Creamed sweet short pastry
1 stick (125 g) unsalted butter,
  softened
½ cup (100 g) granulated sugar
1 egg
2 ¾ cups (250 g) cake flour
1 teaspoon (5 ml) salt

Pastry cream
2 cups (500 ml) milk
1 vanilla bean
3 eggs
⅔ cup (125 g) granulated sugar
6 ⅓ tablespoons (generous
  ⅓ cup or 60 g) cornstarch
A few drops of vanilla essence

TECHNIQUES

Creamed sweet short pastry
  (*pâte sucrée*) **16**
Pastry cream **185**

Preheat the oven to 350°F (180°C).

Prepare the creamed sweet short pastry (see p. 16).
Place the butter, sugar, and egg in the bowl of a food processor
and cream together until smooth. Sift the flour and add it with
the salt to process for 1–2 minutes further, until smooth. Press
down the dough with the palm of your hand, pushing it away
from you, until the ingredients are thoroughly blended. Chill,
covered, for 20 minutes. Roll out the dough very thinly (about
⅛ in./3 mm) to form a disk. Use a rolling pin to transfer it from
the working surface to the baking pan or circle: drape it round
the pin and then unroll it in place. Make decorative patterns
around the edge. Prick the dough with a fork and blind-bake for
20–30 minutes, until it is a light golden color.

Prepare the pastry cream (see p. 185).
Slit a vanilla bean lengthwise and scrape the seeds into the
milk. Place the milk and vanilla bean in a saucepan to heat. In a
mixing bowl, energetically whisk the egg yolks, sugar, and
cornstarch until the mixture is pale and thick. When the milk is
simmering, pour half of it over the egg yolk mixture, beating all
the time. If you are adding a flavoring ingredient, now is the
time to incorporate it, unless you are using a liqueur, in which
case you should add it when the mixture has cooled. Pour in the
remaining milk and return all the liquid to the heat. Bring to a
simmer, stirring all the time. Leave to simmer for 2–3 minutes,
still stirring. Transfer the pastry cream to a mixing bowl and
cover it with plastic wrap flush with the surface. This will
prevent a skin from forming. Cool down rapidly.

When the pastry cream has cooled, spoon it into a piping bag
and fill the cooled pastry shell. Arrange the berries attractively
over the pastry cream. Give them a nice shine by brushing them
with the apricot glaze. If using apricot preserve, liquify a little
over a low heat before use. Serve when cool.

Apple fritters with apricot coulis ✳

SERVES 8

Preparation: **50 minutes**
Resting: **30 minutes**
Cooking: **30 minutes**

INGREDIENTS

Frying batter
2 cups (200 g) all-purpose flour
1 teaspoon (5 g) salt
2 eggs plus 3 egg whites
1 ⅓ tablespoons (20 ml)
  sunflower seed oil
¾ cup (200 ml) milk or beer

2 lb. (1 kg) golden delicious apples
  (about 5–6 apples)
2 teaspoons (10 ml) calvados or
  other apple brandy
Scant ½ cup (80 g) sugar
Generous ½ teaspoon (3 g)
  ground cinnamon
Oil for frying

Apricot coulis
1 ½ lb. (700 g) apricots
1 cup (250 ml) water
3 ⅔ cups (700 g) sugar
1 vanilla bean

TECHNIQUES

Frying batter **25**
Fruit coulis **166**

Prepare the frying batter (see p. 25).
Sift the flour into a mixing bowl and add the salt. Break the whole eggs one by one, and whisk them in to the dry ingredients. Incorporate the oil. Pour in the liquid (milk or beer) and whisk until the mixture is smooth. Stiffly beat the egg whites. Gently fold in the beaten egg whites using a flexible rubber spatula.

Prepare the apples.
Peel, wash, and core the apples. Slice them into disks just over 1 in. (3 cm) thick. Allow 3 slices per person. Combine the calvados, sugar, and cinnamon and place the apple slices in the liquid to marinate.

Prepare the apricot coulis (see p. 166).
Remove the pits from the apricots. Place them in a saucepan with the water and the sugar over low heat. Add the vanilla bean with its seeds scraped. Leave to stew gently. If you wish, add a few drops of the marinade to heighten the flavor of your coulis. Process the stewed fruit using an immersion blender or juicer. Strain through a fine-mesh sieve and set aside.

Begin heating the oil bath. Dip the apple slices in the frying batter. Fry them evenly on both sides. When they are done, remove them with a slotted spoon and drain on paper towel. The fritters should be eaten immediately, accompanied by the apricot coulis.

Gâteau Saint-Honoré ✳ ✳ ✳

SERVES 8

Preparation: **55 minutes**
Resting: **1 hour 20 minutes**
Cooking: **50 minutes**

INGREDIENTS

Puff pastry

1 ⅓ cups (125 g) cake flour
1 small pinch fine salt
⅓ cup (70 ml) water
6 ½ tablespoons (95 g) unsalted
 butter

Choux pastry

1 ¼ cups (125 g) flour
1 cup (250 ml) water
1 teaspoon (5 g) salt
1 scant tablespoon (15 g) sugar
 (optional)
7 tablespoons (100 g) unsalted
 butter, cubed
4 eggs, plus 1 egg, lightly beaten,
 for basting

Chiboust cream

5 sheets gelatin (10 g)
2 cups (500 ml) milk
1 vanilla bean
3 egg yolks
⅔ cups (125 g) granulated sugar
⅓ cup (55 g) cornstarch

Italian meringue

8 egg whites
2 ⅔ cups (500 g) sugar
¼ cup (60 ml) water

Caramel

1 cup (200 g) granulated sugar
¼ cup (60 ml) water

TECHNIQUES

Puff pastry **19**
Choux pastry **22**
Chiboust cream **180**
Italian meringue **51**

Prepare the puff pastry (see p. 19).
Make the puff pastry according to the technique on page 19, using the ingredients listed here. Roll out the dough and cut out a circle with a diameter of about 8 in. (20 cm). Prick it with a fork and leave in the refrigerator until needed.

Prepare the choux pastry (see p. 22).
Preheat the oven to 425°F (210°C). Sift the flour. In a saucepan, bring the water, salt, sugar if using, and cubed butter to a boil. Remove from the heat, pour in all the flour, and stir until combined. It should form a thick paste. Return to the heat and beat energetically with a rubber spatula until the moisture has evaporated. Transfer to a mixing bowl. Add the eggs one by one, and stir in thoroughly using the spatula. Spoon the batter into a piping bag. Take the puff pastry disk from the refrigerator and pipe a ring of choux pastry around the edge of it. Pipe out 8 to 10 small puffs on a lined baking tray. Baste with the remaining beaten egg. Bake for about 20 minutes (for the small puffs) to 30 minutes (for the larger piece).

Prepare the Chiboust cream (see p. 180).
Soak the gelatin sheets in a bowl of cold water. Slit the vanilla bean lengthwise and scrape the seeds into the milk. Add the vanilla bean to the milk and begin to heat. Whisk the 3 egg yolks, sugar, and cornstarch until the mixture is pale and thick. When the milk begins to simmer, remove from the heat and pour half of it over the beaten egg yolks. Combine thoroughly, then pour the egg and milk mixture into the milk and return to the heat. Bring back to a simmer and leave to simmer for 2 to 3 minutes, whisking continuously. Remove from the heat. Drain the gelatin sheets, squeezing out all the water, and incorporate into the milk mixture. Whisk thoroughly, then transfer this pastry cream to a bowl and cover with plastic wrap flush with the surface. Chill to about 60°F (15°C).

Prepare an Italian meringue with the 8 egg whites, sugar, and water, according to the technique on page 51. When the pastry cream has cooled but has not yet set, smooth it out. Carefully fold the Italian meringue into the pastry cream. Spoon this Chiboust cream into a piping bag.

Prepare a caramel with the sugar and water. Make a small hole in each of the puffs using a small sharp knife, and fill them with Chiboust cream. Dip each puff into the hot caramel to close the holes. Place them, caramel side downward, on a sheet of parchment paper to cool. Once cooled, attach the puffs around the outer edge of the choux pastry ring, using a little hot caramel (reheat it, if necessary). Fill the center with the remaining Chiboust cream. Garnish as desired (with spun sugar or chocolate disks, for example) and serve.

Apple upside-down cake (tarte Tatin) ✳

SERVES 8

Preparation: **40 minutes**
Resting: **20 minutes**
Cooking: **55 minutes**

INGREDIENTS

Shortcrust pastry
2 ¾ cups (250 g) cake flour
1 generous teaspoon (5 g) salt
1 stick (125 g) unsalted butter,
  softened
1 egg yolk
4 ½ tablespoons (50 ml) water

10 golden delicious apples
1 stick (125 g) unsalted butter
1 cup (200 g) sugar
Generous ½ teaspoon (3 g)
  ground cinnamon

TECHNIQUE

Shortcrust pastry
(*pâte brisée*) **14**

Prepare the shortcrust pastry (see p. 14).
Sift the flour and add the salt. Blend the butter and the flour together with your fingertips until the mixture forms coarse crumbs. Make a well and incorporate the egg yolk and water. Form a ball with the dough, still working quickly with your hands. Flatten the dough with the palm of your hands, pushing it away from you, until it is quite smooth. Chill the dough, wrapped in plastic, for about 30 minutes. Lightly sprinkle the working surface with flour and roll the dough into a disk shape with a thickness of about ⅛ in. (3 mm).

Preheat the oven to 350°F (180°C).

Peel and core the apples. Cut into thick slices. Place a nonstick cake pan or special tarte Tatin pan on the heat and melt the butter. Add the sugar and caramelize over low heat. When the sugar begins to change color, arrange the apple slices in overlapping circles in the pan. Do not leave any gaps between the pieces. Flatten them slightly using a spatula so that they can poach in the caramel. Sprinkle with cinnamon. Remove the pan from the heat and cover with shortcrust pastry, pressing down firmly at the edges. Prick the pastry with a fork.

Bake for 35–40 minutes. The pastry will be golden. Allow to cool a little in the pan before turning the tart out onto a serving plate. Serve it, still warm, with the apples facing upward.

Tarte Tatin is excellent with slightly sweet whipped cream and vanilla ice cream—a wonderful warm–cold combination.

Didier Stéphan

presents his recipe

The *verrine*, or shot glass, no doubt still has a bright future, even if—just like the omnipresent macaron—we seem to see too many of them in France. There are many advantages to this form of dessert, not the least among them being transparency: we can see—or at least glimpse—what we are about to eat. Next, it allows the pastry chef to make more use of textures that have not set: crispness and melt-in-the-mouth creaminess can be juxtaposed with no difficulty. This gives free rein to the imagination. In my opinion, the verrine should be another means of expression for desserts, just like petit fours, the equivalent of a quarter cup containing multiple and short explosions of tasting pleasure.

In this *verrine* recipe, Pineau wine, an aperitif from the Poitou-Charentes region in southwest France, takes pride of place. Pineau is a grape juice whose fermentation is stopped by adding eau-de-vie before being matured in oak barrels, where it acquires its delightful taste. Pineau rosé, in addition, takes on notes of berries. And diplomat cream, much used in the past, seems almost to have come out of a black-and-white film. Today it is making a comeback and its lightness and subtle creamy texture are once again winning it popularity.

SERVES 4

Preparation:
2 hours
Cooking:
1 hour 40 minutes

INGREDIENTS

Jelled Pineau
Scant ½ cup (100 g)
  Pineau
1 sheet gelatin (2 g)

Diplomat cream
1 cup (250 ml) milk
1 vanilla bean, slit and
  scraped
^{1}/₃ cup (60 g) sugar
2 ½ egg yolks (50 g)
2 tablespoons (20 g)
  cornstarch
1 ^{1}/₃ tablespoons
  Charente butter
¾ cup (200 ml)
  whipping cream, min.
  35% fat, stiffly beaten

Crumble
Scant ½ cup (100 g)
  butter
7 tablespoons (100 g)
  sugar
1 generous cup (100 g)
  ground almonds
1 generous cup (100 g)
  cake flour

Salted caramel sauce
½ cup (100 g) sugar
Scant ½ cup (100 ml)
  crème fraîche
A pinch of salt

Glucose bubbles
2 oz. (60 g) glucose
Food colorant (optional)

Vanilla-Pineau diplomat cream

Jelled Pineau

Soften the gelatin sheet in cold water for 3 minutes. Drain well and dissolve in a few drops of water in a microwave oven for 10 seconds. Combine the Pineau with the gelatin and immediately pour the liquid just under 1 in. (2 cm) deep into each of the 4 glasses.

Diplomat cream

Bring the milk to a boil. Leave the vanilla bean to infuse in the milk for 30 minutes. Beat the egg yolks and sugar together, whisk in the cornstarch, and pour the mixture over the milk. Bring to a simmer and allow to thicken to the texture of a pastry cream. Remove from the heat and whisk in the butter. Cover with plastic wrap and chill for 20 minutes to set. When it has chilled, whisk the cream stiffly and carefully fold it in.

Crumble

Cream the butter and sugar together. If you are not using salted butter, add a little salt. Then incorporate the ground almonds and flour. Chill for 15 minutes and crumble it onto a baking tray. Bake it at 350°F (180°C) for 5–10 minutes, until it turns a light golden color.

Salted caramel sauce

Caramelize the sugar (use the dry method, i.e. without any water). Heat the cream and add it to the caramel. Remove from the heat and adjust the consistency when cold by adding more cream if necessary, until it is syrupy. Add a pinch of salt.

Glucose bubbles

Preheat the oven to 300°F (150°C). Line a baking sheet with parchment paper or use a silicone baking sheet. Spread the glucose out (if you wish to color it, add a few drops of colorant) and bake for 50 minutes.

To assemble

Pour the Diplomat cream (just over 1 in. or about 3 cm) over the jelled Pineau. Then pour in the caramel sauce. Sprinkle the crumble on the top and garnish with a sheet of glucose bubbles.

Didier Stéphan presents his recipe

Raspberry charlotte ✳ ✳

SERVES 8

Preparation: **1 hour 10 minutes**
Chilling: **2 hours 30 minutes**
Cooking: **35 minutes**

INGREDIENTS

Ladyfingers
3 eggs, separated, plus 1 egg white
½ cup (100 g) sugar
Generous ½ cup (50 g) cake flour
⅓ cup (50 g) cornstarch
Confectioners' sugar for dusting

Raspberry syrup
⅓ cup (60 g) granulated sugar
3 tablespoons (40 ml) water
2 teaspoons (10 ml) raspberry
  liqueur
4 ½ oz. (125 g) raspberries, for
  garnish

Raspberry Bavarian cream
10 sheets gelatin (20 g)
1 ¾ lb. (800 g) puréed raspberries
½ cup (100 g) sugar
1 ½ teaspoons (8 ml) raspberry
  liqueur
3 ¼ cups (800 ml) whipping
  cream, min. 35% fat

Raspberry coulis
7 oz. (200 g) raspberries
1 ⅓ tablespoons (20 ml) lemon
  juice
⅔ cup (80 g) confectioners' sugar

Special equipment: a charlotte
  mold, about 8 inches (18 cm) in
  diameter, or individual molds

TECHNIQUES

Ladyfingers **190**
French meringue **51**
Syrup **172**
Fruit-based Bavarian cream **192**
Fruit coulis **166**

Prepare the ladyfingers (see p. 190).
Prepare a French meringue (see p. 51) using four egg whites and the sugar. Fold this in with the egg yolks. Sift the flour with the starch directly into the egg mixture. Carefully fold in using a rubber spatula.

Preheat the oven to 400°F (200°C).

Pipe out the mixture, or spoon it, onto a silicone baking sheet or parchment paper. Each ladyfinger should be about 3 ½–4 in. (8–10 cm) long and ⅔ in. (1.5 cm) wide. Dust them with confectioners' sugar and allow it to penetrate. Sprinkle the ladyfingers again with confectioners' sugar and bake for 10–15 minutes, until a very pale color. Allow to cool.

Prepare the raspberry syrup. Bring the water and the sugar to a boil. When quite dissolved, add the raspberry liqueur.

Line the charlotte mold with the cooled ladyfingers, packing them closely together. Use a pastry brush to moisten them well with the warm syrup.

Prepare the raspberry Bavarian cream (see p. 192).
Soak the gelatin sheets in very cold water to soften them. Bring the raspberry purée and sugar to a boil. Drain the gelatin, wringing out the water with your hands, and add it to the purée. Combine thoroughly. Allow the mixture to cool. When the purée has cooled to about 68°F (20°C) or room temperature, whisk in the raspberry liqueur. Whip the cream until it forms firm peaks. Carefully fold in the whipped cream, little by little, using a rubber spatula, taking care not to deflate the mixture. Pour it into the mold immediately to set. Cover it well with plastic wrap and chill for 2–2 ½ hours.

Prepare the raspberry coulis (see p. 166).
Wash the raspberries and blend them with the lemon juice and sugar. Strain through a fine-mesh sieve. Cover with plastic wrap and chill until needed. Turn the charlotte out of the mold onto a serving plate (use hot tea towels if necessary). Garnish with raspberries and serve with the coulis.

French brioche toast and vanilla stewed rhubarb ✳✳

SERVES 8

Preparation: **50 minutes**
Resting: **1 hour**
Cooking: **1 hour**
Refrigeration: **8 hours**

INGREDIENTS

Brioche
⅕ oz. (5 g) fresh (compressed)
  yeast
2 teaspoons (10 ml) milk or water
2 ½ cups (250 g) all-purpose flour
1 teaspoon (5 g) salt
2 tablespoons (25 g) granulated
  sugar
3 eggs
½ cup (125 g) unsalted butter,
  softened

Sweet custard base for baking
Scant ½ cup (100 ml) milk
Scant ½ cup (100 ml) whipping
  cream, min. 30% fat
2 eggs plus 2 egg yolks
3 ½ tablespoons (40 g) sugar
A few drops of vanilla extract, or
  the seeds from a vanilla bean
A few drops of bitter almond
  extract
5 ½ tablespoons (80 g) butter

Stewed rhubarb
1 lb. (400 g) rhubarb
1 ¾ cups (350 g) sugar
Scant ¼ cup (50 ml) water
A few drops of vanilla extract

TECHNIQUES

Brioche dough 27
Sweet custard base for
  baking 188

A day ahead, prepare the brioche (see p. 27).
Dilute the yeast in the milk or water at room temperature. Sift the flour onto a flat surface and make a well in the center. Sprinkle the salt and sugar outside the well so that they do not come into direct contact with the yeast. Beat the eggs and incorporate them into the mixture using a rubber scraper. Knead the dough energetically to give it elasticity. You may use a stand mixer fitted with the dough hook to do this. If you opt for the stand mixer, use medium speed for about 10 minutes. Then knead in the butter until it is completely incorporated and the dough is smooth, and place the dough in a mixing bowl. Cover with plastic wrap and leave to rise for 30 to 40 minutes at a temperature of 77°F–82°F (25°C–28°C) with a bowl of water. When the dough has doubled in volume, remove from the bowl and turn out onto a lightly floured surface. Flatten it and fold into three. This is known as deflating. Form a ball and shape it to fit the brioche pan. Leave to rise again until it reaches halfway to the top of the mold.

Preheat the oven to 350°F–400°F (180°C–200°C). Bake the brioche. It is done when it is a nice golden color and the tip of a knife comes out dry.

Prepare the sweet custard base for baking (see p. 188).
Combine the milk, cream, whole eggs, egg yolks, sugar, vanilla, and bitter almond extract until just mixed. Do not beat until the mixture forms bubbles. Strain it through a fine-mesh sieve, cover with plastic wrap, and chill.

Prepare the stewed rhubarb.
Trim, wash and peel the stalks, pulling off the hard fibers. Cut them into slices just under 1 in. (2 cm) long and blanch them in boiling water. Drain the rhubarb and rinse it under cold water. Gently stew it over low heat with the sugar, water, and vanilla extract. Test for doneness: it should be soft when pressed between your fingers (allow a piece to cool down before testing). Chill until the next day.

To assemble.
Cut thick slices of brioche, just under 1 in. (2 cm) thick. Dip them in the sweet cream on both sides. Melt the butter in a pan and brown the slices of brioche evenly on both sides. Arrange the brioches slices in plates with the stewed vanilla rhubarb. If you like, you may serve it with vanilla ice cream.

Raspberry ganache tart ✳

SERVES 8

Preparation: **45 minutes**
Resting: **20 minutes**
Cooking: **40 minutes**
Chilling: **2–3 hours**

INGREDIENTS

Creamed sweet short pastry
1 stick (125 g) unsalted butter,
  softened
½ cup (100 g) granulated sugar
1 egg
2 ¾ cups (250 g) cake flour
1 teaspoon (5 ml) salt

Ganache cream
½ lb. (225 g) raspberries, divided
¼ cup (50 g) granulated sugar
2 oz. (50 g) glucose
1 ⅔ cups (400 ml) whipping
  cream, min. 30% fat
7 tablespoons (100 g) unsalted
  butter
Scant ⅓ cup (70 ml) raspberry
  brandy or eau-de-vie
1 ¾ lb. (750 g) dark chocolate,
  64% cacao, chopped

Special equipment: a copper
  saucepan

TECHNIQUES

Creamed sweet short pastry
  (*pâte sucrée*) **16**
Ganache **183**

Prepare the creamed sweet short pastry (see p. 16).
Place the butter, sugar, and egg in the bowl of a food processor and cream together until smooth. Sift the flour and add it with the salt to process for 1–2 minutes further, until smooth. Remove from the bowl. Press down the dough with the palm of your hand, pushing it away from you, until the ingredients are thoroughly blended. Chill, covered, for 20 minutes.

Preheat the oven to 350°F (180°C).

Roll out the dough very thinly (about ⅛ in./3 mm) to form a disk. Use your rolling pin to transfer it from the working surface to the baking pan or circle: drape it round the pin and then unroll it over the tart mold. Make decorative patterns around the edge. Prick the dough with a fork, line it with parchment paper, and fill with baking beans. Blind-bake for 20–25 minutes and allow to cool.

In a copper saucepan, cook 3 ½ oz. (100 g) of the raspberries with the sugar and glucose. Bring to a boil and leave to simmer for a few minutes. Add the cream and butter and bring to a boil again. Remove from the heat and incorporate the raspberry brandy or eau-de-vie and the chopped chocolate. Mix until thoroughly blended. Strain through a fine mesh sieve and pour the ganache into the cooled tart shell. Leave in the refrigerator until set, about 2–3 hours. Garnish with the remaining raspberries and serve.

Floating islands with spun caramel ✳✳

SERVES 8

Preparation: **40 minutes**
Cooking: **30 minutes**

INGREDIENTS

10 egg whites
½ teaspoon (2 g) fine salt
1 ¾ cups (240 g) confectioners'
  sugar
4 cups (1 liter) milk
2 ¾ oz. (80 g) sliced almonds

Custard
½ vanilla bean
5 egg yolks
²⁄₃ cup (125 g) granulated sugar

Spun sugar
1 ½ cups (200 g) sugar

TECHNIQUES

French meringue **51**
Pouring custard (*crème
  anglaise*) **177**

Prepare a French meringue (see p. 51).
Use a round-bottomed mixing bowl that is perfectly clean and
dry. Beat the egg whites together lightly with the salt using a
fork. Then begin whisking them energetically, making sure you
lift up the whisk high to incorporate as much air as possible.
When the whites begin to form stiff peaks, add 1 ¾ cups (240 g)
sugar, blending it in with a circular movement until the
meringue is firm and shiny. It should form small peaks at the
end of the whisk. Bring the milk to a simmer in a fairly large
pot or pan. Dip a soup ladle into the beaten egg whites and form
domes using a plastic scraper. Poach the domes in the milk for
1–2 minutes, depending on their size. Turn them over carefully
to ensure they are cooked through. Remove the cooked
meringue domes, reserving the milk for the custard. Drain them
on paper towel and chill.

Prepare the custard (see p. 177).
Take 2 cups (500 ml) of the poaching liquid and strain it
through a fine-mesh sieve. Slit the vanilla bean and place it in a
saucepan with the milk to heat. Energetically whisk the egg
yolks with the sugar until the mixture is thick and pale. Pour
the milk over the beaten egg yolks, beating constantly, and
return to the heat. Simmer and stir all the time, removing from
the heat from time to time, so that the egg yolks do not
coagulate from too much contact with the heat. Continue until
the mixture thickens and coats the back of a spoon (185°F/85°C
if you have a thermometer). Strain through a chinois and pour
the cream into a mixing bowl. Cover with plastic wrap and
allow to cool. When it has cooled, half fill dessert bowls or cups
with it. Then carefully place a floating island meringue dome
on top of the liquid.

Make the spun sugar: heat the sugar to make a light caramel
and allow to cool just slightly. To make the sugar threads, dip a
fork in the caramel and whisk it energetically in a round-
bottomed mixing bowl. Garnish one of the floating islands.
Reheat the caramel just slightly and repeat the operation as
many times as necessary, garnishing the desserts each time.
Lightly toast the sliced almonds, allow them to cool, and scatter
them over the floating islands. Serve immediately.

DID YOU KNOW?

The recipe for floating islands was first written up by La Varenne in his
Le Cuisinier Français (*The French Cook*) of 1651, and is still popular in its
original form.

Tutti-frutti waffles ✳

SERVES 8

Preparation: **40 minutes**
Resting: **30 minutes**
Cooking: **15 minutes**

INGREDIENTS

Waffle batter
3 ¾ cups (340 g) cake flour
Scant ½ cup (80 g) sugar
Scant ½ teaspoon (2 g) salt
2 ¾ teaspoons (10 g) baking
  powder
2 eggs
2 cups (½ liter) milk
Scant ½ cup (100 g) melted
  butter
A little orange-blossom water

2 apples
4 ½ oz. (125 g) blackberries
8 bunches red currants
4 ½ oz. (125 g) small, tasty
  strawberries (Mara des bois if
  possible)
8 bunches (125 g) black currants
4 ½ oz. (125 g) raspberries
A little confectioners' sugar, for
  coating

Chantilly cream
1 cup (250 ml) whipping cream,
  min. 35% fat, well chilled
¼ cup (35 g) confectioners' sugar
A few drops vanilla extract

TECHNIQUES

Waffle batter **24**
Chantilly cream **179**

Prepare the waffle batter (see p. 24).
Combine the flour, sugar, salt, and baking powder in a mixing bowl. Make a well in the center. Break the eggs into the well and whisk them into the dry ingredients with a little milk. Gradually add the rest of the milk, whisking until there are no lumps. Stir in the melted butter and orange-blossom water. Leave the batter to chill for about 30 minutes.

Prepare the fruit. Peel and wash the apples and cut them into quarters. Wash all the berries. Coat the raspberries and strawberries lightly in confectioners' sugar by placing a little sugar on the tip of a knife and blowing lightly down the blade.

Cook the waffles in the waffle maker according to instructions and leave them to cool.

Prepare the Chantilly cream (see p. 179).
Pour the cold cream into a cold mixing bowl or the cold bowl of a food processor. Whisk briskly or beat at medium speed with the food processor until the cream begins to form peaks. Sift the confectioners' sugar into the cream and then add the vanilla extract. Whisk the cream briskly for a few moments until it forms stiff peaks.

Pipe or spoon the cream onto the waffles and garnish attractively with the fruit.

Cherry clafoutis ✳

SERVES 8

Preparation: **15 minutes**
Resting: **40 minutes**
Cooking: **45 minutes**

INGREDIENTS

1 lb. (500 g) black cherries
½ cup (100 g) sugar, divided
1 ⅓ cups (125 g) cake flour
1 teaspoon (5 g) fine salt
3 eggs, beaten
1 ¼ cups (300 ml) full cream milk
2 tablespoons (30 g) butter, melted
1 vanilla bean, slit, seeds scraped out
Confectioners' sugar, for dusting

Wash the cherries and remove the stalks. Sprinkle them with half of the sugar and leave to rest for 30–40 minutes.

Preheat the oven to 350°F (180°C).

In a mixing bowl, combine the flour and the remaining sugar. Add the salt and energetically whisk in the beaten eggs so that there are no lumps. Stir in the melted butter and the vanilla seeds.

Place the cherries (leave the pits in) in a cake mold or silicone flan mold. Fill it with the batter.

Bake for 40–45 minutes. Test for doneness: it should be very soft, and when you insert the tip of a knife some steam will rise.

Dust with confectioners' sugar as soon as you remove it from the oven and serve hot or warm.

DID YOU KNOW?

A clafoutis is a simple dessert that was traditionally made in the country when cherries were harvested. When cherry season is over, the recipe works equally well with many other fruits.

Cinnamon rice pudding ✳

SERVES 8

Preparation: **20 minutes**
Cooking: **40 minutes**

INGREDIENTS

5 oz. (140 g) round-grain rice
1 small stick of cinnamon (2 g)
1 vanilla bean
4 cups (1 liter) milk
4 egg yolks
¾ cup (150 g) granulated sugar
1 pinch fine salt (2 g)

TECHNIQUE

Rice pudding **200**

Wash the round-grain rice. Place in cold water with the salt and bring it to a boil. As soon as it starts boiling, remove from the heat and refresh under cold running water. Drain.

Preheat the oven to 325°F (160°C).

Break up the cinnamon stick into pieces and slit the vanilla bean lengthwise. Bring the milk to a boil with the vanilla bean and the cinnamon stick pieces. If you are not using a saucepan with an ovenproof lid, transfer the milk to a deep baking dish, pour in the rice, cover, and bake for a good hour. Check for doneness by pressing a few cooled grains of rice between your fingers.

Whisk the egg yolks and the sugar until the mixture is thick and pale. Remove the rice from the oven and stir in the egg mixture. Place over a low to medium heat and bring back to a simmer. Arrange the rice pudding attractively in individual dishes and allow to cool rapidly. Garnish as you wish, with mint leaves, a thin piece of vanilla bean, grated lemon rind, etc.

Red berry *crémet* ✳

SERVES 6

Preparation: **35 minutes**
Chilling: **1 hour minimum**

INGREDIENTS

7 oz. (200 g) *faisselle* cheese (or drained, smoothed cottage cheese, or quark or cream cheese
Scant ¼ cup (30 g) confectioners' sugar
1 vanilla bean, slit lengthwise, seeds scraped
2 egg whites
⅓ cup (60 g) granulated sugar
Scant cup (200 ml) whipping cream, min. 35% fat
7 oz. (200 g) mixed red berries (raspberries, strawberries, red currants, etc.)

If you are using French *faisselle* cheese, drain it well—you might need to drain it overnight. If the type of cream cheese you are using does not have such a high water content, it will not be necessary to drain it so long. Whisk in the confectioners' sugar and the seeds of the vanilla bean.

Beat the egg whites until they form stiff peaks. Add the sugar and whisk until the meringue is firm and shiny.

Whip the cream as for a Chantilly cream (see p. 179).

Gently fold the beaten egg whites into the cheese, and then, equally carefully, the whipped cream. Fold just until all the ingredients are combined. If you used French *faisselle*, return the mixture to the *faisselle* containers (these are tiny colanders). Otherwise spoon the mixture into ramekins or small bowls. Top with the mixed berries and chill for at least 1 hour.

Serve with a red berry coulis (see p. 166) or Breton-style shortbread cookies.

TECHNIQUE

Chantilly cream **179**

Chestnut cream, nougatine, and walnut Succès ✳✳

SERVES 8

Preparation: **50 minutes**
Cooking: **35 minutes**
Chilling: **2 hours**

INGREDIENTS

Succès meringue batter
5 egg whites
²/₃ cup (125 g) sugar
¼ cup (25 g) flour
1 ½ cups (4 ½ oz./125 g) ground
  almonds

Nougatine
2 oz. (50 g) glucose syrup (from
  specialty stores or online)
2 ²/₃ cups (500 g) sugar
10 oz. (300 g) chopped almonds
¹/₃ cup (70 g) unsalted butter,
  melted

Chestnut butter cream
1 cup (200 g) sugar
Scant ¹/₃ cup (70 ml) water
2 eggs plus 2 yolks
2 sticks (250 g) unsalted butter
3 ½ oz. (100 g) chestnut cream
  (from specialty stores or online)

1 cup (4 ½ oz./125 g) shelled
  walnuts

TECHNIQUES

Succès **206**
Butter cream (with cooked
  sugar) **178**

Preheat the oven to 400°F (200°C).

Prepare the Succès meringue batter (see p. 206).
Beat the egg whites until they form firm peaks. Add 1 generous tablespoon (15 g) sugar and beat until dense and shiny. Sift the remaining sugar, flour, and ground almonds together. Pour into the beaten egg whites and fold in carefully so that the mixture does not deflate. Immediately spoon it into a piping bag and pipe out sixteen circles (diameter about 5 in./10 cm) onto a baking sheet. Make a close whirl pattern starting in the center. Bake for 8–10 minutes and transfer immediately to a rack to cool.

Prepare the nougatine.
Melt the glucose syrup over medium heat. Gradually add the sugar, stirring constantly. Toast the almonds and keep them warm without burning them or allowing them to darken. When the sugar mixture begins to turn yellow (the temperature will be around 330°F or 165°C), add the still-hot almonds, stirring them in, and then the melted butter. Stir until all the ingredients are well combined. Pour the mixture out onto a silicone baking sheet and roll out thinly between two baking sheets. Allow to cool.

Toast the walnuts and allow them to cool.

Prepare the chestnut butter cream (see p. 178).
Prepare a sugar syrup with the sugar and the water and cook until it reaches a temperature of 243°F (117°C). With an electric beater, whisk the egg and yolk mixture until is it foamy. Pour the sugar syrup over the eggs, and continue beating for a few minutes to lower the temperature of the mixture. Incorporate the cubed butter using a whisk or an electric beater at medium speed. Stir in the chestnut cream. Spoon the butter cream into a piping bag.

Take a disk of Succès meringue and pipe out the butter cream around the edge of the circle. Coarsely chop the nougatine and rub the walnuts to remove their skin. Place the chopped nougatine and walnuts in the center of the piped chestnut butter cream. Top with a second disk of Succès meringue and chill until needed.

Brown sugar tart ✳

SERVES 8

Preparation: **40 minutes**
Resting: **40 minutes**
Cooking: **30 minutes**

INGREDIENTS

Pastry

½ oz. (15 g) fresh (compressed)
  yeast
Scant ½ cup (100ml) full cream
  milk, warm
2 ½ cups (250 g) all-purpose
  flour
1 egg
1 teaspoon (5 g) salt
¼ cup (50 g) sugar
5 ½ tablespoons (80 g) butter,
  softened and cubed

Filling

5 ¼ oz. (¾ cup or 150 g) brown
  Vergeoise sugar (soft brown
  sugar made from beets)
2 eggs
3 tablespoons (40 g) butter,
  softened
1 cup (250 ml) whipping cream,
  min. 30% fat

TECHNIQUE

Brioche dough **27**

Prepare the pastry dough.
Dilute the yeast in the warm milk. Sift the flour into a mixing bowl and make a well in the center. Add the egg and stir in, followed by the salt, sugar, and the yeast diluted in the milk. Knead until combined, then vigorously knead in the cubed butter. Cover with plastic wrap and leave to rise for 30–40 minutes at a temperature of 77°F–82°F (25°C–28°C) with a bowl of water, as for a brioche (see p. 27), until doubled in volume.

Preheat the oven to 450°F (240°C).

Roll out the dough to fit the tart mold. Sprinkle the brown Vergeoise sugar inside.

Beat the eggs and butter together. Add the whipping cream and pour the mixture over the sugar.

Bake for 25–30 minutes, depending on the size of your tart. It should be a golden color. Serve warm or cool.

DID YOU KNOW?

Until the early nineteenth century, cane sugar was imported into France. Then Benjamin Delessert succeeded in producing another form of sugar using beets. The first factory was located just outside what were then the limits of Paris. The northern regions of France, in particular, made excellent use of the various types of light-colored and brown sugars, known as Vergeoise or *cassonade*, in candies and cakes such as this tart.

French cheesecake (*tourteau fromagé*) ✳

SERVES 4

Preparation: **35 minutes**
Cooking: **1 hour**

INGREDIENTS

Creamed sweet short pastry
4 tablespoons (65 g) unsalted
  butter, softened
½ cup (65 g) confectioners' sugar
1 egg
Scant ½ teaspoon (2 g) salt
1 cup (125 g) all-purpose flour

Filling
6 eggs (10 ½ oz./300 g)
8 ¾ oz. (250 g) fresh goat cheese
  or well-drained *faisselle*
1 scant cup (170 g) sugar,
  divided
½ teaspoon (3 g) salt
3 ½ tablespoons (50 ml) whole
  milk
1/3 cup (60 g) custard powder
1 vanilla bean
2 teaspoons (10 ml) cognac
A few drops orange flower water

TECHNIQUE

Creamed sweet short pastry
  (*pâte sucrée*) **16**

CHEF'S NOTE

– You can add the zest of
½ orange (preferably organic)
to the filling mixture.

Prepare the creamed sweet short pastry (see p. 16).
Place the softened butter and confectioners' sugar in a large
bowl and cream together energetically using your fingertips; if
the butter is quite soft, use a whisk. The mixture should be
smooth. Whisk in the egg and salt, then incorporate the flour
using a spatula or your hands, taking care not to overmix.
Shape the dough into a disk about 1 ¼ inches (3 cm) thick, cover
with plastic wrap, and chill for about 20 minutes.

Grease an 8–8 ½-inch (20–22-cm) round cake pan, or a special
tourteau pan, with butter. Roll the dough to a thickness of about
⅛ inch (3 mm) and fit it into the pan.

Preheat the oven to 350°F (180°C).

Prepare the filling.
Separate the eggs. Place the goat cheese in a large bowl, and add
⅔ cup (125 g) sugar, the salt, and the milk. Whisk until creamy
and smooth. Vigorously whisk in the egg yolks and custard
powder.

Whisk the egg whites with the remaining sugar until they hold
stiff peaks, then gently fold them into the filling mixture. Slit
the vanilla bean lengthwise and scrape in the seeds, then add
the cognac and orange flower water. Gently stir to combine.

Pour the filling into the pastry base and smooth over the surface
using a spatula. Bake for 50–55 minutes, until the filling is
puffed up and very deeply browned, or even slightly blackened,
all over. The cake is done when a knife inserted into the center
comes out clean.

Let the cake cool before removing it from the pan.

DID YOU KNOW?

Known as *tourteau fromagé*, this gem of French patisserie from the
Poitou-Charentes region is a domed cheesecake with a distinctive black
(charred) crust. The interior is moist, spongy, and lightly sweet.

Chocolate mousse ✳

SERVES 8

Preparation: **25 minutes**
Chilling: **1 hour minimum**
Cooking: **10 minutes**

INGREDIENTS

½ lb. (250 g) dark chocolate,
  64% cacao, chopped
5 ½ tablespoons (80 g) butter,
  cubed
3 eggs, separated, plus 3 egg
  whites
½ cup (100 g) sugar
2 oz. (30 g) chocolate sprinkles,
  for garnish

TECHNIQUE

French meringue **51**

Melt the chopped chocolate and the cubed butter in a bain-marie to a temperature of 122°F (50°C). Remove the mixture from the heat and whisk in the three egg yolks until the mixture is smooth. Leave to cool to about 82°F (28°C).

Start whisking the six egg whites. When they start to form firm peaks, add the sugar and whisk until shiny and compact (see French meringue, p. 51). Carefully fold the meringue mixture into the chocolate-butter mixture using a rubber spatula. Take care not to deflate the mixture by breaking the air bubbles.

Spoon the mousse into a piping bag and pipe into ramekins or shot glasses (*verrines*). Chill for at least 1 hour, until set.

Garnish with chocolate sprinkles.

DID YOU KNOW?

Mousses practically disappeared from classic French cuisine toward the end of the eighteenth century, only to reappear with the advent of nouvelle cuisine. There was one notable exception: the chocolate mousse, probably the most popular of all French desserts.

Strawberry gratin with sabayon ✳

SERVES 8

Preparation: **25 minutes**
Marinating: **30 minutes**
Cooking: **20 minutes**

INGREDIENTS

1 lb. (500 g) strawberries
²/₃ cup (125 g) sugar
Zest of 1 unsprayed or organic
    orange
Zest of 1 unsprayed or organic
    lemon
A few sprigs of lemon verbena,
    leaves chopped
1 cup or ¼ lb. (125 g)
    confectioners' sugar

Sabayon
4 egg yolks
Scant ½ cup (100 ml) strawberry
    liqueur

TECHNIQUE

Sabayon (zabaglione) **52**

Wash and hull the strawberries. Roll them gently in the granulated or caster sugar.

Scatter the grated zest and lemon verbena over the strawberries. Stir gently to combine and leave to marinate for 30 minutes.

Set the oven to broil.

Prepare the sabayon (see p. 52).
Place the egg yolks in a saucepan. Add the strawberry liqueur and whisk energetically. Place the saucepan over a low heat. Whisk the mixture continuously until it is creamy.

Arrange the strawberries in small, shallow casserole dishes or in a serving dish with handles. Pour the sabayon over the strawberries and broil briefly, or use a torch to caramelize the top. Dust with confectioners' sugar just before serving. Serve warm.

Alsatian mirabelle plum tart ✳

SERVES 8

Preparation: **40 minutes**
Resting: **20 minutes**
Cooking: **25 minutes**

INGREDIENTS

Creamed sweet short pastry
1 stick (125 g) unsalted butter,
   softened
½ cup (100 g) granulated sugar
1 egg
2 ¾ cups (250 g) cake flour
1 teaspoon (5 ml) salt

Sweet custard base for baking
1 scant cup (200 ml) milk
1 scant cup (200 ml) whipping
   cream, min. 35% fat
4 eggs plus 4 yolks
Scant ½ cup (80 g) sugar
A few drops of mirabelle plum
   brandy
½ vanilla bean

1 lb. (500 g) mirabelle plums
Confectioners' sugar for dusting

TECHNIQUES

Creamed sweet short pastry
   (*pâte sucrée*) **16**
Sweet custard base for
   baking **188**

Prepare the creamed sweet short pastry (see p. 16)**.**
Place the butter, sugar, and egg in the bowl of a food processor
and cream together until smooth. Sift the flour and add it with
the salt to process for 1–2 minutes further, until smooth.
Press down the dough with the palm of your hand, pushing it
away from you, until the ingredients are thoroughly blended.
Chill, covered, for 20 minutes. Roll out the dough very thinly
(about ⅛ in./3 mm) to form a disk. Use a rolling pin to transfer it
from the working surface to the baking pan or circle: drape it
round the pin and then unroll it in place. Make decorative
patterns around the edge.

Preheat the oven to 350°F (180°C).

Prepare the sweet custard base for baking (see p. 188)**.**
Combine the milk, cream, whole eggs, egg yolks, sugar, and
bitter almond extract until just mixed. Do not allow the mixture
to form bubbles. Pour the mirabelle brandy in to the batter and
scrape the seeds out of the vanilla bean to flavor it. Strain it
through a fine-mesh sieve, cover with plastic wrap, and chill.

Wash the plums. Arrange them at the base of the pastry crust
and pour the batter over. Bake for 20–25 minutes. If you are
using a pastry ring, remove it for the last 5 minutes so that the
edges can brown slightly. Remove from the oven and dust with
confectioners' sugar. Turn onto a cooling rack.

This tart is best served warm, and is delicious with ice cream.

DID YOU KNOW?

Mirabelle plums, a small, very sweet variety of plum, are grown in the
Alsace-Lorraine region in eastern France. They are much appreciated for
their juicy flesh and are used to make preserves and eau-de-vie. You can
use other plums or even other fruit to make this tart—but it will no longer
be called a mirabelle tart!

Diplomat cream mille-feuille ✳ ✳ ✳

SERVES 8

Preparation: **50 minutes**
Resting: **1 hour 20 minutes**
Cooking: **40 minutes**
Chilling: **40 minutes**

INGREDIENTS

Puff pastry
2 ¾ cups (250 g) cake flour
1 teaspoon (5 g) salt
½ cup (125 ml) water
1 stick plus 4 tablespoons (185 g)
   unsalted butter

Diplomat cream
5 sheets gelatin (10 g)
1 vanilla bean
2 cups (500 ml) milk
3 egg yolks
²/₃ cup (125 g) sugar
¹/₃ cup (55 g) cornstarch
A few drops of orange-blossom
   water
3 cups (750 ml) whipping cream,
   min. 35% fat

1 scant cup (125 g)
   confectioners' sugar
½ lb. (250 g) white fondant icing,
   optional
2 oz. (50 g) chocolate, 64% cacao

TECHNIQUES

Puff pastry **19**
Diplomat cream **182**

Prepare the puff pastry (see p. 19).
Make the puff pastry according to the technique on page 19, using the ingredients listed here. Preheat the oven to 425°F–450°F (220°C–230°C). Roll out the dough to a thickness of about ⅛ in. (3 mm), ensuring it fits on your baking sheet. Place the dough on a baking sheet lined with parchment paper, trim off any excess from the edges, and prick it at regular intervals with a fork. Bake for about 20 minutes. To obtain very thin, delicate layers of pastry, place a baking tray over your puff pastry halfway through the baking process. This will deflate the air that causes it to rise. At the same time, when the pastry is barely colored, dust it with confectioners' sugar. Repeat this once more, toward the end of the baking time. Be careful not to let it burn—it should remain a nice golden brown.

Prepare the diplomat cream (see p. 182).
Place the gelatin sheets in a bowl of cold water to soften. Slit the vanilla bean lengthwise and scrape out the seeds. Place them in the milk, together with the vanilla bean, and bring to a simmer. Whisk the egg yolks, sugar, and cornstarch briskly together until the mixture thickens and becomes pale. When the milk is simmering, remove it from the heat and pour half of it over the blanched eggs. Mix together. Incorporate the orange-blossom water. Pour the mixture back into the remaining milk, return to the heat, and bring back to a boil. Leave to boil for 2–3 minutes, whisking constantly. Remove from the heat. Wring the water out of the gelatin sheets. Incorporate the gelatin into the mixture and whisk until smooth. Transfer to a bowl and cover with plastic wrap flush with the surface. Cool to about 60°F (15°C). Using a stand mixer or electric beater, whip the cream until it is the same consistency as a Chantilly cream. When the pastry cream is cool but has not yet set, stir it again to loosen it, then delicately fold in the cold whipped cream with a rubber spatula.

Assemble the mille-feuille.
Carefully cut the pastry into three equally sized rectangles, using a knife with a serrated blade. If you are making eight individual portions, cut out twenty-four small rectangles. Spoon the diplomat cream into a piping bag and pipe it out onto the first rectangle of pastry. Place the second rectangle on top and pipe out more diplomat cream over it. Dust the third rectangle of pastry with confectioners' sugar and make crisscross patterns using hot steel skewers, or a caramelizing blow torch. If you prefer, you may coat this top layer with fondant icing; heat the fondant to 95°F (35°C) and spread it over the top. Trace a chocolate design on top. Place this third layer of puff pastry on the top of the mille-feuille. Chill for 30 to 40 minutes before serving.

Opéra ✷✷✷

SERVES 8

Preparation: **2 hours 10 minutes**
Cooking: **35 minutes**

INGREDIENTS

Joconde sponge
1 scant cup (190 g) sugar, divided
1 ²/₃ cups (140 g) ground
　almonds or almond meal
4 eggs plus 4 egg whites
¹/₃ cup (45 g) flour
1 ¹/₃ tablespoons (1 oz./25 g)
　butter, melted

Coffee syrup
¾ cup (200 ml) strong coffee
½ cup (100 g) sugar

Ganache
Scant ¹/₃ cup (70 ml) whipping
　cream, min. 30% fat
¼ cup (50 ml) milk
7 oz. (200 g) dark chocolate,
　64% cacao
1 ½ tablespoons (25 g) unsalted
　butter

Coffee butter cream
2 cups (400 g) sugar
Scant ¹/₃ cup (80 ml) water
2 eggs plus 2 egg yolks
2 sticks (250 g) unsalted butter,
　cubed
A few drops of liquid coffee extract

To finish
4 ½ oz. (125 g) dark chocolate,
　64% cacao, or 7 oz. (200 g)
　glazing paste

TECHNIQUES

Butter cream (with cooked
　sugar) **178**
Ganache **183**
Joconde sponge **196**

Prepare the joconde sponge (see p. 196).
Line a baking sheet with parchment paper. Preheat the oven to 350°F (180°C).

Sift together equal quantities of sugar and ground almonds: ¾ cup (140 g) granulated sugar and 1 ⅔ cups (140 g) ground almonds. Beat this together with four eggs until the mixture reaches the ribbon stage. Fold in the sifted flour, followed by the melted butter. Beat the four egg whites until they form stiff peaks. Add the remaining sugar (¼ cup or 50 g) and beat until the mixture is firm and shiny (it forms a French meringue). Carefully fold this French meringue into the egg and butter mixture. Spread the batter over the baking sheet. It should be very thin, about ¹/₅ in. (3–5 mm) thick. Bake for 8–10 minutes. As soon as it is done, turn it over onto a rack to cool with the parchment paper.

Make the coffee syrup.
Bring the coffee and the sugar to a boil. Cover with plastic wrap and set aside.

Prepare the ganache (see p. 183).
Bring the cream and milk to a boil. Chop the chocolate and pour the boiling cream-milk mixture over to melt it. Remove from the heat, whisk in the butter, and stir until smooth. Leave to cool, stirring from time to time.

Prepare the coffee butter cream (see p. 178).
Prepare a sugar syrup and cook until it reaches a temperature of 243°F (117°C). With an electric beater, whisk the egg and yolk mixture until is it foamy. Pour the sugar syrup over the eggs, and continue beating for a few minutes to cool the temperature of the mixture. Incorporate the cubed butter using a whisk or an electric beater at medium speed. Stir in the coffee extract. Transfer to a mixing bowl and cover with plastic wrap flush with the surface.

Remove the joconde sponge from the baking sheet and cut it into three identical rectangles. Glaze the top of one of the rectangles with melted chocolate or glazing paste, using a pastry brush. Allow to set, turn it over, and moisten the other side with coffee syrup. Cover this layer with coffee butter cream and place a second rectangle of sponge over it. Moisten the second layer with coffee syrup and pour over a very thin layer of ganache. Place the last sponge layer over the ganache and moisten it with coffee syrup. Cover it with butter cream and chill. Slightly heat some glazing paste to smooth over the Opéra, or cover it with a thin layer of ganache. Keep in the refrigerator.

It is a good idea to trim the edges with a sharp knife for an attractive presentation. Coffee-flavored custard makes a refined accompaniment.

Cheesecake ✳

SERVES 4

Preparation: **35 minutes**
Resting: **45 minutes**
Cooking: **1 hour**

INGREDIENTS

Crumbled sweet short pastry
1 cup (125 g) all-purpose flour
4 tablespoons (65 g) unsalted
  butter
¼ cup (50 g) superfine sugar
Scant ½ teaspoon (2 g) salt
1 egg
5 tablespoons (80 g) butter,
  melted until browned
Ground cinnamon

Cheesecake filling
1 scant cup (250 g) *fromage
  blanc*, min. 40% fat
1 scant cup (250 g) crème fraîche
⅓ cup (70 g) superfine sugar
1 ½ tablespoons (15 g) custard
  powder
Zest of ½ lemon
½ teaspoon (3 g) salt
1 vanilla bean
3 eggs (150 g)

TECHNIQUE

Crumbled sweet short pastry
(*pâte sablée*) **15**

CHEF'S NOTE

– For an original twist, you can
make the crust with crushed
speculoos cookies instead of the
short pastry. You could also
flavor the filling with a drizzle
of rum.

Prepare the crumbled sweet short pastry (see p. 15).
Place the flour in a large stainless steel bowl, dice the
4 tablespoons (65 g) butter, and rub it into the flour with your
fingertips, until the mixture resembles coarse sand. Incorporate
the sugar and salt and make a well in the center. Beat the egg
with a fork, pour it into the well, and work it into the dough.
Transfer the dough to a clean work surface and knead it with
the palm of your hand, until just smooth but not elastic. Shape
into a disk about 1 ¼ inches (3 cm) thick, cover with plastic
wrap, and chill for about 20 minutes.

Preheat the oven to 375°F (190°C).

Roll the dough to a thickness of about ¼ inch (5 mm). Place on a
baking sheet lined with parchment paper and blind-bake for
about 20 minutes. Let cool completely on a rack.

Lower the oven temperature to 325°F (160°C). Line an
8–8 ½-inch (20–22-cm) round springform pan or baking ring
with parchment paper.

Grind the short pastry to fine crumbs using a food processor, or
crumble it into a large bowl using your hands. Stir in the
browned butter and cinnamon until well combined. Press this
mixture into the pan, packing it down well using the back of a
spoon. Chill while you prepare the filling.

Prepare the cheesecake filling.
Whisk together the *fromage blanc* and crème fraîche in a large
bowl. Whisk in the sugar, custard powder, lemon zest, and salt.
Slit the vanilla bean lengthwise and scrape the seeds into the
filling. Whisk to combine. Beat the eggs together in a separate
bowl, then gradually pour them into the filling, whisking
continuously.

Pour the filling over the crust and bake for 40–50 minutes, until
a knife inserted into the center comes out clean.

Let the cheesecake cool completely before removing it from the
pan.

Breton flan with dried plums (*far breton*) ✳

SERVES 8

Preparation: **20 minutes**
Soaking: **12 hours or overnight**
Cooking: **40 minutes**

INGREDIENTS

1 tablespoon plus 1 teaspoon
 (20 g) salted butter
1 ¼ cups (125 g) all-purpose
 flour
1 pinch (2 g) fine salt
4 eggs
½ lb. (250 g) dried plums with
 their pits
1 cup (250 ml) well-aged rum
½ cup (100 g) sugar
4 cups (1 liter) full cream milk
1 tablespoon (15 g) unsalted
 butter, to grease the dish

A day ahead, soak the dried plums in the rum and leave overnight.

Preheat the oven to 425°F (210°C).

Butter an ovenproof dish. Melt the butter until it browns. Place the flour and salt in a round-bottomed mixing bowl. Whisk in the eggs one by one, taking care that they are thoroughly mixed in and that there are no lumps. Pour in the browned melted butter and whisk the batter again energetically until it has the light texture of a crêpe batter. Whisk in the sugar and the milk.

Drain the dried plums and arrange them in the dish. Pour the batter over the dried plums. Bake for 20 minutes, then reduce the temperature to 350°F (180°C) and cook for another 20 minutes or so, depending on the diameter of the dish. The tip of a knife should come out dry and some steam will escape from the small hole when it is done.

DID YOU KNOW?

The Breton *far* (literally "flour") is a dense custard flan that is popular as a dessert. There is a variation on this *far*, the *farz fourn* ("oven-baked flan"), which is a savory flan served with meats.

Assorted tuiles ✳

SERVES 8

Preparation: **35 minutes**
Resting: **40 minutes**
Cooking: **15 minutes**

INGREDIENTS

3 egg whites
Generous ¼ cup (25 g) cake flour
2 teaspoons (10 g) unsalted
 butter, melted
⅔ cup (125 g) sugar
½ teaspoon (3 g) vanilla extract
Flavorings—choose from:
4 oz. (125 g) sliced blanched
 almonds, or
4 oz. (125 g) toasted crushed
 pistachios, or
2 oz. (60 g) candied citrus zest,
 or
Scant ½ cup (50 g) cocoa
 powder, or
3 ½ oz. (walnuts)
or any other ingredient you would
 like to try!

Citrus lace tuiles

⅓ cup (80 g) melted butter
½ cup (100 g) sugar
⅓ cup (1 oz., 30 g) cake flour
Scant ¼ cup (50 ml) orange juice
Zest of 1 unsprayed or organic
 orange
1 tablespoon plus 1 teaspoon
 (20 ml) Cointreau or other
 orange liqueur
3 ½ oz. (100 g) chopped almonds

TECHNIQUE

Almond tuiles **207**

Prepare the tuile batter (see p. 207).
Beat the egg whites lightly with a fork. Add the rest of the
ingredients, except the flavorings, using a whisk. Chill for about
20 minutes.

Preheat the oven to 350°F (180°C).

Drop thin layers of batter on a silicone baking sheet or baking
tray lined with parchment paper and flatten using the back of a
spoon. The mixture spreads, so leave plenty of space between
the cookies. Scatter with the chosen flavoring. Bake for
5–8 minutes, until they are a light golden color. Take them off
the baking sheet immediately (an offset spatula will come in
handy) and drape them around a rolling pin while still hot. (If
they become too hard to drape, return them very briefly to the
oven.) Allow to cool.

Prepare the citrus lace tuiles. Melt the butter in the microwave
oven and combine it with the sugar and flour. Stir in the orange
juice and zest, flavor with the orange liqueur. Chill the batter for
20 minutes.

Preheat the oven to 350°F (180°C).

Drop thin layers of batter on a silicone baking sheet or baking
tray lined with parchment paper. Scatter the cookies with
chopped almonds, then bake for 5–8 minutes, until they are the
right color. Remove them from the oven and wait 15–20 seconds
before taking them off the baking sheet and shaping them
around a rolling pin. Leave them to cool.

Bitter almond crème brûlée ✳

SERVES 8

Preparation: **20 minutes**
Chilling: **1 hour**
Cooking: **55 minutes**

INGREDIENTS

10 egg yolks
Generous 1 cup (225 g)
  granulated sugar
2 cups (500 ml) milk
2 cups (500 ml) whipping cream,
  min. 35% fat
1 vanilla bean
A few drops of bitter almond
  extract
A little brown sugar, for
  caramelizing

In a round-bottomed mixing bowl, beat the egg yolks and sugar together energetically until the mixture thickens and becomes pale. Pour in the milk and whipping cream. Whisk together and add the seeds from the vanilla bean. Flavor with the bitter almond extract.

Cover with plastic wrap and chill for about 1 hour.

Preheat the oven to 200°F (100°C).

Strain the liquid through a chinois and pour it into eight small crème brûlée dishes or ramekins. Bake for 45–50 minutes. Test for doneness: the tip of a knife should come out clean.

Allow the crèmes to cool. Just before serving them, set your oven to broil. Sprinkle the top of each one with brown sugar. Caramelize them briefly in the oven, or use a caramelizing iron, and serve.

Pain d'épice ✳

SERVES 8

Preparation: **15 minutes**
Cooking: **40 minutes**

INGREDIENTS

1 cup (125 g) cake flour
Scant 1 ¼ cups (125 g) rye flour
4 teaspoons (15 g) baking
   powder
2 teaspoons (5 g) mixed ground
   spices (cinnamon, ginger,
   nutmeg, clove, and anise)
¾ cup (250 g) honey
2 tablespoons (30 g) butter, plus
   more for the loaf pan
½ cup (100 g) superfine sugar
⅔ cup (150 ml) heavy cream,
   min. 35% fat
3 eggs (5 ¼ oz./150 g)

CHEF'S NOTE

– This French gingerbread loaf
cake improves with time, so plan
to prepare it 2 days before you
serve it. It is excellent with foie
gras.

Preheat the oven to 340°F (170°C).

Sift the flours, baking powder, and spices together into a large
bowl.

Warm the honey, butter, and sugar together over a hot water
bath (bain-marie) until liquefied.

While the honey mixture is still warm, pour it over the flour
mixture. Stir until well combined and smooth.

Beat the eggs together in a separate bowl, then stir them into
the batter.

Grease a 10 × 3-inch (25 × 8-cm) loaf pan with butter. Pour the
batter into the pan and bake for about 40 minutes, until a
toothpick inserted into the center comes out clean.

Turn out of the pan and let cool on a rack.

DID YOU KNOW?

Pain d'épice, or gingerbread, as we know it today is thought to be related
to a tenth-century Chinese bread called Mi-Kong, which literally means
"honey bread."

Financiers ✳

SERVES 8

Preparation: **15 minutes**
Cooking: **8–10 minutes**

INGREDIENTS

1 stick plus 2 teaspoons (125 g)
    unsalted butter
¾ cup (150 g) superfine sugar
¾ cup (75 g) almond flour
4 egg whites (4 oz./120 g)
½ cup (60 g) cake flour

CHEF'S NOTES

– This *financier* batter can also
be spread into a thin layer over a
baking sheet lined with
parchment paper to make a
base for layered desserts.
– If you make small *financiers*,
you can leave them in the molds
until serving. The condensation
keeps them moist.
– You can flavor your *financiers*
with a nut spread or paste (such
as pistachio, hazelnut, or
praline) stirred into the batter.

Preheat a convection (fan-assisted) oven to 340°F (170°C); if
using a regular oven, preheat it to 365°F (185°C).

Prepare browned butter by warming the butter in a saucepan
over medium heat until it melts, turns golden brown, and has
a nutty aroma. Let cool slightly.

Place the sugar, almond flour, and egg whites in a large bowl.
Stir until well blended.

Gradually stir in the browned butter, then sift in the cake flour.
Stir until well blended and smooth.

Pour the batter into a *financier* mold with 3 × 1 ½-inch
(8 × 3.5-cm) cavities, filling the cavities two-thirds full.

Bake for 8–10 minutes, until the *financiers* are golden.

DID YOU KNOW?

This recipe has its roots in a medieval sponge cake, which was revisited
and improved upon by a Parisian pastry chef named Lasne around 1890.
The original small cakes had fallen out of favor during the Renaissance
because they smelled like bitter almonds, which called to mind
arsenic—a potent poison often used against the high nobility. Lasne,
whose boutique was located near the Paris stock exchange, baked his
cakes in ingot-shaped molds, to the delight of his *"financier"* (trader)
clients. Compared to the original oval-shaped cakes, this new form,
according to Lasne, made it easier to keep fingers clean.

Frozen Desserts

Stéphane Augé

presents his recipe

French gastronomy is a combination of tradition and revolution. As the years go by, the great classics remain. It is up to each of us French chefs to transmit our culinary heritage, but we make them our own and give them new life. And so tradition becomes evolution. The Belle-Hélène is a pear sundae that was created around 1864 in honor of Jacques Offenbach's comic opera of that name, and the dessert continues to enjoy popularity. Here, I have reinterpreted what is traditionally served in a sundae glass so that it can be served on a plate. The basic elements—vanilla, pear, and chocolate—are still there, but they are treated differently. The vanilla ice cream has taken in fine leaves of chocolate and becomes a stracciatella (white base with fine chocolate shavings). The poached pears are served in the form of both tiny cubes and jelly, and the crystallized violets have made way for caramelized cocoa nibs and a fantasy caramel-chocolate bow. All the ingredients come together to make up a dessert that is easy to prepare and quick to plate for service. Cold, hot, frozen, melting, crisp, crusty, soft, and creamy—here you have an interplay of textures, temperatures, and intense flavors that will enthrall your palate. Bon appétit!

SERVES 6

Preparation:
1 hour 30 minutes
Cooking: **35 minutes**
Freezing: **12 hours**

Pear Belle-Hélène, revisited

Stéphane Augé presents his recipe

INGREDIENTS

Stracciatella ice cream
1 cup (250 ml) full cream milk
2 ½ tablespoons (¾ oz./20 g)
  skimmed powdered milk
Scant ⅓ cup (2 ¼ oz./65 g)
  granulated sugar, divided
¾ oz. (20 g) glucose syrup
  (liquid glucose)
½ cup (125 ml) whipping cream,
  min. 35% fat
¾ oz. (2 g) ice cream stabilizer
  (available from professional
  suppliers)
1 Madagascar Bourbon vanilla
  bean, slit lengthwise, seeds
  scraped
1 teaspoon (5 ml) Morand
  Williamine® pear brandy
2 oz. (50 g) fine chocolate bits,
  70% cocoa

Cigarette paste tubes
1 ⅓ cup (¾ oz./50 g)
  confectioners' sugar
3 ½ tablespoons (1 ¾ oz./50 g)
  butter, softened
1 ¾ oz. (50 g) egg whites
  (equivalent of approximately
  2 egg whites)
6 ½ tablespoons (1 ⅖ oz./40 g)
  all-purpose flour
1 ½ tablespoons (⅓ oz./10 g)
  unsweetened cocoa powder

Pears poached in syrup
3 Bartlett (also known as Williams)
  pears (10 oz./300 g)
¾ cup (4 ¾ oz./135 g)
  granulated sugar
1 vanilla bean, slit lengthwise
Scant ½ cup (100 ml) water

A DAY AHEAD

Stracciatella ice cream
Heat the milk to 77°F (25°C). When it reaches this temperature, mix in the powdered milk. Continue heating. When it reaches 86°F (30°C), add 3 ⅓ tablespoons (45 g) sugar and the glucose syrup. At 95°F (35°C), add the whipping cream. At 113°F (45°C), mix in the remaining sugar combined with the stabilizer, as well as the slit vanilla bean with its seeds. Bring it to 189°F (87°C) to pasteurize it as you would for a custard. Process it so that it is perfectly smooth.

Place in the freezer at 39.2°F (4°C) for 1–4 hours. Process again and churn. Then add the pear brandy. When you extrude it, incorporate the fine chocolate bits. Spoon the ice cream into a piping bag fitted with a fluted nozzle measuring ½ in. (16 mm) in diameter. Store at 10°F (-12°C) until serving.

Cigarette paste tubes
Sift the confectioners' sugar and cream it with the softened butter. Mix in the egg whites. Sift the flour and cocoa powder together and combine them with the mixture. Leave to chill.

Preheat the oven to 300°F (150°C).

Roll out the mixture very thinly, using a frame if you wish, on a silicone baking sheet to make six rectangles measuring 4 × 5 ½ in. (10 × 14 cm). Bake for 5 minutes. As soon as you remove the rectangles from the oven, roll the pastry around six 4-in. high (10 cm) tubes with a diameter of 1 ¼ in. (3 cm). When they have cooled, carefully remove the tubes. Store the pastry cylinders in an airtight container.

Pears poached in syrup
Peel the pears and dice them very finely (⅛ in./3 mm cubes) to make a *brunoise*. Place them in a bowl with the sugar, slit vanilla bean, and the water. Cover the bowl with plastic wrap and poach the pear *brunoise* in the microwave oven for 4 minutes. Drain carefully, reserving the hot liquid for use for the rest of the recipe. (The pears will give off some of their own liquid, all of which will be needed.) Set aside in the refrigerator.

Bartlett pear jelly

3 g powdered gelatin, 200 Bloom strength (check with your supplier)

½ cup (125 ml) of the reserved poaching liquid, still hot

4 teaspoons (20 ml) Morand Williamine® pear brandy

Caramel-chocolate bow

1 ½ oz. (40 g) pure cacao paste (from specialty stores)

1 ½ oz. (40 g) glucose syrup

2 oz. (60 g) fondant (from specialty stores)

Polignac cocoa nibs

1 oz. (30 g) cocoa nibs (at specialty stores or online)

1 ¹/₃ tablespoons (20 ml) pear poaching liquid

Dark chocolate Chantilly mousse

3 ½ oz. (100 g) dark chocolate, 70% cacao

²/₃ cup (185 ml) whipping cream, min. 35% fat, divided

Custard-style sabayon

2 ½ tablespoons (40 ml) full cream milk

¾ oz. (20 g) egg yolk (about 1 egg yolk)

¹/₃ cup (80 ml) pear poaching liquid

Bartlett pear jelly

Dissolve the gelatin directly in the hot poaching syrup. Flavor with the pear brandy and pour into a shallow tray. Cover with plastic wrap and chill. When the mixture has set, cut out thirty cubes (½ in./1 cm). You will need five per person.

Caramel-chocolate bow

Chop the cocoa paste finely. Cook the glucose syrup and the fondant to a temperature of 325°F (160°C) and mix in the chopped cocoa paste. Roll it out between two silicone baking sheets and leave to cool. To make the bows, break off pieces and soften them slightly in a heated oven. Roll them out thinly and shape into bows. Set aside in an airtight container.

Polignac cocoa nibs

Preheat the oven to 300°F (150°C). Mix the cocoa nibs into the syrup and spread the mixture on to a silicon baking sheet. Bake for 7 minutes, allow to cool, and set aside in an airtight container.

PREPARE AHEAD OF SERVING TIME

Dark chocolate Chantilly mousse

Melt the chocolate to a temperature of 131°F (55°C). While it melts, begin heating

---

¼ cup (65 ml) cream. Remove from the heat before it reaches a simmer. Whisk the heated cream into the melted chocolate. Beat the rest of the cream until it forms soft peaks. When the mixture is at a temperature of 113°F (45°C), incorporate the softly beaten cream. Spoon the mousse into a piping bag and keep in the refrigerator until needed.

PREPARE JUST BEFORE SERVING

Custard-style sabayon

Beat the egg yolk with the syrup until white and pale. Bring the milk to a boil and pour it over the egg yolk mixture. Whisk the mixture over a hot water bath until it reaches a sabayon texture. It should now be served.

To assemble

Fill one third of each tube with chocolate Chantilly and place one in the middle of each plate. Drain the diced pears well and fill the next third of the tubes with the pears. Arrange five cubes of jelly around each tube. Spoon the sabayon into the base of each plate and scatter it with cocoa nibs. Fill the tubes to the top with ice cream and garnish with the chocolate-caramel bow. Serve immediately.

Rum and raisin profiteroles ✳✳

SERVES 8

Preparation: **1 hour 5 minutes**
Baking: **25 minutes**
Freezing: **4 ½–5 hours**

INGREDIENTS

Choux pastry
1 cup (250 ml) water
1 teaspoon (5 g) fine salt
7 tablespoons (100 g) unsalted
  butter, cubed
1 ¼ cups (125 g) all-purpose
  flour
4 plus 1 eggs

Rum and raisin ice cream
½ cup (3 oz./80g) raisins
Rum (sufficient to soak the
  raisins)
1 vanilla bean, slit lengthwise
1 ⅔ cups (400 ml) full cream
  milk
Scant ½ cup (100 ml) whipping
  cream, min. 35% fat
6 egg yolks (4 ¼ oz./120 g)
½ cup (100 g) sugar

Chocolate sauce
1 cup (250 ml) full cream milk
3 ⅓ tablespoons (50 ml) heavy
  cream, min. 30% fat
6 ¾ oz. (190 g) dark chocolate,
  64% cacao, roughly chopped

Special equipment: a sugar
  thermometer

TECHNIQUES

Choux pastry **22**
Custard-based ice cream **211**
Chocolate sauce **170**

Prepare the choux pastry (see p. 22).
Preheat the oven to 400°F (200°C) and ensure there is no residual steam in it. (Choux pastry has to dry out well.)

Sift the flour. Bring the water, salt, and cubed butter to a boil in a saucepan. Remove from the heat and pour in all the flour at once. Return the saucepan to the heat and stir the mixture energetically with a spatula to dry it out. When the moisture has evaporated, put the batter into a mixing bowl. Mix in four eggs, one by one, stirring well each time with the spatula. Spoon the choux batter into a piping bag with a plain tip and pipe out small choux pastries with a diameter of just under 1 in. (1.5 cm). Beat the remaining egg and, using a pastry brush, baste the choux pastries. Dip a fork in water and press down lightly on the surface of the pastries with the tines to make a grid pattern. This will help them bake evenly. Bake for 25 minutes. When the choux pastries are done, leave the door ajar for a few minutes to allow the steam to escape so that they can dry out completely.

Prepare the rum and raisin ice cream (see p. 211).
Macerate the raisins in rum (just enough to cover them in a small bowl). Slit the vanilla bean lengthwise and place it in a saucepan with the milk and cream. Bring the mixture to a boil. Beat the egg yolks with the sugar until the mixture is thick and pale. Pour the hot milk and cream over the eggs, beating constantly, then return the liquid to the saucepan. Heat it as you would a custard, to a temperature of 185°F (85°C), or until it thickens and coats the back of a spoon. Chill the custard cream rapidly over ice and then pour it into an ice cream machine. Follow the instructions for the time, but it will take a minimum of 3 hours. Remove the ice cream from the ice cream maker and stir in the macerated raisins. Place in the freezer for 1 ½–2 hours.

Prepare the chocolate sauce (see p. 170).
Heat the milk and cream on low heat. The temperature of the mixture should not exceed 130°F–140°F (55°C–60°C) (it will be hot but should not burn the tip of your finger). Remove the saucepan from the heat and, using a spatula, incorporate the chopped chocolate until the sauce is smooth. Keep it warm over a bain-marie.

Slit the profiteroles in half horizontally. Fill each one with a scoop of rum and raisin ice cream. Arrange them on a dish and drizzle with the warm chocolate sauce.

Frozen acacia honey parfait ✳

SERVES 8

Preparation: **20 minutes**
Cooking: **10 minutes**
Freezing: **30 minutes**

INGREDIENTS

Scant ⅓ cup (3 ½ oz./100 g)
  acacia honey
4 egg yolks
1 cup (250 ml) whipping cream,
  min. 30% fat

Special equipment: sugar
  thermometer

Using the method for *pâte à bombe* (see p. 212), heat the honey to 244°F (118°C). Pour the honey over the egg yolks, beating constantly, until the mixture cools down completely.

Whisk the cream until it forms stiff peaks and carefully fold it into the honey *pâte à bombe*.

Pour the mixture into ramekins or shot glasses (*verrines*) and leave to set in the freezer for 2–3 hours.

TECHNIQUES

Pâte à bombe **212**
Frozen parfait **212**

CHEF'S NOTE

Lightly oil the measuring cup with a neutral oil when measuring the honey so that you can pour it out without any waste.

Frozen hazelnut parfait ✳

SERVES 8

Preparation: **20 minutes**
Cooking: **10 minutes**
Freezing: **3 hours**

INGREDIENTS

¼ cup (60 ml) water
⅔ cup (4 ⅓ oz./120 g)
  granulated sugar
5 egg yolks
1 ½ cups (375 ml) whipping
  cream, min. 30% fat
2 oz. (50 g) pure hazelnut paste
  (from specialty stores or online)
Toasted hazelnuts, for garnish

Special equipment: sugar
  thermometer

Using the method for *pâte à bombe* (see p. 212), begin cooking the water and sugar.

Place the egg yolks in the bowl of a stand mixer and begin beating them. When the syrup reaches a temperature of about 243°F–250°F (117°C–120°C), begin pouring it over the egg yolks as the mixer continues to beat. Continue beating until the mixture has reached room temperature. It will be dense and shiny, and form a mousse-like ribbon.

Whip the cream until it forms stiff peaks and fold in the hazelnut paste. Carefully fold the flavored whipped cream into the *pâte à bombe*.

Spoon the parfait mixture into molds or small shot glasses (*verrines*) and freeze for 2 ½–3 hours. Garnish with toasted sliced hazelnuts.

TECHNIQUES

Pâte à bombe **212**
Frozen parfait **212**

Frozen strawberry mousse ✳

SERVES 8

Preparation: **20 minutes**
Cooking: **10 minutes**
Freezing: **3 hours**

INGREDIENTS

1 ⅔ cups (400 ml) whipping
  cream, min. 30% fat
1 lb. (500 g) puréed strawberries

Italian meringue
¼ cup (50 ml) water
¾ cup (140 g) granulated sugar
3 egg whites (70 g)
1 pinch salt

Special equipment: sugar
  thermometer

Prepare the Italian meringue (see p. 51). Begin cooking the water with the sugar. When the syrup reaches a temperature of 230°F (110°C), begin beating the egg whites with the pinch of salt in the bowl of a stand mixer. (The bowl should be perfectly clean.) When the syrup reaches 243°F–250°F (117°C–120°C), pour the syrup over the stiff egg whites. Continue whisking until the meringue mixture has cooled down completely. It will be dense, shiny, and form many small peaks.

Beat the cream stiffly to a Chantilly texture. Fold the strawberry purée into the Italian meringue using a rubber spatula. Then carefully fold the whipped cream into the mixture, taking care not to deflate it.

Spoon the mousse into shot glasses (*verrines*) or ramekins and freeze for 2–3 hours.

TECHNIQUES

Italian meringue **51**
Frozen mousse **213**

Champagne granita ✳

SERVES 8

Preparation: **20 minutes**
Freezing: **2 hours 15 minutes**

INGREDIENTS

1 ¼ cups (300 ml) tangerine juice
¾ cup (200 ml) water
1 cup (200 g) granulated sugar
3 cups (700 ml) champagne

In a saucepan, bring the tangerine juice to boil with the water and sugar. Boil for 3 minutes and allow to cool, either on its own or over ice.

Prepare the granita. Add the champagne to the cool syrup. Pour the mixture into a large, shallow dish so that you have a shallow layer of liquid. Place it in the freezer for 15 minutes. With a fork, scratch the surface and stir it to break up any lumps. Return the granita to the freezer and repeat the procedure every 25 minutes for 2 hours.

Just before serving, scratch it well again with a fork to lighten the texture.

Frozen blackberry vacherin ✳

SERVES 8

Preparation: **45 minutes**
Baking: **1 hour 30 minutes**
Freezing: **about 6 hours**

INGREDIENTS

Blackberry sorbet
2 lb. 4 oz. (1 kg) blackberries
1 ¼ cups (240 g) sugar
2 cups (500 ml) water

Meringue
7 egg whites (200 g)
2 cups (400 g) sugar
1 pinch salt

Chantilly cream
1 cup (250 ml) whipping cream,
   min. 30% fat
⅓ cup (40 g) confectioners'
   sugar
A few drops of vanilla extract

8 blackberries, for garnish

TECHNIQUES

Sorbet **211**
French meringue **51**
Chantilly cream **179**

Prepare the blackberry sorbet (see p. 211).
Wash the blackberries. Bring the water to a boil with the sugar. Process the blackberries in a juicer and add the juice to the syrup. Cool rapidly over ice and then pour into the ice-cream maker.

Prepare the meringue shells (see p. 51).
Preheat the oven to 200°F (90°C). Line a baking sheet with parchment paper. Ensure that a round-bottomed bowl is perfectly clean and dry before you pour the egg whites in. Beat the egg whites together with a pinch of salt lightly with a fork. Then begin whisking them energetically, making sure to lift the whisk up high to incorporate as much air as possible. When the whites begin to stiffen, add the sugar, incorporating it with a circular movement until the mixture is firm and shiny. The meringue should be compact and smooth, and should form stiff peaks from the whisk. Spoon the meringue batter into a piping bag and pipe out the shells onto the baking sheet. Dry the meringue shells out in the oven for 1 ½ hours.

When the meringues are perfectly dry and cool, form the sorbet into a single cake shape, or eight individual cylinder shapes, and press the meringues into it around the sides.

Decorate with Chantilly cream (see p. 179) and garnish with the blackberries.

Frozen banana soufflé ✳✳

SERVES 8

Preparation: **40 minutes**
Freezing: **3 hours**

INGREDIENTS

Scant ⅔ cup (120 g) sugar
2 tablespoons (30 ml) water
3 egg yolks (60 g)
10 oz. (300 g) mashed banana
Juice of 1 lemon (to squeeze over
   the mashed banana to prevent it
   from going black)
1 ⅔ cups (400 ml) whipping
   cream

Italian meringue
1 ¼ cups (220 g) granulated
   sugar
Scant ⅓ cup (70 ml) water
4 egg whites (110 g)
1 pinch salt

TECHNIQUES

Pâte à bombe **212**
Italian meringue **51**
Frozen soufflé **213**

Prepare the *pâte à bombe* (see p. 212).
Begin cooking the water with the sugar. Start beating the yolks in the bowl of a stand mixer. When the syrup reaches a temperature of 243°F–250°F (117°C–120°C), pour it over the beaten egg yolks. Continue beating until the *pâte à bombe* has cooled down completely. It will be dense and shiny, and form a mousse-like ribbon. Mix in the mashed banana (with or without the lemon juice).

Stiffly whip the cream and set aside in the refrigerator.

Prepare the Italian meringue (see p. 51).
Begin cooking the water with the sugar. When the syrup reaches a temperature of 230°F (110°C), begin beating the egg whites with the pinch of salt in the bowl of a stand mixer. (The bowl should be perfectly clean before you begin.) When the syrup reaches 243°F–250°F (117°C–120°C), pour it over the stiff egg whites. Continue whisking until the meringue mixture has cooled down completely. It should be dense, shiny, and form many small peaks. Fold the meringue into the *pâte à bombe*, then fold in the stiffly whipped cream.

Line the inside of eight soufflé molds with strips of parchment paper 6–8 in. (15–20 cm) high, depending on the size. Keep the paper in place with paper clips. Pour the soufflé mixture into the molds and freeze for 2 ½–3 hours.

Baked Alaska ✷✷

SERVES 8

Preparation: **50 minutes**
Baking: **25 minutes**
Freezing: **5 ½–6 hours**

INGREDIENTS

Italian meringue
1 ¾ cups (360 g) sugar
6 egg whites (180 g)
1 pinch salt

Vanilla ice cream
1 vanilla bean
1 ⅔ cups (400 ml) full cream
  milk
Scant ½ cup (100 ml) whipping
  cream, min. 30% fat
6 egg yolks
½ cup (100 g) granulated sugar

Genoese sponge
4 eggs
⅔ cup (125 g) granulated sugar
1 ⅓ cups (125 g) cake flour, plus
  extra for the pan
A little butter to grease the pan
Fruit brandy, such as orange or
  cherry, to flambé

TECHNIQUES

Custard-based ice cream 211
Genoese sponge 195
Italian meringue 51

Prepare the vanilla ice cream (see p. 211).
Slit the vanilla bean lengthwise. Bring the milk and cream to a boil with the vanilla bean. Beat the yolks with the sugar in a mixing bowl until they are thick and pale. Pour the milk and cream mixture over the egg yolks, beating constantly, then return all the liquid into the saucepan. Heat it as you would to make a custard, to a temperature of 185°F (85°C). Cool rapidly over ice and then transfer to an ice-cream maker for 2 ½–3 hours.

Prepare a Genoese sponge (see p. 195).
Preheat the oven to 350°F (180°C).

Beat the eggs and the sugar together in a round-bottomed mixing bowl over a bain-marie until the mixture reaches the ribbon stage and a temperature of 140°F (60°C). Sift in the flour and pour half of it in to the mixture, folding it in gently with a rubber spatula. Pour in the remaining flour and fold it in, working quickly and carefully so as not to deflate the batter. Spread the batter out to a thickness of about ⅛ in. (4 mm) on to a silicon baking sheet or baking pan lined with parchment paper. An offset spatula will come in handy here to smooth it. Bake for 10–12 minutes. Test for doneness—it should be a light golden color—and turn it out onto a rack to cool. Remove the vanilla ice cream from the ice-cream maker when it is ready, and shape it into a cube 15 × 4 × 4 in. (40 × 10 × 10 cm). Cut out the Genoese sponge so that you have two layers, each the same size as the vanilla ice-cream cube (15 × 4 in./40 × 10 cm).

Prepare the Italian meringue (see p. 51).
Begin cooking ½ cup (120 ml) water with the sugar in a saucepan. Check that the bowl of the stand mixer is perfectly clean before you pour the egg whites in. When the temperature of the syrup reaches 230°F (110°C), begin beating the egg whites with a pinch of salt. When the temperature of the syrup reaches 243°F–250°F (117°C–120°C), begin pouring it gradually into the egg whites. Continue beating until the meringue has cooled down completely. It will be dense and shiny, and will form many small peaks. Place the ice-cream cube on one layer of the sponge base and then place the second layer on top. Spoon the meringue into a piping bag and decorate your dessert. Freeze for at least 3 hours.

Preheat the oven to 400°F (200°C).

Just before serving, place the dessert in the oven until the meringue browns. Flambé it with the fruit brandy just as you serve it.

Frozen nougat and raspberry coulis ✳✳

SERVES 8

Preparation: **35 minutes**
Freezing: **2 ½–3 hours**

INGREDIENTS

Nougatine
5 ¼ oz. (150 g) glucose
½ cup (100 g) sugar
1 cup (125 g) chopped almonds

Ice cream
Scant ⅓ cup (3 ½ oz. or 100 g) honey
¼ cup (55 g) granulated sugar
4 egg whites (120 g)
2 cups (500 ml) whipping cream, min. 35% fat, well chilled
¾ cup (125 g) assorted candied fruit, cubed
¼ cup (125 g) roasted unsalted pistachios
¼ cup (125 g) chopped nougatine
¾ cup (125 g) candied orange peel, cubed
1 ½ tablespoons (25 ml) Cointreau or other orange liqueur

Raspberry coulis
4 ½ oz. (125 g) raspberries
2 teaspoons (10 ml) lemon juice
Scant ½ cup (60 g) confectioners' sugar

TECHNIQUES

Italian meringue **51**
Fruit coulis **166**

If preparing homemade nougatine, melt the glucose in a saucepan, add the sugar, and cook until it forms a light caramel. Lightly toast the chopped almonds and mix them into the caramel. Pour the caramel on to a silicon baking sheet, spreading it out. When it has cooled, chop it up.

For the ice cream, cook the honey and sugar together until the mixtures reaches a temperature of 243°F (117°C). While the mixture is cooking, beat the whites stiffly. Pour the cooked sugar/honey mixture over the beaten egg whites using the method for an Italian meringue (see p. 51), until it has cooled.

Beat the well-chilled cream in the bowl of a stand mixer. Fold it into the Italian meringue. Then stir in the cubed candied fruit, roasted pistachios, crushed nougatine, and cubed candied orange peel. Stir in the orange liqueur. Pour the mixture into stainless steel dessert rings or other shaped silicon molds. Place in the freezer until it hardens, 2 ½–3 hours.

Prepare the raspberry coulis (see p. 166).
Wash the raspberries and blend them with the lemon juice and confectioners' sugar. Strain through a fine-mesh sieve. Cover with plastic wrap and chill until needed.

Turn the frozen nougat out of the molds or rings and serve it with the raspberry coulis.

DID YOU KNOW?

Nougat is a specialty of the south of France and Montélimar is particularly well known for its nougat. The frozen version combines all the basic ingredients of the traditional recipe.

Index

Acknowledgments

The authors are extremely grateful to the Lycée Hôtelier de La Guerche, in Brittany, for providing the location and supplying the materials featured in the photographs, and to the chefs and Meilleurs Ouvriers de France (Best Craftsmen of France) for their kind contributions to this volume.

They also wish to thank the many partners and suppliers who made this book possible:
· Les Vergers Boiron (frozen fuits): www.my-vb.com
· Boursault (cheeses – Paris 75014)
· Bragard (chefs' clothing): www.bragard.com/en
· Cefimev (training center for meat professionals)
· Céréco (organic cereals): www.cereco-bio.fr
· Ducros (spices, herbs, condiments): www.ducros.com
· Emeraude Marée (fish and shellfish)
· Ercuis (tableware): www.ercuis.com
· Eurolam (knives): eurolam-thiers.com
· Gama 29 (cleaning products): www.gama29.fr
· Gatine Viandes (pork) : www.gatineviandes.fr
· Janzé Volailles Tradition (poultry)
· Louaisil (fresh fruit and vegetables)
· Panzani Food Service (pasta): www.panzani.fr
· Loïc Raison (cider and apple juice): www.loicraison.fr
· Raynaud (Limoges porcelain): www.raynaud.fr/en
· Société Ricard (spirits): www.ricard.com
· Super U (groceries): www.magasins-u.com
· Tendriade (veal): www.tendriade.fr
· Triballat Sojasun (dairy and soy-based products): www.triballat-noyal.com/en